V. S. Naipaul

V. S. NAIPAUL

A Materialist Reading

Selwyn R. Cudjoe

1988

THE UNIVERSITY OF MASSACHUSETTS PRESS

AMHERST

Copyright © 1988 by
The University of Massachusetts Press

Printed in the United States of America
LC 87-35768
ISBN 0–87023–619–9 (cloth); 620–2 (pbk.)

Designed by Susan Bishop
Set in Linotype Times Roman
at Keystone Typesetting
Printed by Thomson-Shore
and bound by John Dekker & Sons

*Library of Congress
Cataloging-in-Publication Data*

Cudjoe, Selwyn Reginald.
V. S. Naipaul : a materialist reading.
Bibliography: p.
Includes index.
1. Naipaul, V. S. (Vidiadhar Surajprasad),
1932–   —Criticism and interpretation.   2. Naipaul,
V. S. (Vidiadhar Surajprasad), 1932–   —Political and
social views.   3. Colonies in literature.
4. Decolonization in literature.   5. Literature and
society—West Indies.   6. West Indians—
Intellectual life.   I. Title
PR9272.9.N32Z65 1988   823'.914   87–35768
ISBN 0–87023–619–9 (alk. paper)
ISBN 0–87023–620–2 (pbk. : alk. paper)

British Library Cataloguing in Publication
data are available

For my wife, Gwendolyn Marie

Black man go pung mata, na mattie head,
Feed dem pickni wid fufu, na mattie flesh,
Coolie grind massala, na mattie bone, stir dhall, na blood.
De air go fill wid curry-smell an roast cassava
Puri an pepperpot
An sitar an steelband go sound when gunfire bin a deh.
Lil pickni go laan plant wara-seed na pelt each odda in de street wid dem,
An when people kill, dem kill only cackroach, centipede, masquita . . .
Hear me dream like birdsaang in yu ear!
—David Dabydeen, "For Mala" (slave song)

Contents

Acknowledgments

A number of persons and institutions assisted in making this work possible. The following have either read it, encouraged me, and/or listened patiently to my ramblings: Arnold Rampersad, Terry Eagleton, Henry Louis Gates, Jr., Biodun Jeyifo, Henry Rosovsky, Michael Colacurcio, Jonathan Culler, Gwendolyn Marie Cudjoe, Yamani Zacharias, Arthur Paris, Wellington Nyangoni, Roy Thomas, and William Cain. I thank Erica Fox and Trudy Calvert, who corrected and typed the final version of this text, Cathy Boyle, who assisted in doing some research in the final days, and the librarians at the West India Collection at the University of the West Indies (Trinidad), Cornell University, and Wellesley College for their patience and assistance. A Harvard University faculty grant and Clark Award and a Wellesley College Faculty Grant allowed me to travel to many collections to gather information, to devote a sustained period of time to writing the manuscript, and to pay for its typing and for research materials.

My wife, Gwendolyn Marie, has been more supportive than any husband has a right to expect. I cannot thank her sufficiently, so I dedicate this work to her. To my daughters, Frances and Kwamena, I would like to say thanks for your understanding. As always, I am thankful for the encouragement and understanding of my mothers, Carmen and Frances, of my sisters Margaret, Roberta, Aneise, and Yvonne, of my late brother Winston, of my brothers Ervin and Cedric, and of all my nieces and nephews. I hope that the people of Tacarigua, Trinidad (especially Nyren -Natch- Evelyn, my aunts Gladys Small and Mildred Cudjoe, and uncles Fred and Hamilton Cudjoe and Victor Bailey) understand how much this book is theirs and a part of them.

Preface

In the spring of 1978 I gave a lecture at Columbia University, New York, to primarily West Indian students, on the manner in which resistance fashioned Caribbean literature. One of the students asked how V. S. Naipaul's work fitted into that pattern. I answered that although the work of some novelists may have been fashioned by the positive dimensions of that tradition (for example, George Lamming), others, such as V. S. Naipaul, had responded to its negative aspects. A fellow panelist commented that Naipaul was "just reactionary." This remark sent me in search of a fuller account of his work, convinced that a writer as important as V. S. Naipaul (even though he was not as well known in the United States then as he is today) could not be discarded by such a simplistic statement. Reactionary he might be, but in that very reaction he had raised many important concerns that serious scholars have to address.

Many concerned persons urged me on and assisted in this study. Arnold Rampersad, professor at Rutgers University, who spent the academic year 1978–79 as a visiting professor of Afro-American Studies at Harvard University, first gave me the confidence to do this study when he suggested that my previous academic experience had prepared me for the task. Terry Eagleton, a reader at Oxford University and visiting scholar at the Society of the Humanities, Cornell University, in the fall of 1980, offered the first systematic criticism of my manuscript and complained about what he called "the disabling dualities of the text." His criticism undoubtedly helped to sharpen the theoretical aspect of this work. Professors Jonathan Culler (Cornell University), Michael Colacurcio (UCLA), and Joel Porte (Harvard) were also very helpful in their comments on certain parts of this work.

This text is informed by four basic postulates. First, Naipaul, more than any other current English-language writer, is a product of a blend of Eastern and Western philosophy and it is this view of the world that has fashioned the vision of his work. Second, his work cannot be understood as self-evident truths ready to be received, absorbed, and understood. As Naipaul understood, it is the critic's function to participate in establishing the meaning of a work. Third, a reading of his work must produce a new knowledge that is independent of though related to what he attempts to say. Fourth, his work can be understood best within the context of the West Indian literary and historical tradition of which it is a part and in relation to other works within the nascent field of postcolonial discourse.

This study, then, is grounded in contemporary concepts of literary criticism, an understanding of Hinduism, a knowledge of West Indian literature and history, and concepts of contemporary psychoanalysis and theories of language. I have relied on the thinking of Caribbean scholars because they have many important insights to offer, particularly with regard to history and sensibility. Although I have made use of some of the most advanced theories of Western literary criticism, they have been tempered by the observations of M. M. Mahood, who argues that while the art of storytelling is universal and while it reached its highest "technical competence in Europe early in this century," non-European writers have added their own peculiarities to the form. I am inclined to agree with C. L. R. James that much of Naipaul's power as a writer is derived from the advanced nature of Caribbean societies, which have been simultaneously influenced by Western culture for the past three hundred years and thrown into what he calls "a very highly developed modern language" from the inception of their history as a plantation economy.

This work is intended as one of the most comprehensive studies of Naipaul's work. Some of the material (those from the BBC Written Archives, for example) is being brought to the public's attention for the first time, as is my discovery in the Guyana archives of the first Trinidadian romance, *Those That Be in Bondage,* a work that examines the position/problem of the East Indian in the Caribbean long before Naipaul did. My work also brings together most of the critical works written on Naipaul and is intended to serve as an interpretive treatment of his fiction and nonfiction. It also places Naipaul's work into the larger field of Caribbean and postcolonial discourse.

Because Naipaul's work occupies such an important place in English literature today, it is necessary to understand the forces that shape his work and the issues with which he is concerned. If this study raises some of the more important questions about Naipaul's work and demonstrates that it cannot be seen as an unproblematic guide to postcolonial "reality," then it would have gone a long way toward opening up the terrain in which the most meaningful discussion of his work can take place. Like it or not, Naipaul's work represents an important postcolonial impulse/response that begs to be understood and interpreted.

V. S. Naipaul

Introduction

The literary work is not a precariously prolonged adventure, a quest for its own vanishing point. The linear simplicity which gives it boldness and freshness is actually only its most superficial aspect; we must also be able to distinguish its real and fundamental complexity. And in this complexity we must recognize the signs of a necessity: the work does not move with the ingenuous freedom and independence that betoken pure invention; it is in fact sustained by a premeditated diversity which gives both form and content.

—Pierre Macherey, *A Theory of Literary Production*

Metropolitan critics have so far failed to serve West Indian literature because they have been unable to resist offering secondhand and superficial analyses of the society, and unwilling or unable to pay close attention to particular texts or to relate their interests in other literature to their interest in West Indian literature.

—Kenneth Ramchand, "Concern for Criticism"

V. S. Naipaul is one of the most popular writers of the English language in the world today. The author of nineteen books and innumerable articles, he stands at the pinnacle of his career. He has been honored throughout the world, won many prestigious awards, and been proclaimed a genius by critics. Fourteen of his books have been translated and his work now appears in sixteen languages. *In a Free State* has been translated into nine European languages, *Guerrillas* into eight, *A Bend in the River* into six; and André Deutsch, his British publisher, has issued a uniform edition of his writings, a privilege that is accorded few authors in their lifetime. His words are quoted by statespersons and peasants alike to describe the condition of the people of the Third World. *Newsweek* has called him "The Master of the Novel," Patrick Swinden has called him "one of the finest living novelists writing in English,"[1] and he has been mentioned several times as a possible nominee for the Nobel Prize in literature.

Born in Chaguanas, Trinidad, in 1932, Vidiadhar Surajprasad Naipaul won a prestigious island scholarship in 1948, which took him to Oxford University in 1950, where he read for a degree in English literature. After spending four years at Oxford, he took a position at the BBC in London, where he worked as an editor and presented a weekly literary program for the Caribbean called "Caribbean Voices." In 1955, from the same room in the Langham Hotel in London where he had begun his career with the BBC, Naipaul commenced his first manuscript, *Miguel Street,* thus launching his literary career.[2]

At least nine books, thirteen doctoral dissertations, and ten master's theses have been devoted to Naipaul's work. Another thirteen studies have compared his work with that of other writers, and two others have discussed his work in the context of the contemporary novel in English.[3] One critic has even been emboldened to argue that "an English writer is what Naipaul is. . . . Naipaul values this [English] culture, and feels himself to be very much a part of it."[4] These dissertations and theses have been produced in the United States, Canada, England, Australia, and Scotland; not one has been produced in the West Indies. Many of these analyses are nonhistorical misreadings that fail to locate Naipaul's work in its tradition and to identify or consider its ideological orientation. Mostly, they seek to reproduce and to reemphasize the self-evident truths of Naipaul's judgments and the brilliance of his observation. I will call such readings idealist. This book will be an examination of Naipaul's work rather than an attempt to understand him as a person. The texts rather than the author will be the center of the study.

A MATERIALIST READING

A reading of V. S. Naipaul's texts is, by definition, a political act. To wrench his texts from the many idealist readings to which they have been subjected one must locate them in their historical context and create a new knowledge in the process. As Louis Althusser argues, "theoretical investigation cannot consist of the simple repetition or simple commentary on already acquired knowledge, and even more importantly, it can have nothing in common with the development of simple ideological themes or personal opinions. Theoretical investigation only begins in the zone which separates already fully acquired and assimilated knowledge from the unknown. To be an investigator one must reach this zone and cross over into it."[5] Thus, in analyzing Naipaul's work, one must not simply repeat what Naipaul says or offers about himself or his society in a noncritical manner. In what I will call a materialist reading, I will dispense with idealistic analyses that claim that Naipaul's work is "politically neutral," "culturally innocent," or unconnected to the Caribbean literary tradition from which it arose.[6] His work is a political intervention within a well-defined historical and cultural space, the product of an emerging tradition in literature.

In this chapter, therefore, I will locate Naipaul's texts within the larger field of their production. From such a position, I will interpret his texts in their intertextuality, arguing as Leonard Green has that "inscribed in a textuality larger than its own, a literary text pre-scribes a domain which is already in excess of the 'merely' literary."[7] Moreover, I will argue that this "excess" is the political and social reality of the colonial and postcolonial world, a situation that led Kenneth Ramchand to observe that "there is a sense in which, even when they are concerned with contemporary reality, nearly all West Indian novels are engaged with history."[8]

I will demonstrate that rather than a mystical conjuring on the part of the writer, Naipaul's work is a product of forms that cannot be subtracted from or understood outside of their immediate environment of knowledge and that what has been called the necessity of the work cannot be perceived as merely "initial datum, but a product where several lines of necessity converge."[9] Such a perspective does not deny the autonomy of Naipaul's work; it simply recognizes its relationship to other works in the larger literary field and defines its specific location in its history.

I will show that the meaning of Naipaul's work is never "given" but "progressively discovered." As such, I will argue that Naipaul's work ought not to be treated as though it were spontaneously given and immediately accessible, ready to be received, described, or modified by the reader. Rather, by allowing the reader to know and to encounter the text as the author himself cannot know and encounter it, this examination will attempt to reveal the "unsaid" of the text, to gather the scattered ideological discourses of the work, and to demonstrate that, indeed, Naipaul's work serves to concretize a well-defined ideological position. In other words, Naipaul must be understood as a product of his history and his time, as a writer who has aligned himself with the values and preoccupations of the dominant Western culture.

V. S. NAIPAUL: PROBLEM AND PROBLEMATIC

The work of V. S. Naipaul is inscribed indelibly with colonial and post-colonial reality. Trinidad served as the initial site for the elaboration of his major problematic ("Who or what am I in this colonial world?"),[10] only to be overtaken by the larger postcolonial world when the author required a larger field in which to develop his doctrines more fully. Trinidad therefore gives way to India, Africa, South America, Iran, Pakistan, Indonesia, Malaysia, and England. The emphasis changed, but the central content of his doctrines remained the same.

Although the impact of colonialism on Naipaul's work must be recognized, the primary influence on his historical-literary vision was his Hindu sensibility. Thus Gordon Rohlehr was correct in suggesting that Naipaul appears to be a "man caught up in two voids," that of Western existentialism and Eastern aestheticism, and that he belongs to neither completely. Wilson Harris, in his book *Tradition, the Writer, and Society,* describes the relationship between the West Indian and his pre-Columbian past as a "series of subtle, nebulous links which are latent within him, the latent ground of old and new possibilities." He argues that the region is steeped in such "broken conceptions as well as misconceptions of the residue of the meaning of conquest."[11] Similarly, in the case of Naipaul the links within him to an uncomprehended past are essential to an understanding of his West Indian experience.

Most critics, particularly those from the First World, attempt a one-dimensional, surface reading of Naipaul's texts and thus reduce the entire critical enterprise to a search for confirmatory and presupposed judgments about their own reality rather than colonial and postcolonial reality as it is revealed through an examination of the texts. The result is a game of mirrored reflections in which the critics attempt to see how well colonial reality confirms their expectations of what it ought to be. At their worst, these critics perceive literary criticism as an opportunity to use Naipaul's texts as pads from which to launch personal attacks against Third World societies. Most First World critics fail to see that their readings of Naipaul are so strongly colored by their values, experiences, and aspirations.[12]

Thus, many of these misreadings present the notion that Naipaul's fiction and nonfiction are privileged discourses that offer their meaning or meanings spontaneously to the reader. These critics do not seem to understand that the text always arrives accompanied, "determined," as it were, "by the existence of other works, which can belong to different areas of production."[13] Naipaul's fictional and nonfictional texts cannot be taken as unproblematic guides to the mapping of our society.[14]

Controversies in interpreting Naipaul's work arise from the almost opposite manner in which the Third World and First World critics interpret it. The preponderance of critiques of Naipaul's work from the First World and their generally favorable responses can be opposed to the generally unfavorable responses of Third World critics. As Elaine Campbell observed in 1981, "Naipaul's attitude has so antagonized both East Indians and British West Indians that his writing is attacked in both India and the West Indies, although it is affirmed in England, and, lately in the United States."[15] For example, while Third World critics argue that Naipaul does not adequately reflect the complexities of life in colonial and postcolonial worlds, First World critics assume that because Naipaul was born in a colonial country, he must be telling the "truth" about that experience. These conflicts are clear in the letters between Michael Thelwell, a Jamaican critic and novelist, and Irving Howe, an American critic and novelist, in which Thelwell attempted to modify some of the effusive encomium with which Howe had greeted *A Bend in the River* (1979).[16]

A similar problem arose between Gordon Rohlehr, a Guyanese critic, and Edward Lucie-Smith, a Jamaican of English parentage who resides in London. The latter attacked Rohlehr's article "The Ironic Approach: The Novels of V. S. Naipaul" for what he called its "most conspicuous and consistent unfairness . . . in its treatment of the work of V. S. Naipaul." Lucie-Smith goes on to make the nonliterary judgment that West Indian critics are likely to be unfair toward Naipaul because of his success.[17]

The Australian critic Helen Tiffin, in an otherwise strong and perceptive reading of Naipaul's work, accused the Indian critic P. D. Narasimhaiah of lacking in "tolerance for any criticism of his country." Moreover, because Narasimhaiah dared to criticize Naipaul's perception of his country, Tiffin charges him with "oversimplify[ing] and fail[ing] to understand the difference between the Trinidad Indian and the Indian who has not emigrated, and two generations previous to that, from his land." Thus, whether one is English, American, or Australian—that is, of European descent and First World—one's response to the colonial critic, be she or he from Jamaica, Guyana, or India, is the same: Naipaul is lucid, coherent, and detached, and as William Walsh said, possessing "a near-Latin order and assurance."[18] If Naipaul's compatriots do not share his interpretation of reality, they are viewed as either lacking in tolerance, oversimplistic, or jealous of his achievements. First World critics never appreciate that Third World critics perceive Naipaul's interpretation of their society in a different light from their own precisely because they see his work in a historical context and tradition.

It would be unfair to say that all First World critics see Naipaul's work in an ahistorical and idealist light. Jean Kramer, for example, in the *New York Times Book Review,* articulated one of the methodological questions that must be addressed in any analysis of Naipaul's work:

By now we [the white world, the First World] embrace Naipaul as a kind of prophet without God, one of those doomsday misogynists who used to wander through Russian novels, raving and shaking their staffs at the gentry in their country houses—*someone whose vision or moral fault has marked him* with a crazed and arrogant and somehow blessed purity. We shudder at his voice, and give him supper, but he is clearly not one of our sane and measured selves. A convenience, certainly. We turn appreciating, even reading Naipaul, into a kind of exemption from his fury. No wonder he forgives no one—not when he is praised so often as that Indian writer who, being "one of them," can expose the depravities of "his" world in ways that we white Westerners, with our colonial past and our complacent present, could presumably never get away with. It is as if his foreignness, his status as "one of them," gives him a license to see, as if our hypocrisies translate into *his* ethnic privilege. . . . There is not much point in reading the Naipaul of the past 10 years if we seize on an ex-colonial's weakness for the "idea" of English civilization and reduce the moral landscape of his books to a map of our own attitudes and narrow politics.[19]

As early as 1963, Gordon Rohlehr observed Naipaul's tendency toward nihilism and argued that "It is only when one reads *The Middle Passage* that one realizes how completely Naipaul has accepted anarchy and absurdity as the norms of his society."[20] Rohlehr could not have perceived the full outlines of Naipaul's vision at that stage of his artistic development nor predicted the direction such a commitment to anarchy and absurdity would lead. Nor, for that matter, could he anticipate Naipaul's embrace of the mother country in 1987 at his second arrival. He called it the enigma of arrival.

Naipaul's work during the period from 1970 to 1980 cannot be dismissed as "an ex-colonial weakness for the 'idea' of English civilization," however, even though an apocalyptic vision began to emerge during this period. Nonetheless, Kramer is undoubtedly correct in her assumptions about Naipaul's growing relationship to the colonizer's world, the nature of his literary work, the surface level of examination accorded it, and his tendency to privilege the ideas of the dominant powers. With the publication of *Among the Believers* (1981), however, First World critics and other thinkers began to interpret Naipaul's work as Kramer did and by 1987 many more searching questions about Naipaul's ideological and racist positions were being raised more openly.[21]

Without a doubt, most idealist readings of Naipaul's work lead, almost inevitably, to misconceptions. None of these critics attempt to locate Naipaul in his tradition or his history and they presume consciously or otherwise that he cannot be circumscribed by a tradition or history. Thus Paul Theroux argues that Naipaul is "wholly original," and that "he may be the only writer today in whom there are no echoes or influences."[22] Theroux does not demonstrate any knowledge of West Indian literature or history and such knowledge does not appear to be important to him. Why, we may ask, is Naipaul so blessed?

Many serious thinkers have recognized the importance of history and tradition in writers' work.[23] Goethe advanced the position that the past hangs over the present so powerfully that not even the most creative genius (or those who are thought to be "exceptional" or "original") can be exempt from its influence. Because of the collective and social dimensions of our humanity and because we borrow and learn from those who lived before and those who live around us, he concluded, "Even the greatest genius would not get very far if he were to try to produce everything out of himself alone."[24] No matter how talented he is, Naipaul cannot be exempt from those influences of the past.

The attempt to show Naipaul as exceptional, unique, and painfully truthful also leads to certain kinds of racist judgments. Not content with arrogant and metaphysical fallacies, such as that Naipaul exists outside historical time and space, idealist critics advance the racist fallacy that Naipaul cannot be a product of the Caribbean tradition of literature because there is none. It is almost to suggest that in spite of all of the Caribbean writers who have preceded him, the West Indies could not produce a literate culture until Naipaul arrived. It was to this attitude that Derek Walcott, the famed West Indian poet, addressed himself in a review of *The Enigma of Arrival* (1987):

The myth of Naipaul as a phenomenon, as a singular, contradictory genius who survived the cane fields and the bush at great cost, has long been a farce. It is a myth he chooses to encourage—though he alone knows why, since the existence of other writers in no way diminishes his gift. . . . There is something alarmingly venal in all this dislocation and despair. Besides, it is not true. There is, instead, another truth. Naipaul's prejudice.

Frankness doesn't absolve him of it. Of course prejudice comes from history, from the hoarded genealogy of the tribe; yet if Naipaul's attitude toward Negroes, with its nasty little sneers . . . was turned on Jews, for example, how many people would praise him for his frankness? Who would have exalted that "honesty" for which he is praised as our only incorruptible writer from the Third World?[25]

Naipaul's work is not a product merely of history and tradition. As Roland Barthes has argued, an author inherits his "mode of writing" or *écriture,* from his society's literary culture. According to Barthes, whether the writer likes it or not, his language is chosen from certain historical possibilities, even though he may claim the *style* is his own. Thus the history of a mode of writing cannot be reduced to an independent, history-less activity from which the writer is free to choose or not to choose. He is implicated irrevocably and cannot arbitrarily negate or deny that bond, and it is in this sense that Naipaul's *écriture,* though free and important, is an integral part of its general history and literary tradition.[26]

This linkage to the past is important in that India's cultural heritage and religious philosophy played a major part in sustaining and shaping the East Indians in Trinidad and Tobago, particularly during the years of their indenture. As early as 1888, J. H. Collens, superintendent of the Boys' Model and Normal School in Port of Spain, Trinidad, observed the diligence with which the East Indians practiced their religion and culture:

Even amongst the humble labourers who till our fields there is a considerable knowledge of them, and you may often in the evening, work being done, see and hear a group of coolies crouching down in a semicircle, chanting whole stanzas of the epic poems, *Ramayan* [sic] etc. In the preface of the *Ramayan* it is stated that "he who constantly hears and sings this poem will obtain the highest bliss hereafter, and become as one with the gods." Hence the wily Babagee who reads to his ignorant countrymen, accounts from the *Ramayan,* or 'Books of the Exploits of Ram,' expects to get, and is tolerably sure of receiving, a large offertory for his pains.[27]

These traditions, according to the Indian scholar J. C. Jha, still inform the cultural life of the East Indians of Trinidad and Tobago who follow the Hindu religion.[28] More importantly, it is this "second-order memory" (myth) or "second-order signification," as Jonathan Culler calls it, resonating with such great persistence in Naipaul's work, that gives it its special brilliance and importance.[29] It is within the duality of "freedom and remembrance" that the author begins to negotiate his liberation from his past and even his present. It is the site from which one ought to begin an examination of Naipaul's work.

This corpus of myth, religion, and philosophy that predominates in Naipaul's early fiction played a strong role in the lives of the East Indians at the time Naipaul was growing up, and this was especially strong in his family. As he remarks in *An Area of Darkness:*

The family life I have been describing began to dissolve when I was six or seven; when I was fourteen it had ceased to exist. Between my brother, twelve years younger than myself, and me there is more than a generation of difference. He can have no memory of that private world which survived with such apparent solidity up to only twenty-five years ago, a world which had lengthened out, its energy of inertia steadily weakening, from the featureless area of darkness which was India.[30]

Naipaul retrieved the philosophical stance of this early world in his later texts. Yet it is the conflict between this second-order memory in the midst of new meaning that characterizes both the content and form of his more persuasive writing.

This conflict was not unique in Naipaul. Mulk Raj Anand, a Hindu novelist and critic from India who read philosophy at the University of London about ten years before Naipaul arrived in London, was plagued by some of the same problems. In 1945 Anand wrote *An Apology for Heroism* to account for the "jig-saw puzzle of my Indian upbringing and Eur-Asian experience." Arguing that "ancient Indian thought . . . gave more rounded answers to life's question," Anand concluded that there is a traditional attitude toward Indian philosophical thought and cultural life expressed in the *Ramayana,* the *Mahabharata,* the *Gita,* and the stories of the *Puranas* that seems to claim the sons and daughters of India.[31] Collens made the same point about the Indians of Trinidad and Tobago in his guide to Trinidad.

In "Old Myth, New Myth: Recital versus Novel," Anand pointed out that the critical literary problem facing many Indian novelists compelled to write in English was how to retain the traditional vision embodied in the old myths while transmitting the truth in contemporary forms of new "myths" as he called them: "The old epic age is over. The novel today is complementary to the other disciplines, for confrontation on another plane, the human situation, and demands a serious mental effort to control it from spilling over into amorphousness. The novel is not for pedagogic learning: it is for the burning and melting till the dross of life falls away and leaves the reader aflame to illuminate the byways of life."[32]

For Anand, then, the task of writers who seek to use the novel to examine their emerging colonial societies is "to relate the old myths to new myths, to synthesize the inner spaces to the outer spaces."[33] The original epic, Anand says, in its received tradition, is unable to reflect upon itself, to signify fully for its society, and so becomes incapable of examining a contemporary society that is seething with revolutionary sentiments.[34] For Anand, in opening up new spaces into history and society—that is, presenting a new discourse about the self and society—and raising questions about society, the novel critiques the writer's activity. In so doing, the novel opens up for exploration new areas of experience about the manner in which an individual functions within his or her society and, as Naipaul has argued, about the manner in which it illuminates "aspects of the human predicament."[35]

For Naipaul and his people, who had been removed from their home for many generations, the pull toward India, though less strong than for Anand and his people, was grounded in nostalgia and was intangible, cloyingly sentimental, and relatively abstract. Naipaul, like his father, was forced to reshape some of the epics and other religious texts of his people so as to examine their attitude toward their former home and their present reality. The short story, the prose-tragedy, the novel, and the nonfictional text became means whereby Naipaul could examine his people's reality in their new world.

The conflict in Naipaul's writing involves the clash between Eastern and Western perceptions of the world. In his *Apology for Heroism,* Anand articulates this conflict:

To me the whole presumption about man being born in sin, which lay at the root of Christian ethics, seemed obnoxious. For whatever criticism may be levelled against the Vedantic Absolute, who is above all human considerations of morality, there is in the Hindu and, particularly, in the Buddhist view, an insistence on light and knowledge as against the Christian insistence on darkness and sin. Guatama became "the enlightened one" when he attained the highest state, whereas from the start Christianity seemed to condemn human beings to an abject and ignominious position.[36]

These contrasting social values produced special problems for the East Indian in Trinidad and compounded the impact of colonialism on him. Although Naipaul ultimately privileged the Christian concept of the world, the conflicting demands of both conceptions subtend his work.[37]

Naipaul's problem therefore extended to the Indian novelists of the 1950s and 1960s who wrote in English and who began to explore, through the novel, the psychic trauma and void that attended the experiences of their people who were exposed to Western culture. According to R. S. Singh, "What was of immense concern to the novelist was the hero's inner being, the metaphysical core shaken to the pores under the stress of an alien culture."[38]

As with these other writers, the major source of tension in Naipaul's work arose initially from the conflict between his Hindu sensibilities and the Christian tradition to which he and his people were subjected. The transition from colonialism to postcolonialism that resulted from the formal independence of the society made the conflict even more dramatic. Forced to choose between these dual demands, he chooses to accept the ideology of the colonizer. As a result, his work has lost its perceptiveness and clarity and is reduced, ultimately, to a repetition of earlier themes and concerns. In ideological terms, he simply elaborates the system of ideas and representation of the dominant culture within his texts.

DISCURSIVE FIELD–SOCIAL CONTEXT

The work of Naipaul must be seen within the larger field of Caribbean literature and history. It must be remembered that in the colonization of the Caribbean a new race of people—a mixture of European, American Indian, and African—came into being: a major synthesis of peoples that brought together the best of their three cultures. The coming of the East Indians to the Caribbean in 1838 as indentured laborers added another dimension to the hegemonic dominance of the African cultural element, particularly in Guyana and Trinidad.[39] Because they came to the Caribbean at a time when wage slavery had replaced physical slavery and when it was not in the immediate interest of the dominant colonial power to suppress their culture, the East Indians remained separate and distinct from the major African groups.[40] As a result, the East Indians were able to preserve much of their customs and traditions. As Naipaul has pointed out,

Living by themselves in villages, the Indians were able to have a complete community life. It was a world eaten up with jealousies and family feuds and village feuds; but it was a world of its own, a community within the colonial society, without responsibility, with authority doubly and trebly removed. Loyalties were narrow: to the family, the village. This has been responsible for the village-headman type of politician the Indian favours, and explains why Indian leadership has been so deplorable, so unfitted to handle the mechanics of party and policy.[41]

In 1917, at the end of indenture, the East Indians' attempt to maintain a separate identity was challenged severely. Feeling the pull of the dominant group and having to participate in the social and political activities of the countries caused increasing strains. The need to act collectively with the Africans in the newly emerging world of capitalism and the imperative that they accept this new land as their home became major concerns for most East Indians, who refused or were unable to return to their motherland. Faced with this new and complex situation in a perverse and alien environment, the East Indians, like other Caribbean peoples before them, were forced to address the dual question of the problematic of being and the quest for meaning in their new environment.

Like the nineteenth century, the twentieth century in the British Caribbean was fraught with upheavals and changes.[42] Many British Caribbean writers, including the East Indians, explored these changes in their fiction. The fictional depictions of the East Indian's experience in the Caribbean in the twentieth century did not begin with Naipaul. A. F. Webber, in *Those*

That Be in Bondage (1917), Edgar Mittleholzer, in *Corentyne Thunder* (1941), Seepersad Naipaul, in *Gurudeva and Other Indian Tales* (1946), and Samuel Selvon, in *A Brighter Sun* (1952) all preceded Naipaul's fictional examination of the East Indian in the Caribbean.[43] In their own ways, particularly in his father's work, they anticipated many of the problems Naipaul has examined.

Naipaul was aware, at least initially, that a knowledge of Trinidad's society was indispensable to understanding his work. In 1958, after the publication of his first three novels, he was explicit about his function as a Trinidadian artist:

I live in England and depend on an English audience. Yet I write about Trinidad, and more particularly about the East Indian community there. Few novels have been written about Trinidad and I cannot deny that this gives me some advantage. . . . My material is abundant, new and easily grasped. I need no gimmicks. But I have certain handicaps. The social comedies I write can be fully appreciated only by someone who knows the region I write about. Without that knowledge it is easy for my books to be dismissed as farces and my characters as eccentrics.[44]

What Naipaul did not anticipate, of course, when he wrote those lines was that his books would be held up as lucid descriptions of the colonial condition and his characters interpreted as representative colonial subjects. What he himself could not know at that time was that he too would grow to disown and to dismiss his society as a meaningless accident of history and need that same England to rescue him from his oblivion. What, then, this analysis seeks to do is to place his work into some meaningful context and to offer a specific manner in which his texts ought to be read.

I will argue that Naipaul's richest and most important fiction emerges in his early period, that is, up to and including *The Mimic Men,* when he seeks honestly to come to terms with the major problematic of his being: what it means to be an East Indian in an alien world. This is the most genuinely creative period of his career. After *Mimic Men,* Naipaul was unable to go beyond an examination of what it means to be a subject in a postcolonial world and thus he repeats the same tirades against these societies. In *A Bend in the River* Naipaul not only condemned these societies to doom and despair but became an apologist for the imperialist world order. And though he may have become more technically proficient in this latter period, his range of examination had narrowed and his insights had become repetitious. In the end, he makes a vain attempt to recuperate and to celebrate his past, but his racist sentiments, unquestioned acceptance of the colonizer's culture, and his imposed exile corrupts that gesture and makes it all but futile.

By 1987 he feels more at home—indeed, is at home—in the colonizer's world.

I have documented Naipaul's contribution to the examination of the subject in colonial and noncolonial societies and argued that *A House for Mr. Biswas* and *The Mimic Men* are his two most important works, even though some First World critics, primarily those from the United States, have tended to grant this honor to *Guerrillas*. Because his loyalties stood midway between the Eastern and Western visions of the world, he gave the world a complex narrative of Eastern acceptance and Western striving: a complex retelling of the greatest epic of the East in language and cadence that the West could understand and accept. To put it another way, the tension in his work is created by the fundamental opposition between the deep linguistic structures of his culture and the elective models (fictional and nonfictional) through which he chooses to express himself.

At its best, this opposition between culture and form produces rich and exciting fiction. When the former—the very object that is the source of his work's richness and beauty—is scorned, ridiculed, and defamed, then the latter is compromised and fiction(s) of a dubious order are produced. His writing thus becomes ephemeral, enigmatic, elliptical, and obtuse. It promises much but offers little. Writing in the *New Republic,* Walcott noted that *The Enigma of Arrival,* Naipaul's last novel, "began as a healing"—it promised much—but then sadly it degenerates into banality.[45] And this is the final absurdity of both Naipaul and his work. They are absorbed, deracinated, and, finally, fetishized by the very dislocation and disruption that produced them in the first place, and that is paradox indeed. How his work arrives at that seemingly paradoxical position and why it moves toward an increasing identification with the dominant imperialist ideology and racist preoccupation of the time are the subject of this book.

1. Tradition, *Miguel Street,* and Other Short Stories: The First Period of Naipaul's Development

The only independence which they [the Africans and East Indians] would desire is idleness, according to their different tastes in the enjoyment of it; and the higher motives which actuate the European labourers . . . , that to be industrious is a duty and a virtue; that to be independent in circumstances, whatever his station, raises a man in the moral scale amongst his race; and that his ability to perform his duties as a citizen, and, we may add, as a Christian, is increased by it. These, and such motives as these, are unknown to the fatalist worshippers of Mahomet and Brahma, and to the savages who go by the names of Liberated Africans.
—Lord Harris, quoted in Eric Williams, *History of the People of Trinidad and Tobago*

I suppose . . . there is barely a society without its major narratives, told, retold and varied; formulae, texts, ritualized texts to be spoken in well-defined circumstances, things said once, and conserved because people suspect some hidden secret or wealth lies buried within.
—Michel Foucault, *The Archaeology of Knowledge*

THE NEED FOR A TRADITION

The movement toward literary and cultural autonomy in Trinidad and Tobago roughly parallels the social and political development of the society.[1] The only discernible cultural activity during the period from 1833 to 1870 was the struggle to continue the annual carnival celebrations. From 1870 to 1890, however, interest in cultural pursuits arose among the more progressive black and colored citizens. As Bridget Brereton has argued, "The coloured and black intelligentsia prided itself on its literary and intellectual attainments and boasted of being more 'cultured' than the whites, who were accused of crass materialism. Often movements of a literary character were initiated by non-whites; for instance, the Athenaeum Club or, the *Trinidad Monthly Magazine.*"[2]

Publications such as the *Trinidad Monthly Magazine* (1870), the *San Fernando Gazette* (1874–95), and the *Indian Kohinoor Gazette* (1898) served as avenues for the rudimentary literary productions of some of the island's inhabitants and defended the interests of the oppressed black and East Indian masses. *Public Opinion,* first published in 1884, edited by Philip Rostant and designed to reach the lower classes, "speedily obtained a large circulation among all classes, both on account of its cheapness, the soundness of its views on matters of importance and the excellence of its literary matter."[3] In his autobiography, *Trinidad and Trinidadians* (1919), L. O. Lewis noted that dramatic plays were being performed as early as 1870; Brereton's history alludes to two satirical sketches by J. J. Thomas written around 1890; Grenidge produced his *Bohemian Sketches* in 1890; and Ignacio Bodu produced his *Trinidadiana* in 1890. Thus the literary activity during this period in addressing the need for national autonomy paralleled the impulse of the masses to regain their cultural autonomy.

In the period from 1900 to 1940, the movement toward nationalism and self-determination among the working people had its counterpart in the literary and cultural arena in the struggle to create an authentic literary tradition, as evidenced by the influence of radical literature on the public. The Sedition Ordinance, which was passed in Trinidad in 1920, to stymie industrial and political unrest, prescribed severe penalties for the circulation of newspapers and publications deemed subversive, and publications such as *Negro World, Crusader,* and the *Messenger* were banned.[4] Alfred Mendes, a leading figure in the literary movement of this period, argued that the individuals who spearheaded the literary movement were veterans returned from World War I who were influenced by the achievements of the Russian Revolution.[5] The content and form of the literature, however, were a part of and were fashioned by the larger movement toward nationalism and self-determination.

This twentieth-century literary movement began as an attack against what were thought to be the recalcitrant elements of the dominant culture and the members of the oppressed class who believed all things foreign and European were inherently superior. As a result, most of the writers used as their subject matter the residents of the barrack yards of Port of Spain. The termination of the indenture system and the fragmentation of the traditional Indian way of life also became sources of much East Indian writing. Thus emerged an urban proletarian literature that dealt primarily with the Africans and a peasant literature that dealt primarily with the East Indian.

A debate in two periodicals, *Trinidad* and the *Beacon,* published in Trinidad between 1929 and 1933, "formulated basic postulates for an indigenous West Indian literature."[6] The short story, which remained the dominant form of West Indian literature until 1949,[7] was the vehicle through which this tradition and the incipient nationalism best expressed themselves, whereas the periodicals provided a forum in which writers could discuss the parameters of West Indian literature.[8]

Writers such as C. A. Thomasos argued that when the West Indies produced a literature of its own, it would "use a tradition, culture, and temperament of its own to pass judgment on its literature." Ernest A. Carr argued for the universality of tradition in general and commented that "the artist who attempts a new formula will deserve success only if the content of this formula draws its sustenance from the well of the past, in other words, if the artist pays due respect to tradition."[9]

More spirited critics condemned the imitativeness of West Indian writers, and the editors of the *Beacon* criticized the attempt by some critics to force Trinidadian writers to conform to English and American practices. In one of its early editorials, "Local Fiction" (1932), the editors accused young writers who had submitted short stories to its local fiction-writing competition of copying these models and warned:

We fail utterly to understand, however, why anyone should want to see Trinidad as a miniature *Paradiso,* where grave-diggers speak like English M.P.'s and vice-versa. The answer is obviously that the average Trinidadian writer regards his fellow-countrymen as his inferiors, and uninteresting people who are not worth his while. He genuinely feels (and by this, of course, asserts his own feeling of inferiority) that with his people as characters his stories would be worth nothing. It is for this reason that he peoples them with creatures from other planets, American gangsters and English M.P.'s and revives familiar plots and characters from *True Story* and other *n*th rate periodicals.[10]

They were just as acerbic in their editorial on poetry, complaining that "intellectual dropsy is a popular form of ailment."[11] The periodical also castigated the literary pretensions of some Trinidadians who imitated the English "classics" and waged war on any intellectual production from the island. In encouraging the production of a literature that reflected the local landscape and used local themes, the editors of the *Beacon* argued that they were "able to squeeze more beauty out of watching Ramirez glide rhythmically over the fresh, green grass of the [Queen's Park] Savannah than in witnessing the pathetic spectacle of a group of pretentious and artificially-spirited young men and women dissecting Keats."[12]

The editors of the *Beacon* realized, as perhaps V. S. Naipaul never did, that a national literature would grow out of the confluence of social forces peculiar to the island and, in fact, shape its growth. Thus they attacked Dr.

Laurence for comparing C. L. R. James's short story, a local piece, to the works of Charles Dickens and Sir Walter Scott on the grounds that "the sociological forces" at work in the islands were so different from those of Dickens's or Scott's England that no comparison was valid.

Inherent in the struggle to articulate the indigenous tradition in literature was the attempt by the more progressive elements of the emerging nationalist movement to anticipate, through literature, a sense of national consciousness. As a result of the agitation in the society and the insistence on a national tradition in the literature, a large body of local short stories, a few novels, and other literary works emerged in the period from 1929 to 1949. Of particular importance were the short stories of C. L. R. James, Alfred Mendes, W. Therold Barnes, Daniel Samaroo Joseph, Frank Collymore, Edgar Mittelholzer, Claude Thompson, Roger Mais, H. D. Carberry, Seepersad Naipaul, Samuel Selvon, and Cecil Gray, who concentrated primarily on local themes. Of special importance to V. S. Naipaul's development were his father's *Gurudeva and Other Indian Tales* (1946), Joseph's "Taxi Mister" (1947), Selvon's "The Baby" (1949) and "Cane Is Bitter" (1950), and Gray's "Merely for the Record" (1951), in which one encounters many of the topics V. S. Naipaul later examined in his early short stories and the local style he emulated.[13]

When V. S. Naipaul began to write, he thus drew upon a collective tradition for both his style and his content. And although his father's work must have had some influence on him simply because of its proximity and familiarity, he drew heavily from the island's folk life and stories. As Landeg White has suggested, "Much of the material in *Miguel Street* is based on anecdotes which are still widely current in Trinidad. I myself . . . had heard the adventures ascribed to Bolo many times before I read *Miguel Street,* and 'Man-Man' exists in other versions."[14] Many of the themes in *Miguel Street* are found in short stories written from 1929 to 1951 by other writers, and Miguel Street itself is a composite of streets in Port of Spain.

To be sure, the immediacy, urgency, urban focus, and rhythm of Naipaul's early stories and the definite break with the East Indian tradition which he suggested and Selvon undertook were not found in the fiction of other writers of this period or in the work of Seepersad Naipaul. Even *The Mystic Masseur* and *The Suffrage of Elvira,* in which Naipaul returns to the themes of his father, bear the unmistakable imprint of the short stories of the period from 1929 to 1949. *A House for Mr. Biswas* is a more complex exercise than Seepersad Naipaul's "They Named Him Mohun," despite the "cannibalization" of the latter, of which V. S. Naipaul speaks in his introduction to his father's stories.[15] V. S. Naipaul preferred to use the artistic unity and vision of the short story to give his world a sense of order. In *Miguel Street* and his early short stories, we first see Naipaul's tendency to consolidate and reshape his early experiences.

THE EARLY SHORT STORIES

When Naipaul went to Oxford in 1950 he became a privileged colonial subject thrust into the colonizer's world of "learning" and "culture." In that year he wrote a poem entitled "Two Thirty A.M.," which was read by John Figueroa on "Caribbean Voices" on September 24, 1950.[16] Because the poem is little known and has been reproduced in a dissertation that is not easily available (see n. 18), I planned to reproduce it here, but unfortunately, V. S. Naipaul, through his literary agent, denied permission to reproduce the full poem (Gillion Aitken to the author, Feb. 12, 1988). I therefore must limit myself to a few lines. Yet one cannot read those lines without recognizing the darkness that possessed Naipaul's soul when he arrived in England. In her very courteous response to a letter I wrote requesting permission to quote this poem, Patricia Naipaul noted that her husband "says that this poem, written by him at school before he left Trinidad, was a joke poem, 'a prank,' not to be taken seriously, about modern poetry—showing how things could be written, words strung together without feeling" (Patricia Naipaul to the author, Jan. 11, 1988). Aitken, in his "official" response to my letter, claims that Naipaul "views" this poem as his "juvenilia" that ought not "to be published just yet." Both these claims, it seems, reflect retrospective readings of what may be Naipaul's later embarrassed response to his first encounter with London. Certainly when the poem was read over the BBC no indication was given that it was a prank about modern poetry. Indeed, it was aired because it so *truly* represented colonials' fears as they encountered the "reality" of the [m]other country. The fact that similar sentiments, the sense of being lost, alone, and afraid, are repeated in many of his early works, tends to support the conclusion that "Two Thirty A.M." represents Naipaul's authentic feelings when he arrived in London.

The poem itself is very revealing. It is sparse, cryptic, and economical in its sentiments. Viewing that dreadful world and the frenzied activity of that ghost-laden time of morning/mourning, the poet recoils at the immensity of the city and his seeming helplessness in coming to terms with the endless sense of "futility" that it engenders. He asks: "does it [the futility] begin today / tomorrow or last night" or is it ever present, "an overpowering now," re-presenting "eternity transfixed"? This inability to control his time or to locate himself in that "overpowering now [world]," generates a sense of fear that leaves him feeling trapped, as though it is "forever," as though it were "death / and nothing / and mourning."

The poem reflects the powerful fear and dread that pervaded Naipaul's soul when he arrived in that at once most sought after and indifferent country of the master. Years later he still felt the same fear of London. In *An Area of Darkness,* he lamented: "I came to London. It had become the centre of my world and I had worked hard to come to it. And I was lost. London was not the centre of my world. I had been misled; but there was nowhere else to go."[17] Helen Tiffin has argued that, on one level, "Two Thirty A.M." is about "time, darkness, and futility—concerns (and even images) which become more pervasive in Naipaul's later work."[18] This powerful poem conveys the ambivalence and dread Naipaul felt in those early years, which would set the tone for everything he wrote afterward.

"This Is Home" (1951), the first of Naipaul's short stories to be broadcast on "Caribbean Voices," tells of man's solitary condition and his terrible desire, despite his doubts and fears, to cling to extraneous emotions (in this case, love) to hold him together. The story reflects Naipaul's continuing desire to examine the fear expressed in "Two Thirty A.M." It is about a man and a woman who go to the top of a hill to begin their lives together and is told from the point of view of a man who is trying to reconcile the twin emotions of fear and joy. Beset by a growing panic, he looks at the woman and is overcome by "a weight of immense solitude."[19] As the narrator reflects on the man's condition, he expresses the fear and aloneness the man feels: "We are always so much alone; the crowd gave us solace for the moment, yet the crowd was stronger than the individuals who made it up. And always within us was a whole private life, that was stark and solitary. The responsibility was too great. Whatever we did, we could never free ourselves from that solitude—the solitude of one's mind." The same sense of dread of tomorrow is also encountered in "Two Thirty A.M." Here it anticipates an emotion that would come full circle when Naipaul tried to find his center.[20]

In the end, the major character of "This Is Home" tries to overcome his fear of the future—the solitude he expects to darken his days—by assuring his woman that "this [the top of the hill] is home." But even as he tries to comfort her, the man feels that "he was lying." The questions of the proper relationship between the East Indian man and woman which is raised here occurs in other early short stories. Although Naipaul does not deal as explicitly with Hindu culture in "This Is Home" as he does in some of his later stories, he alludes to it when the major protagonist says:

He saw the tasks of the world split in two. Man the author, man the worker. Woman the anvil of man's passion: the feeder and lover of her master. Good God! The responsibility was too much for him. It wasn't the mere physical satisfaction that disturbed him. It was the idea of fitting into a primaeval pattern of living to mate, and mating to create that filled him with dread. Sex was the whole works and he knew it; and it hurt him. He was ashamed. Why must flesh be so weak and so powerful at the same time? Why couldn't people be made out of rubber, insensitive to touch and passion? He sought to control his own passions, but he had failed. It cropped up, triumphant, again and again. . . . We never can live alone. We need protection. We created a mutual protection society and called it love: called it marriage and home.

Naipaul's second story, "The Mourners," confronts his concerns more concretely. The story is about an East Indian couple who have begun to acquire many of the traits of the creolized or Western world. The story is told from the point of view of Ann, a young East Indian girl just beyond her tenth year, who seems to be confused by the behavior of adults. It hints at the caste/class conflicts within the East Indian community, the relations between the poorer and richer sides of the extended family, and the changing social attitudes. These incidents reflect the changing world of the East Indian in Trinidad and Tobago and the resulting conflicts. Ravi participates in carnival, a predominantly Negro festival, Sheila shortens a servant's name from Soomintra to Soomin ("a thing that was ordinarily forbidden, even to the children"), and the doctor wishes to have his son enter the "Cow and Gate Baby Contest."[21]

The conflict between the Western and Eastern worlds, the creolized and the Hindu, which would become central to Naipaul's work, is examined in greater detail in his next short story, "Potatoes" (1952). Most of Naipaul's early concerns are included in this eight-page story, thus making it central to an understanding of the stories of this period. Here can be seen the seeds of *A House for Mr. Biswas.* The story centers upon Mrs. Gobin, who comes from a leading Hindu family on the island and is trying to free herself from her mother's dominance by entering the potato business. Her father "had been recognized as the leader of the new Hindu aristocracy in the island; the family was venerated for its caste, its piety, and its wealth. Mrs. Gobin, nevertheless, was poor."[22] Her poverty had disgraced her family, and she also had become somewhat ashamed of herself. She was determined, however, once her husband was dead, to remove herself from poverty and to become "independent" of her family. As she tells her mother: "I say it now, I say it before, and I will always say it, it never does pay to be dependent on anybody. But mark my words, Ma. I am going to make myself independent."[23]

In her effort to become independent, Mrs. Gobin experiences the same isolation the man in "This Is Home" felt:

The cart jogged away; Mrs. Gobin felt that she was alone, felt it poignantly—alone in a big, bad world. The people she met walked with firm feet, always knowing where they were going, and, most importantly of all, how they were going about it. But always she was lost. If she could have formulated her thoughts, Mrs. Gobin would have cursed the life she had been brought up to live. Perhaps her method of thinking, her way of life, was all right in an all-Hindu society, but in this cosmopolitan hotch-potch where nothing was sacred and everything was somehow flat and unsatisfying, in this hotch-potch, it is totally inadequate.

The conflict between the sacred and the profane and Mrs. Gobin's painful awareness that she is neither trained nor prepared to act in the creole world creates the powerful sense of aloneness and loss first encountered in "Two Thirty A.M." This conflict between East and West, the feudal and the colonial-capitalist, runs through all of Naipaul's work.

This social conflict is evident even in the descriptions of landscape, a technique Naipaul would use frequently. Mrs. Gobin's home, for example, became familiar to many of Naipaul's readers. The house, it can be assumed, is in the country district.

She came from a family that prided itself on its business skill. Her father, starting from almost nothing, had established himself as a prosperous landowner and businessman. Before he died he had erected, as a monument to his enterprise, and unquestionable proof of his wealth, a magnificent white palace, built in a mongrel Hindu style by architects who had come all the way from India. The walls were four feet thick; the balustrades were lavishly ornamented with religious carvings; and figures of elephant gods and monkey gods appeared in the most unlikely places. On the top of the grand facade two stone lions stared forever in different directions.

A new phase of her life begins when Mrs. Gobin goes to the city to begin her potato business. The shop to which she goes to transact her business contrasts sharply with "the magnificent white palace built in a mongrel Hindu style":

On Thursday morning she went to the city, and entered the shop of an Indian merchant, a man she knew. The shop was a small, square room that smelled of curry and onions. An obsolete cash register was opened by a venerable-looking man with a beard, who could pass for a religious prophet, but who was, in fact, merely a Hindu of mediocre caste. The two girl assistants who glided skillfully among the crates of onions, the sacks of flour, and the barrels of potatoes were conveniently tiny, underfed creatures.

The city is inhabited by that feared other, "the nigger world." The fear this world evokes is first made known to the reader when Mrs. Gobin informs her mother that she intends to be independent of her. Her mother mutters some quotations from the *Gita* and then responds: "I know what you will do. I know what your type always does. Well, go ahead, go to hell, and walk the streets. I wash my hands of you since I married you off. . . . Your father used to warn me all the time about you; and ever since you have been living in the town, you have been playing white woman. Well, go ahead, and turn nigger. I am not going to stop you."

In the story the "nigger world" is represented by a nameless "old negro man," whom Mrs. Gobin engages to carry her potatoes home, and his family, to whom Mrs. Gobin goes when the Negro man is late in delivering the potatoes. On one occasion when he is two days late, she goes to his home and is terrified by his alien world. She is greeted by the familiar taunts the Negro directs against Indians. The old Negro's wife, who is also nameless, tells Mrs. Gobin: "All you Indians smart as hell. Making money like hell, and not spending a cent. Just saving up to be rich. I don't know an Indian who ain't rich. All you people does always help one another." The irony of this statement is that it expresses a stereotype of the East Indian. Mrs. Gobin is indeed poor, has no help from anyone, and is trying to survive on her own. The author's concern, however, is the misconceptions about the "other" and the fear that ensues when the East Indian encounters that other world of the profane. The Negro world is painted as threatening and intrusive. Mrs. Gobin fails in her business venture, but she does attempt to break out of the rigid hold that "the magnificent white palace" and its major occupant have on her.

In the end, the vehemence Mrs. Gobin's mother feels toward the "nigger world" reflects the changes that seem to threaten the somewhat closed East Indian community. The fear in "Potatoes" is not so much of the "nigger" or the "nigger world" as what they represent: the encroachment of the colonial-capitalist way of life on the ordered feudal world Mrs. Gobin's mother had known. In Mrs. Gobin we see the first sign of rebellion that is so celebrated by Mr. Biswas, the first attempt to break out of a way of life that seemed "fated."

Naipaul's next short story, "The Old Man" (1953), opens up another theme that became important to his work: the isolation of individuals in Trinidad, especially those who emigrated around the middle of the nineteenth century, and their difficulty in calling the island "home." In this story, the major characters are Chinese, and like the East Indians, they seem to feel an isolation and lack of attachment to the island.

In "The Old Man," the Chengs, a family of ten, save money to return to China. They are forced to abandon that ambition when Mr. Cheng dies.

(The theme of a man dying and leaving women to face the world alone is typical of Naipaul's early stories.) The children soon forget their parents' plan and begin to reconcile themselves to the remoteness and isolation of Trinidad. The items on the society page of the *Trinidad Guardian* assume more interest to them than the important events of the outside world. The narrator observes:

In Trinidad, the grand affairs that rock the hemispheres are remote, and do not have any immediate interests for us. Besides, we are worried by our own political problems. Should we kill off tubercular cows? One member of the Legislative Council thinks it is a wicked plan to impoverish a large part of the community. Another thinks it is a grand step forward.

We find life in Trinidad full and trying. We are not greatly disturbed by the world's great week-end crisis. We are amused and detached. It is only when we leave Trinidad for some time that we see how truly [in the original manuscript the words "unimportant we are" and "how" are deleted] amusing we have been. Tubercular cows dwindle into their proper importance. But we realize, too, that our approach to world affairs was correct. For when we are abroad, you see, we realize that Trinidad, with its blending of peoples, and with its burning political problems of no significance, is really the world in small.[24]

To Naipaul, even at this stage in his career, Trinidad is remote and unimportant. No group other than the Africans can call the island home. When Mary Cheng is asked, "Why don't you stay here [in Trinidad], as so many other Chinese have done?", she responds disdainfully: "Stay in Trinidad? What for? I want to go home. Nobody can call Trinidad home, even if he is born here. The place is like one big camp. That is all. I want to go home." The narrator comments: "Yes, Mary wanted to go home. Home meant very much. In Trinidad she was an exile, not belonging to any group, and feeling separated by ages from the smart Chinese set, who belonged to exclusive clubs, who owned race horses, and who had completely adopted what they considered the Western way of life."

In this story, as in "Potatoes," the separation of the parents from the younger generation is very evident. The children, for example, speak Chinese only when they are at home, and Mr. Cheng seems utterly "indifferent to the world" around him. Mrs. Cheng owes all her allegiance to Mao Tse-Tung, who to her was the only true leader. She, it seems, keeps up with important world affairs. According to the narrator, Mr. Cheng "kept Mary and her family thoroughly Chinese in an atmosphere that would otherwise have swamped them with the frustrating emptiness of a [here "Trinidad" is crossed out in the manuscript] isolated existence." Both Mary and Mr. Cheng wished to return to mainland China, where life was more secure and ordered and where, presumably, the civilization was older and more ordered. The problem remains the same as in the other stories: isolation in a remote and unimportant island. And even though the privileged Chinese seek to lose themselves in the emptiness of Western culture, the older, more traditional members feel sadly misplaced. The younger Chinese, with much difficulty, attempt to adapt "themselves to their new social environment."

The breakdown of the Hindu family is spelled out in "A Family Reunion" (1954), which tells the story of a dispersed family coming back to their modest house for Christmas and the problems they confront. Although Naipaul addresses some of his central concerns in this story—the breakdown of the Hindu family, East versus West, the conflict between the sacred and the profane—the story is more about the injustices within the East Indian family than those it meets in the outside world. The text hints at the traditional injustices against women, particularly daughters who are dominated by their mothers and mothers-in-law.

The tension in the story involves the injustices experienced by daughters who have served their mothers faithfully, while sons, who have done little for their mothers and have discarded their traditional Hindu ways, receive the best their mothers can offer. This treatment of daughters is exemplified by the concern accorded the boys' education and the neglect of the well-being of the daughters:

The old woman had given her sons a good education. Suraj was a doctor, and he had a flourishing practice. Krishna occupied a good position in the Civil Service. They, the women, were barely literate, and they had been married not because they wanted to, but because of their mother's will. Hindu sense had been scandalized that girls of eighteen should wander around unmarried.[25]

When the mother's property is divided, the bulk of it goes to her sons and very little to the daughters, even though they know they have served her well. Although the daughters do not rebel outwardly, they recognize that their mother has wronged them gravely, for, as the narrator observes, "In their hearts they considered their mother malevolent and intriguing." Yet they are accepting and placid. They know their mother has wronged them and that their brothers are indifferent and cruel to them, yet they are constrained from expressing their feelings. Unlike Mrs. Gobin, they tend to accept their lives, which have been "fated to them." This fate, the author suggests, is the terrible injustice to which the Hindu woman is a victim. As the narrator observes: "In a way the women accepted, as natural, that their brothers should be treated with great respect, and should get most of any legacy. It seemed so right, so proper."

The problem of stasis and decay and the persistence of obsolete social practices that deny and negate the personhood of these women is at the root of this story. One must break out of that "destined position" to be free. It is within this context that we must understand the decaying nature of the landscape, of the very house to which the family returns for the reunion. Indeed, on their return, they recognize that decay, symbolized by the house. In the end the mother lives alone in the same wooden house, which had "faded like herself . . . [where] everything smelled of dampness and decay." In the broken-down house, blind and close to death, the old woman dispenses her not-too-kind justice and bemoans that education turns girls into prostitutes. "The boys," she says, "never let you down."

The old order is dying. Something is fundamentally wrong with the social arrangement. There is the feeling that a historical wrong has been committed against the daughters, yet their acceptance of their fate seems to suggest compliance, which adds an unsatisfactory dimension to the text. Naipaul does not explore the feelings of the daughters, and he depicts the mother only as a malevolent figure. The women's fate seems to be unalterable. Clearly, the author is struggling with some of the problems of his society, particularly the role of women and the decay of the world order.

"My Aunt Gold Teeth" (1954) is a much more comprehensive examination of the conflict between Eastern and Western ways of life. Like "The Mourners," this story is told through the eyes of a young person who is bewildered by the conflict of cultures. His aunt Gold Teeth, knowing "little apart from the ceremonies and the taboos" of Hinduism and childless at the age of forty, is willing "to trap and channel the supernatural Power"[26] of both Hinduism and Christianity to give birth to a child. In the alien wilderness of Trinidad she is forced to compromise between these two cultures. Fearing that her praying to "Christian things" may have led to the illness of her husband, a Hindu pundit, she asks Pundit Ganesh (who is reintroduced in *The Mystic Masseur*) whether she has committed an error of judgment. He replies:

"And do you think God minds, daughter? There is only one God and different people pray to Him in different ways. It doesn't matter how you pray, but God is pleased if you pray at all."

"So it is not because of me that my husband has fallen ill?"

"No, to be sure, daughter."

Although Gold Teeth calls upon both Hinduism and Christianity, her husband dies, leaving her believing that her infidelity (nay, idolatry) caused his death. In a fit of self-abnegation she destroys "every reminder of Christianity in the house." Her mother forgives her for turning to Christianity, yet its intrusion into the highest level of the Hindu world—"for Gold Teeth's husband was a Brahmin among Brahmins, a *Panday,* a man who knew all five Vedas"—left an indelible mark. Like his counterpart in "The Mourners," the young narrator is left confused by the behavior of his elders.

Naipaul's early stories clearly present a more creolized version of East Indian life than does Seepersad Naipaul's work. The society of "The Mourners" is opening itself up to the influence of the larger community and thus presents the changing behavior of the Trinidadians of East Indian descent. In "This Is Home," "Potatoes," "The Old Man," "A Family Reunion," and "My Aunt Gold Teeth" the author expresses an ambivalent position toward his society. Although his ideas are still tentative, they are nonetheless being articulated.

NAIPAUL AND HIS ART

Naipaul confessed in 1964 that he wrote *The Suffrage of Elvira* to prove to himself that he could construct a sustained text around one central incident.[27] The short stories, however, preceded that effort by about seven years. He may have been motivated to write the novel by the comments he made about Samuel Selvon's inability to construct a much longer and sustained narrative.[28] Speaking about Selvon's work in "The Literary Output of West Indian Writing in 1955," Naipaul argued, "It is curious that the West Indian whose inventiveness and humour and gift of repartee is shown up so advantageously in the calypso . . . should be so uninventive in his novels."[29] Writing much later, in 1968, about the difficulty West Indian writers had in using the novel form, Naipaul said: "The trouble about novel writing is that it is such an artificial form. It is something that people in my culture have borrowed from other people and the danger is that we tend, when we are beginning, however honestly we may work—we tend to recreate an alien form, an alien novel, the whole form and concept of life is totally alien to the society. We impose one on the other. My attempt has been, in a way, to dredge down a little deeper to the truth about one's own situation." And even though he found "the confirmation of simple societies . . . inadequate to a serious writer immersed, as he [was], in the English literary tradition,"[30] this conscious struggle to find the appropriate form in which to express his experiences characterized Naipaul's early (and, perhaps, his entire) art.

In speaking about his place in West Indian literature in 1960, Naipaul declared unequivocally that he was a Trinidadian writer—"a writer from Trinidad"—and in discussing the nature of the society about which he wrote, he announced that he was writing about "an Indian society in Trinidad, which is still, to a certain degree, a coherent society, with its own flavour and without, yet, an American flavour . . . [a] people set in a certain society within a certain framework. That framework is now breaking up, but that is giving me materials for fresh work."[31] Clearly, when Naipaul began his career as a writer he was well aware of his own position in a particular tradition, which he perceived to be in transition. Naipaul's perception of his relationship to his society changed as he became a more sophisticated craftsman. Indeed, even in this early period a certain ambivalence in his relationship to his society is evident. When Naipaul began his career, however, he was particularly aware of his Trinidadianness, and this fact cannot be dismissed simply in light of his later realizations or rationalizations.

Certain themes that related directly to his early experiences prevailed throughout his early stories: a sense of being lost and alone, a sense of isolation and exile, a recognition that his society was decaying and that it committed injustices against its members, and the conflicting pull of the Eastern (Hindu) and Western (Christian) worlds, a subset of which was the rising conflict between the feudal world of the Hindus and the colonial-capitalist world. As an inescapable result of these concerns, the subtheme of home (what or where is home?) and displacement (trying to find a center) arose with enormous force, persistence, and urgency in these early texts. Adaptation and change carried a price; the resulting psychic pain subtends his work.

In a way, these stories represent Naipaul's attempt to make coherent and intelligible his early experiences and to form some meaningful link with his parents' generation. As he explained to Nigel Bingham in a radio discussion in New Zealand:

I grew up with about fifty cousins and that was like a crash course in the world. You learn then about cruelty, about propaganda, about the destruction of reputations. You learn about forming allies. It was that kind of background to which my father was reacting. This world—I have written about this—to a large extent, and certainly for most of my childhood—appeared to me in my own mind to exclude what was outside, although one was living in a multiracial society. I don't think the child formulated it like that. I think the child simply understood that what was outside that large clan was somehow not it. It was outside. It was something else. No judgment was to be made on it and I perhaps didn't make any judgments on it as a child. . . . It was different. The food would be different, the manners would be different, that was all, a sense of difference, great difference.[32]

Naipaul's childhood was very unhappy, "largely," he says, "because of feeling a kind of helpless unit in this large family organization." Naipaul therefore passionately wanted to become an adult, "to be responsible for myself, to be able to look after myself and to look after my father as well."[33] His early texts attempted to capture the urgency, helplessness, and unhappiness of those early years.

In May 1954, just two months after he had finished writing "A Family Reunion," Naipaul wrote to Grenfell Williams of the BBC for a job. Naipaul had stayed on at Oxford for a few months to complete a B. Litt., but, as he phrased it in his letter, "with one thing and another, I no longer have the desire to go through with the work." It was time to face the world, to be responsible for himself. Perhaps the most important decision he made was not to return to the West Indies, as he explained to Williams:

One thing I certainly do not want to do: go back to Trinidad or any other island in the West Indies if I can help it. I very much want to go to India. But there are many difficulties. I cannot be employed on the Indian side because I am British, and on the British side, I cannot be employed because I am not English. I think it is almost impossible for me to do anything worthwhile in this country, for reasons which you doubtless know. . . . I am applying for jobs in places as far apart as Turkey and Indonesia, but with little hope of success.[34]

There is a myth, perpetuated by Naipaul particularly in his writings of the 1980s, that he never wanted to or gave very little thought to any other career but writing. His letter to Williams and his attempt to do a B. Litt. certainly contradict that position. Writing came very hard to Naipaul. As he said to Jim Douglas Henry, "I don't think of myself as a born writer. I've learnt the very hard way."[35] In 1954, however, Naipaul's life and his direction as a writer were at a crossroad. His not getting a job was the best thing that happened to him. At any rate, the themes of his stories began to resonate with the choices that he had to make. As he developed and matured as a writer, the interplay of these two dimensions became the base of his work.

MIGUEL STREET

By the time Naipaul wrote *Miguel Street* (the text was completed in 1955 but was not published until 1959), he was a much more conscious artist than he was when he wrote his first short story some four years earlier.[36] He could speak much more authoritatively than he could in his earlier efforts. Some years later he wrote about the stories in *Miguel Street:*

It was through them that I began to appreciate the distorting, distilling power of the writer's art. Where I had seen a drab haphazardness they found order; where I would have attempted to romanticize, to render my subject equal with what I had read, they accepted. They provided a starting point for further observation; they did not trigger off fantasy. Every writer is, in the long run, on his own; but it helps, in the most practical way, to have a tradition. The English language was mine; the tradition was not.[37]

In 1983, Naipaul said that he wrote *Miguel Street* to "ease" himself into knowledge. He asserted that the book "seemed to have been written by an innocent, a man at the beginning of knowledge both *about himself* and about *the writing career* that had been his ambition from childhood."[38] Yet these stories represented a West Indian tradition of which he was a part.

The stories in *Miguel Street* are set in Port of Spain. The characters are modified products of the barrack yard whose social existence has been twisted severely because of the social pressures of the city's slum. But because the book lacks sustained dramatic tension and a coherent plot and unified theme of a novel, it is more in the tradition of the early short stories of Trinidad and the West Indies.[39]

Miguel Street examines a colonial society in which the characters' traditional values have no organic connection with the social environment and their quest for a meaningful existence seems to be denied because of the apparent chaos that surrounds them—hence the major theme that one cannot achieve anything in Trinidad because of the futility and the sterility of the society. This position is exemplified best in the story "How I Left Miguel Street," when, in response to his mother's complaint that he was "getting too wild" and by his own recognition that he was drinking too much, the character asserts: "Is not my fault, really. Is just Trinidad. What else can anybody do here except drink?"[40] This sentiment also appeared in the earlier story "The Old Man." It is expressive of an ideological position that informs much of Naipaul's later work.

At the beginning of the book, Bogart, one of the major characters, is described as "the most bored man I ever knew" (*MS,* 10). Almost inevitably, Bogart, as well as all the other characters, have to do something insane to relieve the tedium of their existence. More important, this boredom, taken to an extreme, makes all the characters absurd reflections of the social totality.

Such is the case of Man-man, who tries to reenact the crucifixion of Christ, which for him is the only way to escape the meaninglessness of his existence. When this crucifixion act is taken seriously by other inhabitants of Miguel Street, he reverts to his normal existence and finally goes insane because he is unable to withstand the pressures of the changing social order. The tensions between the real and the unreal and the attempt to separate the meaningful from the meaningless exact too high a price in a colonial society.

Two major concerns emerge from this text that further structure Naipaul's work. First, he presents absurdity as the normal mode of behavior for the inhabitants of Miguel Street and, in so doing, commences to construct an elaborate philosophical and ideological superstructure on which to ground his work. Second, he presents the alienating aspects of a colonial society and how it marginalizes its subjects. As Geoffrey Broughton observed: "Here is the first statement of the theme of cultural deprivation; a first sketch of individuals struggling for a new way of life, both within the ambit of colonial society, and within the strangling grip of an isolated community within that society."[41]

Miguel Street is Naipaul's first sustained piece of work. As he argued in 1964, it was through *Miguel Street* that he discovered "the trick of writing after a lot of fumbling and the book was written out of the joy of that discovery."[42] Elaborating on this theme in 1983, he said that in writing *Miguel Street* he achieved "self-awareness" and "self-knowledge." The language of the text takes shape because of his enlightened and surer perception of the society. Somewhat in the tradition of Cecil Gray's "Merely for the Record," his sentences are terse and crisp, and repetitions abound, which make his assertions believable. There is a lightness and frivolity of tone that tends to obscure the central concerns of the text and accentuate the natural patterns that characterize Trinidadian speech.

"The Perfect Tenants" at first seems to be outside the pattern of Naipaul's development, but it in fact fits into his overall work. In many ways it is simply an examination of the social concerns Naipaul addressed in his first collection of stories—social status, behavior, and attitudes—which he felt he had left behind when he left Trinidad and Tobago. Indeed, the story can be seen as Naipaul's attempt to understand his home situation through an imaginative projection into another society, a device he would use again in *Mr. Stone and the Knights Companion.* Written at a time when a great deal of discussion about social status, behavior, and attitudes was taking place in England, it helped Naipaul work out some of his specific, local concerns against the larger background of the English landscape.[43] The articulation of such problems within an English background was particularly important for Naipaul because previously he had identified them only within his local Trinidadian landscape.

The early stories, *Miguel Street,* and "The Perfect Tenants" constitute the first stage of Naipaul's writing career when the short story predominated. These stories served to establish Naipaul's perception of the colonial society, which he would expand as his writing career developed. In particular, the incident of Man-man in *Miguel Street* is expanded and refined in *The Mystic Masseur.* Whereas Man-man goes from politics to the priesthood, Ganesh goes from the priesthood to politics. Whereas Man-man is fascinated by the world and spends entire days poring over and shaping one word, Ganesh attempts to appropriate his world through writing and by studying books. Whereas Man-man is taken away and considered insane (the logical progression of his development, as it were), Ganesh becomes a statesman and a respected member of the community because he is able to manipulate words and his social environment. Many of the thematic concerns of *The Mystic Masseur* are already evident in *Miguel Street.* So, too, is the manner in which Naipaul perceived his society.

NAIPAUL AND HIS PERCEPTION OF HIS SOCIETY

Writing in the *Times Literary Supplement* in August 1958, Naipaul articulated his views about the society that would shape his work:

Superficially, because of the multitude of races, Trinidad may seem complex, but to anyone who knows it, *it is a simple colonial philistine society.* Education is desirable because it may lead to security, but any unnecessary acquaintance with books is frowned upon. The writer or the painter, unless he wins recognition overseas, preferably in England, is mercilessly ridiculed. This is only slowly changing. Respectability and class still mean very little. Money means a good deal more, and the only nonfinancial achievements which are recognized are those connected with sport and music. For these reasons Trinidadians are more recognizably "characters" than people in England. Only a man's eccentricities can get him attention. It might also be that in a society without traditions, without patterns, every man finds it easier "to be himself." Whatever the reason, this determination of people to be themselves, to cherish their eccentricities, to reveal themselves at once, makes them easy material for the writer.[44]

Naipaul was not alone in condemning what he regarded as the philistine nature of West Indian society. Bridget Brereton refers to its presence in very early Trinidad society, and two eminent West Indian scholars, C. L. R. James and the martyred Walter Rodney, shared many of Naipaul's concerns in this regard. But whereas James and Rodney identified this condition as residing at the top of the society, Naipaul saw it as plaguing the entire society, with the inhabitants at the bottom of the social ladder being both the worst offenders and the victims.

To demonstrate his position, James used the example of the Mighty

Sparrow, the calypsonian. James makes three important observations about his artistry. First, "He is in every way a genuine West Indian artist, the first and only one I know." Second, "He is the living proof that there is a West Indian nation." Third, his artistic achievement compares favorably with the highest literary achievements of the colonizer's culture, and even though the calypso would not be "ranked very high in the hierarchy of the arts. . . . I believe that Shakespeare would have listened very carefully to him, and Aristophanes would have given him a job in his company." Sparrow's work was important within the overall context of the culture, James argued, because it extended the calypso medium. He concluded: "When our local dramatists and artists can evoke the popular response of a Sparrow, the artists in the Caribbean will have arrived."[45]

Rodney contended that all the creativity of the society came from what had been considered its "dregs." In his book *The Groundings with My Brothers,* Rodney paid tribute to the creativity of the masses of the Caribbean and argued that the black masses (Africans and East Indians) had produced all its culture. He argued that "some of the best painters and writers are coming out of the Rastafari environment. The black people in the West Indies have produced all the culture that we have, whether it be steelband or folk music. Black bourgeoisie and white people in the West Indies have produced nothing!"[46] Further, whereas Naipaul sees the society as being static, depicts the inhabitants as generally philistine, and perceives existence in the Caribbean (and, by extension, in all colonial countries) as futile, both James and Rodney take the opposite view. In structuring his arguments against colonial peoples, Naipaul uses the social and cultural values of the colonizers' culture as the norm by which to measure the behavior of the colonial person. Anything that does not conform to those standards becomes futile, meaningless, and worthless. This position is demonstrated by Hat, one of the more eccentric characters of Miguel Street, who reflected the rather ambivalent relations that many of the characters felt toward their social environment when, in appreciation of the 150 runs Gerry Gomez and Len Harbin (both Trinidadians of European descent) scored to save Trinidad from defeat against Jamaica in an intercolonial cricket match, Hat dances gleefully and shouts, "White people is God, you hear!" (*MS,* 155).

Rodney, however, makes the most telling case against this perception of the society when he insists that it is perpetuated by the dominant culture through an elaborate ideological system of manipulation and control. Thus he argues in his article on black power that "white people have produced black people who administer the system and perpetuate the white values. . . . This is as true of the Indians as it is true of the Africans in our West Indian society." He concludes that "the road to Black Power here in the West Indies and everywhere else must begin with a revaluation of ourselves as blacks and with a redefinition of the world from our own standpoint."[47]

For Rodney, part of the tragedy of West Indian society was that certain elements had appropriated and become entrapped by the ideological apparatuses of the dominant class. Part of the process of social reconstruction lay in revaluating those judgments through ideologies such as black power and the imperative that West Indian society be viewed through West Indian eyes.

Naipaul, however, was prepared to see West Indian society through the eyes of the English. This is the dominant perspective from which he analyzed and judged it, and it may be one reason why he attacked the concept of black power so savagely. His three years at Oxford tended to magnify the ills of West Indian society and to structure his method of analysis and his manner of depicting it. The additional years he spent in London did not change his view significantly. Where Rodney was prepared to conduct his analysis of West Indian society (and colonial reality) at the level of what Edward Schillebeeckx calls the plane of "conjectural" history, Naipaul was content to leave his arguments at the "ephemeral" level of history and culture. He remained secure in the judgment that English culture was the standard against which social, historical, and cultural development should be measured.[48]

Yet a paradox stands at the center of Naipaul's work and that of many other colonial writers who left their societies to practice their craft in the home of the colonizer. They left, in Naipaul's words, because the society was "unimportant," "uncreative," and "cynical"; one could not practice one's craft. Yet as Nancy Fitch pointed out in referring to James Joyce, Edna O'Brien, and Naipaul, "The force which propelled them outwards remained in their consciousness and formed their art, providing a theme in their work."[49]

The first phase of Naipaul's work belongs to a specific historical tradition in literature. That Naipaul, from the inception of his writing, gave a privileged status to the culture of the colonizer and chose that site in which to anchor his work should not detract from his central dependence on the experiences of the colonial world to fashion the content of his work and the historical tradition of West Indian literature to shape his specific "mode of writing." The central tension between his Eastern sensibility (subjective) and the material condition of his Western experiences (objective) had not yet begun to articulate itself with any insistence, even though it can be perceived in its nascent form. As his career unfolds, this central tension generates the major problematic of his work.

2. The Colonial Society:
Opening Up the Social Space

I am not sure one really knows what one does in one's writing. One knows what one is trying to do, but this is not always the same as what comes out. It is very much for other people who read one's work to judge, though probably it is wrong for them to look for philosophies or basic beliefs.

—V. S. Naipaul, "V. S. Naipaul Tells How Writing Changes a Writer," *Tapia*, 1973

Language is not a mere tool, one of the many which man possesses; on the contrary, it is only language that affords the very possibility of standing in the openness of the existent. Only where there is language, is there world, i.e., the perpetually altering circuit of decision and production, of action and responsibility, but also of commotion and arbitrariness, of decay and confusion. Only where world predominates is there history. Language is a possession in a more fundamental sense. It is good for the fact that (i.e., it affords a guarantee that) man can *exist* historically. Language is not a tool at his disposal, rather it is that event which disposes of the supreme possibility of human existence.

—Martin Heidegger, "Holderlen and the Essence of Poetry," in Vernon W. Gras, *European Literary Theory and Practice*

ASRAMAS IN THE WILDERNESS: THE TRANSITION FROM FEUDALISM TO CAPITALISM

Naipaul's focus on the lives of individuals in *Miguel Street* and his other short stories gives way to a broader focus on the East Indian community in *The Mystic Masseur*. First published in 1957, the novel spans the period from 1929 to 1954, the first generation of East Indians after the termination of indentureship. Distinguished by its alienation from the larger society, the community of *The Mystic Masseur* shares the sociocultural openness to other cultural influences typical of the African communities in the West Indies. *The Mystic Masseur* takes place entirely within an East Indian community in transition from feudalism to capitalism.[1] The novel concerns the problems of arranged marriages, the inevitability of one's *karma* or fate, tradition versus modernity, and the act of writing as a means of appropriating one's reality. The text examines Ganesh Ramsumair's rise to prominence from masseur to mystic to the position of an MBE (Member of the British Empire), one of the highest honors a colonial subject could hope to achieve.

As in *Miguel Street,* the characters in *The Mystic Masseur* are not well developed. Instead, the novel uses five parallel themes or movements to reveal the social development of the East Indian in Trinidad.

The first movement presents the major problematic of most of Naipaul's work: the duality of the East Indian's experience in Trinidad, as exemplified in the description of Ganesh's hut:

> Nothing had prepared me for what I was to see inside Ganesh's hut. As soon as we entered my mother winked at me, and I could see that even the taxi-driver was fighting to control his astonishment. There were books, books, here, there, and everywhere; books piled crazily on the table, books rising in mounds in the corners, books covering the floor. I had never before seen so many books in one place. . . .
>
> I tried to forget Ganesh thumping my leg about and concentrated on the walls. They were covered with religious quotations, in Hindi and English, and with Hindu religious pictures. My gaze settled on a beautiful four-armed god standing in an open lotus.[2]

At one pole is Ganesh's attempt to appropriate the Western world through books; at the other is the centrality of Visnu, the Hindu icon, representing the traditional Eastern dimension of his social reality.[3] This theme is both emblematic and paradigmatic of Naipaul's early approach to the representation of the East Indian's dual position in Caribbean society. The five parallel themes of the text encompass Ganesh's working out of this dual position.

The picture of Visnu "standing in an open lotus" on Ganesh's wall would suggest a number of meanings to the East Indian, thrust as he is into the Wilderness of the Caribbean. Although Visnu symbolizes the eternal qualities of the East Indians' existence—man's common origin, the limitless powers of his mind, the illusion of the world and its powers, and the sovereignty of man's individuality—he also represents man's transitory nature and existence in a changing universe. Yet Visnu also suggests the asramas that each Hindu must make in the Wilderness to assume his being in this new world; the goal toward which all beings must tend, the symbolic compromise all must make to survive.[4] Thus the icon of Visnu structures the novel, suggesting the way of life of the East Indian within the feudal-communal world of Trinidad and Tobago. The life of Ganesh Ramsumair in *The Mystic Masseur* can thus be considered as a signification of "the history of our [Trinidad's] times" (*MM,* 14).

The second movement of the text depicts Ganesh's first encounter with the capitalist world as he departs from the countryside, emblematic of the feudal-communal world, for Queen's Royal College in Port of Spain, emblematic of the dawning of new capitalist relations. The safety and identity granted him by the country district and his Hinduism give way to insecurity and a threatened loss of identity in the city.

The sense of alienation created by his confrontation with the urban center is contrasted with his people's attempts to revive the rituals of their former Indian world, that is, to be "good" Trinidadians yet to remain faithful to their Indian tradition. This point is clearly made when Ganesh is ridiculed by the college principal for disturbing a class on his return from being initiated into Brahminism. The contradiction of these two worlds exists not only at the level of mythology but also at the level of social practice.

The third movement of the text begins when Ganesh, unable to cope with the urban world, returns to the countryside and meets Mr. Steward, an Englishman, who advises him to find the "spiritual rhythm" of his life. Steward reminds Ganesh how ordinary his life is and tells him about the beauty and wonder of foreign lands: "He can't help being involved there. Here there is no such need" (*MM*, 37). Because this incident occurs at a time when Ganesh is particularly vulnerable psychologically, Steward's ideas have a significant influence on him.

The fourth movement develops during Ganesh's marriage. Life for him and his wife, Leela, is bleak and arid:

The villagers went to work in the cane-fields in the dawn darkness to avoid the heat of day. When they returned in the middle of the morning the dew had dried on the grass; and they set to work in their vegetable gardens as if they didn't know that sugar-cane was the only thing that could grow in Fuente Grove. They had few thrills. The population was small and there were not many births, marriages, or deaths to excite them. Two or three times a year the men made a noisy excursion to a cinema in distant, wicked San Fernando. Little happened otherwise. (*MM*, 63)

Writing is the only means Ganesh has for imposing some sense into this world, though at this point in his development the act of writing is a curiosity whose implications Ganesh does not yet grasp.[5] The tension between the spoken (the word/world that is given) and the written (the word/world that is received) exists until Ganesh becomes a pundit.

In this transitional phase of Ganesh's life, education begins to assume importance. When his wife, Leela, leaves him, an action unheard-of in Ganesh's traditional society, Suraj Mooma blames this trouble on the new tendency to educate East Indian women. According to Suraj Mooma: " 'Leela spend too much of she time reading and writing and not looking after she husband properly. I did talk to she about it, mark you' " (*MM*, 87). Education was decisive in transforming the society from feudalism to capitalism.

World War II further eroded feudal relations in the East Indian society and opened up new possibilities for the East Indians. More important, it encouraged Ganesh to undertake a deep examination of the *Gita:*

> It gave a new direction to his reading. Forgetting the war, he became a great Indologist and bought all the books on Hindu philosophy he could get in San Fernando. He read them, marked them, and on Sunday afternoons made notes. At the same time he developed a taste for practical psychology and read many books on The Art of Getting On. But India was his great love. It became his habit, on examining a new book, to look first at the index to see whether there were any references to India or Hinduism. If the references were complimentary he bought the book. Soon he owned a curious selection. (*MM*, 108)

The acts of writing and reading open up a new world of thought for Ganesh and increase his understanding of his own world. It is because he must know about the past before he can investigate and explore the present that he develops an interest in practical psychology ("The Art of Getting On") and in Hindu philosophy. An understanding of English empiricism and Hindu metaphysics becomes indispensable for his future undertakings.

The fifth movement of the text brings together the two modes of perception—the Eastern and the Western, the spoken and the written word—in a united act of cognition. This moment occurs when Ganesh, having failed to achieve financial success by his writing, becomes a pundit. As the Great Belcher warns Ganesh, "He must realise by now that he have to use his learning to help out other people" (*MM*, 110).

Becoming a pundit enables Ganesh to investigate the past more closely. In a significant gesture of solidarity, the Great Belcher gives him his uncle's great books, so he can use the legacy of the past to guide himself and his people in the newly emerging capitalist world. It requires a mystic to unravel the knowledge that is buried in the old books and to transmit it to his people in an enlightened manner. As Ganesh wrote: "We never are what we want to be . . . but what we must be" (*MM*, 70).

At this point the narrative enters more fully into the life of Ganesh. The mythology of the East is combined with that of the West as Ganesh attempts to save the life of Hector, an African boy who believes that a cloud is following him. In preparing to welcome Hector to his home, Ganesh converts his bedroom into a study in which he places a picture of Kakshmi, the goddess of fortune and the consort of Visnu, in a prominent place. Below the goddess Ganesh places a candle. He burns the camphor and incense, and, in his new persona, the tenets of Hinduism and Christianity, the theology of feudalism and capitalism, respectively, merge. The ritual symbols of both worlds are placed at the service of Ganesh's new enterprise in the Wilderness: that of participating in a newly emerging social order and, in the process, retreating from the narrow confines of the East Indian feudal order.

The combined strengths of both worlds are used to exorcise the demon from Hector so that the child can become psychologically liberated. Thus, in one bold stroke, a young boy is liberated from the crippling superstitions of the past and Ganesh makes his final break with his feudal past. After this point of the text Ganesh acquires his new name, G. R. Muir, Esq., a symbol of his new identity.

Ganesh's entrance into the capitalist world is signaled by the alacrity with which the "Niggergram" spreads the word of his success throughout the country. Through a process of ritual and magical incantation, Ganesh is brought into the mainstream of society. As his popularity spreads, his preaching and healing, which initially were primarily religious and social, begin to merge with the history and politics of the country. What begins as a purely particular and parochial matter becomes a general and national matter, and in the process that which is purely Hindu merges with the general and sociopolitical history of the country.

The text moves the reader toward an understanding of the entire history of the country, and thus the sociopolitical and historical development of the Hindus becomes, as it should, the sociopolitical and historical development of Trinidad. A search for personal liberation through the acquisition of a vocation ultimately becomes a search for the national liberation of an entire people. Ganesh's personal liberation closely parallels the national liberation of his people, reaching its climax in the election of 1946, the first to be conducted with universal adult suffrage.

Ganesh's running for the Legislative Council in this election is the result of his new consciousness and involvement in the newly emerging social order. Indeed, the election of 1946 allows Ganesh to combine his religious, social, and political convictions. Pitted against Indarsingh, who was educated at Oxford and whose demeanor seems to suggest disdain for Trinidad, Ganesh wins the election and continues along his path toward becoming a Trinidadian. Ganesh's transformation to Trinidadianism is complete when he decides to stop studying "Indology and psychology and [buys] large books on political theory." Undoubtedly, "political theory" is the new gospel for an emerging capitalist world.

After eleven years, Ganesh leaves Fuente Grove and, consistent with his new posture, goes to live in Port of Spain. Initially Ganesh had rejected Port of Spain as representative of capitalism, in favor of the countryside, representative of feudalism. Now his priority has changed. As Ganesh leaves for Port of Spain, the two stone elephants on the balustrade of his home "stared in opposite directions" (*MM*, 206),[6] gestures of enormous symbolic significance, for, in calling upon Ganesha (his namesake), Ganesh seems to be asking for assistance and guidance in making the transition to nascent capitalism.

Just as important, that the elephants are looking away seems to suggest Ganesh's ambivalence toward his undertaking. As Ganesh enters his new world he needs both the wisdom of the elephant and the prudence of the rat. As he concludes the second part of his asramas in the Wilderness, he maintains a balance between what he was and what the social order demands that he become. Ganesh's new journey can be prefaced with the words: "Sri-ganesh-nama" (Praise be to the divine Ganesha), which are used at the beginning of many Hindu religious books.

THE MYSTIC MASSEUR AND SECOND-ORDER MEMORY

A complex Hindu consciousness is evident in *The Mystic Masseur* in the spiritual guidance of Mahatma Gandhi, in the teachings of the *Gita*, and in the role of mysticism. Indeed, although Gandhi is the spiritual guide of the text, Ganesh derives his learning primarily from the *Gita*, and mysticism provides a means to unify the characters with their social environment.

The importance of Mahatma Gandhi in the text as well as in Ganesh's life is best comprehended by understanding the significance of the teachings of the *Gita* for Gandhi. Louis Fischer's *The Life of Mahatma Gandhi*, which Naipaul cites in *The Mystic Masseur*, examines this influence. Drawing heavily on Mahadev Desai's *The Gospel of Selfless Action According to Gandhi*, Fischer demonstrates how the *Gita* became Gandhi's "spiritual reference."[7] For Gandhi, the most important principle of the *Gita* is the idea of desirelessness, which culminates in the attainment of self-realization or freedom. But although the concept of self-realization or freedom involves complete indifference toward the rewards of one's actions, it does not necessarily imply an indifference to the results of one's actions. Indifference to rewards, then, does not mandate a disregard for material goods.

Thus interpreted, Ganesh is seeking self-realization or freedom. He is not prevented from attempting to acquire material goods, even though he may choose to be indifferent to their power. Thus when Ganesh discovers the *Gita*, he develops "a fuller appreciation [for] the dialogue between Arjuna and Krishna on the field of battle [which] . . . gave a new direction to his reading" (*MM*, 108).

Soon after this "conversion," Ganesh becomes a "mystic" and is forced to carry the legacy of his people: "If he is a Hindu, he must realize by now that he have to use his learning to help out other people" (*MM*, 110). At this point, the Great Belcher gives him his uncle's old books, "some in Sanskrit, some in Hindi" (*MM*, 112). From now on, Ganesh devotes his life to desirelessness, and his teaching in the Wilderness exemplifies renunciation in the service of his people:

His main point was that desire was a source of misery and therefore desire ought to be suppressed. Occasionally he went off at a tangent to discuss whether the desire to suppress desire wasn't itself a desire; but usually he tried to be as practical as possible. . . . At other times he said that happiness was only possible if you cleared your mind of desire and looked upon yourself as part of Life, just a tiny link in the vast chain of Creation. (*MM*, 157)

The teaching of desirelessness that is embodied in the *Gita* and that was the central message of Mahatma Gandhi's life becomes the central focus of Ganesh's. Indeed, Gandhi's attempt to synthesize the dichotomy between Western and Hindu culture, which lay at the heart of his greatness, is also Ganesh's central concern during Trinidad's transitional period. W. T. Stace has observed, in regard to Gandhi's capacity to synthesize the cultures of the East and West, that

the secret of Gandhi is that, although his basic inspiration, like that of the Buddha, came from the spiritual plane—and in this he remained characteristically Indian—yet he perceived that the alleviation, though not the destruction, of suffering is possible on the material plane and is to be achieved by social and political action. This has now been understood, not only by Gandhi but by India in general. And this fact, which found its most perfect expression in the life of Gandhi, must be regarded as one of the most hopeful examples of that synthesis of Eastern and Western philosophies and values of which we all ought to be in search. Gandhi's enormous stature is in part due to the fact that he combined in his personality all that is greatest and strongest and noblest in both East and West.[8]

Therefore, as the life of Gandhi demonstrated and that of Ganesh reveals, the achievement of self-realization requires participation in a combination of religious and social and political activities. Unlike Gandhi, however,

Ganesh discards his religious mantle when it is no longer appropriate to his social and political aspirations.

The synthesis of the best of the East and the West is connected closely to the notion of mysticism, also an integral part of the text and its title. More than most religious beliefs, mysticism pervades the minds of its Hindu adherents. Evelyn Underhill defines mysticism as "the art of union with Reality" and the mystic as a "person who has attained that union in a greater or lesser degree; or who aims at and believes in such attainments."9 R. C. Zaehner, in *Mysticism: Sacred and Profane*, argues that "the keynote of the [mystical] experience has always been one of reconciliation and of union with all things."10 But although the concept of mysticism involves both union and reconciliation, it also involves an appeal to a layer of one's consciousness that, as Underhill points out, "has lain fallow in the past."11 Inherent in the text, and therefore in its title, are the concepts of union, reconciliation, and the raising of consciousness.

Naipaul's concern with the specific form necessary to convey Ganesh's new world experience remains paramount. Here again mysticism operates at both the levels of form and content. The mystical experience of the East, specifically of India, differs from that of the West, however, even in its mode of writing. According to Zaehner, "The Hindu mystical classics are not autobiographical and are not the record of actual experiences undergone by given individuals. They are either mystico-magical tracts like the earlier, Upanisads, or the exposition of mystical doctrines in verse like the later Upanisads and the Bhagavad-Gītā."12 *The Mystic Masseur* is not in keeping with the tradition of "Hindu mystical classics" because it is couched as an autobiographical statement and records the activities of Ganesh. The author, however, is forced to use this autobiographical style precisely because he is in the Wilderness. "The mystic" in a new land is forced to compromise.

To conclude, *The Mystic Masseur* examines the reconciliation Ganesh must make with his social environment and his linguistic legacy. Although he examines the "mystical experiences" of the East Indian in an alien land through an autobiographical mode, he is constrained to use the "mystical doctrines" of the Bhagavad Gita (the authentic Hindu content of his East Indian experiences) to explore his changing consciousness in his new land.

Because Ganesh felt compelled to explain the reality of the East Indian condition at a particular moment in history, he "found himself a mystic when Trinidad was crying out for one" (*MM*, 200). He was able to offer his people "spiritual solace and comfort" because he was "the only true mystic in the island" (*MM*, 134). Ganesh's life, then, becomes a reflection of Trinidad's social evolution at that particular historical moment.

The life of Mahatma Gandhi also embraced the union of two seemingly contradictory principles. As a mystic, he preferred to live among the masses of his people rather than achieve self-realization apart from them, as some Indian mystics did by returning to the caves of the Himalayas. As such, he became the symbol of the Indian liberation movement, a representation of the attempt to synthesize the traditional world of Hinduism and mysticism (feudalism) and the contemporary world of Christianity and pragmatism (capitalism).

Ganesh's life parallels that of Gandhi in many essential details. Most important, his participation as a mystic in social and political life becomes the point of departure for understanding his life in the Wilderness. It is also the point of departure in Naipaul's second book, *The Suffrage of Elvira,* in which the examination of the political is more important than that of the social or religious and in which the mysticism of feudalism gives way to the pragmatism of capitalism.

THE SUFFRAGE OF ELVIRA: THE POLITICAL DIMENSION

Like *The Mystic Masseur, The Suffrage of Elvira* examines the confrontation between feudalism and capitalism. Whereas *The Mystic Masseur* is concerned primarily with the internal dynamics of the East Indian experience in Trinidad, however, *The Suffrage of Elvira* examines the political dimension of the colonial experience. Thus, whereas the community of *The Mystic Masseur* is closed and insulated, "practically lost . . . so small, so remote, and so wretched" (*MM,* 68), that of Elvira opens up into the larger Trinidad community. As the narrator suggests, "From the top of Elvira Hill you get one of the finest views in Trinidad, better even than the view from Tortuga in South Caroni."[13] In a sense taking up where *The Mystic Masseur* left off, *The Suffrage of Elvira* is set during the 1950 general elections, and the community has expanded to include Negroes and Spanish-speaking people. The novel's central thematic concerns are the problems of a community in transition. As Geoffrey Broughton has suggested: "This world of Harbans, Chitteranjan and Baksh looks backward in the same way as those of Ganesh and Uncle Bhacku to the tight constraints of a society narrowly ruled by religion and superstition. Once more the pundit and the small shopkeeper form the nodes of the traditional social structure, with the schoolmaster, journalist and local businessman representing more modern foci."[14]

Much more tightly crafted than *The Mystic Masseur, The Suffrage of Elvira* examines the East Indian community within the context of the newly emerging colonial-capitalist society during a period of growing social awareness. Specifically, the text examines East Indians' dispossession in the society, the manner in which the Hindu-Muslim conflict mitigated against the liberation of the East Indian from the colonial society, and the relationship of the East Indian to the larger society as its feudal ties began to unravel. As in *The Mystic Masseur*, the reader is introduced to the major conflict of the text through a central image. Here it is on the wall of "the big drawing room" of Chitteranjan's home, where the Indian leaders of the community, Chitteranjan, Baksh, Foam, and Harbans, have gathered for the first time to develop an election strategy. Above them is "a large framed picture of the Round Table Conference with King George V and Mahatma Gandhi sitting together, the King formally dressed and smiling, the Mahatma in a loincloth, also smiling. The picture made Harbans easier. He himself had a picture like that in his drawing-room in Port of Spain. Then Foam had an accident. He knocked the Negro waiter down and spilled his red sweet drink on the floor" (*SOE*, 31). This picture, like the one in Ganesh's hut, becomes the novel's major controlling device.[15]

For Baksh, Chitteranjan, Harbans, and the others at this meeting, Gandhi's presence is very important, symbolizing the position he took at the Round Table Conference. In his only address to the conference, at the second plenary meeting, Gandhi stated that the coming of the English and particularly the capitalist relations they engendered among the Indians caused strife among his people by disrupting their relatively peaceful way of life. The picture of the Round Table Conference is mentioned at strategic moments during *The Suffrage of Elvira*, serving to demonstrate the concerns mitigating against the development of the East Indian community in Trinidad. The Indians in Trinidad, like those in India, attempted to solve their problems through elections. The only difference was that the Indians in Trinidad had to solve their problems thousands of miles from home.

Like Gandhi in India, *The Suffrage of Elvira* suggests that East Indians could solve their problems in the Wilderness only by rejecting such feudal practices as the taking of child brides, the proscription against educating girls, and the belief in fate and the preordination of events. These practices are dramatized by the many supernatural powers the community attributes to Tiger, the black bitch. Having thus established the connection between how feudal practices enslave the East Indians in Trinidad, Naipaul changes his methodological approach. The older generation—those characters who were born before the termination of indenture—represents the recalcitrant practices of feudalism. The younger generation—those who were born after indentureship ended—are given the task of breaking out of the feudal mode and seeking a freer, more individualistic participation within the new social order.

Prominent among the younger generation is Nelly Chitteranjan, who is intent on living free of the proscriptions that bound her father to the older world. Although she is a victim of ethnic superstition, she also embodies the rising sense of liberation that pervades the political climate. Nelly's psychological development is not fully worked out in the text, but she does negotiate some of the problems of the old world–new world dichotomy. Thus at the end of the novel she is enjoying her long-cherished dream of dancing at the Poly, and the birds she sent her parents are flying "on the wall next to the picture of Mahatma Gandhi and King George V" (*SOE*, 207). Nelly Chitteranjan has liberated herself from the feudal atmosphere of Elvira.

Pundit Dhaniram and his daughter-in-law, the "doolahin," who was deserted by Dhaniram's son only two months after their marriage, also demonstrate this liberation from feudal relations. Although Hindu tradition demanded that the doolahin remain with and serve her father-in-law, she deserts him and runs away with Lookhoor, her new lover, to live "in a dingy furnished room in Henry Street in Port of Spain" (*SOE*, 206). She refuses to be bound by feudal obligations.

Dhaniram also embodies some of the contradictory tendencies in the two competing social orders. A Hindu priest, he was educated at one of the Presbyterian schools of the Canadian Mission, "where he had been taught hymns and other Christian things" (*SOE*, 48). He takes a certain delight in his dual heritage because, as he says, " 'It make me see both sides' . . . and even now, although he was a Hindu priest, he often found himself humming hymns like 'Jesus loves me, yes, I know' " (*SOE*, 48). Inherent in this duality is the conflict between the new capitalist order and the old feudal order. A picture on the wall of Dhaniram's home introduces the symbolic dimension of the conflict:

In the light of the Petromax he [Mahadeo] studied Dhaniram's veranda walls. There were many Hindu coloured prints; but by far the biggest thing was a large Esso calendar, with Pundit Dhaniram's religious commitments written in pencil above the dates. It looked as though Dhaniram's practice was falling off. It didn't matter; Foam knew that Dhaniram also owned the fifth part of a tractor and Baksh said that was worth at least two hundred dollars a month. (*SOE*, 44)

On the one hand, the Hindu colored prints represent Dhaniram's Hindu culture and his declining commitment to its practice; on the other hand, the large Esso calendar is symbolic of the nascent capitalist order and Dhaniram's growing attachment to the spoils of that system—two world orders competing for dominance.

The election offers the people of Elvira a chance to recognize their cultural diversity and to rejoice in its richness. There is no need to wage a divisive struggle to achieve temporary power. Lookhoor, for example, rhapsodizes about the unity of the races and the religions as the most important prerequisite for the realization of the liberation and identity of Elvira's people:

"People of Elvira, the fair constituency of Elvira. . . . Unite! You have nothing to lose but your chains. Unite and cohere. Vote for the man who has lived among you, toiled among you, prayed among you, worked among you. This is the voice of the renowned and ever popular Lookhoor begging you and urging you and imploring you and entreating you and beseeching you to vote for Preacher, the renowned and ever popular Preacher. Use your democratic rights on election day and vote one, vote all. This, good people of Elvira, is the voice of Lookhoor." (SOE, 66)

This mixture of utopian and Marxist slogans, somewhat analogous to the brand of "Socialinduism Socialism-cum-Hinduism," which Indarsing offered in *The Mystic Masseur,* is meant to be comic at one level. At another level, it is meant to demonstrate the need for the society to work out a creative and original formula through which to speak about its aspirations. The strange mixture of the borrowed and the indigenous, the fantastic and the practical, is indicative of the insecurities that inhere in that transitional period of social development. In *A House for Mr. Biswas* this transition is seen more clearly.

In the end, the legend of the ghost that haunts Elvira House, emblematic of Trinidad's condition, speaks to another part of the colonial legacy in Trinidad: the bastardy between Europeans and Africans at the foundation of the nation. Naipaul elaborates upon the East Indians' fears of this contamination in *The Mimic Men.* The ghost in Elvira, which is the basis of social relations in the country, is this same fear, an unconscious fear that undergirds the text at all times.

Yet it is in Elvira House, an abandoned cocoa house (symbolic of the colonizer's glory), where they find the mother of Tazan (superstition), whom Harbans had killed at the beginning of the novel. Harbans was responsible for killing the superstition of the past but, as Hurbert, the little boy, says: "Everybody only know how to say 'mash, dog!' . . . Nobody know how to feed it" (SOE, 118). For the narrator as well as the author, the *Swaraj* task is not simply to destroy but to rebuild. And as the narrator seems to imply, one of the major defects of colonial man is his inability to build a new social order once he has destroyed the old.

The gradual dissolution of feudalism in Trinidadian society in 1950 created new problems for its citizens: it required the older generation (the Chitteranjans, the Bakshes, the Ramloogans) to discard their old superstitions as a necessary prerequisite for nationhood. For the younger generation (the young Miss Chitteranjan, Lookhoor, the doolahin, and Foam), who had broken with the older order by violating the past, it meant mustering the courage to begin to shape something new, wholesome, and lasting, free from the superstition of the old, and to use creatively the new conditions the nascent capitalist society offered.

Before the younger generation could realize this dream of harmony, they had to free themselves from the parochialism and age-old fears of their elders. The elections simply revealed the problems to be overcome. As Gandhi said: "It is *Swaraj* when we learn to rule ourselves."[16] Harbans's election to political office, like Ganesh's, seems to indicate an acceptance of the colonialist-capitalist system, an individualistic approach to liberation through personal aggrandizement and a betrayal of the people's hope of total liberation. By changing his name, Ganesh betrays his people's hopes; by driving a new Jaguar, Harbans accepts the oppressor's culture.

The confusion that greets Harbans on his return to his constituency emphasizes the backwardness from which the society had to liberate itself. For as the crowd gathers, a young man, a symbolic embodiment of the darkness of the past, rises out of the crowd and reveals, in grotesque proportions, the country's predicament:

It was a moonless night and the occasional oil lamps in the houses far back from the trace only made the darkness more terrible. At the heels of Harbans and his committee there was nearly half the crowd that had gathered outside Chitteranjan's shop. Tiger ran yapping in and out of the procession. One horrible young labourer with glasses, gold teeth and a flowerpot hat pushed his face close to Harbans and said, "Don't worry with the old generation. Is the young generation like me you got to worry about." (*SOE*, 204)

This deformed relationship with the past must be clarified. The greed, chicanery, and bribery of the declining social order must give way to a structured and "civilized" response to the past and the achievement of "soul-force," which Gandhi indicated was the chief prerequisite for independence.[17] The suffrage of the people of Elvira can be a progressive social phenomenon only if it is used in a constructive manner rather than to manipulate prejudices, disguise false sentiments, or perpetuate obsolete superstitious practices. It can be accomplished only if the people truly accept the principles manifested in the life and practices of Mahatma Gandhi in his struggle to attain *Swaraj* in their ancestral home.

In *The Suffrage of Elvira* no one character responds fully to the problematics of the East Indian in the Wilderness. The text is diffused and occasionally uncertain, and the various strands of the narrative seem forced together to create a tentative harmony. No character is developed fully, nor does any character display great psychological depth. Yet the text manifests the complexity of the East Indian experience in the Caribbean and the problematic nature of social transformation in Trinidad and Tobago.

Reflecting on *The Suffrage of Elvira* in an early interview, Naipaul remarked: "I wrote *The Suffrage of Elvira* to prove to myself that I could invent, invent a story constructed carefully round a given incident."[18] Geoffrey Broughton, in his examination of the early novels of Naipaul, has suggested that *The Suffrage of Elvira* discloses "a new unity . . . and it clearly is the most highly organized of the four Trinidad novels."[19] The novel represents the culmination of a period of preparation that was consummated with *A House for Mr. Biswas*.

3. A Prose-Tragedy: Mr. Biswas
and the Original Myths

And all about the greenwood came and went the monkey hosts, weird with a more than human wisdom, able at a word to make the leafy branches blossom into beauty, and yet unhappy strugglers with their own hot monkey-nature, ever imposing on them, like a spell, a strange, unspeakable destiny of mischief and futility.
—A. K. Coomaraswamy and Sister Nivedita, *Myths of the Hindus and the Buddhists*

> "Deeds we do in life, Kausalya, be they bitter, be they sweet,
> Bring their fruit and retribution, rich reward or suffering meet.
>
> Heedless child is he, Kausalya, in his fate who doth not scan
> Retributions of his *karma,* sequence of a holy plan."
> —*Ramayana*

THE REALISM OF V. S. NAIPAUL

The continuing quest for order and meaning in the new world of Trinidad and Tobago which Naipaul evinced in his earlier work becomes much more serious and structured in *A House for Mr. Biswas,* in which the social and political concerns of *The Mystic Masseur* and *The Suffrage of Elvira* give way to a deeper ontological examination of the colonial subject and his relationship to his world. Locating the subject in the changing contours of his world as it emerges from the stasis of a feudal order to the fluidity of a nascent capitalist society is the central concern of this novel. The transformation of the inner world of the individual is examined as it relates to the changing social environment.

A House for Mr. Biswas must also be seen as a product of Naipaul's Hindu sensibility. The Hindu epic the *Ramayana* adds a philosophical dimension to the text, enabling the author to manipulate the epic form to illustrate the themes already introduced in *The Mystic Masseur* and *The Suffrage of Elvira:* the East Indian problematic in the Wilderness, the Hindu concept of self, and the nature of self-realization. Moreover, the contradictions of Mr. Biswas's life reflect the changing conditions of his society and his age, and in this sense he comes to represent every colonial person caught up in the transition from feudalism to capitalism.

Contrasted with the feudal stasis of the Tulsi family of Hanuman House, Mr. Biswas's struggles are an attempt to liberate himself from the obsolescence of that world. As Patrick Swinden notes, "Biswas has to settle for a life which is awkwardly shot through with memories of a Hindu past and the complex ambition roused by a modern Westernised present."[1] "Told against an episodic framework of several houses,"[2] *A House for Mr. Biswas* is located solidly in the geography and history of Trinidad and Tobago during the period from 1931 to 1948. One is presented with the details of a world where child labor, rigid caste relations, and child brides are the norm.[3] Economically underdeveloped, it is an almost Dickensian world where colonialism has made children old before they can enjoy their childhood (Mr. Biswas himself appears never to have had a childhood in that he is never called anything but Mr. Biswas), malnutrition is an everyday fact of life, life expectancy is short, and ambition is not a part of the natural order.

As one looks at the world of Mr. Biswas one is struck by the absolute sense of fate—that everything is preordained—that underlies the social philosophy of his people.[4] At the beginning of the novel, Mr. Biswas's grandfather is depicted as a futile man who accepts the conditions of his life, including his asthmatic illness, without question. "Fate," he says; "there is nothing we can do about it." As the narrator observes: "Fate had brought him from India to the sugar estate, aged him quickly and left him to die in a crumbling mud hut in the swamplands; yet he spoke of Fate often and affectionately, as though, merely by surviving, he had been particularly favoured."[5]

In this feudal world, the social status of the Tulsis was clear. Pundit Tulsi, a man of the highest caste (Brahmin), had retained his link with his people in India and communicated with them. As a consequence, the Tulsis symbolized, to the extent that such was possible, the solidity and continuity of the East Indian community in Trinidad. Governed by a strong sense of communal organization, individuals were subordinated to the group, which offered them a degree of emotional and spiritual security in their alien world, a sense of wholeness, order, and meaningful continuity. To maintain the smooth functioning of this well-ordered hierarchical world, however, each member of the clan not only had to know his place within and outside that world but had to remain within it.

Internally, the Tulsis' world was also well structured: Mrs. Tulsi ("the old queen," as Mr. Biswas called her), the head of the family, lived in the Rose

Room and imposed harmony and order upon the house. Seth ("the big boss") ruled the family under Mrs. Tulsi's guidance. Next in line were Mrs. Tulsi's sons ("the two gods"), who were being prepared for the changing world of Trinidad and upon whom the future of the family depended. The rest of the family, which consisted of the Tulsis' daughters and their families, known simply as the Tulsis, formed the bottom of the pyramid.

The family followed most of the dogmas of Hinduism: they believed that the caste system was of utmost importance to the maintenance of the social order, converts should not be accepted into the religion, idols should be worshiped, women should not be educated, the children's spouses should be selected by the family, *pujas* should be observed, and Hindu ceremonies should be respected. Even though the Tulsis had transgressed in some of these areas (such as "marrying off [their] favorite daughter in a registry office [or] sending the two little barbers to a Roman Catholic college" (*HFMB*, 117), these were merely concessions to the rising colonial-capitalist order.

Yet, as solidly entrenched as the Tulsis appeared, they, like some of the earlier inhabitants of Naipaul's novels, never felt really safe in Trinidad. The narrator gives this assessment of their situation:

[Trinidad] was no more than a stage in the journey that had begun when Pundit Tulsi left India. Only the death of Pundit Tulsi had prevented them from going back to India; and ever since they had talked, though less often than the old men who gathered in the arcade every evening, of moving on, to India, Demerara, Surinam. Mr. Biswas didn't take such talk seriously. The old men would never see India again. And he could not imagine the Tulsis anywhere else except at Arwacas. Separate from their house, and lands, they would be separate from the labourers, tenants and friends who respected them for their piety and the memory of Pundit Tulsi; their Hindu status would be worthless and, as had happened during their descent on the house in Port of Spain, they would only be exotic. (*HFMB*, 390)

The Tulsis' inability to feel truly a part of the society in which they lived resulted in their psychological displacement. It was as though their social existence was not synchronized with the sociopolitical realities of their new environment. Because of this tension, or sense of emotional displacement, the Tulsis initially could make temporary concessions to the new environment. For them, Hanuman House represented the external symbol of an inner reality.

Mr. Biswas was of the new generation, and his life was therefore diametrically opposed to that of the Tulsis. Bereft of either security or solidity in his family life and feeling responsible for his father's death and his family's misfortune, he was forced to leave his home at Parrot Trace and become a strafe and wanderer. From the moment he left the house,

he was to be a wanderer with no place he could call his own, with no family except that which he was to attempt to create out of the engulfing world of the Tulsis. For with his mother's parent dead, his father dead, his brothers on the estate in Felicity, Dehuti as a servant in Tara's house, and himself rapidly growing away from Bipti, who, broken, became increasingly useless and impenetrable, it seemed to him that he was really alone. (*HFMB*, 401)

Certainly, this sense of insecurity is emblematic of the newly emerging social order. Marriage, however, introduced Mr. Biswas to the Tulsis of Hanuman House. For him, this liaison represented a transition from instability to stability, from a state of permanent homelessness to an apparently safer haven.[6]

In contrast to his previous life of misfortune and loneliness, Hanuman House offered an apparent solidity, peace, and impregnability. Physically, it resembled an "alien white fortress," constructed of "concrete walls" that made it look "bulky, impregnable and blank." Hovering above it was the "statue of the monkey-god Hanuman," which looked "slightly sinister" and gave the building a cold, frightening appearance. The inside of the house, by contrast, seemed warm and comfortable. Filled with illusions, Mr. Biswas entered the world of the Tulsis unaware that his romantic ego would be crushed by a hierarchical order that did not allow for the expression of individuality.

As soon as he enters that impregnable fortress, the Tulsis attempt to reduce him to a "non-entity," for, as Gordon Rohlehr has argued, "Tulsi-dom depend[ed] for its existence on the psychic emasculation of the man [and woman] and the maintenance of their sense of inferiority. At the most humiliating moments of his struggle, Biswas nearly surrenders to this sense of inferiority."[7] Like the other brothers-in-law, Mr. Biswas is expected to succumb to fate as his grandfather had done. Immediately, he recognizes his situation: "He had no money or position. He was expected to be a Tulsi. At once he rebelled" (*HFMB*, 97). At that point, his liberation begins.

To repulse the assaults against his personhood, he clings tenaciously to his self-effacing humor and his occupation as a sign painter. When his brother-in-law Govind suggests that he give up sign painting and become a driver in the Tulsis' estate, Mr. Biswas recoils in horror and responds. "Give up sign-painting? And my independence? No, boy. My motto is: paddle your own canoe" (*HFMB*, 107).

His independence and manhood are further threatened when he is forced to apologize for insulting members of the family, thereby disrupting the order and unity of the Tulsi household. Mr. Biswas is appropriately remorseful until he is required to apologize to the "two gods" for his remarks. He then lashes out, criticizing the entire arrangement of Hanuman House and explodes: "The whole pack of you could go to hell! . . . I am not going to apologize to one of the damn lot of you. . . . Having that damn little boy talk to me like that! He does talk to all your brother-in-laws like that?" (*HFMB*, 111). This act of rebellion releases him temporarily from the grips of the Tulsi family and signals his determination to be independent and take whatever action is necessary to maintain his individuality.

His next act of disloyalty or disobedience occurs when he attempts to subvert the Tulsi organization by introducing foreign doctrines. Becoming a proselytizer for the Aryans, a group of revisionist Hindu missionaries from India, Mr. Biswas advocates the education of girls, the abolition of the institution of child brides, and freedom of choice in the selection of a mate. Mr. Biswas also approves the Aryans' method of peaceful persuasion and nonviolent conversion to Hinduism and blithely refuses to speak Hindi.

These acts of disloyalty which Mr. Biswas introduces into the feudal world of the Tulsis embody some of the central doctrines of capitalism: the equality of men and women and the freedom of choice. Seth, who recognizes the potency of these ideas and the threat they pose to the Tulsis' world, recoils in horror, exclaiming: "This house is like a republic already. . . . The Black Age has come at last. Sister, we have taken in a serpent" (*HFMB*, 123–24). By advocating these capitalist ideas Mr. Biswas has become a direct threat to the feudal world of the Tulsis.

Mr. Biswas's first move toward an independent existence comes when he takes his family to live in the village called the Chase. Even though his six years there are filled with "boredom and futility" (*HFMB*, 182), Mr. Biswas manages to pursue a purposeful existence. Having discovered the speculative wisdom of philosophy, he decides that life should not emphasize the sensuous but should be contemplated and accepted. Thus, though "his philosophical books gave him solace, he could never lose the feeling that they were irrelevant to his situation" (*HFMB*, 182–83).

With the birth of his fourth child, Mr. Biswas begins to feel trapped by a future that is closing in on him. The romance, sense of invention, and reflective wisdom of philosophical discourses cannot dissipate his gloom. The uncertainty he feels in the Wilderness is exemplified by a feeling of void.

The future he feared was upon him. He was falling into the void, and that terror, known only in dreams, was with him as he lay awake at nights, hearing the snores and creaks and the occasional cries of babies from the other rooms. The relief that morning brought steadily diminished. Food and tobacco were tasteless. He was always tired, and always restless. He went often to Hanuman House; as soon as he was there he wanted to leave. Sometimes he cycled to Arwacas without going to the house, changing his mind in the High Street, turning round and cycling back to Green Vale. When he closed the door of his room for the night, it was like an imprisonment.

He talked to himself, shouted, did everything as noisily as he could.

Nothing replied. Nothing changed. *Amazing scenes were witnessed yesterday when.* The newspapers remained as jaunty as they had been, the quotations as sedate. *Of him I will never lose hold and he shall never lose hold of me. Of him I will never lose hold and he shall never lose hold of me.* But now in the shape and position of everything around him, the trees, the furniture, even those letters he had made with brush and ink, there was an alertness, an expectancy. (*HFMB*, 227–28)

His inability to situate himself fully in his world leads to further alienation from that world and to the deepening psychological crisis this condition engenders.

The first part of the text ends with Mr. Biswas in this state of gloom. He is clearly unable to fit into the changing social world and is unsure what course to follow. He does not know what constitutes a satisfactory life, nor can he explain or understand the subtle breaking down of the previous order, which he has never fully known. His inability to reconcile his essence with his existence constitutes the major source of tensions in the first part of the novel.

The fragmentation of his psyche brings him to the dramatic realization that he is beginning to function at the level of his animal being.[8] The intense uncertainty he feels about the future is revealed most graphically when he forlornly surrenders himself to his condition, finding solace only in his dog, Tazan, who awaits his return:

"You are glad to see me," he thought. "You are an animal and think that because I have a head and hands and look as I did yesterday I am a man. I am deceiving you. I am not whole."

Tazan wagged his tail.

He opened the lower half of the door.

People!

Fear seized him and hurt like a pain.

Tazan jumped upon him, egg-stained, shining-eyed.

Grieving, he stroked him. "I enjoyed this yesterday and the day before. I was whole then."

Already yesterday, last night, was as remote as childhood. And mixed with his fear was this grief for a happy life never enjoyed and now lost. (*HFMB*, 268)

At Green Vale, where Mr. Biswas lives after the Chase, he undergoes an acute depression that eventually ends in a nervous breakdown. Brought back to Hanuman House, he is relieved temporarily from this state by the warmth and protection it offers. The morning after his arrival is "like the morning after a birth in the Rose Room" (*HFMB*, 296). Significantly, the physician who attends Mr. Biswas represents the two antagonistic worlds that continue to plague him.

Port of Spain, the major city of the island, provides Mr. Biswas with a new beginning. Yet because he carries within him the seeds of his feudal past, his transition to a capitalist way of life will entail as much pain and difficulty as his struggle with his previous way of life. In Port of Spain, therefore, his initial feeling of freedom and release is illusory:

His freedom was over, and it had been false. The past could not be ignored; it was never counterfeit; he carried it within himself. If there was a place for him, it was one that had already been hallowed out by time, by everything he had lived through, however imperfect, makeshift and cheating.

He welcomed the stomach pains. They had not occurred for months and it seemed to him that they marked the return to the wholeness of his mind, the restoration of the world; they indicated how far he had lifted himself from the abyss of the past months, and reminded him of the anguish against which everything now had to be measured. (*HFMB*, 316)

A chance encounter leads him to write for the *Trinidad Sentinel* and allows him to make some sense of his mental chaos and to deflect the anguish he feels in Port of Spain. Equally important, it gives him a belief in future possibilities, no matter how slight, and he begins to impose some order in his domestic life and to take a new sense of pride in himself. For the moment, there is a glimmer of hope.

At the same time, a crack appears in the solidarity of Hanuman House. The nascent capitalist order enters the world of the Tulsis. Shekhar, the wife of the elder god, who had treated the "Tulsi patronage with arrogant Presbyterian modernity" (*HFMB*, 365) from the day of her marriage, flaunts her education: "She called herself Dorothy, without shame or apology. She wore short frocks and didn't care that they made her look lewd and absurd" (*HFMB*, 365). Seth, the pillar of the Tulsi organization, and his family leave Hanuman House to live in a back street nearby. The rest of the family also leaves to live in a new estate at Shorthills in the northeastern part of the island. The breakup of Hanuman House is complete.

At this juncture of the text, we observe the same movement that took place in the two previous novels, from the countryside to the city, that is, from a feudal to a capitalist society. Like Hanuman House, the physical appearance of the Shorthills estate is symbolic of the social order:

In the grounds of the estate house there was a cricket field and a swimming pool; the drive was lined with orange trees and gri-gri palms with slender white trunks, red berries and dark green leaves. The land itself was a wonder. The saman trees had lianas so strong and supple that one could swing on them. All day the immortelle trees dropped their red and yellow bird-shaped flowers through which one could whistle like a bird. Cocoa trees grew in the shade of the immortelles, coffee in the shade of the cocoa, and the hills were covered with tonka bean. Fruit trees, mango, orange, avocado pear, were so plentiful as to seem wild. And there were nutmeg trees, as well as cedar, *poui*, and the *bois-canot* which was light yet so springy and strong it made you a better cricket bat than the willow. The sisters spoke of the hills, the sweet springs and hidden waterfalls with all the excitement of people who had known only the hot, open plain, the flat acres of sugar cane and the muddy ricelands. Even if one didn't have a way with land, as they had, if one did nothing, life could be rich at Shorthills. There was talk of dairy farming; there was talk of growing grapefruit. More particularly, there was talk of rearing sheep, and of an idyllic project of giving one sheep to every child as his very own, the foundation, it was made to appear, of fabulous wealth. And there were horses on the estate: the children would learn to ride. (*HFMB*, 391–92)

This idyllic setting is symbolic of an idealized colonial past. And Naipaul uses these stylized images to present one version of colonial ideology. The cricket field, for example, is symbolic of the imposition of British colonialist-imperialist values upon colonial peoples. The delicate gri-gri palms, the orange trees, and the berries, the strength of the saman trees, and the subtleness of the lianas and the immortelle are all symbolic of the ordered nature of the capitalist system. The comparison between the colonizer's culture and "the hot, open plain, the flat acres of sugar cane and the muddy ricelands," which was the Tulsis' world, implies a judgment that the exploitive activity of the colonizers is to be admired, not the noble work of the laborers.

In the new capitalist world order, which Shorthills represents, values are inverted: people gain dignity not from hard, honest work but from their capacity to exploit others and represent those parasitic activities as the height of civility. The estate's previous owners, the French creoles of the island, represent the bourgeois civilization that the Tulsis are depicted as violating. The clash of these two cultures is represented as follows:

The solitude and silence of Shorthills was violated. The villagers bore the invasion without protest and almost with indifference. They were an attractive mixture of

French and Spanish and Negro and, though they lived so near to Port of Spain, formed a closed, distinctive community. They had a rural slowness and civility, and spoke English with an accent derived from the French patois they spoke among themselves. They appeared to exercise some rights on to the grounds of the house. They played cricket on the cricket field most afternoons and there was a match every Sunday, when the grounds were virtually taken over by the villagers. For some time after the coming of the Tulsis courting couples strolled about the orange walks and the drive in the afternoon, disappearing from time to time into the cocoa woods. But this custom soon ceased. The couples, finding themselves surprised at every turn by a Tulsi, moved further up the gully. (*HFMB*, 400)

In this alien order, the Tulsis are unable to function in a purposeful and ordered manner. They begin to neglect the estate and ultimately abandon it. As the narrator suggests, there was no one who was capable enough to "plan and direct" its activities (*HFMB*, 404). The feudal order gives way to the new capitalist order, as each detail of the new life emphasizes the slow demise of the old society and the inability of its members to act creatively in the new social order. The society's values are utilitarian, and its people have none of the saving graces of civilization. At Shorthills, nascent capitalist relations triumph.

The disintegration, which at first is depicted at the adult level, is quickly reflected in the behavior of the children. For them, Shorthills becomes a virtual nightmare:

Daylight was nearly always gone when they returned [from school], and there was little to return to. The food grew rougher and rougher and was eaten more casually, in the kitchen itself, where the brick floor had been topped with mud, or in the covered space between the kitchen and the house. No child knew from one night to the next where he was going to sleep; beds were made anywhere and at any time. On Saturdays the children pulled up weeds; on Sundays they collected oranges or other fruit.

At week-ends the children submitted to the laws of the family. But during the week, when they spent so much time away from the house, they formed a community of their own, outside family laws. No one ruled; there were only the weak and the strong. Affection between brother and sister was despised. No alliance was stable. Only enmities were lasting, and the hot afternoon walks which Mrs. Tulsi had seen lightened by song were often broken by bitter fights of pure hate. (*HFMB*, 411–12)

In this world of budding bourgeois social relations, the laws of capitalism—the survival of the fittest and bourgeois individualism—begin to dominate. The older bonds of solidarity cease to exist, replaced by divisiveness, fragmentation, disloyalty, and competitiveness.

Unable to understand the new land and without Hanuman House to protect them, individual family members begin to prepare their offspring for the new capitalist world. Education is the key to admittance: "Everyone had to fight for himself in a new world, the world of Owad and Shekhar had entered, where education was the only protection. As fast as the children graduated from the infant school at Shorthills they were sent to Port of Spain. Basdai boarded them" (*HFMB*, 436). At this point, the Tulsis' fear of education which we saw in the earlier texts is gone. Education is the sine qua non of one's liberation.

The disintegration of the feudal world of the Tulsis brings Mr. Biswas to another crisis, for he must confront himself and his feelings. Reflecting upon his social condition at the death of his mother, he realizes that "no one could escape from what he was . . . [and] concluded that no one could deny his humanity and keep his self respect" (*HFMB*, 483). Trapped by a social history from which he cannot escape, he has to reconcile his personal history with a heritage from which he feels alienated.

This confrontation with himself—and the various forms of alienation that are generated by the society—leads Mr. Biswas to face his society and question his place within it. Unable to reconcile the feudal aspects of his past with the capitalist order of the present, Mr. Biswas, in an important moment of his life, becomes frozen between two points of existence. Unable to take any physical action to bridge the chasm between the two conflicting worlds, he turns to the metaphysical act of writing in an attempt to unify his social being and complete himself as a person. This "coming into consciousness," as it were, is marked out by three phases: "the apprenticeship of writing, the composition of unfinished stories, and the improvisation of a poem about his mother's death."9 As in the fifth thematic moment of *The Mystic Masseur*, the written and the spoken word—emblematic of the two warring dimensions of his being—are brought together to effectuate some existential balance and to attempt a closure in time; an attempt to cut what one critic has called "the figurative umbilical cord with India."10

MR. BISWAS AND THE ACT OF WRITING

The death of Mr. Biswas's mother, which serves as the climax of the second part of the novel, causes Mr. Biswas to take stock of his existence and allows him to express his true feelings toward his mother. To honor her and their mutual past, which he had violated during her lifetime, he composes a prose-poem. Placing himself on a spiritual pyre, he seeks to confront that aspect of his past that he denied:

To do honour he had no gifts. He had no words to say what he wanted to say, the poet's words, which held more than the sum of their meanings. But awake one night, looking at the sky through the window, he got out of bed, worked his way to the light switch, turned it on, got paper and pencil, and began to write. He addressed his mother. He did not think of rhythm; he used no cheating abstract words. He wrote of coming up to the brow of the hill, seeing the black, forked earth, the marks of the spade, the indentations of the fork prongs. He wrote of a journey he had made a long time before. He was tired; she made him rest. He was hungry; she gave him food. He had nowhere to go; she welcomed him. The writing excited, relieved him; so much so that he was able to look at Anand, asleep beside him, and think, "Poor boy. He failed his exam."

The poem written, his self-consciousness violated, he was whole again. And when on Friday the five widows arrived in Port of Spain for their sewing lessons at the Royal Victoria Institute, and the house resounded with clatter and chatter and shrieks and singing and the radio and the gramophone, Mr. Biswas went to the meeting of his literary group and announced that he was going to read his offering at last.

"It is a poem," he said. "In prose." (*HFMB*, 484)

In this prose-poem, Mr. Biswas writes of a journey his people had made a long time ago, a journey that embodied all of the old values of his people. Unable to break the bonds of that past, the dependence that characterized his social relations, he writes to externalize and objectify the past so he can examine it. Once having externalized the past, he can bear the pain caused by such an examination. Yet he is forced into contact with the present world of capitalism represented by the "clatter and chatter and shrieks and singing and the radio and the gramophone." Mr. Biswas is able to use language to transcend the sense of loss he feels.

This mental synthesis and metaphysical reconciliation constitute the limitation of Mr. Biswas's vision. Unable to perceive any meaningful activity arising out of his colonial reality, Mr. Biswas cannot go beyond abstractions. The solution to the problem of the colonial person can be found only in concrete and sensuous activities. Therefore, as soon as the poem is read and the necessary catharsis is completed, Mr. Biswas "disgraces himself":

Thinking himself free of what he had written, he ventured on his poem boldly, and even with a touch of self mockery. But as he read, his hands began to shake, the paper rustled; and when he spoke of the journey his voice failed. It cracked and kept on cracking; his eyes tickled. But he went on, and his emotion was such that at the end no one said a word. He folded the paper and put it in his jacket pocket. Someone filled his glass. He stared down at his lap, as if angry, as if he had been completely alone. He said nothing for the rest of the evening, and in his shame and confusion drank much. When he went home the widows were singing softly, the children were asleep, and he shamed Shama by being noisily sick in the outdoor lavatory. (*HFMB*, 485)

This outcome was inevitable, for escape could not be found through abstract words alone. Words may be the necessary starting point for articulating one's condition of alienation, isolation, and emotional dissonance, but social reality can be transcended only through concrete activity. Mr. Biswas takes only the first step of mental abstraction; he is unable to proceed to the second step of practical activity to resolve his conflicts. As a result, he can only recede into obscurity and slow decay. His demise is inevitable, and much of the rest of the novel becomes anticlimactic, tying up stray strands of the text.

Like the other men at the *Sentinel*'s office who consider their lives ended at the age of forty, Mr. Biswas quickly begins to age and to deteriorate physically. To him, the city began to lose "its romance and promise" and he began "to consider himself old, his career closed, and his visions of the future became only visions of Anand's future" (*HFMB*, 494). His offspring, Anand, will most likely not face a frozen and impotent position as his father had and will be better equipped to be a Trinidadian.

At the same time that Mr. Biswas is condemning himself to a life of blight, waste, and long-term debt, the kingdom of the Tulsis is disintegrating. Mrs. Tulsi, who heretofore has been the family's major cohesive force, begins to lose faith in her own people: "Never trust your race, Blackie. Never trust them," she confides to her Negro servant. "I have no luck with my family. I have no luck with my race" (*HFMB*, 519–20). Surely, such confessions to one who is of neither Mrs. Tulsi's race nor caste must signal the demise of Hanuman House.

The next bastion of Mrs. Tulsi's feudal world to disintegrate is her religion. Thrusting her beliefs aside, she takes refuge in Roman Catholicism:

Regularly too, she had *pujas*, austere rites aimed at God alone, without the feasting and gaiety of the Hanuman House ceremonies. The pundit came and Mrs. Tulsi sat before him; he read from the scriptures, took his money, changed in the bathroom and left. More and more prayer flags went up in the yard, the white and red pennants fluttering until they were ragged, the bamboo poles going yellow, brown, grey. For every *puja* Mrs. Tulsi tried a different pundit, since no pundit could please her as well as Hari. And, no pundit pleasing her, her faith yielded. She sent Sushila to burn candles in the Roman Catholic church; she put a crucifix in her room; and she had Pundit Tulsi's grave cleaned for All Saints' Day. (*HFMB*, 521–22)

Surely, there can be no greater profanation than to turn from Hinduism to Catholicism. Mrs. Tulsi's loss of faith signifies the final crumbling of the feudal world of the Tulsis and the desperate attempt of the feudal aristocracy to become a part of the new capitalist order. As Mrs. Tulsi laments to Mr. Biswas, "The old ways have become old-fashioned so quickly, Mohun" (*HFMB,* 527).

In the end, the old ways of India must give way to the new ways of Trinidad as feudalist relations give way to those of a colonialist-capitalist society. Mr. Biswas, who has struggled to release himself from the old ways, still feels captured by their power and so he becomes a frozen victim between the two social worlds. The socialism of Owad, Mrs. Tulsi's son, which is perceived at first to be a curiosity, soon turns into callous individualism and arrogance. Finally, he enters the capitalist world by marrying Dorothy's cousin, "a handsome young woman who had graduated from McGill University and had all the elegance of the Indian girl from South Trinidad [with her] . . . Canadian degree, her slight Canadian accent and her musical skills" (*HFMB,* 546).

As for Mr. Biswas, he believed that things would get better financially when Anand returned from England and so all he does is wait. When Anand's letters to Mr. Biswas became less frequent, Mr. Biswas began to lose his zest for life and simply awaits his death. As the narrator notes: "He grew dull and querulous and ugly. Living had always been a preparation, a waiting. And so the years had passed; and now there was nothing to wait for" (*HFMB,* 586–87). When death comes, his life is summarized in a headline of three words: JOURNALIST DIES SUDDENLY and two announcements over the radio.

A House for Mr. Biswas exemplifies Naipaul's capacity to capture the "contradictory unity of crisis and renewal, of destruction and rebirth" that characterizes a society in transition. For as Georg Lukács has argued in his *Studies in European Realism,* it is the unique capacity and talent of the great realist writers "to penetrate deeply into the great universal problems of their time and inexorably to depict the true essence of reality as they see it."[11] In *A House for Mr. Biswas* Naipaul captures that East Indian world in transition as so many great realist writers have done with other worlds, capturing the "concrete totality" of a society that was forging a new social era. But, as Homi Bhabha has observed, *A House for Mr. Biswas* also resists being totally "appropriated into the Great Tradition of literary Realism" in that the text "abounds with references to loss, circularity and the demoniacal." Thus he argues:

The narrative of 'Biswas' and the discourse of 'character' satisfy those ideological and formal demands of realist narrative that in displacing the ascriptive totalitarian

discourse of Hanuman House foregrounds the values of individualism, progressiv-
ism, and the autonomy of characters. . . .

To the extent to which stasis and romance are in a dynamic relation, the narrative
can play one discourse off against another in the manner of classical realism,
generating irony and humor, conjuring up the *comedie humaine*. But the driving
desire of 'Biswas' conceals a much graver subject: the subject of madness, illness
and loss; the repetition of failure and the deferral of desire; the trauma of being
always inscribed between the unwritten—Biswas' unfinished narcissistic fables; and
the endlessly rewritten—the beginning of the novel re-writes the end and in that
sense it never really begins or ends. It is here that the fantasy of the text lies; a fantasy
that is resistant to the tension releases of humor, and so to the structural resolutions
of comedy.[12]

This duality explains the ambivalent response to *A House for Mr. Biswas*
and its inability to be absorbed completely by one world or another and, in
this case, by one literary category. In any reading, the excesses of the story
have to be accounted for, and it is in an understanding of the Eastern
dimension of its telling that one can more fully explain the text. The
psychoanalytic analysis that Bhabha applies to *A House for Mr. Biswas*
draws very heavily upon this "unspoken/unsaid" dimension of the text.

The novel, then, is not so bleak as to be completely hopeless nor so
hopeless as to be lacking in compassion for its protagonist. We empathize
with him as he struggles against forces he cannot fully understand or
control. Yet, bowed down as he is by his feeling of alienation from his
society, isolation from his fellow man, the slow dissolution of his internal
fortitude, and a sense of primal loss, Mr. Biswas keeps going. The novel is
the tragic conception of the individual who is contained in the original myth
of the *Ramayana* (Eastern) and forced to respond to the demands of the
contemporary Western world. This tension, independent of Naipaul's intention and attitude toward his art, informs the central content and form of *A
House for Mr. Biswas*.

V. S. NAIPAUL AND THE CREATIVE TRANSFORMATION
OF THE *RAMAYANA*

The creative transformation of the *Ramayana* in *A House for Mr. Biswas*
gives us a parallel and complementary source for interpreting Naipaul's
text.[13] As we have seen, the creative transformation of Hindu classical
literature within Naipaul's work first occurred in *The Mystic Masseur*,
which relied heavily on the *Bhagavad Gita*. In the present text, the author
inverts and distorts the *Ramayana* to express his new historical reality.[14]
More important, the unity of the old epic, which tells of the noble lives of

Rama and Sita, must be destroyed to capture the disunity of the new world and the apparent helplessness of a man and his wife caught up in the ambiguity of a new social situation.[15] Paralleling the story of the *Ramayana*, *A House for Mr. Biswas* tells of a colonial man who has been banished from his homeland and is destined to wander in the Wilderness of Trinidad and Tobago. More specifically, the novel examines the colonial person caught in a drama of exile and alienation.

George Steiner, in his introduction to Walter Benjamin's illuminating text *The Origin of German Tragic Drama*, distinguishes between two concepts useful in understanding the tragic nature of both the *Ramayana* and *A House for Mr. Biswas: Tragödie* and *Trauerspiel*.

Tragödie and *Trauerspiel* are radically distinct, in metaphysical foundation and executive genre. Tragedy is grounded in myth. It acts out a rite of heroic sacrifice. In its fulfillment of this sacrificial-transcendent design, tragedy endows the hero with the realization that he is ethically in advance of the gods, that his sufferance of good and evil, of fortune and desolation, has projected him into a category beyond the comprehension of the essentially "innocent" through materially omnipotent deities (Artemis' flight from the dying Hyppolytus, Dionysus' myopia exceeding the blindness of Pentheus). This realization compels the tragic hero to silence. . . . The *Trauerspiel*, on the contrary, is not rooted in myth but in history. Historicity, with every implication of political-social texture and reference, generates both content and style. Feeling himself dragged towards the abyss of damnation, a damnation registered in a profoundly carnal sense, the baroque dramatist, allegorist, historiographer, and the personages he animates, cling fervently to the world. The *Trauerspiel* is counter-transcendental; it celebrates the immanence of existence even where this existence is passed in torment. It is emphatically "mundane," earthbound, corporeal. It is not the tragic hero who occupies the centre of the stage, but the Janus-faced composite of the tyrant and martyr, of the Sovereign who incarnates the mystery of absolute will and of its victim [so often himself]. Royal purple and the carmine of blood mingle in the same emblematic persona.[16]

Tragödie is thus more consistent with the earlier epoch of mankind. The hero is grounded in myth, aspires to transcendence, is ethically and morally in advance of the gods, and need not explain his purpose on earth to common mortals. The hero is essentially beyond human comprehension. In the *Ramayana*, Rama is depicted as being "God-assisted"; he possesses "god-like might" and is accepted as "the Spirit of God descended on earth, as an incarnation of Vishnu, the Preserver of the World."[17] Therefore, Rama is in advance of the gods in that he represents God incarnate, the immanent manifestation of a transcendent form. As such, the *Ramayana* is akin to a *Tragödie*. The *Trauerspiel*, on the other hand, is situated more in the contemporary epoch, and its hero is a product of history. He derives his nature from the sociopolitical complex of his existence, and even though he finds himself dragged to damnation, he celebrates the immanence of his existence—even when it is passed in torment—and clings fervently to this world.

It is in this latter category that *A House for Mr. Biswas* belongs. Neither transcendent nor ethically in advance of his time, Mr. Biswas is historically embedded in his time and place and is damned by his social context, even as he clings to his world and seeks to comprehend it. Because content brings forth its own form, consistent with the demands of its time and place, Naipaul uses the novel to express Mr. Biswas's relationship to his colonial-capitalist environment. In combining the content of the classical epic with the contemporary form of the novel, he thus creates a *prose-trauerspiel,* or, more simply, a prose-tragedy.

Against this background, a comparison of the texts is instructive. As the *Ramayana* opens, the reader meets Dasa-ratha, the great king of Kosalas, who lives in the city of Ayodhya, the ideal seat of righteousness, and is celebrated for his noble deeds and just actions. In this ordered society each person knows his rank and, with blissful acceptance and obedience, follows his *varna* faithfully.

Kshastras bowed to holy Brahmans, Vaisyas to the Kshatras bowed
Toiling Sudras lived by labour, of their honest duty proud.

To the Gods and to the Fathers, to each guest in virtue trained,
Rites were done with due devotion as by holy writ ordained.

Pure each caste in due observance, stainless was each ancient rite,
And the nation thrived and prospered by its old and matchless might,

And each man in truth abiding lived a long and peaceful life,
With his sons and with his grandsons, with his loved and honoured wife.[18]

In due course, four sons are born to the three wives of Dasa-ratha. Of all the sons, Rama becomes the idol of his father and much beloved by all his people. His brother Lakshman devotes himself to Rama, and they become very close. Because Rama has a tremendous sense of duty toward his father, care for his mother, faith and respect for the gods, and the love of the people of Ayodhya, Dasa-ratha names him heir-apparent to his throne. The good news brings much rejoicing, but as preparations are being made for the coronation celebration, dark intrigue follows, which leads to the exile of Rama, Sita, and Lakshman into the forest.

Rama accepts his fate calmly. Neither grief nor anger touches his heart and, in obedience to his father's will, he prepares for his lonely exile in the cold of Dandak's forest. The loyal people of Ayodhya, on hearing of Rama's exile, follow him to the banks of the Tamasa River, and Rama, Sita, and Lakshman go to the hermitage of Bharad-vaja, where they stay for a while. For fourteen years Rama wanders in the forest, fulfilling the work of his father to which he had committed himself.

Upon his return to Ayodhya, Rama is greeted by his people and his brother Bharat, who had reigned in his absence. Placing the "jewelled sandals," symbol of kingship, at Rama's feet, Bharat humbly returns the kingdom to his brother with the following words:

"Tokens of thy rule and empire, *these* have filled thy royal throne,
Faithful to his trust and duty Bharat renders back thine own,

Bharat's life is joy and gladness, for returned from distant shore,
Thou shalt rule thy spacious kingdom and thy loyal men once more,

Thou shalt hold thy rightful empire and assume thy royal crown,
Faithful to his trust and duty,—Bharat renders back thy own!"   (R, 144)

All the people rejoice at the return of the true king. The ancient sages would tell you that while Rama reigned there was neither sickness nor woe, pain nor suffering, and that he was the most magnificent king India had ever known.

The parallels with *A House for Mr. Biswas* are clear. For one, as in the *Ramayana,* the concepts of fate (*karma*) and duty (*dharma*) are important. Rama and Mr. Biswas are of Raghu's line (Mr. Biswas's father's name is Raghu). But unlike Rama, who becomes the symbol of his people's aspirations, Mr. Biswas rejects his duties of allegiance and obedience to his parents and his people. In fact, Mr. Biswas is the cause of his father's death, as the men call out derisively to "Raghu's son" while they dig for the wealth they believe Raghu buried. Unlike Dasa-ratha, Raghu left no wealth, spiritual or material, from which Mr. Biswas could draw. (Although Bipti, Mr. Biswas's mother, claims that Raghu had trained his children in piety, the behavior of Pratap, Raghu's oldest son, seems to belie this notion when he is with Tara. The search for the remains of Raghu's wealth is futile:

They searched. They pulled out Raghu's box from under the bed and looked for false bottoms; at Bipti's suggestion they looked for any joint that might reveal a hiding-place in the timber itself. They poked the sooty thatch and ran their hands over the rafters; they tapped the earth floor and the bamboo-and-mud walls; they examined Raghu's walking sticks, taking out the ferrules, Raghu's only extravagance; they dismantled the bed and uprooted the logs on which it stood. They found nothing. (*HFMB*, 36)

Thus Raghu, who, unlike Dasa-ratha, bequeathed no legacy to his son, is a miser, in stark contrast with Dasa-ratha's largesse. So too Rama's performance of his duty to his parents, the strength of his character, the courage of his convictions, and his capacity to carry out an assigned task are in contrast to the behavior of Mr. Biswas. The law of Raghu's race is made quite clear when Queen Sumitra bids Lakshman good-bye and tells him the laws by which his people are bound:

"Dear devoted duteous Lakshman, ever to thy elder true,
When thy elder wends to forest, forest-life to thee is due,

Thou hast served him true and faithful in his glory and his fame,
This is Law for true and righteous,—serve him in his woe and shame,

This is Law for race of Raghu known on earth for holy might,
Bounteous in their sacred duty, brave and warlike in the fight!

Therefore tend him as thy father, as thy mother tend him wife,
And to thee, like fair Ayodhya be thy humble forest life,

Go, my son, the voice of Duty bids my gallant Lakshman go,
Serve thy elder with devotion and with valor meet thy foe." (R, 39)

Clearly, Raghu's sons are expected to be truthful and devoted, to serve their elders unquestioningly, to perform their duty well, and be brave at all times. Mr. Biswas does not have any of these qualities. He has not fulfilled his obligations and his duty (his own *dharma*) toward his mother or his land. He certainly has formed no ties to her and does not feel responsible for her social condition. In being remiss in the performance of his duty to his mother, he has committed the most heinous crime in his culture and therefore deserves to be punished by the gods. It is no wonder he feels no pain when his mother dies:

He called the children away from school and they went with Shama to Pratap's. From the road the open verandah and steps, thick with mourners, appeared to be draped with white. He had not expected such a crowd. Tara was there, and Ajodha, looking annoyed. But most of the mourners he didn't know: the families of his sister-in-law, his brother's friends, Bipti's friends. He might have been attending the funeral of a stranger. The body laid out in a coffin on the verandah belonged more to them. He longed to feel grief. He was surprised only by jealousy. (HFMB, 480)

In contrast to Mr. Biswas, Rama is resolute, noble, dutiful, respectful, and concerned for his elders, particularly his parents. Moreover, whereas Rama is the eldest son and the pride of the Raghu line, Mr. Biswas is the youngest son of Raghu and the bane of the line. Thus, whereas Rama can boast proudly that he is "Duteous to my father's bidding, duteous to my mother's will, / Striving in the cause of virtue in the woods we wander still" (*R*, 7), Mr. Biswas is estranged from his mother and feels no grief when she dies. All he can do is bewail his loneliness in exile and pontificate about the futility of his life and the boredom his exile in the Wilderness has brought him.

The second inversion-distortion in the novel revolves around a curse. Dasa-ratha was cursed by the hermit when he killed his son in the forest, and it was prophesied that only Dasa-ratha's death would cleanse him of this accidental murder. Dasa-ratha drew the following moral from the crime:

Deeds we do in life, Kausalya, be they bitter, be they sweet,
Bring their fruit and retribution, rich reward or suffering meet.

Heedless child is he, Kausalya, in his fate who doth not scan
Retribution of his *karma*, sequence of a mighty plan!

Oft in madness and in folly we destroy the mango grove,
Plant the gorgeous gay *palasa* for the red flower that we love,

Fruitless as the red *palasa* is the *karma* I have sown,
And my barren lifetime withers through the deed which is my own!   (*R*, 49–50)

Whereas the curse in the *Ramayana* is upon the father, Dasa-ratha, and leads to his death and his son's exile, the curse in *A House for Mr. Biswas* is upon Mr. Biswas and leads to Raghu's death and Mr. Biswas's exile. With the death of Dasa-ratha, Rama begins his wanderings, just as Mr. Biswas begins his wanderings with the death of Raghu. Rama goes into the Wilderness to fulfill his fate, buoyed with the conviction that

In his father's sacred mandate still his noblest Duty saw,
In the weal of subject nations recognised his foremost Law!

And he pleased his happy mother with a fond and filial care,
And his elders and his kinsmen with devotion soft and fair,

Brahmans blessed the righteous Rama for his faith in gods above,
People in the town and hamlet blessed him with their loyal love!   (*R*, 12)

Mr. Biswas, however, wanders "with no family except that which he was to attempt to create out of the engulfing world of the Tulsis. For with his mother's parents dead, his father dead, his brothers on the estate at Felicity, Dehuti as a servant in Tara's house, and himself rapidly growing away from Bipti who, broken, became increasingly useless and impenetrable, it seemed to him that he was really quite alone (*HFMB*, 40). For Mr. Biswas, there was no "father's sacred mandate," "mother's filial care," "faith in gods above," or concern from his fellow citizens for his welfare. Mr. Biswas's fate was predictable, the resultant chaos inevitable.

In his search for Sita, Rama first goes to Surgriva, king of Vanars, and his brave lieutenant, Hanuman, for help. He forms an alliance with Surgriva, and Hanuman is placed in charge of the search for Sita. So too Mr. Biswas goes to Hanuman House in search of his bride, Sharma, and makes a temporary alliance there as he sets out into the Wilderness of Trinidad to realize himself. Throughout his wanderings Hanuman House provides him with succor and comfort. But whereas Rama had to depend on Hanuman to lead him to Sita and to defeat the enemy, Ravan, Mr. Biswas wages a violent spiritual war against Hanuman House to free himself from feudal enslavement. Indeed, Hanuman House becomes the measure against which Mr. Biswas's liberation can be judged, rather than the ally Hanuman is to Rama in his struggle for liberation.

Even Hanuman's physical appearance is an inversion-distortion in the text. In speaking about the symbolic construct of Hanuman in the *Ramayana*, Ananda Coomaraswamy and Sister Nivedita (Margaret E. Noble) have argued that

there moves through the *Ramayana* one being who, though also a monkey, is of a different order. In those parts of India where, as in the Himālayas or the interior of Mahārāshtra, the symbols of primitive Hinduism still abound, little chapels of Hanuman are as common as those of Ganesha, and the ape, like the elephant, has achieved a singular and obviously age-old conventionalism of form. He is always seen in profile, vigorously portrayed in low relief upon a slab. The image conveys the impression of a complex emblem rather than of plastic realism. But there is no question as to the energy and beauty of the qualities for which he stands. It may be questioned whether there is in the whole of literature another apotheosis of loyalty and self-surrender like that of Hanuman. He is the Hindu ideal of the perfect servant, the servant who finds full realization of manhood, of faithfulness, of his obedience; the subordinate whose glory is in his own inferiority.[19]

This description contrasts with the description of Hanuman in *A House for Mr. Biswas:* "The balustrade which hedged the flat roof was crowned with a concrete statue of the benevolent monkey-god Hanuman. From the ground his whitewashed features could scarcely be distinguished and were, if anything, slightly sinister, for dust had settled on projections and the effect was that of a face lit up from below" (*HFMB*, 80–81). Whereas Hanuman has traditionally been portrayed as vigorous, in low relief, in profile, and suggesting complexity, in *A House for Mr. Biswas* he is undistinguished and "slightly sinister."

The relationships that are formed in Hanuman House are equally distorted, beginning from the moment Mr. Biswas enters the gate. In contrast to the Hindu ideal presented upon Mr. Biswas's arrival at Hanuman House is the slow deterioration that occurs as a result of the forces of capitalism and modernity. Mr. Biswas denies all the external practices and internal values of Hinduism (that is, feudalism) and opts for, and subsequently comes to represent, the central moral and spiritual principle of Christianity (that is, capitalism): that it is possible to be socially mobile and to reject the static, hierarchical position ordained by Hindu tradition. The major contradiction of the text is rooted in this denial. In renouncing his *dharma* and following his conscience, Mr. Biswas, damned though he may be, clings tenaciously to the historical dictates of his time and is determined to *be*.

Thus the tragedy of Mr. Biswas is that because he has not fulfilled his *dharma* (the duty and morality that befits his caste) and his own *dharma* (his personal morality and duty) toward his mother and his kind, his *karma* becomes predictable and inevitable. He is condemned to a life of death and damnation. Unlike Rama, who has been dutiful to his father and to the gods and is therefore able to overcome evil and realize himself, Mr. Biswas, the contemporary anti-hero, is destined to wander in an alien land, unable to realize himself. In the process, however, he develops a self that is staunchly rooted in his world, that is a product of his history and times.

SYMBOL, ALLEGORY, AND THE TRAGIC VISION OF MR. BISWAS

The use of Hanuman House as a central symbol in *A House for Mr. Biswas* is not unintentional. Writing about the importance of symbols within a text, Walter Benjamin observed:

The most remarkable thing about the popular use of the term [symbol] is that a concept which, as it were categorically, insists on the indivisible unity of form and content, should nevertheless serve the philosophical extenuation of that impotence which, because of the absence of dialectical rigour, fails to do justice to content in formal analysis and to form in the aesthetics of content. For this abuse occurs wherever in the work of art the "manifestation" of an "idea" is declared a symbol. The unity of the material and the transcendental object, which constitutes the paradox of the theological symbol, is distorted into a relationship between appearance and essence.[20]

As a theological symbol, Hanuman is just such a distortion of the "indivisible unity of form and content" and of the "relationship between appearance and essence." On one level, the statue of Hanuman at the top of Hanuman House brings to mind an important religious personage in the Hindu religion; on another level, he is depicted as sinister and in an alien world, unable to transcend the "apparent" impregnability of the house over which he stands. At this level of symbolic construction, the statue and by extension the house represent the relationship between the transcendental nature of the religious ideal of Hinduism and the material and alien culture of Trinidad. Thus while the symbol insists upon the "indivisible unity of the form and content" of the Hindu experience in Trinidad and Tobago, it is able to situate simultaneously the general dichotomy that results from the outward appearance of harmony of the East Indian condition with the gradual fragmentation and dissolution of their social being in the necessary secularization that results from their living in Trinidad.

The symbol gives way to allegory as the narrative moves from Hanuman House into the world of Mr. Biswas, who is a new recruit into the apparently solid world of Hanuman House. Thus, from this fundamentally theological and plastic symbol of Hanuman (House) we move on to the theosophical aesthetic of Mr. Biswas's world, and here we find yet another important inversion-distortion of the text. Placed under the guidance of Pundit Jairam, Mr. Biswas desecrates the holy place with his faeces.

Sent out into the world and from Pundit Jairam's protection and guiding care, Mr. Biswas returns to his mother, who, rather than greeting her long-lost son, seems angry that he has thrown away a fortunate and favorable position. Finally, however, overcome by maternal affection, she welcomes him home. The imagery approximates that of the return of the Christian prodigal son:

She poured water for him to wash his hands, sat him down on a low bench and gave him food—not hers to give, for this was the communal food of the house, to which she had contributed nothing but her labour in the cooking—and looked after him in the proper way. But she could not coax him out of his sullenness. (*HFMB*, 57)

At first, he interpreted his mother's behavior as ironic. In retrospect, however, he perceived the allegorical character of this moment in his life:

He did not see at the time how absurd and touching her behavior was: welcoming him back to a hut that didn't belong to her, giving him food that wasn't hers. But the memory remained, and nearly thirty years later, when he was a member of a small literary group in Port of Spain, he wrote and read out a simple poem in blank verse about this meeting. The disappointment, his surliness, all the unpleasantness was ignored, and the circumstances improved to allegory: the journey, the welcome, the food, the shelter. (*HFMB*, 57)

As in the climax of the novel, Mr. Biswas turns to writing to organize his feelings. More important, the text moves from irony to allegory to explain much of his subsequent development.

Because allegory "is that aesthetic genre which lends itself par excellence to a description of a man's alienation from objective reality,"[21] and rejects the relative importance of the immanent nature of human existence in favor of man's transcendental existence, Mr. Biswas is in precisely that predicament of stasis that he wishes to avoid.

But allegory does not concern itself only with alienation and transcendence. It also comments on the process of history and individualization in place and time. The form moves from the depiction of the noble and divine being of classical allegorical literature to the depiction of the common man, which is embodied in contemporary literature. Drawing heavily on the work of Friedrich Creuzer, Walter Benjamin explained the use of allegory as follows:

In allegory the observer is confronted with the *facies hippocratica* of history as a petrified, primordial landscape. Everything about history that, from the very beginning, has been untimely, sorrowful, unsuccessful, is expressed in a face—or rather in a death's head. And although such a thing lacks all "symbolic" freedom of expression, all classical proportion, all humanity—nevertheless, this is the form in which man's subjection to nature is most obvious and it significantly gives rise not only to the enigmatic question of the nature of human existence as such, but also of the biographical historicity of the individual.[22]

The first movement of the allegory, then, is concerned with the "enigmatic question" of human existence; the emphasis is on a general concept ("man," for example) rather than a particular phenomenon ("Mexican man"). In the second movement, which is concerned with the particular individual and embodies the mythic, the person is shown to have a social history.

By reducing Mr. Biswas's life to an allegory, Naipaul anticipates the four stages that Mr. Biswas's life in Trinidad takes: the journey through the Wilderness, the welcome by the Tulsis of Hanuman House, the search for spiritual and physical food, and the tragic inability to find a safe shelter in the alien land. Mr. Biswas's life is thus presented in four stark dialectical movements: his alienation, the immanent nature of his social existence, the particularity of his social being, and the historical dimension of his existence. More specifically, Mr. Biswas's life dramatizes the question of how man in general (East Indian man) becomes particularized (Trinidadian) in a specific historical context (colonialism) and culture (Western and Eastern).

Such a reading is tragic rather than pessimistic. Unlike Naipaul's subsequent novels in which tragedy and human shortcomings are reduced to pessimism and gloom, the internal logic of *A House for Mr. Biswas* is tragic. Given the Hindu sensibility that informs the text, Mr. Biswas's tragic dimension can be perceived as a poetic necessity. His tragedy therefore ought not to be perceived as sad or futile but as an ennobling part of his vision. As Satischandra Chatterjee has argued: "For one who believes in the law of karma, sorrows have a greater moral value than the pleasures of life. While the latter have a tendency to corrupt the mind and deaden the higher and nobler faculties, the former act as incentives to the mind to put forth its best efforts to overcome evil and suffering."[23] Seen within this context, a purely Western reading of *A House for Mr. Biswas* as a metaphor of futility, nothingness, and absurdity is only a partial reading. Read apart from its Eastern/Hindu origins, the text is rendered incomplete and its meaning is diminished. Mr. Biswas's Hindu origins have defined his position within the capitalist-colonialist world and explain his fear, despair, and alienation. As a prose-tragedy, *A House for Mr. Biswas* better explains Mr. Biswas's dilemma in the Wilderness of Trinidad and Tobago.

4. The Conflict of World Views: The Second Period of Naipaul's Development

It used to be said that facts speak for themselves. This is, of course, untrue. The facts speak only when the historian calls on them: it is he who decides to which facts to give the floor and in what order or context. . . . The facts of history never come to us "pure," since they do not and cannot exist in a pure form: they are always refracted through the mind of the recorder. It follows that when we take up a work of history, our first concern should not be with the facts which it contains but with the historian who wrote it.
—E. H. Carr, *What Is History?*

History, as a number of West Indian artists seem to be depicting it, is the study of human survival in the teeth of suffering. Finally, Naipaul the novelist has a more complex vision of West Indian history than Naipaul the social commentator, who tends toward an almost histrionic despair. A friend of mine describes Naipaul as a man who travels about the world looking for despair. The despairing vision of both Naipaul and [Eric] Williams derives in part from their closeness to a European way of seeing.
—Gordon Rohlehr, "History as Absurdity"

The leading of the wise few, the willing obedience of the many, is the beginning and the end of all right action. Secure this, and you secure everything. Fail to secure it, and be your liberties as wide as you can make them, no success is possible.
—J. A. Froude, *The English in the Indies*

Publication of *A House for Mr. Biswas* completed the first phase of Naipaul's writing. The ambivalent feelings Naipaul expressed in his first four novels gave way to a much more systematic, nonfictional examination of Caribbean society. Thus in 1961, the year he completed *A House for Mr. Biswas,* Naipaul wrote his impressions of five Caribbean countries—Trinidad, Guyana, Surinam, Guadeloupe, and Jamaica—which he visited on a grant from the Trinidad and Tobago government. These impressions are included in *The Middle Passage.*

Naipaul returned to the Caribbean in 1960 for the second time since he left in 1950. During his eleven years abroad, he maintained consistently negative feelings toward Trinidad. When he aborted his studies at Oxford, he wanted to go any place but the Caribbean. His writing following his return, *The Middle Passage* and *An Area of Darkness,* was an attempt to understand the harrowing experiences of slavery and indenture that had shaped the social consciousness of Caribbean peoples, particularly those of East Indian descent.

Before we examine the nonfictional writings of V. S. Naipaul it is necessary to note that there is a tension between Naipaul's fictional and nonfictional texts and so one cannot accept Naipaul's testimony about his own work in an unproblematic manner. In differentiating between the purely fictional and nonfictional aspects of his work, Naipaul argues in his introduction to *The Middle Passage* that the "novelist works towards conclusions of which he is often unaware; and it is better that he should. To analyse and decide before writing would rob the writer of the excitement which supports him during his solitude and would be the opposite of my methods as a novelist." Yet writing some twenty years later, Naipaul seemed to ignore most of these considerations when he argued in the introduction to *The Return of Eva Perón: with the Killings in Trinidad* that the pieces which were contained in that text "bridged a creative gap, when no novel offered itself to me. That perhaps explains the intensity of some of the pieces, and their obsessional nature. The themes repeat whether in Argentina, Trinidad or the Congo. Out of these journeys and writings novels did in the end come to me." It is clear that even though Naipaul offers contradictory evidences as to the motives that underlie his nonfictional discourses and the manner in which they fashion his fictional texts, there is really no substantive difference between these two modes of writing in Naipaul's work: one informs the other and vice versa and in these matters Naipaul is not always the best judge. The "obsessional nature" of the nonfictional does intrude upon the fictional. There can be no such purity of intent as Naipaul would have us believe. As Dominick La Capra argued with regard to Sartre's nonfictional work, "A text has no pure virginal 'inside' that may find sanctuary in formalistic interpretation. Its 'inside' is 'always already' contaminated by an outside: the outside of internal self-questioning other texts, and the text of life. Nor does the putative intention of the writer unproblematically govern what the text does, especially when the intention is a retrospective one provided by a self-reading or self-commentary."[1] Thus understood, Naipaul's nonfictional text ought to be interpreted as parallel rather than privileged. Stated in other terms, Naipaul's nonfictional texts serve as an alternative method of disclosing his meaning which is presented later in a fictional manner. The differences that remain unanswered in his fictional texts are subjected to close scrutiny in his nonfictional writings.

In *The Middle Passage* Naipaul articulates the concepts that had fashioned his earlier fiction and to a large extent the ideas he would attempt to work out in his later fiction. In his travel books Naipaul outlined his perceptions of the history and culture of his society, with emphasis on the ways slavery and colonialism had shaped its moral and ethical standards. Following in the tradition of Anthony Trollope, Charles Kingsley, and James Anthony Froude, Naipaul stated his views about the West Indies with an inflexibility and dogmatism that gave them weight and authority. He was determined to demonstrate that little had changed in the West Indies since the visits of these early English travel writers. As he said early in the text:

No attitude in the West Indies is new. Two hundred years before, when he would have been a slave, the tourist would have said the same. "The creole slaves," says a writer of 1805, "looked upon the newly imported Africans with scorn, and sustained in their turn that of the mulattoes, whose complexions were browner; while all were kept at a distance from the intercourse of the whites." On this ship only the Portuguese and the Indians were alien elements. Mr. Mackay and his black fellers, the tourist and the wild cows: these relationships had been fixed centuries before.[2]

The text is primarily devoted to demonstrating that the West Indies had remained a philistine society, bereft of history and standards, and therefore "unimportant except to themselves" (*MP,* 30).

The West Indies, according to Naipaul, exist in a static condition, which he attributes to their early history: "For nothing was created in the British West Indies, no civilization as in Spanish America, no great revolution as in Haiti or the American colonies. There were only plantations, prosperity, decline, neglect; the size of the islands called for nothing else" (*MP,* 27). Drawing on the ideas of Trollope and Froude, Naipaul continued:

How can the history of this West Indian futility be written? What tone shall the historian adopt? Shall he be as academic as Sir Alan Burns, protesting from time to time at some brutality, and setting West Indian brutality in the context of European brutality? Shall he, like Salvador de Madariaga, weigh one set of brutalities against another, and conclude that one has not been described in all its foulness and that this is unfair to Spain? Shall he, like the West Indian historians, who can only now begin to face their history, be icily detached and tell the story of the slave trade as if it were just another aspect of mercantilism? The history of the islands can never be satisfactorily told. Brutality is not the only difficulty. History is built around achievement and creation; and nothing was created in the West Indies. (*MP,* 28–29)

Naipaul's view that history consists primarily of the recapitulation of the "great deeds" of the "great men" who make civilizations and create new worlds is taken from Thomas Carlyle and Froude, who condemned the orator and saw the man of action as the supreme embodiment of history.[3]

That some deeds are only the physical manifestation of historical activity and, as such, represent only one side of a given social phenomenon did not seem to occur to Naipaul; nor did he care that his interpretation of history represented only one aspect of English intellectual thought in the nineteenth century—and the most reactionary. Thus his nonfictional work is a uni-dimensional view of history. As Sylvia Wynter has stated:

It is logical that a Naipaul, although using the title *The Middle Passage* for this travel book about the Caribbean, should avoid making mention of the economic connection and implications. Nor in fact does he seem ever to have bothered to read [Eric] Williams' book [*Capitalism and Slavery*]. Steeped in the English interpretation of their own history, he is able to criticize the "lack of culture" in Trinidad, measuring it against an English "norm"; and without ever understanding that the lack of the one and the norm of the other are equally the results of a single and common historical process. He averts his gaze from the guilt of the strong; and concentrates his contempt of the degradation imposed on the victim by the aggressor.[4]

Froude's influence on Naipaul's understanding of history is also evident in the emphasis he places on the "material" or physical dimension of the history and culture of the Caribbean as opposed to the "spiritual" dimensions. Whereas such writers as Gordon Rohlehr and Wilson Harris see strength in the "spiritual" culture of the Caribbean people, Naipaul sees only the physical manifestations of the culture, which he reduces to absurdity. Thus he writes:

Outside the Royal Victoria Institute in Port of Spain an anchor, still in good condition, stands embedded in concrete, and a sign says this might be the anchor Columbus lost during his rough passage into the Gulf of Paria. So much, one might say, for the history of Trinidad for nearly three hundred years after its discoveries. . . . So Trinidad was and remains a materialist immigrant society, continually growing and changing, never settling into any pattern, always retaining the atmosphere of the camp; unique in the West Indies in the absence of a history of enduring brutality, in the absence of a history; yet not an expanding society but a colonial society, ruled autocratically if benevolently, with the further limitations of its small size and remoteness. All this has combined to give it its special character, its ebullience and irresponsibility. And more: a tolerance which is more than tolerance: an indifference to virtue as well as to vice. (*MP*, 52–54)

Material artifacts of culture, to Naipaul, are the essence of history. For him, the spiritual dimension of the culture plays no part in the lives of the

Negroes, for it does not exist. There is only indifference toward moral or ethical standards, the result, no doubt, of the absence of doers in the society.

If there is no history because there have been no recorded historical deeds and there are no material artifacts of culture, what then is the legacy of slavery? Naipaul draws on Trollope for assistance:

"But how strange is the race of creole Negroes—of Negroes, that is, born out of Africa! They have no country of their own, yet they have not hitherto any country of their adoption. They have no language of their own, nor have they as yet any language of their adoption; for they speak their broken English as uneducated foreigners always speak a foreign language. They have no idea of country, and no pride of race. They have no religion of their own, and can hardly as yet be said to have, as a people, a religion by adoption. The West Indian Negro knows nothing of Africa except that it is a term of reproach. If African immigrants are put to work on the same estate with him, he will not eat with them, or drink with them, or walk with them. He will hardly work beside them, and regards himself as a creature immeasurably the superior of the newcomer."[5]

Naipaul draws the following moral from Trollope's analysis:

This was the greatest damage done to the Negro by slavery. It taught him self-contempt. It set him the ideals of white civilization and made him despise every other. Deprived as a slave of Christianity, education and family, he set himself after emancipation to acquire these things; and every step on the road to whiteness deepened the anomaly of his position and increased his vulnerability. "He burns to be a scholar," Trollope observed, with an unusual insensitivity, "puzzles himself with fine words, addicts himself to religion for the sake of appearances, and delights in aping the little graces of civilization." Everything in the white world had to be learned from scratch, and at every stage the Negro exposed himself to the cruelty of the civilization which had overpowered him and which he was mastering. "These people marry now," a white lady said to Trollope in Jamaica. "In the tones of her voice," he comments, "I thought I could catch an idea that she conceived them in doing so to be trenching on the privileges of their superiors." (*MP*, 66–67)

According to Naipaul, slavery, the mulatto population, the absence of national pride, and the closed nature of the society "re-created the attitudes of the Spanish picaroon world" (*MP*, 73). Naipaul perceived the same ill effects of slavery in British Guiana (now Guyana) and Surinam. His observations of Jamaica, however, were pertinent only because he repeated them, almost verbatim, in *Guerrillas:*

Every day I saw the same things—unemployment, ugliness, overpopulation, race— and every day I heard the same circular arguments. The young intellectuals, whose gifts had been developed to enrich a developing, stable society, talked and talked and became frenzied in their frustration. They were looking for an enemy, and there was none. The pressures in Jamaica were not simply the pressures of race or those of poverty. They were the accumulated pressures of the slave society, the colonial society, the under-developed, over-populated agricultural country; and they were beyond the control of any one leader. (*MP*, 224)

Naipaul concluded that because of slavery there was no upper society to guide the taste of the island's inhabitants, to give them cultural taste or social standards. Everything was second-rate, minds remained "rigidly closed," and Trinidadians became mimic men, "remaking themselves in the image of the Hollywood B-man" (*MP*, 61). Because of his social history, the Negro was condemned to "permanent inferiority": "Colonialism distorts the identity of the subject people, and the Negro in particular is bewildered and irritable. Racial equality and assimilation are attractive but only underline the loss, since to accept assimilation is in a way to accept a permanent inferiority" (*MP*, 165). This distortion of identity, which presumably is equated with "permanent inferiority," has caused the Negro to have a "deep contempt . . . for all that is not white; his values are the values of white imperialism at its most bigoted" (*MP*, 165).

In his doctoral thesis, "The Uncommitted Artist," A. C. Derrick documents approximately twenty references to the derogatory manner in which Naipaul describes the Negro in *The Middle Passage* and argues:

Every single allusion suggests that Negroes appear to V. S. Naipaul as grotesque, exotic and alien. Brilliantly effective though these skin portraits may be, they usually, in time, settle into the type—high bottoms and all. What perhaps may be more important, however, is that interest seldom goes beyond physical exterior. . . . It seems to me that Naipaul is unable or unwilling to explore the Negro consciousness in any depth. The Negro in Naipaul becomes a symbol, a seemingly apt peg on which to hang the denuded and misshapen reality of the West Indian experience.[6]

Naipaul, it seems, could not describe the Negro in other than physical terms because he could not grant that African peoples in the Caribbean had a spiritual or mythological tradition. Accepting the notions of the English racists, he could not move beyond the colonizer's confined vision of the society. Thus, even though he had been around Negroes in his youth, he promulgated the tradition begun by early English writers of denigrating African peoples in the Caribbean.

After discussing the Negro, Naipaul turned his attention to the East Indians, whom he knew more intimately and who would become the subject of his most insightful fiction. Although he saw this group as possessing a greater sense of cultural autonomy, he also saw them as disintegrating:

Islam is a static religion. Hinduism is not organized; it has no fixed articles, no hierarchy; it is constantly renewing itself and depends on the regular emergence of teachers and holy men. In Trinidad it could only wither; but its restrictions were tenacious. Marriage between unequal castes has only just ceased to cause trouble; marriage between Hindu and Muslim can still split a family; marriage outside the race is unthinkable. Only the urban Indian, the Indian of the middle class, and the Christian convert were able to move easily out of the Indian framework. The Indian Christian was more liberal and adaptable in every way; but, following far behind the Negro on the weary road to whiteness, he was more insecure. . . .

A peasant-minded, money-minded community, spiritually static because cut off from its roots, its religion reduced to rites without philosophy, set in a materialist colonial society: a combination of historical accidents and national temperament has turned the Trinidad Indian into the complete colonial, even more philistine than the white. (*MP*, 82)

Naipaul argues that the West Indian "needs writers to tell him who he is and where he stands" (*MP*, 68). Most West Indian writers, he claims, have failed because they have pandered to "the prejudices of their race or colour groups" (*MP*, 68). Naipaul wanted no such group flattery. The writer, he said, must commit himself to removing the veil of self-delusion that exists in the West Indies. As a writer, Naipaul attempted to explore and to expose the strengths and weaknesses of his people with as much savage and unblinded fury as possible.

But herein lies a paradox. If, indeed, the spiritual and emotional aspects of West Indian reality constitute important areas of concern for a West Indian writer, why then does Naipaul place so much emphasis on the physical achievements and the material artifacts of his culture while over-looking the spiritual qualities that have enabled this "immigrant colonial society" to withstand the trauma and torments of the middle passage, the physical degradation of slavery and indenture, and the attempt to fashion a new society in the midst of poverty and want?

Surely the West Indians' spirit must be counterposed with the ravenous appetites of men who, because of the times in which they live, are concerned only with building empires, regardless of the human or psychological cost. If achievements and physical creations are the criteria by which dominant, oppressive, and imperialist societies measure and are measured, should not the "oppressed colonial society" measure and be measured by different standards of achievement and creation?

Because Naipaul admires the values of the dominant colonialist-capitalist society and has a corresponding disdain for the values of the society in which he grew up, he cannot successfully promulgate any of the enduring values of the oppressed culture. He has an almost unnatural love for and justification of the culture of the other. Yet at this early period in his work, his emotional response to Hinduism, which played an important part in his youth, is stronger than the culture of the other.

A second and parallel point arises. Naipaul's vaunted attempt to tell the West Indian who he or she is or where he or she stands is not as unproblematic as he would have us believe, for he has not yet formulated an unambiguous response and relationship to his society and himself. His "truthtelling," as *The Middle Passage* reveals, is as ambivalent as it is complex. *An Area of Darkness* allows for a further elaboration of this contradictory response.

AN AREA OF DARKNESS

Naipaul's inability to apprehend his social being in purely Western and external (that is, historical) terms led him to shift dramatically toward an Eastern and internal (that is, psychological) orientation. Visiting the Indian village his grandfather had left sixty-two years before as an indentured laborer, Naipaul concluded that his ancestor's home was "an area of darkness." A tender and lyrical book, *An Area of Darkness* is an honest account of Naipaul's anguished search into his past for his roots and his self. The painfully self-revealing and self-critical text marks a crucial turning point in his life and art.

Written three years after *The Middle Passage, An Area of Darkness* complements the former text in two important ways. First, *The Middle Passage* examines only the external dimensions of West Indian reality. In contrast, *An Area of Darkness* is an intimate and delicate probing into Naipaul's self and the psyche of his people in an effort to understand how the legacy of the past fashioned his feelings of alienation. Second, whereas *The Middle Passage* draws heavily on English imperialist writers to explain the West Indian world, *An Area of Darkness* draws upon the *Bhagavad Gita* and other Indian religious texts to explain the Eastern world and thereby reveals Naipaul's ambivalent relationship to both Trinidad and India and his people.

Whereas *The Middle Passage* represents Naipaul's attempt to understand the African world of Trinidad and the West Indies, *An Area of Darkness* is his attempt to understand the East Indian dimension of his world. Such a search was an effort to gain perspective on his self and his relationship to the colonial world of Trinidad. He begins his journey to India by announcing his relationship to the place:

India had in a special way been the background of my childhood. It was the country from which my grandfather came, a country never physically described and therefore never real, a country out in the void beyond the dot of Trinidad; and from it our journey had been final. It was a country suspended in time; it could not be related to the country, discovered later, which was the subject of the many correct books issued by Mr. Gollancz and Messrs. Allen and Unwin and was the source of agency despatches in the *Trinidad Guardian*. It remained a special, isolated area of ground which had produced my grandfather and others I knew who had been born in India and had come to Trinidad as indentured labourers, though that past too had fallen into the void into which India had fallen, for they carried no mark of indenture, no mark even of having been labourers.[7]

Naipaul's elders, the first generation of Indians to come to Trinidad, shared his ambivalent relationship to the island. His mother's friends, for example, did not so much ignore Trinidad as deny it, and they "made no effort to learn English, which their children spoke" (*AD*, 30). Because they attempted to deny the country in which they lived so as to cling to a world they brought with them, they became remote from their children, who were forced to forge a new world on the island. Unable to converse with their elders, the children began to see them as "rustic oddities," exiled forever from the land of their birth.

For Naipaul, Trinidad was a narrow-minded world characterized by outmoded caste relations and irrelevant Indian deities. His trip to India confirmed these sentiments, reinforcing his view of the East Indian world of Trinidad as a distorted and imperfect image of an old and distant past covered in darkness. Thus it would remain, no matter how much the East Indians tried to replicate their home life in Trinidad. As he acknowledged:

To me as a child the India that had produced so many of the persons and things around me was featureless, and I thought of the time when the transference was made as a period of darkness, darkness which also extended to the land, as darkness surrounds a hut at evening, though for a little way around the hut there is still light. The light was the area of my experience, in time and place. And even now, though time has widened, though space has contracted and I have traveled lucidly over that area which was to me the area of darkness, something of darkness remains, in those attitudes, those ways of thinking and seeing, which are no longer mine. (*AD*, 32)

This confession, uttered with tenderness and passion, makes Naipaul seem almost vulnerable. Unlike his grandfather, who "went back to India . . . to return with more things of India" (*AD*, 32), or his character Gold Teeth, who tried to deny Trinidad and sought "to recreate an Eastern Pradesh village in central Trinidad," Naipaul and his generation could not afford to deny Trinidad. They had to accept that the society was multiracial, even though they remained a separate cultural entity and, in Naipaul's case, unaware of its racial differences.

As Naipaul continues to examine his condition in the alien world of Trinidad, he speaks of a sense of violation he and his people encountered beyond the protected world of the immediate family. In trying to come to grips with his Hinduism, Naipaul argues that he was born an unbeliever even though he may have received "a certain supporting [Hindu] philosophy" (*AD*, 34). Yet of one thing he is certain: by the time he was fourteen or so, the world was disintegrating:

The family life I have been describing began to dissolve when I was six or seven; when I was fourteen it had ceased to exist. Between my brother, twelve years younger than myself, and me there is more than a generation of difference. He can have no memory of that private world which survived with such apparent solidity up to only twenty-five years ago, a world which had lengthened out, its energy of inertia steadily weakening, from the featureless area of darkness which was India. (*AD*, 37–38)

Despite Naipaul's aversions and disavowals, the process of cognition and the formation of conceptual thought that he went through are a direct function of the social, historical, and cultural development of a people and are transformed at various stages of the social development. In his path-breaking studies of central Asia, Aleksandr Luria has demonstrated that some mental processes cannot develop if the appropriate forms of social life do not exist. As he observed, the most important aspect of conceptualization takes place at the formative stages of a child's life, as his social history establishes a system of language and abstract codes that enable him to make the leap from the sensory to the logical (that is, from the graphic-functional to the conceptual and theoretical) and that indeed one's consciousness is the product of one's social history. One cannot prevent or not-will that process. It occurs independent of the will of the subject.[8] It is no wonder then that in India Naipaul discovered much about the nature of his consciousness. He explains:

And in India I was to see that so many of the things which the newer and now perhaps truer side of my nature kicked against—the smugness, as it seemed to me, the imperviousness to criticism, the refusal to *see*, the double-talk and double-think— had an answer in that side of myself which I had thought buried and which India revived as a faint memory. I understood better than I admitted. And to me it is an additional marvel that an upbringing of the kind I have described, cut short and rendered invalid so soon, should have left so deep an impression. Indians are an old people, and it might be that they continue to belong to the old world. That Indian reverence for the established and ancient, however awkward, however indefensible, however little understood: it is part of the serious buffoonery of Ancient Rome, an aspect of the Roman *pietàs*. I had rejected tradition; yet how can I explain my feeling of outrage when I heard that in Bombay they used candles and electric bulbs for the Diwali festival, and not the rustic clay lamps, of immemorial design, which in Trinidad we still used? I had been born an unbeliever. Yet the thought of the decay of the old customs and reverences saddened me when the boy whispered "real brahmin," and when, many years later, in London, I heard that Ramon was dead. (*AD*, 38)

In India Naipaul's world of imagination gave way to the sensuous reality of people and landscape, and the conflict between the two left a painful impression. But more than just landscape separated Naipaul from India. He had lost his ability to speak the language, and as an unbeliever he was shut off from the Hindu religion. More important, he did not feel linked to the people of India in any way.

   Yet India also reminded Naipaul that he was an outsider in England even though he had tried hard to assimilate himself and had espoused many English attitudes in *The Middle Passage*. India painfully revealed to Naipaul his own emptiness and loneliness:

I was lost. London was not the centre of my world. I had been misled; but there was nowhere else to go. . . . Here I became no more than an inhabitant of a big city, robbed of loyalties, time passing, taking me away from what I was, thrown more and more into myself, fighting to keep my balance and to keep alive the thought of the clear world beyond the brick and asphalt and the chaos of railway lines. All mythical lands faded, and in the big city I was confined to a smaller world than I had ever known. I became my flat, my desk, my name. (*AD*, 45)

He quickly realized that London had robbed him of his identity. His confrontation with India made him reflect on his being and, in spite of the negative emotions it evoked, he felt "some little feeling for India as the mythical land of [his] childhood was awakened" (*AD*, 45). In India he felt a new sense of awareness and came to realize the extent to which his identity had been circumscribed in Trinidad and England.

   Nothing had prepared Naipaul for what he would see in India. The filth of the cities and the rigidity of the caste system struck him as major evils. Try as he might, Naipaul was unable to identify with a society that eluded him at every point. Nor could he relate to the landscape, which was very different from Trinidad's. And even though he could recognize aspects of behavior in Kashmir that reminded him of Trinidad, the distance between the two cultures made him sad and he realized that "three generations and a lost language lay between us" (*AD*, 150).

   The Himalayas, however, brought him great joy, for the mountains were "a part of the India of [his childhood] fantasy" (*AD*, 176). He could also compare India's absorption by England with the colonial status of his native Trinidad and this helped him understand his alienation in Trinidad:

For in the India of my childhood, the land which in my imagination was an extension, separate from the alienness by which we ourselves were surrounded, of my grandmother's house, there was no alien presence. How could such a thing be conceived? Our own world, though clearly fading, was still separate; and an involvement with the English, of whom on the island we knew little, would have seemed a more unlikely violation than an involvement with the Chinese or the Africans, of whom we knew more. Into this alienness we daily ventured, and at length we were absorbed into it. But we knew there had been change, gain, loss. We knew that something which was once whole had been washed away. What was whole was the idea of India. (*AD*, 197–98)

Thus India's colonization by England was a double humiliation for him: first because he was born in Trinidad and thus had been an alien in that land, and second, because English colonialism had desecrated his ancestors' home. English violation of the purity and sanctity of Indian culture seemed "more creative and more vulgar" (*AD*, 200) than that of the displaced Indians in Trinidad.

Because of his perception of a double humiliation, Naipaul's judgments of India and Trinidad are increasingly similar from this point in the narrative. In India, he saw "a nation at play, acting out of a fantasy" (*AD*, 210). He saw a people who were able neither to look at their country directly nor to preserve their own history. Thus whereas Trinidad did not have a history because it lacked the material artifacts of culture, India, which had those material artifacts, had to be told that she possessed a history before it could become a reality. Thus, "In India these endless mosques and rhetorical mausolea, these great palaces speak only of a personal plunder and a country with an infinite capacity for being plundered" (*AD*, 217).

Paradoxically, the rapacious behavior of the heroic and the brave made colonized countries virtuous; in the West Indies and Trinidad, the colonizer could endow the colonized with meaning, virtue, or value. Thus "it was Europe that revealed India's past to India and made its veneration part of India's nationalism. It is still through European eyes that India looks at her ruins and her art" (*AD*, 217). According to Naipaul, Trinidad, like India, mimics the West, and a resultant futility pervades both countries. Ironically, even though Naipaul relied on familial ties with India to help him in his search to find himself, India inspired in him the same emotions as did Trinidad, and like *The Middle Passage, An Area of Darkness* is a biased account.

After a year of trudging through India, Naipaul went to the village of Dubes, where his grandfather was born, to make his peace, as it were, with his past. But this intensely emotional experience yielded only a sense of denial, withdrawal, and shame: "I had not learned acceptance. I had learned my separateness from India, and was content to be a colonial, without a past, without ancestors" (AD, 266). To him, India would always be "an area of darkness . . . a land of myth . . . [which] seemed to exist in just the timelessness which I had imagined as a child, into which, for all that I walked on Indian earth, I knew I could not penetrate" (AD, 266).

Naipaul's response to India is similar to his response to Trinidad. C. D. Narasimhaiah, professor of English at the University of Mysore, India, and editor of Literary Criterion, a prestigious Indian periodical, offered an evaluation of An Area of Darkness. Although he accepts that Naipaul "is largely correct in his observation of life on the surface," he finds that Naipaul "has not shown any conspicuous ability to penetrate the deeper layers of the Indian mind." Accusing Naipaul of using many "half-truths," "unrepresentative" examples of Indian society, and a certain unscrupulousness ("he will not hesitate to say certain things for effect"), he sees An Area of Darkness as the response of a man who is "fight[ing] for self-preservation . . . by looking down upon Indians if necessary. Which means to understand India is to understand Mr. Naipaul."[9] Narasimhaiah comments further on Naipaul's journey: "It starts in Greece—'even in Greece I had felt Europe falling away'—increases as he travels through the Middle East, and reaches its breaking point in India. The farther from Europe, the more hellish it is—so thorough has been the European loot and impoverishment of Asia and Africa throughout history."[10]

The editors of the Times Literary Supplement, however, saw Naipaul's work and criticism of India as a manifestation of the best impulse of England's imperialist experiment. Writing on September 24, 1964, they argued:

It is interesting that the dominant kind of preoccupation that both our literature and our criticism have had in recent years does seem, on Mr Naipaul's showing, to have a real relevance to the growth of a healthy new consciousness in countries like India. This is the faith in which so many teachers have worked abroad and they will be glad to see the small meed of confirmation which An Area of Darkness brings.

Speaking about the need of thinkers in the Third World to "apply the critical western consciousness to the problems of their country," the editorial concludes by arguing:

This is exactly the spirit [the sense of purpose as opposed to dilatoriness] that Mr Naipaul looks for, largely in vain in Indian literature today. Indonesian foreign policies at present may not show the same sense of realism. But everywhere in the East it is the attitude of men like Pramudya [a proponent of purposefulness] which will do most to put the new nations on the right road.[11]

Inescapably, Naipaul's analysis is influenced by the politics of the colonial world, in which the responses of the colonizer and the colonized are invariably at opposite poles. Naipaul attempts to chart his way out of the ambivalence of these extreme feelings and responses. *An Area of Darkness,* called "a personal testament" by one reviewer, speaks to that anguished quest for roots and for solidity in an alien universe.

Yet, as a reviewer of the *Times Literary Supplement* argued, at the end of *An Area of Darkness,* "repulsion and alienation triumph; he cannot even eat the food that is offered to him [by his distant relatives of India]."[12] Naipaul is yet to reconcile the warring parts of his social consciousness.

A PARADOX CONFRONTED: *MR. STONE AND THE KNIGHTS COMPANION*

The inability to reach a reconciliation with one's past becomes the subject of Naipaul's next novel, *Mr. Stone and the Knights Companion.* Bounded by a traditional Hindu world view, represented by India, and a rational Western world view, Naipaul found it difficult to understand the creative impulses in Trinidad and India. All that he saw in both societies was persistent negation.

In *Mr. Stone and the Knights Companion,* written in Srinagar, Kashmir, in the "Doll's House on the Dal Lake," Naipaul attempted to come to grips with the problems of stasis, negation, and divided loyalties confronting him. Naipaul confessed in *An Area of Darkness* that India "was a journey that ought not to have been made; it broke my life in two" (*AD,* 280). His Indian experience had truly fractured his perception of the world and left him a prisoner of his warring dichotomous impulses: one that kept him a prisoner of the past, subjected to the Indian perception of the world; the other that willed him to break out of that past and merge with the contemporary Western world to which he longed so intensely to belong.

This vision and sensibility led to the writing of *Mr. Stone and the Knights Companion.* The book thus can be regarded as a creative metaphor for the ambiguity, ambivalence, and internal confrontation Naipaul felt at that moment of his development. As he noted, it was his "most autobiographical book," up to that point of his career and, as Peggy Nightingale has observed, in *Mr. Stone and the Knights Companion* Naipaul "appears to create the fictional character, Mr. Stone, in an attempt to resolve his own difficulties and perspective."[13] Larry Husten has argued that there is some indication that there are autobiographical details in *Mr. Stone and the Knights Companion* and that it reveals what he calls a "hermetic perspective" on Naipaul's fiction. Like *A House for Mr. Biswas,* it suggests the inevitable breakup of a homogeneous society. As John Thieme has noted: "Mr. Stone is as much a displaced person in his native English environment as any of Naipaul's earlier colonial protagonists were in theirs."[14] Like Naipaul, Mr. Stone is bereft of a conception of his self and faces the prospect of his ordered life coming to an end. Both Naipaul and Mr. Stone must do something creative to regenerate their lives. Naipaul writes; Mr. Stone creates the Knights Companion.

The parallels between Naipaul and Mr. Stone do not end here. When we meet him, Mr. Stone is sixty-two years old, the number of years that had passed since Naipaul's grandparents left India. Mr. Stone is a man for whom "life had gone by in an orderly fashion," and everything around him speaks of "solidity, continuity and flow."[15] He detests "frenzied home building" and takes pleasure instead "in the slow decay of his own house, the time-created shabbiness of its interiors, the hard polish of old grime on the lower areas of the hall wallpaper, feeling it right that objects like houses should age with their owners and carry marks of their habitation" (*MSKC,* 18).

Now, at the age of sixty-two, Mr. Stone is beginning to feel uneasy about his morning rituals. "As it happened, [everything] seemed to belong to the past. It was not an event which was attaching itself to his hoard of experience, but something to which he was saying good-bye" (*MSKC,* 19). Like Naipaul's past, Mr. Stone's life is beginning to unravel and lose its meaning. Only through his new relationship with Mrs. Springer and then his attachment to the Knights Companion could his life gain new meaning. Mr. Stone begins his relationship with Mrs. Springer at "a private hotel in one of the crescents off the Earl's Court Road [where] a small typewritten 'Europeans Only' card below the bell proclaimed it a refuge of respectability and calm" (*MSKC,* 26). Because Naipaul was writing in the cool of the Indian mountains, he became more nauseated by the raw, open sewage that he had seen in some Indian cities and the injustices of India's caste system. These things made him more despairingly aware that London was not the center of his world. One can see how the exclusiveness of European civilization could have both attracted and repelled him.

His marriage to Mrs. Springer (somewhat analogous to Naipaul's new relationship with India) allays Mr. Stone's fears of the future for a while, but soon his feeling of uneasiness returns. With it comes "a realization, too upsetting to be more than momentarily examined, that all that was solid and immutable and enduring about the world, all to which man linked him-self . . . flattered only to deceive. For all that was not flesh was irrelevant to man, and all that was important was man's own flesh, his weakness and corruptibility" (*MSKC*, 42). Naipaul has begun to retreat somewhat from his position of *The Middle Passage* that only material artifacts are important in a culture. He is beginning to accept the notion that man's spiritual capacities also play a substantive role in his social development.

Mr. Stone's Knights Companion are depicted as "pensioners of his fantasy [with] long white beards, thick, knotted sticks and Chelsea Hospital uniforms . . . tramping about the country lanes, advancing shakily through gardens in full bloom, and knocking on the doors of thatched cottages (*MSKC*, 64). Likewise, in *An Area of Darkness,* Naipaul describes "fabu-lous personages [in the medieval town of Srinagar] of whom little was known except that they were very handsome or very grave or very wise, with wives who were very beautiful" (*AD*, 132). And in the Kashmir mountains "there were cave-dwellers, thinly bearded and moustached, handsome, sharp-featured men, descendants, I felt, of Central Asian horse-men; in the summer they came down with their mules among the Kashmiris, who despised them" (*AD*, 137). Thus the legend of the central Asian horsemen becomes a primary motif in *Mr. Stone and the Knights Compan-ion.* Through these mysteriously exciting personages, Mr. Stone (and Nai-paul) recapture the spark of wonder and excitement and the possibilities of a new beginning. The sense of release these legends generate can therefore be seen as symbolic of Naipaul's attempt to signify the possibility of generating a more meaningful response to life.

It is no wonder that in undertaking the Knights Companion as a project Mr. Stone changes his relationship with those around him and feels a new sense of belonging. The success of his plan brings him glory and happiness. Yet, in spite of his success, he recognizes that his achievements have only postponed his demise, and gradually he begins to feel "emptiness and the darkness to come" (*MSKC*, 106). In the end, he returns to the quiet of his home. "In the empty house he [is] alone" (*MSKC*, 126), as he was at the beginning of the novel and as Naipaul was at the end of *An Area of Darkness.*

In an effort to avoid his pain, Mr. Stone retreats into the act of writing, which offers him some solace. He is forced to admit:

Nothing that was pure ought to be exposed. And now he saw in that project of the Knights Companion which had contributed so much to his restlessness, the only pure moments, the only true moments were those he had spent in the study, writing out of a feeling whose depth he realized only as he wrote. What he had written was a faint and artificial rendering of that emotion, and the scheme as the Unit had practised it was but a shadow of that shadow. All passion had disappeared. It had taken incidents like the Prisoner of Muswell Hill to remind him, concerned only with administration and success, of the emotion that had gone before. All that he had done, and even the anguish he was feeling now, was a betrayal of that good emotion. All action, all creation was a betrayal of feeling and truth. And in the process of this betrayal his world had come tumbling about him. There remained to him nothing to which he could anchor himself. (*MSKC*, 118–19)

The act of writing offers Mr. Stone a sense of relief from the intense feelings of void and alienation. These sentiments closely approximate those Naipaul expresses in the last paragraph of *An Area of Darkness:*

The world is an illusion, the Hindus say. We talk of despair, but true despair lies too deep for formulation. It was only now, as my experience of India defined itself more properly against my own homelessness that I saw how close in the past year I had been to the total Indian negation, how much it had become the basis of thought and feeling. And already, with this awareness, in a world where illusion could only be a concept and not something felt in the bones, it was slipping away from me. I felt it was something true which I could never adequately express and never seize again. (*AD*, 280–81)

The "faint and artificial rendering of that emotion," which was barely reflected in the practice of the Knights Companion, is contrasted with that "true despair [which] lies too deep for formulation" and which, in its mere awareness, dissipates into the void. Both these descriptions of the intangible nature of these emotional-spiritual qualities reflect an Eastern sensibility, which renders all things as illusions.

Naipaul's attempt to articulate what was purely an Eastern sentiment in a novel set in England demonstrates his dilemma with great clarity. His Eastern perception presumes the interconnectedness of all phenomena and the predominance of intuitive knowledge, whereas the Western conception of the world presumes a duality of all reality and the predominance of rational knowledge. In *An Area of Darkness*, Naipaul drew upon Albert Camus and argued that the novel is of the West and is concerned with the condition of men and women. As was typical, he belittled non-Western literature, arguing that the East possesses a mythical and fairy-tale literature that could be construed as a literature of consent. In articulating this distinction, however, Naipaul reflects the duality of his heritage and the difficulties that he encounters in trying to untangle them. In *The Tao of Physics* Fritjof Capra describes the manner in which the Eastern mode of perception and expression function:

First of all, [Eastern] mystics are mainly interested in the experience of reality and not in the description of it. They are therefore generally not interested in the analysis of such a description, and the concept of a well-defined approximation has thus never arisen in Eastern thought. If, on the other hand, Eastern mystics want to communicate their experience, they are confronted with the limitations of language. Several different ways have been developed in the East to deal with this problem.

Indian mysticism—and Hinduism, in particular—clothes its statements in the form of myths, using metaphors and symbols, poetic images, similes, and allegories. Mythical language is much less restricted by logic and common sense. It is full of magic and of paradoxical situations, rich in suggestive images and never precise, and can thus convey the way in which mystics experience reality much better than factual language. . . .

The rich Indian imagination has created a vast number of gods and goddesses whose incarnations and exploits are the subjects of fantastic tales, collected in epics of huge dimensions. The Hindu with deep insight knows that all these gods are creations of the mind, mythical images representing the many faces of reality. On the other hand, he also knows that they are not merely created to make the stories more attractive, but are essential vehicles to convey the doctrines of a philosophy rooted in mythical experience.[16]

Naipaul bemoaned the fact that the Indians lacked any "descriptive" gifts (*AD*, 87) and lauded Gandhi for his direct vision, which he argued was not so much Indian as "a colonial blend of East and West, Hindu and Christian" (*AD*, 87). It is this blend of East and West, reflected in his ontological dilemma and the stylistic renderings of his experiences, that Naipaul seems to be working through at this point of his career. In this work, however, the necessity of choosing between the two worlds does present itself as a likely option. Elaine Campbell suggests that *Mr. Stone and the Knights Companion* "is the no-man's land of the soul where Naipaul contests action against withdrawal. The contest is close, but the victory appears to be in favor of withdrawal." She argues further that "Mr. Stone was seventeen when he lost his mother; he continues living his entire life mourning his maternal loss. Stone associates the 'stretch of the way home' which he can only recapture in memory with life before losing his mother. Naipaul was eighteen when he left Trinidad, but he claims never to have entertained any grief over his homeland."[17] In discussing the manner in which Naipaul depicts mothers in his fiction, Sanna Dhahir notes that "many of Naipaul's protagonists never completely outgrow the need for the mother figure" and goes on to argue that "Mr. Stone's need for a mother is analogous to his obsessive desire for regeneration. His creative act in the course of the narrative (the idea of the Knights Companion) is deeply rooted in his subconscious yearning for rebirth and continuity."[18]

Up to this point, the entirety of Naipaul's work seems to be an attempt to "cancel" his life before he left Trinidad and to insert himself into the warmth and security of the motherland. In *The Enigma of Arrival* (1987) he would attempt to make permanent that cancellation, but at this juncture of his career his experiences remain inchoate, anxious, and unformed. All of his subsequent writings would be an attempt to consolidate his stance of cancellation of and withdrawal from his homeland.

The movement, therefore, which we observe from the prose-tragedy of *A House for Mr. Biswas* to *Mr. Stone and the Knights Companion* can be perceived as an attempt to express a complex colonial heritage in a language and form that is faithful to the direct experience and conditions of his people. The ambivalent nature of Naipaul's work, signified in *An Area of Darkness* and reflected in *Mr. Stone and the Knights Companion*, brings it to a radical epistemological break. The almost metaphysical rendering of the East Indian experience gives way to the political examination of the colonial subject in a postcolonial society. More important, *An Area of Darkness* signals the end of the second phase of Naipaul's career.

5. At the "Rim of the World":
The Postcolonial Society

In the great demoralization of the land he had kept up
his appearance. That's backbone.
—Joseph Conrad, *Heart of Darkness*

In the discourse he pronounces on himself, the subject moves
progressively away from the truth of his essence.
—Anika Lemaire, *Jacques Lacan*

THE POLITICAL TEXT

The year in which the Cuban Revolution triumphed, 1959, marked a milestone in the development of Caribbean peoples, for the event awakened in them a social consciousness and resulted in a shift in the sensibilities of many writers and artists.[1] East Indians were no less affected than other Caribbean people. Thus, whereas Naipaul characterized the East Indian community in Trinidad as insular during the period from 1920 to 1960, he stressed in his writings from 1960 to 1980 the complete breakdown of that community and its assimilation into the larger society. Radical periodicals of this period reflect an increasing concern with local subject matter. Periodicals in Trinidad and Tobago such as *Tapia* (currently the *Trinidad and Tobago Review*) became valuable outlets for the creative energies of West Indian writers, and articles on calypso, folklore, Indian and East Indian culture, and related matters appeared regularly.

Yet, while all these creative activities were taking place at home, most of the important West Indian writers, including Naipaul, were maturing abroad, separated from the creative source of their people and unaffected by the national awareness and nation building that was taking place. As Edward Brathwaite has observed, their generation had fled the "limiting influences" of their society, and their sojourn abroad had increasingly cut them off from "the metaphorical and stylistic explosions" occurring on the island. Thus, while writers such as the Jamaican Roger Mais were "interpret[ing] the other world to which the majority belong for the rest of us to see and to understand,"[2] Naipaul was safely ensconced at Oxford University marching to a different drummer. Surrounded by ivied leisure and bourgeois comforts, Naipaul assumed most of the learned responses that his British education had taught him. The longer he stayed in London, the more he became alienated from the sources that had nourished his earlier work. The farther removed he became from his native culture, the more he assumed the values of the Western imperialist world and its rationalist method of apprehending social reality. More important, the conflict that marked the first period of his work gave way to a neurotic indulgence and lack of identification with the national struggles of Third World peoples.

Naipaul's return to Trinidad in 1960 was important in his development as a writer. Interviewed by Marchi Myer on the BBC program "World of Books" on October 28, 1961, Naipaul observed that when he returned, "the people of various races [were] getting together, particularly at higher levels [and] . . . a new middle class [was] emerging." At the end of this interview, Naipaul made the following observation:

I'd really like to write about this new middle class . . . because . . . it is a middle class with such a strange background, in that it is so racially mixed and its influences are so diverse, and then all living together in this former colonial society. Another aspect of that society which I'd like to do—do more seriously than I've done so far—is the political side. Because in a place like Trinidad—immigrant society, various peoples—there hasn't been, and this couldn't really be, any national struggle as there was in India, or even in certain parts of Africa. And the new politician who emerges from this is very interesting, and to me is very often a tragic figure.

Naipaul realized that because Trinidad was not undergoing a physical struggle for independence a unique political culture had emerged. It was this new subject on which Naipaul increasingly focused his attention. Political questions became uppermost in his literary examination, informed by the values of the Western world.

Naipaul's emphasis cannot be attributed solely to the political activities taking place in Trinidad. It also represented his attempt to answer the nagging question of what it means to be a colonial subject. Earlier in his career, Naipaul had confronted this question from a metaphysical and historical perspective. Now the emphasis had shifted to the political.

Naipaul's examination of postcolonial societies began with the long story "A Flag on the Island" (1965), although "A Christmas Story" (1962) anticipated this political interest. Unlike his work on the colonial epoch, which was concerned primarily with the relationship between the colonial subject and his society, the fiction of the postcolonial period focused more centrally on the manner in which the postcolonial subject responded to his new political environment. As a result, Naipaul paid more attention to the psyche of the postcolonial subject.

"A CHRISTMAS STORY"

"A Christmas Story," one of Naipaul's strongest short stories, contrasts the progressive tendencies of Christianity ("the grace and dignity" of its ceremonies, "the peace and culture" of its marriage ceremony) with the backwardness of Hinduism, which, as the narrator contends, is a "religion that deadens its devotees" and is "little fitted for the modern world."[3] The story is to an extent a continuation of A House for Mr. Biswas, in which these two world views struggle for dominance.

In "A Christmas Story," the narrator (who has changed his Hindu name, Choonilal, to Randolph) tells of the pain and humiliation he suffers after he converts to Presbyterianism. Although his adoption of Christianity can be perceived as an arbitrary acquisition of a superior religion and culture, it also represents a strategic adaptation to the postcolonial world, a necessary means of surviving under capitalism. Thus, whereas the breakup of Hanuman House in A House for Mr. Biswas signaled the breakdown of the feudal world of Hinduism, Randolph's upward social mobility demonstrates the capacity of Trinidad's emerging capitalist society to draw the East Indian out of his social isolation and place him squarely within the ambit of the new social order.

Just as important, "A Christmas Story" suggests that Hinduism is not an appropriate ideology for the new world. As in Naipaul's other fiction during the postcolonial period, the major characters are the younger members of the Hindu community who have freed themselves from the bonds of their religion and culture. Whereas the fiction of the first period centered upon characters who were embedded firmly within their culture and looked toward India almost nostalgically (Chittiranjan of The Suffrage of Elvira, Gold Teeth of "My Aunt Gold Teeth"), here we find the children of the first generation of freed Indians (1917–47), whose conception of their world has been shaped by the rupture of the old feudal bonds and the arrival of the capitalist order.

"A Christmas Story," which examines the striving for middle-class respectability, can thus be seen as a logical culmination of a process that began at the end of A House for Mr. Biswas, for Randolph's conversion to Christianity, though it may be perceived as a betrayal of his people, reflects the changes the East Indian is forced to make if he or she wishes to enjoy any of the liberating possibilities of the new capitalist order.

"A FLAG ON THE ISLAND"

"A Flag on the Island" is the first of Naipaul's fictional texts to be set in postcolonial Trinidad. Although the title of the story symbolizes the divided loyalties of the inhabitants of Trinidad ("a floating suspended place to which you brought your own flag, if you wanted to" [*FOI*, 132]), the text is concerned more with the unreality of life on the island and the lack of identity that arises when one's loyalties are divided. Here, in incipient form, mimicry and identity are first posed as mutually related.

To demonstrate the unreality of postcolonial society (there are "toy drums," "a toy [telephone] directory," the "new funny island money," and the "very little people attending to their very little affairs"), Naipaul describes the changes the colonial subject undergoes. The three major characters of the story—Mr. H. J. Blackwhite, Priest, and Selma, identifiable from *Miguel Street*—during the colonial period led aimless lives. Here, they have been transformed by their new political status, symbolized by the coming of the American soldiers to the island. By the story's end, the Americans have left, and Blackwhite, Priest, and Selma assume new roles as leaders in the postcolonial society.

Blackwhite, Priest, and Selma are incapable of internal transformation and, as a result, are unable to perceive their society as in a new stage of development. They assume new names—H. J. Blackwhite becomes H. J. B. White, and Priest becomes Gary Priestland—and new titles—Mr. Blackwhite gives up his position as principal of the Premier Commercial College of Shorthand and Bookkeeping to become the principal of the University College; Priest ceases being a wayside preacher and worker of *obeah* to become a TV personality; and Selma is no longer a *wabeen* (an inexperienced and casual prostitute) but a lady of the first rank. But although they take on new roles, these characters remain their old inconsequential and hollow selves, unable to see their society except through old eyes.

Mr. Blackwhite seems typical of his class. As his name implies, he is a product of a black and white heritage. His most successful novel, *I Hate You: One Man's Search for Identity,* undoubtedly indicates the nature of his search for an identity among a people he does not believe can have meaningful lives. Mr. Blackwhite is the embodiment of everything English. He writes about the English and in fact pretends he is English. Such paranoia over being a colonial, the narrator suggests, can be sublimated only through the "lunacy" of the island's annual carnival celebration. On Carnival Monday, therefore, Mr. Blackwhite assumes the character of General Douglas MacArthur, and on Carnival Tuesday, William Shakespeare. Carnival, it is suggested, provides the means for a collective exorcism of the paranoia of the colonial experience.[4]

It takes an American visitor, in the person of the narrator, to endow Mr. Blackwhite with a meaningful purpose. He tells him what to write about, and Blackwhite becomes famous. Because he has no firm conception of himself, he operates only in extremes. So great is his desire for (re)cognition that when the celebration of blackness becomes popular, he moves from his uncritical acceptance of whiteness to an equally uncritical acceptance of blackness. This easy assumption of an identity becomes his downfall and reflects his inability to endow himself with a purpose. He is, as it were, the entire creation of the other, a toy, one of the latest fads in the hands of an American foundation.

Inherent in this examination of the postcolonial subject's search for an identity is the major assumption that without the guidance of "real people" (that is, the other), all will revert to gloom and destruction. Aimless living and confused identities will lead inevitably to frenzy and paranoia, which constitute the "real" condition of the people of the island. Priest's proclamations of apocalyptic gloom reflect this condition: "There is a way which seemed right unto man but at the end thereof are the ways of death. Repent! Rejoice! How shall we escape, if we neglect so great a salvation" (FOI, 204). Ultimate destruction is the only means through which the inhabitants of the island can escape the unreality of their lives, and the departure of the birds from the island becomes prophetic of their final abandonment. According to the narrator, it is their "ultimate benediction" (FOI, 212). Spared destruction, the colonial person must participate in the anarchy that is sure to follow. At the end of the story, "each exhausted person had once more to accommodate himself to his fate, to the life that had not been arrested" (FOI, 215).

Because the story is sparsely textured, specific aspects of overdetermination are not explored in any sustained manner, particularly the concepts of mimicry and what I call "psychic crampedness." The former is evident, however, in the island's annual carnival celebrations and the latter in Mr. Blackwhite's acknowledgment of the intellectual limitations of his society. Both of these concerns are developed more fully in The Mimic Men.

THE MIMIC MEN

The concept of identity is examined much more comprehensively in The Mimic Men than in earlier works. Whereas in A House for Mr. Biswas Mr. Biswas is situated within the social formation, the narrator of The Mimic

Men, Ralph Singh, seeks to understand what it means to be a colonial subject in a postcolonial society.[5] Moreover, in *The Mimic Men* we find the most comprehensive social development of the first generation of freed East Indians, who, bereft of the culture that nurtured the earlier generation, float aimlessly in the shifting social relations generated by the changing social order. No relationship is certain, and unlike Mr. Biswas and the earlier generation of East Indians, the characters are fragmented and uncertain of their positions within the society.

Ralph Singh's fragmentation and loss contrast with Mr. Biswas's strivings to establish himself within the colonial society; formal independence, as it were, demands a new positionality of the subject within the society. In this sense, *A House for Mr. Biswas* and *The Mimic Men* examine the same subject at different moments in time and space, at different points in their social evolution. Whereas Mr. Biswas starts out from Parrot Trace in Trinidad and strives continuously to locate himself in his colonial world, Ralph Singh stays in London and from there reflects upon what it means to be a subject in a postcolonial world. Whereas Mr. Biswas is a signification of the social dimension, Ralph Singh is a signification of its political dimension.

Two significant methodological points arise in *The Mimic Men*. First, whereas Ralph Singh writes so as to examine the manner in which his *subjectivity* has been constituted by the colonial experience, Mr. Biswas writes to escape, to lose himself within himself: a self he can neither understand nor express. The act of writing begins as an experiment in *A House for Mr. Biswas*. In *The Mimic Men* it is a much more conscious and skillful act, and although it does not function independently of the subject it seeks to reconstitute, the discourse cannot, as we learn from psychoanalysis, "be reduced to what is being said explicitly; [for] like thought itself and behavior, it bears the weight of the 'other,' the 'other' of which we are all unaware or which we half refuse."[6] Further, the nature of Singh's subjectivity is mediated as he tells his story and seeks to understand his relationship to his world.

Second, the narrator in *The Mimic Men* is decidedly distant from the object upon which he mediates (and meditates). As in "A Flag on the Island," in which the narrator is an American, the narrator here is separate from his society and thereby able to make certain objective judgments about it. Although the process of distancing creates a number of conflicts that separate the narrator from his society, it also enables him to examine, in specific terms, the manner in which his identity has been shaped by his economic class position. More so than Mr. Biswas, Ralph Singh is a specific product of a particular socioeconomic formation called colonialism.[7]

In *The Mimic Men* colonialism is depicted as a self-generating process that consciously creates it own specific subject. The language is strikingly similar to that in "A Flag on the Island," in which the theme is abandonment and loss. Thus Ralph Singh can describe the island of Isabella as "set adrift yet not altogether abandoned, where . . . controlled chaos approximates in the end, to a continuing order. The chaos lies all within."[8] Because Ralph Singh, unlike his predecessors, understands the colonial process, he is able, much more consciously, to construct his identity. Unlike the inhabitants of the colonial world, the characters in *The Mimic Men* can make a choice, even if it is the incorrect one.

Precisely because he has the capacity to choose his identity (and, by extension, the course of his social development), Singh appears to be in control of the choices he makes about his life. Yet, because the author has given a privileged position to the ideological assumptions and behavioral practices of the colonizer, the acts of the colonial subjects and the choices they make at the end of "A Flag on the Island" are depicted as meaningless and suggest the controlled frenzy of colonial subjects. As a consequence, the society Ralph Singh describes is very much like that in "A Flag on the Island." He remembers it as being "horribly, man-made; . . . exhausted, fraudulent, cruel and, above all, not mine" (*MM*, 50). Only fragmentation and loss are possible, and, as Singh discovers after independence, only chaos can follow from such social arrangements.

I had never thought of obedience as a problem. Now it seems to me the miracle of society. Given our situation, anarchy was endless, unless we acted right away. But on power and the consolidation of passing power we wasted our energies, until the bigger truth came: that in a society like ours, fragmented, inorganic, no link between man and the landscape, a society not held together by common interests, there was no true internal source of power, and that no power was real which did not come from the outside. Such was the controlled chaos we had, with such enthusiasm, brought upon ourselves. (*MM*, 206)

When the colonizer abandons the society, chaos and disorder ensue as in "A Flag on the Island." Order can be brought to the society only through outside authority.

As the society develops, every act of the colonial subject becomes a statement of despair with little meaning. Given the ethical and moral bankruptcy of the people, they become incapable of conceiving any "larger" ideas of social reconstruction. They move from one "sensation" to another, and the struggle for formal independence is presented as nothing more than a new "stage of the old war between master and slave." There can be no new permutations of thought and relations. Mass political mobilization is seen as "less a political awakening than a political anxiety" (MM, 190) and colonial peoples as incapable of political action.

Against this background, political independence is perceived as nothing more than the culmination of play-acting on the part of the leaders and the people. Both are depicted as children and the entire political process as a game. The "terrible" realization that they could have effected social transformation gives the people a sense of emptiness. The narrator feels a "terrible" sense of "exhaustion, even distaste: [a] dissatisfaction that nags and nags and at last defines itself as apprehension and unease" (MM, 199). In "A Flag on the Island," such exhaustion leads to abandonment and gloom.

The narrator's distance from his subject enables him to depict the achievement of independence in idealist terms. The "mobs," we are told, cannot be organized for trade union activity or as a nationalist force. The organization of financial, rather than human, capital takes on primary importance during the transition from colonialism to postcolonialism. It never occurs to the narrator that because slavery and colonialism reduce people almost exclusively to their economic functions, the primary goal of independence should be to enable them to realize their social functions. Changes in economic practices may be the major determinant in carrying the society forward, but, for colonial subjects, concern for the cultural and social dimensions of their lives is just as important.

Unable to play a constructive role in rebuilding their society, colonial people were, according to the narrator, "without skills" and "unproductive" and as such "offered nothing and were in the end without power" (MM, 204). Such an evaluation hearkens back to Singh's earlier proposition that colonial people can only feel sensations and mouth slogans, not effect change. The logic of the text and the privileged status of the narrator's vision lead the reader to the same conclusion.

Independence brought only a sense of drama to Isabella, not the possibility that a new social environment could be created in which people would realize their potential. To be sure, independence has its rewards:

[It] sharpens our perception of the world, gives us some sense of our selves, makes us actors, gives point and sometimes glory to each day. It alters a drab landscape. So it frequently happens—what many have discovered—that in conditions of chaos, which would appear hostile to any human development, the human personality is in fact more varied and extended. And this is creation indeed! (*MM*, 214)

Such superficial transformations do not substantially challenge the deep-seated ideological premises and behavior of colonialism. As a result, change is not possible in Isabella or in any other colonial territory. So hopeless is the cause of the inhabitants of Isabella that their once vibrant call for nationalism is reduced to merely "an emotive sound" (*MM*, 220) and the people to a state of mimicry. It is not possible for them to transcend this dependent relationship with the former colonizer and structure an alternative discourse for their liberation. As Ralph Singh concludes: "We, here on our island, handling books printed in this world, and using its goods, had been abandoned and forgotten. We pretended to be real, to be learning, to be preparing ourselves for life, we mimic men of the New World, one unknown corner of it, with all its reminders of the corruption that came so quickly to the new" (*MM*, 146). According to the gospel of Naipaul and Ralph Singh, colonial people are doomed forever to be pale reflectors of the dominant power.

The Mimic Men cannot be viewed only in its political context, however. A psychoanalytic perspective gives strength to Naipaul's observations and helps explain Ralph Singh's struggle.[9] Further, because Ralph Singh's transformation is examined as the society moves from one stage of social development to another, the reader is able to observe both Ralph Singh and the society in their transition from a position of nonidentity to a definable identity. Part of the paradox of the text, therefore, is that the narrator (and thereby the author) is unable to see that the identity for which he searches is closely related to the concept of mimicry, for which he seems to condemn his people. By linking the concept of mimicry with the act of writing, or, more precisely, with the discourse of the subject, Naipaul reveals the unconscious world of Ralph Singh and the pain he suffers as he attempts to move from one stage of development to another. Thus the act of writing, which at first is perceived by the narrator as a "substitute for what it then pleased me to call life" (*MM*, 244), becomes the instrument through which Singh begins "to impose order on [his] own history, [and] to abolish that disturbance [within him]" (*MM*, 243). As he says: "It never occurred to me that the writing of this book might have become an end in itself, that the recording of a life might become an extension of that life" (*MM*, 244). As he writes the book, a process of creation begins to take place: "one order, of which I form part, answering the other, which I create" (*MM*, 245). Eventually, the very act of writing, despite "its initial distortion, clarifies, and even becomes a process of life" (*MM*, 251). In other words, a process designed to organize and give meaning to life becomes life itself and thus the basis upon which to chart Singh's and his society's development. That is creation indeed. In the end, the narrator becomes the subject of his own discourse and the text a political discourse on the postcolonial subject as he moves from the narcissism of the Imaginary into the Symbolic Order.[10] The crisis Singh experiences in his personal life is nothing more than the crisis that the individual subject undergoes as the society moves from a colonial to a postcolonial status.

Ralph Singh's discourse, a manifestation of his unconscious, reveals the obstacles that prevented him from achieving social identification. This process can best be understood in the context of Jacques Lacan's description of what he called the "mirror phase" of human development.[11] Indeed, a careful examination of a few key psychoanalytic moments in the text help in understanding the painful and ambivalent struggle Ralph Singh undergoes as he attempts to realize his social identity. The tremendous libidinal energy that accompanies his attempt to emerge from his early stage of social development, the proliferation of sexual images and language, and the constant relapses into childhood fantasies and dreams at each critical moment when he must make a choice to be free from the "other" (phase of his development) illustrate the intense psychic struggle that takes place as he moves from the undifferentiated stage of the colonial era to the groping moments of self-recognition of postcolonialism. Indeed, the tremendous libidinal energy manifested in this text reveals the need to impose psychic and institutional order and direction upon the postcolonial experience to ensure its orderly evolution. As we will see, such a position is inherent in the savage manner in which Naipaul describes the colonial and the post-colonial condition.[12]

It is important, then, that Singh begins his search for his social identity in London, the bosom of the mother country, where he has gone to further his understanding of who he is. The search is aggressive[13] and takes the form of profanatory, or violating, sexual behavior. He keeps a diary that he says developed into "a type of sexual autoeroticism," as he recorded his most "intense reactions" (*MM*, 25–26). It is from this narcissistic state that he begins his struggle. Such behavior corresponds to the prematurity of the mirror stage of life in which the individual garners satisfaction from itself, a period in which he or she needs no outside object to establish identity. It is from this undifferentiated stage that Ralph Singh begins his quest to achieve his social identity. As he pursues his search for a self through the writing of his biography, he is granted several opportunities to declare his autonomy— that is, to break out of the mirror stage; but each time he relapses into childhood fantasies and dream phases so that he can postpone the pain that accompanies this necessary moment of separation.

In the course of the novel, three significant attempts at separation take place, one at the local, one at the national, and one at the international level, a spiraling outward, as it were. The first such moment occurs at a school sports meet. After preparing for some time, Singh decides on the day of the meet to withdraw. In retrospect, he "recalled, with shame," the dream that had caused him to make this decision:

I had dreamt that I was a baby again and at my mother's breast. What joy! The breast on my cheek and mouth: a consoling weight, the closeness of soft, smooth flesh. It had been at dusk, in a vague setting, no lights, in a back veranda, all around a blue of dark bush. My mother rocked and I had the freedom of her breast. A dream? But no, I was not dreaming. What pain then, what shame, to awaken! (*MM,* 116)

It is significant that he begins his search by way of a dream. Because dreams are the fulfillment of repressed wishes, they serve as a point of departure for an individual to examine his or her psychic life and they become a "privileged path, a royal road back to that mythical moment at which 'difference' is established and the global calibration of signifier to signified almost obscures the continuing effect of the death drive, of 'affect,' as it operates with redoubled fury in the very heart of representations."[14] Clearly, Singh's identification with his mother and his regression to infant-hood can be read as a return to the original compact between the colonizer (the mother) and the colonial subject (the baby) and "the breast on my cheek and mouth" as the consolation offered by the master. Surely, the threat of "the dark bush" from which he is protected can be seen as the "barbarity" from which the colonial subject has been taken and to which he is afraid to return. He must break away from the warmth of the mother, yet he cannot. Assuming an identity, inserting himself into the Symbolic Order, is too painful and so he retreats. The bond between him and his mother is too strong. His failure to make a significant break with his "Ideal I" at school (that is, among his peers) leads him to believe that the obscurity of his location in the world makes him a nonentity—that is, he lacks an identity. Shortly after this incident, he decides to seek his identity in London because he believes he cannot achieve one on the shipwrecked island of Isabella.

The next significant moment when he is offered an opportunity to declare his autonomy occurs when his party is victorious at the polls and independence is achieved. Such independence means, among other things, a formal break with the mother country and a discontinuation of her tutelage. At that moment of supreme achievement, Singh reverts once more to images of childhood to express his hopelessness: "The play was over. Exhilaration went. We could no longer draw strength from one another. It was one of those occasions when each person looks into himself and finds only weakness, sees the boy or child he was and has never ceased to be" (*MM*, 199–200).

The government's attempt to nationalize Lord Stockwell's estate—one of the most significant acts of the new government in that it symbolized the recapturing of an important part of the people's resources—demonstrates once more Singh's failure to break out of his narcissistic relationship with the master. Singh, who had to go to London to negotiate this economic break with Lord Stockwell, a representative of the colonial power, refuses to break with the colonizer and depicts this moment of rupture as "a private loss" that leads to frenzy and pain and that can be contained only by reverting to childhood:

I struggled to keep drama alive, for its replacement was despair: the vision of a boy walking on an endless desolate beach, between vegetation living, rotting, collapsed, and a mindless, living sea. No calm then: that came later, fleetingly. Drama failing, I knew frenzy. Frenzy kept me silent. And silence committed me to pretence. (*MM*, 221)

Certainly the images of "desolate beaches" and "rotting vegetation" signify the aridity of the colonial experience in the absence of the mother.

After the proposal for nationalization fails, Singh is seduced by Lady Stella, the daughter of Lord Stockwell, the master. Here Singh's identification is with the master or the father. By reducing Singh to a small boy and making him identify with the master, the text clearly stresses the alienating function of identification when it is closely linked with a potential rival that seeks its elimination. Freud explained that "identification, in fact, is ambivalent from the very first; it can turn into an expression of tenderness as easily as into a wish for someone's removal. It behaves like a derivative of the first, *oral* phase of the organisation of the libido, in which the object which we long for and prize is assimilated by eating and is in that way annihilated as such."[15] Here is the perfect opportunity for Singh to remove the master (his colonial father) from the island and to begin independence on a new footing, but he is unable to do it. Instead, he is seduced by the daughter of the master—à la Caliban—and thereby opts for a continued subservient relationship with the colonizer, further affirming the master's superior vision and insight. In other words, Lord Stockwell via his daughter makes Singh recognize that he is still a subject of (and subjected to) his discourse and power and the beneficiary of the master's largesse. After all, Lord Stockwell points out that he knew Singh's father when the "very savage" did not even know his name; when, indeed, "he was just wearing a yellow dhoti. His chest was bare. His skin had a shine" (*MM*, 239). How, indeed, could Singh question his master's power, his inherent right over his property?

A few minutes after Singh's conversation with Lord Stockwell (he is invited to Lord Stockwell's home), Lady Stella gives him a copy of *The Oxford Nursery Rhyme Book*, "a link with the past" as he calls it. When he reads it at his hotel, it brings him "that limpid, direct vision of the [colonizer's] world, neither of which had been mine, neither vision, of delight, nor world, of order" (*MM*, 230). Contained in that vision, however, was a warning:

> But when they are clean,
> And fit to be seen.
> She'd dress like a lady.
> And dance on the green.

If the colonial subjects behave themselves properly, they too can receive the master's blessings. In other words, Lady Stella demands that he accede to her people's vision of the past, even under independence, in the same manner as Miranda, acting on her father's behalf, demanded that Caliban accept her father's vision of life. Back in his London hotel, after reading *The Oxford Nursery Rhyme Book,* Singh relapses into a state of childishness and is lulled into a calm provided by the mother country. The colonizer has the power to control even the sexuality of the colonial subject.

Singh's last attempt at identification occurs with a prostitute in Spain, where the separation between self and subject is depicted through a genital fantasy. Here, childlike fantasies give way to a more mature form of representation. "Walking, as in a dream, through the streets of the city," he meets a prostitute whom he describes as "ghastly, tragic, a figure from hell with a smiling girl's face" (*MM*, 236). In his sexual encounter with her, characterized by its lack of human or personal concern, Singh is all but annihilated by the profusion of her flesh. It is appropriate that such an aggressive sexual encounter should occur as Singh attempts to seal (that is, to pin down) the pain that results when the "social I" tries to separate itself from the objectified, narcissistic relationship with the self.

In his description of this encounter Singh equates this final closure with a psychological probing and the almost total effacement of his being:

No damp, flat, smothering embrace came; only the softest of words, the sweetest of breaths, a brushing—of those breasts?—against my nipples, the barest touch of a fingernail circling my areola. I never touched; my hands still lay at my side. Yet I was already turning in on myself; judgment was disappearing. Nails, tongue, breath and lips were the instruments of this disembodied probing. . . . The probing went lower; no effort of concentration was now required, no need to shut out the world, the liquid sighs and sounds. Judgment disappeared, I was all painful sensation. Flesh, flesh: but my awareness of it was being weakened. I was turned over on my belly. The probing continued, with the same instruments. The self dropped away, layer by layer; what remained dwindled to a cell of perception, indifferent to pleasure or pain; neutral perception, finer and finer, having validity, existing only because of that probing which, growing fainter, yet had to be apprehended, because it was the only proof of life: fine perception reacting minutely only to time, which was also the universe. (*MM*, 236–37)

The self, the "Ideal I," drops away during this encounter and the subject or, as Singh puts it, "a cell of perception . . . the only proof of life," emerges. Whereas in the first sequence the identification of the subject is defined as a reflection of an image, here it is defined as differentiation, the cutting away of the flesh, layer by layer. This revelation of the social I is not a pleasurable experience but "a moment of horror," which suggests the pain experienced by the emerging postcolonial subject. This intense revelatory moment is counterposed with the autoeroticism Singh experiences at the beginning of the text. And even though the undifferentiated colonial subject may be resistant to immediate symbolization and representation as it moves from the "ideal I" to the "social I," the reduction of the individual to a "cell of perception" may be perceived as the beginning of the interjection of the postcolonial subject into the social totality where he begins to construct his own identity.

In a way, the text sketches the three moments the colonial subject passes through as he goes from the self to the acquisition of an identification: moments of privation, in which he attempts to dispossess the object; moments of frustration, in which he attempts to reach a full equivalence between himself and the former master but realizes that he is still subjected to the colonizer's power; moments of castration, in which he recognizes that although he has been separated from the master and has become a subject for scrutiny in a new world, that recognition is filled with horror. He cannot return fully and completely to his society. The movement from colonialism to postcolonialism is fraught with psychic pain. It is this dimension of the emerging consciousness Naipaul wanted to examine in *The Mimic Men*.

Undoubtedly, the text is concerned not only with the pain that ensues when the self and the subject (or the self and the world) are separated but with the nature of consciousness that is created when the subject enters a new social realm of language and culture and the uncertainties and ambivalences surrounding this important moment of social and political transformation. Singh's position, necessarily, brings us full circle, back to Ganesh and Mr. Biswas, who, as colonial subjects, entered the world as already given, thrust into the colonial society to make their way. Unlike his predecessors, Singh must make the painful transition at yet another remove from his original home. Out of the complexities of the Isabella experience, he must find a way to explain his world. It is questionable whether living in London allows him to do so in a way that is helpful to the society from which he has departed.

Closely related to the question of the mirror stage and mimicry is the concept of psychological space as it relates to the emergence of the social I. Lacan has argued that "the notion of the role of spatial symmetry in man's narcissistic structure is essential in the establishment of the bases of a psychological analysis of space . . . [and] animal psychology has shown that the individual's relation to a particular spatial field is, in certain species, mapped socially, in a way that raises it to the category of subjective membership."[16] In the texts of his second period, Naipaul persistently raised the question of psychological space as it relates to the colonial's quest for freedom and liberation.[17] In his work the need to conquer *inner* (personal/subjective) and *outer* (external/material) spaces is related directly to his notion of the "placelessness" of the colonial person; hence his constant concern, as echoed in *The Mimic Men,* that "to be born on an island like Isabella, an obscure New World transplantation, secondhand and barbarious, was to be born to disorder" (*MM,* 118). I have called this apparent lack of social, cultural, intellectual, and psychic space engendered by the condition of colonialism (particularly in small territories) "psychic crampedness."[18] At the inner, subjective level, this condition, according to Consuelo López de Villegas, suggests that one's (the colonial's) identity "is determined by one's existential space; that is to say, that as one possesses space, one creates a center, a point of departure from which one can set goals. Hence, freedom presupposes security, for some [*sic*] must be aware of one's identity before one can journey outward."[19] At the outer, material level, psychic crampedness also creates a sense of insecurity and uneasiness which makes the colonial person feel that his or her achievements must always be measured against those of the colonizer and have no merit unless they have the approval of the colonizer. Invariably, the accomplishments of the colonized person are always second-best when measured by those criteria.

Psychic crampedness cannot be attributed solely to the size of the colonies, however, or to the people's biological or social development. Rather, this condition is related directly to European imperialism and colonialism, which, among its other attributes, made the "symmetry of space" an important dimension of its rule.[20] Not merely descriptive of a unique aspect of the colonial condition, the concepts of mimicry and psychic crampedness are characteristic of the entire colonial experience. At one level of analysis, mimicry can be interpreted as a statement of the intensely painful moment of psychoanalytic knowledge of self-awareness, the necessary precondition for the reconstitution of the colonial subject; psychic crampedness is a concomitant condition of recognition and response, as a necessary moment in the social development of the colonial subject in which he or she realizes the limitations imposed by the condition of colonialism.

As a consequence, mimicry and psychic crampedness constitute a simultaneous moment in the social development of the colonial subject, a double inscription that assumes tremendous importance in the transition from colonialism to formal independence, particularly in countries that did not achieve their independence through violent struggle. In this context, Frantz Fanon's notion of the cathartic value of revolutionary violence for the colonial subject in the transition from colonialism to postcolonialism is an important point of comparison in any study of the relation of the colonial subject to mimicry and psychic crampedness.[21] The condition of mimicry that is Naipaul's particular concern in this text does not take place in a historical vacuum, however, but involves a reassembling of one's subjectivity in relation to the former colonizer and in response to one's social space in the new independent society. Consequently, any attempt to interpret and understand the postcolonial subject must be seen in relational rather than absolute terms.

Naipaul's inability to see Isabella's society in relational or, for that matter, its own terms, leads to difficulties in the text. Singh, for example, sees only the behavior of the colonized people as savage and sympathizes entirely with the colonizer. Whereas in Joseph Conrad's *Heart of Darkness*— another text on colonialism and one to which Naipaul is indebted[22]— Marlow is tentative in promulgating his truths, Ralph Singh is never at such a loss and thus becomes an all-knowing, condemnatory presence who demonstrates the absurdity of the behavior of the colonial person. Even though Singh tries to distance himself from the Africans, as if to illustrate that he, a "picturesque Asiatic," has no stake in the outcome of the primitive struggle between the master and the slave and thus can be neutral, his attitude toward the colonized population undercuts such a strategy at each critical moment of the text. Moreover, Naipaul never questions the assumptions of the colonizers or their ideological formulation about the state.

This major constraint prevents Naipaul from giving the reader the comprehensive truth about the postcolonial subject, a difficulty that is made manifest in the discourse of Ralph Singh. Truth does not lie on the surface of Ralph Singh's conscious discourse but must be sought out in its lacunae. As Lacan counseled: "The unconscious, a second structure, cannot be apprehended in its truth by the logical analysis that the patient makes of his being, his Ego or his past. The 'I' of the discourse is radically separated from the Other of the subject, the unconscious. As a mediator, language distances the 'I' which speaks and believes itself to be telling the truth about its essence from the unconscious reality which founds it in its truth."[23] As we have seen, Ralph Singh's conscious discourse reveals only partial truths about the colonial subject and his social reality.

Another difficulty that arises is the manner in which Naipaul mediates the discourse of the subject. Antoine Vergote, in his foreword to Anika Lemaire's *Jacques Lacan,* has argued that "simply setting up human relationships does not liberate. It is the technical speech of the analyst which restores to these relationships their alienated truth."[24] In a text, the author is responsible for structuring the discourse of the subject, which in turn is determined by his relationship to the society. Because Naipaul feels so negative toward his society (he begins to laugh at it), he is unable to structure the discourse of Ralph Singh in a sympathetic manner. Because "the technical speech of the analyst" is not disinterested, Ralph Singh cannot take a liberating attitude toward his society. Not only is it true that *all* subjects do not live in accordance with their fantasies and the dreams that separate them from their truth. Separation is multiplied when the analyst himself has to struggle to find a language through which to express the particularity of his social reality. His profoundly alienated vision of the society makes it difficult for him to structure discourses with which to disclose and fully apprehend the condition of that society.

The further Ralph Singh moves away from an organic relationship with his society, the further he moves away from understanding his self or his society's truth. Moreover, Singh's decision to abandon his society drives him even further from it and thereby prevents him from establishing a liberating relationship with it. His eventual residence in London is the ultimate statement of his alienation and a reflection of his unresolved (and somewhat unhealthy) relationship with the island.

The narrator's unresolved relationship with his society distorts his vision of it. Naipaul has argued that "most imaginative writers discover them-selves, and their world, through their work." Later in the same essay, he argues that "Conrad is too particular and concrete a writer. . . . He sticks too close to the facts; if he had meditated on those stories he might have turned them into case histories." In the end, Naipaul could not tell us about the "other" aspect of himself that Singh "half-refuses" and that he could not possibly have known. By seeing only the immediate "facts" of the colonial experience and removing himself from "these dark or remote places . . . the world's half-made societies that seemed doomed to remain half-made," he could provide no more than surface responses to postcolon-ial reality.[25]

Naipaul's desire to understand the colonial subject and the manner in which she or he functions in the social totality pushes him further toward a historical explanation, but his inability to move fully out of the mirror stage of development and assume a social identity separate and distinct from that of the mother (country) results in his feelings of fragmentation and loss, disorder and helplessness, isolation and unease. Until he can remove him-self from his incestuous relationship with the mother (country), he cannot articulate an autonomous subject or comprehensively understand how that subject functions in the era of independence.

THE LOSS OF EL DORADO

Naipaul's inability to effect a closure in *The Mimic Men* led him to look for a more "informed" rationale to explain the colonial subject and resulted in his use of what can be called colonial discourse.[26] Because Naipaul took a more genuine approach to the colonial subject in the first part of his work, he did not have to resort to stereotypes, binary opposites, or an ideology as he did in the second part. Thus the nature of his examination, particularly after *The Mimic Men,* led him back again to the origins of the colonial enterprise to seek to describe the behavior and nature of the colonized person. But precisely because he ceased to examine the colonial experience within its own terms, he did not examine the conditions that produced the colonial subject in the first place. Therefore, he simplified the colonial experience and relied on the myth that masked colonial power as a gift of freedom, education, and civilization given to a bestial "other." Such an approach, of necessity, hides the ambivalent nature of the colonial experience and falsely represents its reality. The stereotype, which is its major discursive strategy, is presented as "a form of knowledge and identification that vacillates between what is always 'in place,' already known, and something that must be anxiously repeated . . . as if the essential duplicity of the Asiatic or the bestial sexual license of the African that needs no proof, can never really, in discourse, be proved."[27] Paradoxically, as one observer has noted, the very discourse that announces the triumph of civility constantly reproduces the condition that created the stereotype in the first place: the stereotype that declares "the other" to be inferior and barbarous.[28]

Naipaul's search for origins took him to the origins of colonial society. In the account of the fabled city of El Dorado at the end of the sixteenth century and the implantation of slaves into Trinidad at the beginning of the nineteenth century, he uses his theories of mimicry and psychic crampedness in relation to the colonial subject. Because Naipaul needed historical focus, he chose the Trinidadian, of whom he had much knowledge, as the subject of his examination. *The Loss of El Dorado,* then, emerges as Naipaul's attempt to understand the colonial subject in his or her historical specificity.

This quality distinguishes *The Loss of El Dorado* from *The Middle Passage* and *An Area of Darkness.* The latter two texts are simply travelogues in which he records his subjective and, by definition, nonscientific responses to his society. Because in *The Loss of El Dorado* Naipaul is more "objective," his judgment takes on the scientific mode and the authority that are possible in history. History can speak without being condemned by the contemporaneous. Universalizing and thereby "naturalizing" the behavior of the colonizer as "proper" enabled him to point to the behavior of the colonial subject as a deviance rooted in the historical. It does not matter that he restated many of the conclusions he arrived at in "A Flag on the Island" or *The Mimic Men.* More important, he moved from, or removed the mask of, his subjective responses and spoke in the name of historical authority. He could legitimately arrange his facts to arrive at the meanings he desired. Like Stendhal, he could be a snob and state his dislike of his society as he pleased.[29] Likewise, he could admire Trollope's "unapologetic display of outrageous prejudices . . . that fairness, that cruel humour without a tinge of self-satire, that deep sense of religion and good business"[30] and that sense of racial bias that Trollope stated so unequivocally in *The West Indies and the Spanish Main*. If Caribbean peoples (Africans and East Indians) are "inferior," "absurd," "unimaginative," and so on, it was his (Naipaul's) duty to state these truths "unapologetically" and with the full knowledge that he would be disliked.

Naipaul's concern with the colonial subject in *The Loss of El Dorado* goes much deeper than a desire to be snobbish. One does not research two essential movements in a people's history simply to prove that they are "absurd," "unimaginative," and so on. Undoubtedly Stendhal's positions buttressed Naipaul in unabashedly stating his views, but his inability to believe unequivocally the conclusions he reached in "A Flag on the Island" and *The Mimic Men*—or, for that matter, that the nature of the postcolonial subject was problematic—drove him on to this historical excavation. He had to convince himself that his attitudes toward his society lay deeply buried in the collective psychology of his people and were not the paranoic conclusions of a disillusioned colonial person but reasoned analysis based on historical evidence. If the conclusion he reached made him a snob, then so be it. For, as he concluded in "What's Wrong with Being a Snob," "the sad fact about prejudices, between classes, castes or indeed races, is that they are an accretion of observation and cannot be destroyed by simple contradiction. Improvement begins with the recognition of difference; it begins with the direct vision and the compassion of a Chekov or a Dickens."[31] Naipaul gives much weight here to historical certainty. This position is captured fully by Derwent May, who argued that in *The Loss of El Dorado* Naipaul "found a psychological and cultural history of colonialism reflected, as it were, in some broken, half-buried scrap of mirror."[32] Naipaul had to unearth these treasures and arrange them in a manner that suited his intention and attitude toward his society.

The Loss of El Dorado, therefore, becomes a reconstruction of the historical evolution of the colonial subject, an attempt to understand how the concepts of "mimicry" and "psychic crampedness" were historically founded and implanted in the colonial. Whereas "A Flag on the Island" and *The Mimic Men* examine what it means to be a colonial subject, *The Loss of El Dorado* attempts to tell how those historical subjects became so constituted in the first place.

Naipaul chose to see colonial society from the eyes of the colonizer rather than those of the colonized. As *The Loss of El Dorado* shows, the text is concerned primarily with the activity of the colonizer; the activity of the colonized person is depicted as a mere reflection of the colonizer and, as such, assumes no spontaneous or self-actualizing subjectivity. The activity of the colonial subject remains fixed, predictable, and repeatable regardless of the changing social or cultural situation; this is a product of the ambivalence central to the colonial situation.

As a historical narrative, *The Loss of El Dorado* simultaneously achieves two methodological purposes: as history, it enables Naipaul to satisfy his psychological need to be a historically constituted human being (that is, a colonial man from Trinidad); as a narrative, it enables him to fulfill his aesthetic-literary concern of achieving "direct vision." This technique is the reason for his formal failure. Since history is generally concerned with articulating facts, it depends on clarity and directness for the achievement of its ends. Narrative, on the other hand, depends on descriptions, emotions, and ambiguity. As such, it is concerned more with the effects of its message than with conveying information. Such cross-purposes tend to confuse and obscure the intention of the work.

Intent on demonstrating the double failure of the society, Naipaul begins with the earliest recorded moment in Trinidad's history: the search for El Dorado by Antonio de Berrio and Walter Raleigh. De Berrio, "the dispossessed conquistador" who made three trips to Trinidad and Guiana at the beginning of the sixteenth century in search of El Dorado, ended up a failure and died a "lunatic" on a forgotten island on the Orinoco River. Raleigh, who was intent on building "an empire of Guiana in which Indian numbers and English skill would destroy the power of Spain at its source, in the Indies"[33] and whose last voyage to Guiana was perceived as an "act of madness," came to the same ignominious fate as de Berrio: he was hung in the Tower of London for his failure in the Caribbean. Speaking of Raleigh's failure, Naipaul mentions de Berrio's failure as well and concludes: "It had begun as a dream as large as the New World itself; it ended in this search for a mine no one had seen, in an action of amateurs, in which all the great ones, and few of the lesser ones, perished" (*LED*, 85).

All Naipaul remembers about the victims, the Amerindians and the first colonized subjects, is their cannibalism, which he condemns not so much as an inherent evil as for its power to arouse in the Spaniards "the same wish to mutilate, destroy, and enslave as did sodomy, another open Indian practice" (*LED*, 60). Because of their practice of cannibalism, the Amerindians are "declared slaves and hunted down," as the "niggers" are hunted down in the second part of the text. The Spaniards in Trinidad did not request assistance to exterminate the Caribs because the Spanish Empire was more concerned with its more important territories of Peru and Mexico. Even at this point in its history, Trinidad was already sliding into obscurity; the island "had almost dropped out of the Spanish Empire; but it had become an English word" (*LED*, 60). The roots of psychic crampedness had begun. Trinidad was nowhere. At the end of the first part of the text, the last image we get of the island is one of violation: "The ships from Europe came and went. The plantations grew. The brazilwood, felled by slaves in the New World, was rasped by criminals in the rasp houses of Amsterdam. The New World as medieval adventure had ended; it had become a cynical extension of the developing old world, its commercial underside. No one would look at Trinidad and Guiana again with the eye of Ralegh or Robert Dudley or Captain Wyatt" (*LED*, 86).

In the second part of the text, we see the further degeneration of the Spaniards, and Trinidad becomes the "ghost province, remoter than it had been a century before" (*LED*, 93), a place where no one wanted to become governor. The Amerindians were butchered by the Spaniards (from a population of forty thousand at the end of the sixteenth century they had dwindled to four thousand at the end of the seventeenth century), and by the end of the eighteenth century, with the arrival of the French and Africans, "the slave colony was already getting its tone, of bustle and acuteness" (*LED*, 106). More important for Naipaul, a new generation of slave suppliers was becoming the aristocracy of the island.

The end of the eighteenth century also saw the victory of the Negroes in Haiti (of whom Trollope had spoken so unflatteringly in *The West Indies and the Spanish Main*, which Naipaul used in the preface to *The Middle Passage*). Rather than speak of their self-liberating capacities, Naipaul depicted their mimicry in *The Loss of El Dorado*:

Negroes wore the tricolor cockade and sang the "Marseillaise." It was part of the French absurdity: the slave revolt was not wholly a slave revolt, the race war not wholly a race war. All the local hatreds were entangled with the revolutionary politics of France. Paris supplied each side with the same simple vocabulary of revolution, words that were like part of the drama and the promise: even the pretty climatic names—*germinal, brumaire*—of a new calendar of the North. (*LED*, 114)

According to Naipaul, the impetus for the Negroes' revolutionary self-liberating activity came from outside the society rather than from within. Nor did these slaves have a language with which to express the content of their new activity. The victims were imprisoned by the language of the other.

In the third section of the text Naipaul continues to sketch the failure of these colonial subjects, locating their sense of failure at a much deeper level of the cultural, psychological, and intellectual history of the country. This time the victims were the Negroes, and, as he argues, the introduction of the East Indian in 1838 merely continued to reproduce the pattern of "human dereliction" (*LED*, 324) characteristic of the history of the country. The major focus of this section of the text, however, is the failure of the society at the end of the eighteenth century to channel its intellectual vigor and socially meaningful activity into a permanent historical legacy upon which the subjects could draw. The failure rests, of course, on the upper classes— the whites and the coloreds—since the Negro slave did not exist in any meaningful sense for Naipaul.[34] Yet Naipaul saw such failure within the entire social history of the colony.

Naipaul begins the section by depicting Francisco Miranda, the famous South American revolutionary, as capable of "applying the concepts of Europe as words alone, accurate but misleading, to a simpler world" (*LED*, 150). The revolution of Gaul and España established much of what was to follow in the social and cultural history of the island: "the borrowed words that never matched the society, the private theatre of disguises and false names that ended in blood and the heads spiked in public places" (*LED*, 153).

When Naipaul describes the Negro community of 1800, which supplanted the man-eating Caribs, he is no less flattering. Although the Negroes of 1800 had "remained as anonymous as the Indians of Las Casas three centuries before" (*LED*, 253), their silence was only the silence of a life of fantasy in which all of the Negroes ("creole Negroes and new Negroes, French Negroes and English Negroes" [*LED*, 254]) came together in bacchanal and pagan orgies, a world of "make believe . . . [a] Negro fantasy life [that] changed and developed":

In Trinidad, an immigrant island, it [this Negro fantasy life] had become many-featured, a dream beyond labor and more real than labor, of power and prettiness, of titles, flags and uniforms, kings and queens and courtiers. The planter, looking at his Negroes and seeing only Negroes, never knew. He might know that certain Negroes dressed up in cast-off clothes and received other Negroes, fed and danced and jumped up together: a mimicry in the Negro yards of white entertaining. (*LED*, 254)

A whole new society was coming into being, but because the Negroes remained inarticulate and no one bothered to chronicle their history, their existence remained unacknowledged. Their struggle for freedom, a part of the impetus of the age reflected in the French and American revolutions, was relegated to the realm of fantasy. Thus the Negro uprising, planned for the second week in December 1805, can be described as "only an aspect of Negro fantasy; but an adequate leader could make it real. The moment would occur when secrecy became its own assurance, when fantasy submerged and ridiculed the world of labor and property" (*LED*, 254).

Such activity could not be taken seriously. It did not matter that the Africans, in spite of their enslavement, kept their social order intact by forming their own councils, judging each other, electing their kings, and so on and organized in a constructive manner to secure their liberation. They were black and they lived in a colonial outpost, and so such activity was dismissed as "a whole underground of *Negro* fantasy," as Naipaul called it. Such attempts at social liberation were the product of the "confusion of philanthropy and Jacobinism among the English settlers, London talk from London people" (*LED*, 261).

All Naipaul could perceive in early eighteenth-century society was the great want of moral principle in the colonial character. As George Smith, an Englishman, argued, "Generally colonies are peopled by the refuse of the Mother Country, but Trinidad is peopled by the refuse of the other colonies" (*LED*, 290). Not even the activity of the free people of color is exempted from Naipaul's criticism. Their petition to Governor Hislop condemning Smith's excesses only reflects their submissiveness and their capacity for hero worship.

In his epilogue Naipaul draws a number of conclusions about the society. He posits that with the departure of the few Europeans from the island, the "intellectual liveliness" of the Fullartons, the Hislops, and the Smiths disappeared, "Port of Spain dropped out of history" again, and Trinidad returned to "what it was, an outpost, a backwater":

As a British colony Trinidad was as much an error and a failure as it had been as part of the Spanish Empire, "these provinces of El Dorado." And again, separate from the life of the Empire elsewhere, the imperial cycle was speeded up: a special virtue and vigor swiftly followed by the special decay which they contained. (*LED*, 322)

Hence Trinidad, which entered history as a result of a "joke" (*LED*, 333), wound up an "error" destined for slow decay and oblivion. Without imperial attention, no history was possible; without imperial activity, no real people were possible. People, purpose, and meaning could be defined only through a relationship with the other. Such a relationship, however, was one-dimensional.

Naipaul updated his story, however. *The Loss of El Dorado* was not so much a historical narrative as a historical-political narrative, and thus there was an intention. Naipaul updated the conclusions he reached in his earlier text and somehow separated himself from the stereotype he was depicting. Thus he concludes: "Today I am a stranger in the city myself. Port of Spain is bigger, brighter, noisier and better educated than it was when I was at school there, between 1939 and 1948. Then, in spite of the war and the United States base, it felt like a place at the rim of the world" (*LED*, 324).

He had come full circle from the search he began in *The Mystic Masseur* and that culminated in *The Mimic Men*. Was it not the feeling of being "at the rim of the world," outside the concourse of meaningful human activity, that impelled him to leave the island in the first place, as he recorded in *The Middle Passage*? And was not *The Loss of El Dorado* supposed to be his final historical-political justification for his condemnation of his society, his condemnation of the "mimicry," the "barbarity," that lay buried beneath the cultural and social history of his people? He had not—perhaps could not—explore the evolution of the social consciousness of the Negro, for it remained enigmatic, unable to yield to the stereotypic explanation he offered. This weakness is the major problem of the text and represents the continuing crisis in his search for his identity. *A House for Mr. Biswas* and *The Mimic Men* examined, if not successfully at least enlighteningly, the contradiction inherent in being Indian in a creolized society and, as I have argued, in being a colonial subject in a colonial world. But what about the Negro? After cramming 350 years of history into three hundred pages, Naipaul could only conclude: "The slave [the Negro] was never real. Like the extinct aboriginal, he had to be reconstructed from his daily routine. So he remains, existing, like Vallot's jail (of which no plan survives), only in the imagination. In the records the slave is faceless, silent, with an identification rather than a name. He has no story" (*LED*, 325). This is an incredible admission of failure. After three hundred pages, we are told that the slave was not real. To whom, he does not say. Naipaul concludes that the slave had no story to tell. Perhaps Naipaul was looking in the wrong place.

Does not such a conclusion reside somewhere near the point where we began, when Naipaul declared that prejudices "are an accretion of observations and cannot be destroyed by simple contradiction"?[35] Is there not an alternative tradition that Naipaul neglected? And does he not rely too heavily on the written rather than the oral tradition?

The Loss of El Dorado, however, is not only about the lack of materials to construct the evolution of the colonial subject. It also reveals the limitations of Naipaul's ideological approach and the inherent limitations of colonial discourse. For although he was able to reconstruct a superstructure (the ideological apparatus, as it were) in which to insert the colonial subject, he suddenly realized that even if he understood the East Indian well enough to make some statements about him, he was unable to penetrate deeply into the Negro culture and psyche and for that reason the African remained unreal, residing only within Naipaul's imagination. Because Naipaul was unable to locate the African in his "real social world," he was unable to reveal him as a fully constituted colonial subject. As a consequence, his work, particularly as it relates to the African person, is of limited value.

The Loss of El Dorado, therefore, serves more as a forum for Naipaul to justify his attitudes toward his society than as an authentic examination of that society. To accomplish this end, he had to distort significantly the history of the country and present a purely ideological interpretation. In another context and with a different emphasis, the historical facts could have yielded quite different conclusions.

Finally, all Naipaul does in *The Loss of El Dorado* is to mark the subject with the racist practices and discourses of a purely colonial culture and fix him irredeemably into a position from which there can be no release. As Homi Bhabha says:

The legends, stories, histories and anecdotes of a colonial culture offer the subject a primordial Either/Or. *Either* he is fixed in a consciousness of the body as a solely negating activity *or* as a new kind of man, a new genus. What is denied the colonial subject, both as coloniser and colonised, is that form of negation which gives access to the recognition of difference in the Symbolic. It is that possibility of difference and circulation which would liberate the signifier of *skin/culture* from the signifieds of racial typology, the analytics of blood, ideologies of racial and cultural dominance or denigration.[36]

To understand the colonial subject, he must be positioned differently within the colonial culture. This Naipaul could not do and would find increasingly more difficult in his more recent work.

6. Ideology, Culture, and National Identity

Ideology is a false totality because it has not appointed its own limits, because it is unable to reflect the limitations of its limits. . . . Like a planet revolving around an absent sun, an ideology is made up of what it does not mention; it exists because there are things which must not be spoken of.

—Pierre Macherey, *A Theory of Literary Production*

> Can't beat me drum
> In my own, own native land
> Can't have we Carnival
> In my own, my native land
> Can't have we Bacchanal
> In my own, my native land
> In my own, my native land.
>
> In my own native land,
> Moen pasca dancer, comme moen viel
> (I cannot dance as I wish)
>
> —Calypso composed in the 1880s (quoted
> in *Race Relations in Colonial Trinidad, 1870–1900*)

IDEOLOGY AND CULTURE

It was not inconsistent that in trying to unearth the nature of the colonial subject V. S. Naipaul went back to the origins of the colonial experience, to the myth of savagism and civility. His inability to understand colonial people and his growing psychological distance from them led him to stereotype them. Indeed, one cannot understand the condition of savagery and barbarity ascribed to colonial peoples without understanding the historical concepts of civility and order associated with European civilization. After all, when Raleigh went to the New World he was in search not only of gold and silver but of paradise; gold and imperial domination were largely the "symbols of his impassioned search for the boundless dreamworld of paradise and El Dorado."[1] For Raleigh, El Dorado symbolized paradise, and it became his obsession.

The paradisiac myth, unimaginably remote and as old as European civilization itself, was a fundamental part of Western civilization and, in part, accounted for the ambivalence Europeans felt toward non-European people. As Henri Baudet has pointed out, this myth celebrated the "glorification of all things primitive, the cultureless as a characteristic of the true, the complete, the only and original bliss: that is one of the fundamentals of our Western civilization." This myth, of course, was originally related to Christianity and its past, but as long as Christianity remained spiritually and geographically sealed off from the rest of the known world, "it went on relating its images of the primitive age, which were just as real as its own faith, to itself, projecting them all back to 'the beginning.' "[2] Eventually, this myth became closely associated with the Western view of the world.

In this sense, then, paradise was the hoped-for condition, and as Bernard Sheehan pointed out, human beings were defined "largely by negation." Because men yearned for this original condition of paradise, savagism embodied all that these men were not and thus "offered the savage nothing of his own. Instead, it deprived him of the elements of culture and bound him irretrievably within the skein of the European thought process."[3] Savagism explained people as having failed to attain or replicate the European mode of life.

This concept, then, was not racist. It simply depicted a particular theory of life. It may have praised the savage or endorsed the Indian's progress, but it did not acknowledge the integrity of the native's culture. Savagism, therefore, inverted the civil condition. Civil men, in contradistinction to savages, lived an ordered and disciplined life characterized by political authority, a system of law, and the presence of religious morality. According to Sheehan, "Civil men labored for their bread, pacified their sexual urges in marriage, and formed a complex pattern of social arrangements."[4]

When Columbus traveled to the New World he therefore brought with him all the psychological baggage that was implied in that European position, updated, as Baudet noted, to fit the needs of the fifteenth century. He too was chosen to serve God and the Christian cause even though his mission was an economic and political one. As Baudet notes, "In October 1492, Columbus was convinced that he had arrived in Old Testament country and was not far distance from earthly Paradise."[5] It was precisely at that moment, at the dawning of the "Atlantic" era, that the American Indian was admitted to the ranks of the noble savage. He too was the creation of the European imagination, a being free from the burdens of civilization, knowing neither human wickedness, human suffering, nor human wants.

The savage, then, was a European creation and its definition a product of European culture. Naipaul was indebted to this notion when he went back to the origins of Trinidad's history to attempt to define the colonial subject. The savage is always before culture and history and is perceived always as having no history or culture. When he does, it is always presumed to be meaningless. Because he lacks letters, the savage cannot enjoy intellectual life, and thinking leads invariably to unhappiness. The savage state required no system of law, no social organization, and no political order, and people lived without the benefit of kings. "Noble savages," according to Sheehan, "enjoyed a life without bound and apparently substance."[6] Theirs was an ideal state of perfect happiness.

Naipaul's response to the experience of the colonial subject was profoundly ideological in that he interpreted it from the eyes of a European. He saw the culture of the colonizer as the universal culture and, as a result, all other cultures, particularly those of the colonized, as needing to be reinterpreted on that basis. This methodology precluded any radical interrogation of European culture. In fact, the difference between European and colonial culture became the latter's defect, its almost incurable disease. Such an approach to analysis or interpretation, perforce, naturalized the concept of culture and vulgarized ideology. Needless to say, Naipaul labored to reproduce the image of European society for every part of the world that he tried to interpret. This tendency became more apparent as he lost touch with his own society.

Naipaul's inability to see anything worthwhile in the society of *The Mimic Men* and his subsequent attempt to seek justification for his negative posture in *The Loss of El Dorado* can be understood within the context of his growing acceptance of the ideology and culture of the former colonizers and his assumption of their method of analysis and perceptions. This transformation can be observed in the manner in which Naipaul described these societies and the nature of the laughter that occurs in the latter part of his work. From a laughter that originates with or within the people in his earlier texts he turned to a laughter at the people in the fiction of his later period. Thus, although he may have objected to certain aspects of his society's behavior in his earlier novels, he did not feel the intense disdain that he revealed in *The Middle Passage* and *An Area of Darkness*. And though Gordon Rohlehr has argued that even in his earlier texts Naipaul regarded the people "with more contempt than compassion . . . the same people whom he described in *The Middle Passage* as being 'like monkeys pleading for evolution,' "[7] his laughter with the people during his early period can be seen as genuine and evidence of a tolerance for their foibles. During his early period he felt some bond with Trinidadian society, particularly in 1964, when he asserted that "no writer, however individual his vision, could be separated from his society."[8]

The comic laughter in Naipaul's first three texts gives way to tragic laughter in *A House for Mr. Biswas.* By "A Flag on the Island," the nature of that laughter has changed substantially. It has become privatized, sterile, and, most of all, derisively ideological.[9] From laughing *with* his people, Naipaul shifts to laughing *at* his people and positions himself above his society in both his intelligence and his responsiveness to the culture of the colonizer, which he believes is absent in the colonial society.

Such a transformation cannot be accounted for simply by arguing that Naipaul was disdainful of his society. He was disdainful long before he left Trinidad. Rather, his distaste for the folk culture of his people arose primarily because he acquired the ideology and culture of the dominant colonizing power, accepted its values, and adopted a European perspective in his writing. Although some scholars have argued that Naipaul's acceptance of the values of the colonizing power was evident as early as *The Middle Passage,* I do not believe he had yet internalized those ideas fully or formulated them into a coherent epistemological position until "A Flag on the Island."[10]

Naipaul's negative ideological posture toward Trinidad is clearest in *The Loss of El Dorado,* in the overdetermined nature of the text and the privileged positions he gave to the values of the colonizer's culture. Rather than being concerned primarily with the plausibility of the South American revolution, he wished to explain his attitude toward his society, the superiority of the colonizer's culture, and the total debasement of the culture of the colonized people. To Naipaul, "The revolution was a farce, Miranda a fraud: Miranda wanted to be the Emperor of Spanish-America" (*LED,* 153). Such fraudulence made the revolution prophetic of all that was to follow in the society and in most colonial territories, where such revolutions reflected only "borrowed words that never matched the society, the private theatre of disguises and false names that ended in blood and the heads spiked in public places" (*LED,* 153).

Against this background, Naipaul offers his attitude toward the Negro society in Trinidad. It is a world of witchcraft, sorcery, divination, and poisoning, a "Negro underground" that is the horror and bane of the French and English aristocracy of the island. Such abomination had to be uprooted at any cost, so when Governor Thomas Picton turned from the Spanish invasion that threatened from Venezuela, he devoted himself to the "suppression" and "subordination" of the Negro underground.

From the time Naipaul began to speak about the Negro underground, it was clear that he did not find any validity in that society or believe it necessary to study it. It was, after all, a world that was already known. To him, as in the popular myth, that world was permeated by fear, deceit, and treachery. Like the society of *The Mimic Men* and "A Flag on the Island," there could be no redeeming qualities in Negro society. He takes delight in describing the outer veneer of the society by depicting the brutality and degeneration of the "alguazils," or policemen, who were called upon to pick up and impound "a curfew-breaking Negro or a Negro who walked about after dark without a light" (*LED*, 159). The Negroes were subjected to particular victimization at the hands of the creoles and the alguazils.

Naipaul describes the countless acts of brutality perpetrated against the Negroes and those they perpetrated against themselves, but he has nothing to say about their alternative inner life and world. According to Naipaul, their existence was characterized only by confused fantasy and make-believe into which they receded when they withdrew from the "real world."[11] In their world of make-believe they became "kings and courtiers, generals and judges, so many suffering from sores, [when they] visited and exchanged courtesies" (*LED*, 254). In their confused state, "they blessed, they punished. France, England and Africa, the plantations themselves, the church and the Council provided the ritual, the titles, the ceremonies of power" (*LED*, 254). In the Negro world, "kings exchanged polite messages" and kings and queens visited formally with each other and feasted on "callaloo, beef and rum" (*LED*, 255). Bakhtin tells us that every feast symbolizes a philosophy of life; all Naipaul saw was confusion and stupidity.

Nor was Naipaul impressed by the "other formalities" of Negro life, which he described so well:

Old Michel, the Grand Judge, punished offenders by beating them like a plantation overseer; or he fined them, or made them kneel for two hours, knocking stones together; or he expelled them from the regiment for a fortnight. Sometimes King Noel and his queen, Marie, levied a subscription. Then a large loaf of bread was baked and pieces were sent to all the king's subjects and sometimes also to another king. Sometimes a "communion," a biscuit without salt, was administered to a king and queen; King Samson's subjects paid two dollars each to attend the ceremony. Money was always important to a king. Samson sold rum at twenty-seven cents a bottle. (*LED*, 255)

Although Naipaul contrasted this fantasy life of the colonized with the "real world" of the colonizer, Negro society could never become "real," even though it changed and developed, because "real" life was not possible as long as the Negroes were dominated by the European world view. The savages could not possibly be like the English, who, according to the discourse of savagism and civility, had to be inverted to exist in the first place. Thus Naipaul could say of the European immigrants:

The English were not yet colonial; they were still a part of England. Their drives were more complex, and the colony offered liberation of a sort. English tradesmen took up duelling; "the humbler the grade of duellists, the more sanguinary were their encounters." And the English fight against Picton in Trinidad soon went beyond gossip and became like an extension of the political agitations in England. The English immigrants claimed rights; they talked of writing to London newspapers and London lawyers. They wanted a British constitution in Trinidad. They planned a petition. They announced a public meeting. (*LED*, 166)

The "drives" of the colonized could not be considered "complex" because the colonial world was one fantasy. The resistance of the English immigrants to Picton takes on the form of "political agitation," whereas Negro insurrection is merely "an aspect of Negro fantasy." The practices of the English became hallowed because they were "written." The activity of the colonized was not written down in any book, and so it did not have the authenticity or the validity of a written document that was sent up to the motherland to be authenticated. As Naipaul argued as early as 1964 in his essay "Jasmine," landscape and societies do not exist in any ordered or coherent sense until they have been documented in a book. As far as he was concerned, "the stored wisdom of [the colonial society] was only about cocoa, tobacco, sugar and the management of Negroes" (*LED*, 283). Everything else came from the mother country: "The wines, the manners and the graces, the books and the art and the ideas of a living culture came from the outside. The simple society bred simple people" (*LED*, 283).

So constructed and constituted, the colonial society was the product of the colonizer, and all culture and intellectual knowledge came from outside the society. While the English immigrants remained in that displaced setting, they were distinguished not only "by their wealth and commercial adventurousness (sometimes folly), their clothes, the ritual of their English-style meals and the other emblems of a finer domestic self-cherishing, but also by their intellectual liveliness" (*LED*, 316). When they left the island, such "intellectual liveliness," "a carry-over from the metropolis," died, "the quality of controversy declined, and the stature of men" (*LED*, 316).

In the absence of "intellectual liveliness" all that was left was the savagery of a slave society in a place where there could be no independent thought or indigenous cultural life. In this colony, this world of fantasy and make-believe, vulgarity and void, are found the seeds of the twentieth-century Caribbean, a world of bacchanals and orgies, of "voodoo, the Negro dances and the cynical Negro songs, the bands at carnival time: the underground Negro life the slave-owner had tried to suppress" (*LED*, 316), a world sanctioned by the colonizer and defiled by the author. According to Naipaul, this is the sum total of the "unreal" world of the Negro.

It is this perception of reality that Naipaul brings to his interpretation of the history and politics of Caribbean life. He does not look beneath the surface experiences of the "underground life" of the Negro or examine "the Negro underground kingdoms" with any seriousness. He simply reduces the culture and history of colonized people to a pale reflection of that of the dominant culture. But can such an understanding of history or politics be accepted as adequate or "scrupulous scholarship,"[12] or is it not an ideological history that privileges the discourses and practices of the dominant culture without granting any validity to the culture of the oppressed?[13] Naipaul's approach to colonial societies simply continues a process outlined at the beginning of the chapter. He interprets the culture of the colonized "within the skein of the European thought process." The savage can have nothing of his own. Neither his culture nor his history (which is not his own) can be of any importance.

In presenting history and politics in such a manner, Naipaul never stopped to ask a fundamental question: How can a society that began in enslavement and indentureship follow the same dialectical path and use the same ideological assumptions as that of another society that grew through conquest and was sustained by brutality and oppression? How can one ascribe the same values to the social activities of both the enslaved and the enslaver when each was designed to secure entirely different results? Necessarily, each society ascribed different values to the same activities. The results could not possibly be the same. One need only suggest another dialectical path the culture of the colonized might have taken to understand the ideological approach behind Naipaul's analysis.

The dominant power that colonized Trinidad—the slave master and later the colonizer—possessed the inherent right to oppress the slave, steal his labor, despise his work, denigrate his culture, and deny his humanity. Under this system, the colonized person and the slave had no rights except those defined by the dominant power. Inherent rights did not exist. To rationalize the nonrights of the colonized person, the colonizer erected a system of scientific and humanitarian knowledge. This body of knowledge became the truth of the entire society. To achieve this end, an established order of scholarship (both ecclesiastical and lay) was put in place to defend and protect this body of knowledge, now called the "truth," "standards," and so on. All knowledge that did not originate within the official world of the colonizer could therefore be disregarded and called "untruth." All knowledge of the world of the colonized was negated and said to make no sense. Such nonsanctioned knowledge was "fantasy" or "make-believe" because it did not exist in any essential sense within the context of the colonizer's culture.

So defined, the "truth" or "knowledge" of the activities of the colonized is neither "unreal" nor fantasy. It is nonsanctioned knowledge. But, more important, this unofficial, nonsanctioned world of the colonized—call it the culture of carnival—has important characteristics. The validity of the colonized's culture or of his activities does not depend on the sanctioning of the dominant culture. The colonized culture possesses an integrity of its own.[14]

In this context, we can draw on Bakhtin's impressive study of Rabelais in which he distinguished between the unofficial world of the "carnivalesque folk humor" and the official world of the ecclesiastical order of the Middle Ages. Bakhtin demonstrated not only that carnival was important but that the life of carnival and the marketplace existed separately and distinctly from that of the official world order. The world of the former, he said "offered a completely different non-official, extra-ecclesiastical and extra political aspect of the world, of man, and of human relations; they built a second life outside officialdom, a world in which all medieval people participated more or less, in which they lived during a given part of the year."[15] This unofficial world of carnival and the marketplace provided a temporary liberation from the prevailing truth of the established order, suspended all hierarchical rank and privileges, became a symbol of renewal and change, and always stood for the element of *becoming* in opposition to the immovable, unchanging stability of the official world.

Bakhtin, unlike Naipaul, understood the coherence and congruence of this unofficial world of carnival and argued its importance in understanding any era of oppression. Without an understanding of this two-world consciousness, Bakhtin argued, "neither medieval culture nor the culture of the Renaissance can be understood. To ignore or to underestimate the laughing people of the Middle Ages also distorts the picture of European culture's historic development."[16] The same case can be made for the culture of carnival in the Caribbean. The irreducible nature and integrity of such a culture exists within its own terms and cannot be reduced simply to "an underground of fantasy" or "an underground kingdom." In so characterizing it, Naipaul failed to understand the capacity of this Symbolic Order to create its own meaning-producing subjects.

Viewed from this perspective, it becomes clear why the discourse and practice of the oppressed and the oppressor alike take on their own determinate significance within the context of each specific culture. Marx argued, for instance, that all aspects of ideology (morality, religion, and so on), as well as the forms of consciousness that correspond to them, are not merely independent entities: "They have no history, no development; but men, developing their material production and their material discourse, alter, along with this their actual world, also their thinking and the products of their thinking."[17] Because Naipaul presents his analysis in an idealist manner, he is unable to present a comprehensive picture of the social relations of the slave society and thereby relate them to the specific development of Caribbean peoples. Only by removing the veil of "fantasy" and studying the life processes of real, active men as they participated in concrete activities could he have arrived at the "real history" of Caribbean people and recognized the truth of their existence. In these terms, the existence of Caribbean people would never have been perceived as the mere echo of another culture. An analysis of Caribbean societies demands that the myth of savagism be rejected and an nonideological perspective be the basis of analysis.

Inescapably, another important consideration arises when we counterpose the European world view to that of the African and ask what is meant by "an underground of fantasy" within the context of Caribbean culture. The Indian scholar Homi Bhabha, for example, has argued for a "Terrestrialism" of the African world view, distinct from the rationalism of the Western world view. He says,

It is the Terrestrialism of the African (Yoruba) world-view that established its identity and distinguishes it from western rationalism. Terrestrialism locates man in a cosmic totality, presenting a unified sensibility, where his earth-boundedness is indispensable from the entire cosmic phenomenon. Antithetical to this is the Platonic-Christian tradition which creates a compartmentalized mind that hypostasises "separatist myths" and elaborates them in all-pervading truths. The separation of the secular and the sacred is one such myth, the elevation of the syllogism as the *natural* model of thought is another. But these insubstantial "creative impulses . . . directed by period dialectics" are a reflection of the absence in western culture of a cohesive, irreducible truth in which the roots of African reality are deeply sunk. For Terrestrialism makes no issue of contradiction or dialectic, as the very nature of African essence . . . is protean and changing—Ogun himself is transitional and contradictory. But change is not viewed as it is in the West, as a linear, teleological process. Past and Present, Mind and Body, Myth and History, Ritual and Fiction coexist in an alchemy that doesn't demand hierarchies of hypostasisations, or any such rationalist notions of Order.[18]

One cannot simply transfer the values of one civilization to that of another without attempting to explain the reasons for the specific character of that civilization.[19] Such an alternative vision of colonized societies never seems to occur to Naipaul because he presumes that the colonizer's truth is the universal truth of all societies. Such an approach distorts the reality of the colonial experience and makes that which begins in ideological terrain with pregiven values and verdicts appear as though it possesses eternal, disinterested, and unbiased "truths" about social life, built on the solid "accretion of observation," rather than the narrow idealist biases from which they are generated in the first place. Sectional interests are indeed presented as universal. Stated in such terms, it becomes highly unscientific to condemn one civilization or society on the basis of values and practices developed by another civilization to serve its own particular ends. Naipaul could have depicted these societies in an innovative or creative manner only if he stopped seeing them as extensions of European societies that did not match the European ideal.

THE OVERCROWDED BARRACOON

As early as 1965, one year after Naipaul wrote *An Area of Darkness,* Nissim Ezekeil observed that Naipaul had presented the communal life of India as "hidebound, inimical to personal development, fantastically ignorant and prejudiced about the world's outside community, and hopelessly uncreative in every conceivable area of life."[20] In that same year, Naipaul, in an article entitled "East Indian," chronicled the disintegration of the East Indian in the New World and argued that "to be an Indian from Trinidad, then, is to be unlikely . . . exotic . . . [and] a little fraudulent" (*OB,* 38). Generally, however, in this early period, Naipaul saw the Indians as possessing the same characteristics of mimicry as the Negroes of Trinidad.

In 1976 Naipaul made a second visit to India and suggested that the Indians had become "a people grown barbarous, indifferent and self-wounding, who, out of a shallow perception of the world, have no sense of tragedy" (*OB,* 93). This problem, according to Naipaul, resulted from "the intellectual failure" (*OB,* 94) that manifested itself in "a nation exchanging banalities among itself" (*OB,* 97) and that was symptomatic of a "larger crisis, which is that of a decaying civilization, where the only hope lies in further swift decay" (*OB,* 106).

In "A Second Visit," Naipaul argued that because the Indians lacked the capacity for self-analysis, the Indian novelist had no descriptive capacity.

More specifically, he argued that because the humanities are borrowed disciplines "there can be no effective writing. The ritual of Indian life smothers the imagination, for which it is a substitute, and the interpretation of India in the Indian novel, itself a borrowed form, is at a low, unchanging level" (*OB*, 98). This lack of imagination and absence of descriptive powers show up more clearly in the novel and the Indian autobiography, in which this "Indian deficiency" is magnified:

The world in these books is reduced to a succession of stimuli, and the reacting organism reports codified pleasure or pain; the expression of an egoism so excluding that the world, so far from being something to be explored, at times disappears, and the writers themselves appear maimed and incomplete. All Indian autobiographies appear to be written by the same incomplete person. (*OB*, 98)

It never occurs to Naipaul that he could explore Indian writing (be it the novel or the autobiography) from within its own indigenous boundaries, its own mode of looking at itself.

In contrast, might it not be possible to offer an aesthetic mode based on the Eastern vision that would argue that because the Eastern world view seeks to acquire a direct insight into reality (as opposed to the conceptual, dialectical thinking of the Western world), it always privileges the intuitive manner of knowing and perceiving? One could argue that, in the words of Fritjof Capra, "Eastern art forms, too, are forms of meditation. They are not so much means for expressing the artist's ideas as ways of self-realization through the development of the intuitive mode of consciousness." Such a conception of art, perceived as an irreducible whole, necessarily occasions its own manner of telling. As Capra reminds us, "The Eastern mystics, too, are well aware of the fact that all verbal descriptions of reality are inaccurate and incomplete. The direct experience of reality transcends the realm of thought and language, and, since all mysticism is based on a direct experience, everything that is said about it can only be partly true." Concerned primarily about "the experience of reality" rather than the "description of reality," the mystic (and by definition the literary expression of this culture) reveals its experiences through mythical language, "which is much less restricted by logic and common sense."[21]

Could it be that the manner of seeing closely approximates the manner of telling in the Indian autobiography? In this case the "experience of the reality" would be more important than the "description of the reality," the former much more concerned with the development of the internal, intuitive world of the subject (a form of self-realization) than with a description of outer, conceptual reality, a way of excluding, denying, and compartmentalizing the concrete reality of the external world.

Was it not this dichotomy that Naipaul described in the Indian autobiography when he complained that "the world in these books is reduced to a succession of stimuli, and the reacting organism," which expressed "an egoism" that so excluded the world that was being discussed that it disappeared or was denied? Of course Naipaul arrived at different conclusions. He saw such writing as an expression of the "Indian deficiency" and the autobiographical statement as the expression of an "incomplete person." But was not this effect intended, given the specific historical development of the Indian people?

Because Naipaul treats the Western experience as the universal experience, a final closure of all knowledge and the beginning and end of all history, even that which is to come, he cannot perceive, nor would he allow himself to believe, that the Western experience, like the African or Indian, was only a partial experience of the social totality called world. As a part of this whole, each individual experience possesses its own irreducible essence and is complete unto itself. Because Naipaul failed to appreciate this position, we are forced to listen to his repetitious tirades against the people of India, many of which appeared in *The Mimic Men*. We are told that

India is fragmented; it is part of her dependence. This is not the fragmentation of region, religion or caste. It is the fragmentation of a country held together by no intellectual current, no developing inner life of its own. It is the fragmentation of a country without even an idea of a graded but linked society. . . .

So Indians, the holy men included, have continually to look outside India for approval. Fragmentation and dependence are complete. Local judgment is valueless. It is even as if, without the foreign chit, Indians can have no confirmation of their own reality. (*OB*, 101–3)[22]

In *The Mimic Men* this capacity for fragmentation that lies within is called chaos and leads to disorder; in "A Flag on the Island" the lack of social bonds leads to the final abandonment of the island and the regret that the lives of the people were not finally "arrested." In India, the cause of fragmentation is internal; it is the "self-destructive malice which startles and depresses the visitor" (*OB*, 103). Like the inhabitants of "A Flag on the Island," the malady and the remedy are the same: "This dependent frenzy nowadays finds its expression in flight" (*OB*, 103).

And so the link is complete. India joins hands with Trinidad, and from Naipaul's vantage point, they share the same social disease. The East Indian people still needed to be situated, however, within the social history of

Trinidad, where they had become a part of the "new human dereliction." They were a people who "had little sense of history, were governed and protected by rituals which were like privacy; and in the Trinidad countryside they created a simple, rural India. They were an aspect of the colony. The colony became an imperial amalgam, the Empire in little" (*LED*, 318).

Trinidad and India were fragmented societies that depended on the outside imperial world for guidance. *The Loss of El Dorado* would not be Naipaul's last attack on the colonial world; he would transfer the sentiments expressed in this text, almost verbatim, to the Islamic world.

Meanwhile, against the backdrop of the eruption of the black power movement at the end of the 1960s, Naipaul linked his concept of carnival with that of black power and used the combined metaphors as a means of expressing the postcolonial realities of the Caribbean. He also continued to examine the Negroes of the Caribbean, as he had done in *The Loss of El Dorado*.

BLACK POWER AND THE CULTURE OF CARNIVAL

In the article "Power?" (1970) Naipaul brought together the concepts of psychic crampedness, mimicry, and the lunacy of the culture of carnival that he had first advanced in "A Flag on the Island." In "Power?" Naipaul used the concepts of carnival and black power, manifestations of the unofficial culture and both possessing the characteristics of mimicry and psychic crampedness, to demonstrate the essential points he made in the latter part of the 1960s. In the article, he reechoed many ideas he had explored before. As in *The Loss of El Dorado*, he argued that when the official culture of the white planter class fell away it was replaced by

a securer, secret world of fantasy, of Negro "kingdoms," "regiments," bands. The people who were slaves by day saw themselves then as kings, queens, dauphins, princesses. There were pretty uniforms, flags and painted wooden swords. Everyone who joined a regiment got a title. At night the Negroes played at being people, mimicking the rites of the upper world. The kings visited and entertained. At gatherings a "secretary" might sit scribbling away. (*OB*, 267)

He repeated the scene about the Negro uprising planned for December 1805 and reached a conclusion that the demands of "scrupulous scholarship" would not have allowed him to make in *The Loss of El Dorado*: in "Power?" he concluded that the uprising broke up "the Negro kingdoms of the night" (*OB*, 268).

But the fantasies remained. They had to, because without that touch of lunacy the Negro would have utterly despaired and might have killed himself slowly by eating dirt; many in Trinidad did. The Carnival the tourist goes to see is a version of the lunacy that kept the slave alive. It is the original dream of black power, style and prettiness; and it always feeds on a private vision of the real world. (*OB,* 268)

Once more we are asked to contrast the "real world" of the colonizer with the "unreal world" of the colonized, and we see the conflict between the "official" and the "unofficial" cultures continue unabated. Whereas Naipaul was implicit in *The Loss of El Dorado,* here he is explicit.

In "Power?" Naipaul's description encompasses the entire Caribbean region. As in previous articles ("Columbus and Crusoe" [1967], "The Ultimate Colony" [1969], "Anguilla: The Shipwrecked Six Thousands" [1969], "St. Kitts: Papa and the Power Set" [1969]), he states once more that "something of the Carnival lunacy touches all these islands where people, first as slaves and then as neglected colonials, have seen themselves as futile, on the other side of the real world" (*OB,* 268).[23] Paradoxically, this notion of being on the "other side" of the "real world" is linked to the concept that dominated the first part of Naipaul's work: that the Indian is an alien in the New World. It also harks back to the concept of savagism outlined at the beginning of this chapter. In both cases the sense of the "unreality" of the life of the Negroes and the exclusion of their culture from the circumscribed world of the colonizer shapes his notion of civility and officialdom.

What is most significant at this point in Naipaul's literary development, however, is that although he was now more inclined to examine the conditions of the black masses in the Caribbean, he was not ready to examine the culture of carnival or to legitimize it. Because he could only compare the aspirations of the black masses, embodied in the concepts of black power and the culture of carnival, with those of the official culture, he could only repeat new versions of the same myths in the guise of a new formula. The rise of the black power movement simply gave Naipaul a new vehicle by which to articulate old views. To him, black power was simply a repetition of the "old apocalyptic mood of the Black masses" (*OB,* 269) done up in a new form.

In "Power?" we find elements from *The Mimic Men* (independence brings only drama to the island) and "A Flag on the Island" (the people are threatened with imminent chaos), but in many ways it anticipates *Guerrillas* (anarchy is at hand). Thus black power is depicted as having something for everyone, as almost a carnival of the folk:

Black Power as rage, drama and style, as revolutionary jargon, offers something to everybody: to the unemployed, the idealistic, the drop-out, the Communist, the·

politically frustrated, the anarchist, the angry student returning home from humiliations abroad, the racialist, the old-fashioned black preacher who has for years said at street corners that after Israel it was to be the turn of Africa. Black Power means Cuba and China; it also means clearing the Chinese and the Jews and the tourists out of Jamaica. It is identity and it is also miscegenation. It is drinking holy water, eating pork and dancing; it is going back to Abyssinia. There has been no movement like it in the Caribbean since the French Revolution. (*OB*, 270)

Naipaul's commitment to the official version of Caribbean culture is so strong that although he links the black power movement to the "old apocalyptic mood of the Black masses," his only paradigm is the French Revolution. The Haitian Revolution, which many scholars cite as the most significant event in Caribbean history, must give pride of place to it.[24] For Naipaul, Europe must always be the standard by which everything is measured.

Black power gave Naipaul an opportunity to collapse his previous concerns on psychic crampedness, mimicry, and the lunacy of the culture of carnival into a major epistemological moment. Black power became the metaphor for everything he had expressed before. It enabled him to state the conclusion for which his long, tortuous path had prepared him:

Black Power in these black islands is protest. But there is no enemy. The enemy is the past, of slavery and colonial neglect and a society uneducated from top to bottom; the enemy is the smallness of the islands and the absence of resources. Opportunism or borrowed jargon may define phantom enemies: racial minorities, elites, "white niggers." But at the end the problems will be the same, of dignity and identity.

In the United States Black Power may have its victories. But they will be American victories. The small islands of the Caribbean will remain islands, impoverished and unskilled, ringed as now by a *cordon sanitaire*, their people not needed anywhere. They may get less innocent or less corrupt politicians; they will not get less helpless ones. The island blacks will continue to be dependent on the books, films and goods of others; in this important way they will continue to be the half-made societies of a dependent people, the Third World's third world. They will forever consume; they will never create. They are without material resources; they will never develop the higher skills. Identity depends in the end on achievement; and achievement here cannot but be small. Again and again the protest leader will appear and the millennium will seem about to come. (*OB*, 271–72)[25]

In this statement, all history, culture, and colonized life are subsumed to a simple formula and the "real, active lives" of millions of people summarily dismissed to eternal damnation. A position that was first enumerated in "A Flag on the Island" and stated and restated in *The Mimic Men* and *The Loss of El Dorado* is brought to a culmination in this essay. Even the notion of "achievement" and "creation," first raised in *The Middle Passage* and which, to quote Bhabha, was a vivid indication of "the complete success of the colonialist values and of the complete despair of the colonized,"[26] is given one last hurrah. "Power?" is the final summing up and entrance into the society of the apocalyptic vision most fully articulated in *Guerrillas*.

All the evidence Naipaul gathered throughout the 1960s led him to the inescapable conclusion that Trinidad and all the islands are "condemned, not necessarily as individuals, but as a community, to an inferiority of skill and achievement" (*OB,* 274). To release themselves from such condemnation, the people need "access to a society, larger in every sense, where people will be allowed to grow" (*OB,* 274) and to mix themselves with the "larger world." Without this option, the society is destined to remain as it always has been:

manufactured societies, labour camps, creations of empire; and for long they were dependent on empire for law, language, institutions, culture, even officials. Nothing was generated locally; dependence became a habit. How, without empire, do such societies govern themselves? What is now the source of power? The ballot box, the mob, the regiment? When, as in Haiti, the slave-owners leave, and there are only slaves, what are the sanctions? (*OB,* 275)

Thirteen years later, in October 1983, seventeen days after the United States invaded Grenada, Naipaul swooped down on the island to continue his observations of mimicry and the black fantasy of Caribbean peoples. It did not bother him that he had uttered the same words in other contexts. The Grenada Revolution, a direct outgrowth of the black power movement of the 1960s, according to Naipaul, was "an imposition," the use of "people's speech" to make all of the activity of the revolution "appear carnival-like and Grenadian and black."[27] To him, the Grenada Revolution was nothing more than "socialist mimicry . . . proof of the naturalness and rightness of the cause. . . . Socialism absorbed the racial idea, purified, did away with the corruption inherent in it. Socialism, doing away with the racial issue, left men free to be men" ("IB," 63, 69). Socialism, then, was just another form of black fantasy, "a reawakening of old racial anxiety" that was taking place in one of the small, remote corners of the world, just another joke to the "real socialist, the people of the great world outside" ("IB," 70).

The Grenada Revolution, then, was just another variation of the theme of "black redemption." Both Eric Gairy, the former prime minister of Grenada, and Maurice Bishop, the slain prime minister of the revolution, offered "the vision . . . of sudden racial redemption" ("IB," 68). The revolution was nothing more than "big new words" to explain "old attitudes" ("IB," 68, 70). It depended on language and thus, "at one level it used big, blurring words; at another, it misused the language of the people" ("IB," 72). Thus, "the revolution was a revolution of words. The words had appeared as an illumination, a shortcut to dignity, to newly educated men who had nothing in the community to measure themselves against and who, finally, valued little in their own community. But the words were mimicry. They were too big; they didn't fit; they remained words" ("IB," 72).

As Chris Searle demonstrated, Naipaul's report turns out to be nothing but lies.[28] Like most enemies of the Grenada Revolution, Naipaul arrived in Grenada with many preconceived ideas about what caused the failure of the revolution. Unlike the fifty or so leading Caribbean cultural figures who visited Grenada in 1962 (among whom were writers such as George Lamming, Martin Carter, and Earl Lovelace) while the revolution was in progress and pledged solidarity with the revolution, Naipaul, according to Searle, went to Grenada on "a mission of solidarity with the imperialist media network that had systematically lied about and libelled the Grenada Revolution for four and a half years."[29]

Given his solidarity with imperialism, Naipaul could not see that the revolution, by attempting to change the material basis of the society, had also "extend[ed] the language resources"[30] of the society; it found new ways to use words, and, through the struggle for liberation, opened up new possibilities for the language. As Searle noted, Naipaul did recognize that something had happened to the language during the years of the revolution. But, "obsessed with the death of the Revolution, he refused to acknowledge its life. He sees words in a vacuum, words without achievement, without practice, without production, without progress." What Naipaul could not see is that "there is a dialectic between language, work and material progress and they move in and out of each other as they advance as a part of the same process, whether that means more fields under the hoe, more agro-industrial plants, increased electrification, more new schools or an eye clinic."[31] As the revolution became more a part of the people, the language of the people broke out of the old dysfunctional mold that retained all of the values of the decadent colonial-capitalist culture.

Naipaul has not moved very far, either in content or in style, from *The Middle Passage,* in which he asked: "How can the history of this West Indian futility be written? What tone shall the historian adopt? . . . The history of the islands can never be satisfactorily told. Brutality is not the only difficulty. History is built around achievement and creation; and nothing was created in the West Indies" (*MP*, 28–29). Because his ideas were taken from James Anthony Froude and other British historians, Naipaul is entrapped by the same perception of Caribbean realities as he was in 1960. The settings and events have changed, but his conclusions remain the same.

Fame, time, and cynicism made Naipaul harsher in his judgments. Rather than simply asking questions about Caribbean society, he condemned it. As he says at the end of "Power?", "With or without Black Power, chaos threatened. But chaos will be only internal. The islands will always be subjected to external police. . . . These islands, black and poor, are dangerous only to themselves" (*OB*, 275). Such condemnation, indicative of the changed satire of his work, indicates his further distance from the truth of his society and his deeper entrenchment in his ideological method for interpreting history. The distortion of his vision grows ever more intense.

Naipaul is not, however, without insights into colonial society. He sees the specific problematic of mimicry as characteristic of the colonial condition (or the colonial subject) at the early stages of independence. He is correct to suggest that intense mimicry occurs during the phase of transformation from colonialism to independence, particularly when independence is granted without violent confrontation.

Many Caribbean and Third World scholars have not looked at or clearly delineated the manner in which the colonized subject functions, or ought to function, in the age of independence. To be sure, many grandiose and important economic and political strategies are designed to enhance the social and cultural development of the newly freed colonized person, but the specific manner by which this "new person" ought to be reconstituted in the new social order has not been examined. This limitation occurs in many cases because of the exigencies of the historical situation rather than callousness or indifference on the part of political leaders. During the independence era, people were more concerned with freeing the population from foreign control than with the specific function of the colonized subject in the social totality. As such, the society tended to emphasize the problems of the masses of the oppressed rather than those of the individual subject, and most plans and programs revolved around material rather than spiritual well-being.[32]

Thus, although the material conditions of the colonial society prevented an examination of the specific problems of the individual subject, Naipaul did ask, What does it mean to be an autonomous subject in a free state? Critical insight into the process of our social development, though fraught with limitations, should shed some light on this aspect of social relations in newly independent societies.

Posing the question was an important first step. But because Naipaul accredited no value to the unofficial culture of the folk, he could not structure the question comprehensively. The constraints on Naipaul's ideological approach to the historical evolution and present condition of colonial reality prevented him from offering an authentic, liberating response.

The colonized subject, like any other, is a product of his history. His real-life activities are structured by certain practices that give meaning to his life. For the colonized subject, a product of slavery and colonial violence, meaning always issues forth from the unofficial culture, which, as Amilcar Cabral and other Third World scholars understand, gave colonized peoples the strength to withstand the cruelties of slavery and colonialism.[33] It is therefore to the integrity of the unofficial culture that we must return in order to restructure and reconstitute the autonomy of colonial people in the age of independence.

When independence is not achieved through a violent struggle, the question of individual autonomy takes on a different hue and mimicry becomes more important. The need to define the "social I" induces a comparison with the "other," and, as Naipaul proposed for a limited time, the phenomenon of mimicry becomes intensified, particularly for the society's petit-bourgeois elements, who became government leaders at the moment of independence. Where, as in the case of Trinidad, the colonizer's culture made many inroads into the unofficial culture, especially via the media, mimicry penetrates into many of the social activities of the people. Given the intensity of capitalist exploitation, such tendencies can drive the culture to vulgarity.

The mimicry on which Naipaul anchors his case ought not to be seen as a one-sided process, however. Errol Hill has pointed out that during the early carnival celebrations the masters took the place of the slaves, mimicked them, and required the slaves to whip them. Such reverse mimicry continued until as late as 1894.[34] It would seem, therefore, that the autonomy of the social self required both the colonizer and the colonized to recognize the importance of the other, particularly at the important moment of separation.

Although the subject is essentially the product of his colonized past, he is also contingently the product of the colonizer's culture. His subjectivity, therefore, can only be understood as receiving its essence from the unofficial culture of his people and its contingent qualities from the creative borrowing (what Naipaul calls mimicry) and the sum total of all human culture which others throughout the long history of social development have created. The latter, of course, is the patrimony of all persons.

In expressing this relation, Hegel observed that "self-consciousness exists in itself and for itself, in that, and by the fact that it exists for another self-consciousness; that is to say, it *is* only by being acknowledged or 'recognized.' "[35] Thus, although the slave and the master exist in an antagonistic relationship in colonial society, both measure themselves (that is, their subjectivity) in contrast to each other. Because history has so decreed, there is no way the former slave can know himself (that is, his own subjectivity) on the eve of independence without some referent to the master—the "other"—and his culture. Therefore, for the colonized person to establish his own unique identification in the aftermath of independence, identification with the master is absolutely necessary.

To be sure, Naipaul does not make this point explicitly. Nor does he recognize the implications of his insights, as evidenced by his derisive and derogatory portrayal of the colonized person. In fact, Naipaul's ideology prevents him from seeing the contradictions. Yet, because he recognized and chronicled the condition of mimicry as an important moment in the transformation from colonialism to independence, he made an invaluable contribution to the literature of colonial and postcolonial societies. In so doing, he has helped us further our understanding of the complexities that occur in one's subjectivity as one's society moves from colonialism to postcolonialism. Undoubtedly, as Naipaul's texts suggest, a new discourse is needed to examine the problematics of this condition.

Because Naipaul was concerned only with the negative aspects of this condition, he was unable to take his insights to a more complex level. Consequently, an apocalyptic gloom and the notion that there can be no escape from stasis and mimicry characterize most of his work after this period. That Naipaul was able to focus on this important question of the social development of colonized man and to provide a mirror in which his society could see its own undifferentiated *imago* is the most significant aspect of his work during this period. That he was unable to take his insights to the next level proves to be the shortcoming of his literary development and marks the end of the most significant part of his career as a novelist.

7. The Postcolonial Society and the Individual Subject: The Third Period of Naipaul's Development

For a time, I stood there thinking most of the living who, buried in remote places out of the knowledge of mankind, still fated to share in its tragic or grotesque miseries. In its noble struggles, too—who knows? The human heart is vast enough to contain all the world. It is valiant enough to bear the burden, but where is the courage that would cast it off.
—Joseph Conrad, *Lord Jim*

Consciousness finds itself inevitably facing the necessity of *having to choose a language*. With each literary-verbal performance, consciousness must actively orient itself amidst heteroglossia, it must move in and occupy a position for itself within it, it chooses, in other words, a "language." Only by remaining in a closed environment, one without writing or thought, completely cut off the maps of socio-ideological becoming, could a man fail to sense this activity of selecting a language and rest assured in the inviolability of his own language, the conviction that his language is predetermined.
—Mikhail Bakhtin, *The Dialogic Imagination*

THE SECOND SYNCHRONIC BREAK

In a Free State (1971) brings us to the third and most recent phase of Naipaul's literary development, a phase characterized by brilliant craftsmanship but also repetition of much he had said in his earlier work. Although his later texts bridge the formal gap between his Eastern and Western modes of apprehending and expressing his social reality, Naipaul clearly not only moved closer to accepting the latter view of life but was unable to break his incestuous relationship with the mother country. Thus, apart from accepting the ideological assumptions of the dominant colonial powers about former colonial peoples, he also reflects the sense of pessimism and gloom that characterizes the worst aspects of bourgeois life and aesthetics.

What is particularly distinctive about this phase of Naipaul's development is the deep sense of hysteria generated by his inability to understand the nature of social transformation taking place in Third World societies and his profound alienation and distance from them. As a result, the wholesomeness that permeated the world of his earlier work, even though the world he described was beginning to disintegrate, is not found in the last phase of his work. At this point, his world has become eclectic, fragmented, and bereft of the organic plentitude and richness of the earlier phases. Even the sense of wonder that he posits as the raison d'être of the novel is absent.

Thus the cultural comprehensiveness that informs *A House for Mr. Biswas* and the psychoanalytic awareness and introspection of *The Mimic Men* are lacking in *Guerrillas*. Indeed, the semantic openness characteristic of Naipaul's earlier period is not found in his latest texts. The novels and novellas recoil into themselves and become self-sufficient entities devoid of any particular historical context. When they do open up to the society, they reveal an emptiness and hopelessness inconsistent with the constitutive nature of the novel.

Closely related to the sense of isolation, Naipaul's texts of the late period lack the seriocomical elements that gave richness and freshness—the sense of wonder—to his earlier work. This absence can be accounted for only by Naipaul's distance from Trinidadian society, which led to his cynicism and hopelessness. As Bakhtin correctly argued: "As a distanced image a subject cannot be comical; to be made comical it must be brought close. Everything that makes us laugh is close at hand, all comical creativity works in a zone of maximal proximity."[1] Undoubtedly, Naipaul's estrangement from his society prevented him from realistically depicting its development in that period.

This distance and estrangement led Naipaul to render his society in a naturalistic manner and prevented him from capturing the psychic trauma and emotional development experienced by the newly freed subjects or recognizing the human psyche as a specific social entity that is reorganized and reconstituted into a more specific unity in historical time. In fact, Naipaul's inability to readjust his apprehension of colonial reality led him to an apocalyptic interpretation of history which saw only hopelessness in the aspirations of colonial and postcolonial peoples. Edward Schillebeeckx has argued,

The basic substance of apocalypticism bears the stamp of a long experience of human life, an experience which has ceased to look to a man's history for any improvement. Suffering and every kind of misfortune, whether individual or national, are so persistent that one has to postulate at the source of mankind's history a

Fall of the first man, which then rolls through history like a snowball. . . . It is no longer possible, therefore, to hope for any final good from our human history.[2]

Naipaul's apocalypticism differs somewhat from the traditional form in which the intervention of God is seen as the only means of salvation and *metanoia* (repentance and conversion) as the prerequisite for salvation. In the apocalyptic context, "expectation of the End and the call to *metanoia* go hand in hand" and the concept of *paraenesis* or moral uplift, which allows men and women to endure during the period of apocalypticism, is also present. Naipaul, in his wrath, allows neither *metanoia* nor *paraenesis* for Third World peoples. They are without hope, and nothing can prevent their doom. It is this obsessive aspect of his work that heralds the apocalyptic vision. As Schillebeeckx notes, the experience of apocalypticism is "existential and realistic, even 'modern.' "[3] It is this contemporary dimension of the experience that Naipaul's work reflects so well.

As we observe the apocalyptic gloom and absolute hysteria in Naipaul's later work, it becomes clear that he is unable to move beyond the manipulation of imposed binary ethical oppositions to a dialectical interpretation of postcolonial reality. Moreover, his inability to change the conceptual framework on which his analysis is based leads to a kind of banality: a prose that evinces a brilliant sense of craftsmanship even though the content of the social reality he examines is narrowly circumscribed.

In this changed "text" created by postcolonial reality, the question of language and the motivation of the "revolutionary subject" also come under intense scrutiny. But although Naipaul interprets language as largely the mimicry and repetition of metropolitan utterances, a more rigorous examination suggests that the language of postcolonial liberated subjects is closely bound up with their struggle for social and political transformation and, more specifically, with the nature of structural transformation itself.

Mikhail Bakhtin, in his "Discourse in the Novel," has argued that language becomes a victim of the onslaught of the transformations that take place in any society and assumes new meanings in the process. As he pointed out, the living language that takes its meaning and shape from a particular historical moment within a specific social environment "cannot fail to brush up against thousands of living dialogic threads, woven by socio-ideological consciousness around the given object of an utterance; it cannot fail to become an active participant in social dialogue." It is from this dialogue that language continues to grow and develop:

As a living, socio-ideological concrete thing, as heteroglot opinion, language, for the individual consciousness, lies on the borderline between oneself and the other.

The word in language is half someone else's. It becomes "one's own" only when the speaker populates it with his own intention, his own accent, when he appropriates the word, adapting it to his own semantic and expressive intention. Prior to this moment of appropriation, the word does not exist in a neutral and impersonal language (it is not, after all, out of the dictionary that the speaker gets his words!), but, rather it exists in other people's mouths, in other people's contexts, serving other people's intentions: it is from there that one must take the word, and make it one's own.[4]

Against this background we can begin to see the dichotomy in Naipaul's analysis of postcolonial reality. He can see only how language "uses" the colonized person rather than how the newly freed subjects use and expand language as they live their new reality and realize themselves through their language.[5] It is clear that because Naipaul understood only the first level at which language operates he was unable to appreciate the new subject's struggle to appropriate language and to shape it to his contemporary needs. Indeed, as Chris Searle has stated in talking about the Grenada Revolution, "Cracking apart the contradictions of language itself . . . decolonising and demystifying [it and] . . . tear[ing] out all those expressions, images and deformities within the coloniser's language that only appeared to legitimise racism, mimicry, dependence and other colonial complexes that gave to the people a fear of themselves" became the indispensable tasks of the revolution.[6] The postcolonial experience is a process in which the people appropriate language and use it for new and expanded purposes.

There is yet another dimension of language in the postcolonial experience that Naipaul misses. In his work on language development during the Grenada Revolution, Searle notes that apart from overturning the political and economic structures of the old colonial society, the revolution was faced with the problem of overthrowing the "colonising language," which had become an institution in itself. The postrevolutionary society therefore had to transform language from a "private means of communication between individuals" to "an organised form of connection and synthesis, whereby previously unconfident and sometimes reticent people" began to speak out openly in an effort to take their country forward collectively.[7] In that context, language was perceived as the fundamental guarantee of popular, participatory political democracy.

It is within this context that Lawrence Carrington, one of the foremost linguists in the Caribbean, distinguished between "languaging" and "communicating" during the colonial era. During that latter period language was seen as a barrier to communication in that it assumed a certain class content. The colonizer spoke in a particular manner whereas the colonized spoke in another. As Carrington pointed out, during that period, it was presumed that a person who spoke standard English "had to be talking sense," whereas someone who spoke in Creole, the language of the people, had "to be talking 'stupidness.' "[8] The first task of the revolution was to free the language of such class biases.

I do not mean to suggest that one cannot learn anything from the language and culture of the colonizer. Amilcar Cabral, in a very insightful essay on people's revolutionary culture, recognized that in the construction of a new language, although the revolution borrows from the "positive accretions from the oppressor and other cultures," the road toward genuine liberation leads a society back to the "upward paths of their own culture, which is nourished by the living reality of its environment, and which negates both harmful influences and any kind of subjection to foreign culture." Mikey Smith, the Jamaican dub poet who was killed in 1983, stated the matter in the following way: "Me really believe seh you have fi learn the ABC of Babylon fi destroy them. So you know you haffi really have a sense of awareness of what's happening around, so you can explain to people wha a gwaan."[9]

Thus, although Naipaul examined the individual subject *within* the context of his history and culture during the first two stages of his development, he examined the individual subject *outside* that context during the last phase. Naipaul examined the postcolonial subject as though he were a fragmentary and isolated entity bereft of organic interconnectedness with his society, as though he could extract no positive accretions from the oppressor's culture. Indeed, Ganesh, Harbans, Mr. Biswas, and Ralph Singh had an organic unity within their communities that gave them a sense of meaning from which they derived their tone, resonance, and raison d'être.

The same cannot be said for Santosh ("One out of Many"), Frank and Dayo ("Tell Me Who to Kill"), Jimmy Ahmed (*Guerrillas*), or Salim (*A Bend in the River*). They all exist outside, or on the periphery, of the society in which they are examined and seem to be only a collection of social attributes and speech types who function merely as vehicles through which Naipaul imposes his already established judgments. As a result, these characters are *individual subjects* rather than *transindividualized historical* subjects of a new society.

Finally, in the late period, Naipaul began to draw upon the example of Joseph Conrad, who Naipaul argued covered much of the same ground he did. In fact, much of Naipaul's description of the function of the novel, particularly in "Conrad's Darkness," is taken from Conrad's 1897 preface to *The Nigger of the Narcissus.* He shared with Conrad the feeling of the immigrant who attempts to divest himself of his culture so that he can acquire the culture of the other. They may even have shared the same guilt at having betrayed their country, a position Naipaul seems to have reflected most explicitly in the hysteria of *Guerrillas.* [10]

Increasingly, Naipaul seemed overtaken by Conrad's preoccupations: the seeming lack of imagination of the colonial subject, the dependent nature of the primitive psyche, and the depiction of the white man as the bearer of all light and knowledge. In fact, Naipaul empathizes so much with Conrad that one wonders whether he may have created "a public personality . . . to camouflage his deeper and more problematic difficulties with himself and his work." [11] Certainly his many references to his ignorance about the meaning of his work, the nature of his identity, and his problematic relationship with the country of his birth may attest to the same difficulties Conrad confronted.

IN A FREE STATE

The process of examining the individual colonial subject outside the context of his sociohistorical reality begins with *In a Free State,* in which three short stories are enclosed by a personal prologue and epilogue. Because Naipaul employs style to answer a genuine aesthetic problem at the concrete level of his work, the ambiguity in *In a Free State* reflects the problems he faced at this moment of his development. Linda Anderson, in a perceptive article on some similarities and differences between Naipaul and Conrad, argued that the characters in their work are "depicted as solitary subjectivities in the sense that they are conscious of their separation from the surroundings in which they find themselves placed. Far from being able to accommodate themselves to their societies, they experience these as the hostile environments to which their authentic identity is perpetually opposed. The discovery of a social role does not coincide, therefore, with a discovery of self, rather it implies the adoption and maintenance of a mask." [12]

Thus, though Naipaul announced that *In a Free State* was "a rather final statement" on his vision of placelessness, lingering doubts remained about whether he could define the "place" and nature of the postcolonial subject given his distance from and unsympathetic attitude toward that subject and whether he could "create" rather than "make" a novel that would examine the complexities of what it means to be a liberated colonial subject. [13] And even though he anticipated the problem of the postcolonial subject in *The Mimic Men,* by 1971 events had so far outstripped him that he could not answer the question satisfactorily. By 1975, when he wrote *Guerrillas,* most of these complex problems were outside his ken.

It is not inconsistent, then, that of the three stories in *In a Free State,* two ("One out of Many" and "Tell Me Who to Kill") are set outside the colonized society, and the major story, "In a Free State," examines the activity of a member of the dominant colonial group within the colonial society. Because Naipaul could not locate the problematic of the liberated colonial subject within the real, concrete history of the colonial society, he was unable to carry forward the dialectic he began in the first two stages of his work. Most of the texts of this period, therefore, couched as they are in caricatured forms, grant us only stereotypical responses to the conditions of the subject in postcolonial societies. Moreover, because Naipaul so fully accepted the tenets of the dominant imperialist culture, he was unable to move beyond the strictures imposed by these "superior" societies and cultures.

"ONE OUT OF MANY"

"One out of Many," an intensely racist story, is as much an examination of the liberation of the colonized subject within the context of a "free" society as it is an indictment of the activities of the *hubshi* (the blacks in the United States).[14] Indeed, although the problems of the liberation of Santosh, the protagonist, are the apparent subject of the text, the narrative reiterates the stereotypic pictures of blacks Naipaul expressed in *The Middle Passage, The Mimic Men,* and *The Overcrowded Barracoon.* Santosh's emerging sense of liberation is sketched against the background of the *hubshi,* who are lost and live in a world of make-believe.[15] The pattern of symbols that Naipaul established in his earlier fiction is changed somewhat in this text. Whereas in the earlier period the country areas and the city symbolized feudalism and capitalism respectively, in this phase the hills and the colonial territory symbolize backwardness and the illusion of liberty, and metropolitan imperialist centers the notions of progress and freedom. Naipaul seems to support the political link between these two notions when he acknowledges that Santosh's view of the world is very much "the immigrant's view of the capital of the world, the view of a man from another, enclosed culture, rather like my own of London, twenty years ago."[16]

When the story opens, Santosh is faced with the choice of returning to his village in the hills, to his wife and children "not just for a holiday but for good" (*IFS*, 26) or persuading his employer to take him to Washington, D.C., to take up a new post. In Washington, Santosh becomes aware of his own "self" and gradually realizes that he can become a "liberated" subject. As he reminisces about his life, he acknowledges:

Once my employer had been to me only a presence. I used to tell him then that beside him I was as dirt. It was only a way of talking, one of the courtesies of our language, but it had something of truth. I meant that he was the man who adventured in the world for me, that I experienced the world through him, that I was content to be a small part of his presence. I was content, sleeping on the Bombay pavement with my friends, to hear the talk of my employer and his guests upstairs. I was more than content, late at night, to be identified among the sleepers and greeted by some of those guests before they drove away. (*IFS*, 40–41)

The colonial relationship between master and servant and the sense of dependency and nonidentity are shattered when Santosh is exposed to the ideas inherent "in a free state." In Washington, Santosh breaks "faith" with that dependent relationship and opts to establish an independent presence and changed set of social relations with his employer. In the process, he recognizes his subjective consciousness, the "I" of his existence, and abandons his relationship of dependency. Such a condition of liberation, however, is analogous to that of the colonial condition, which was characterized by a sense of excitement and promise during the early days of formal independence.[17]

Santosh's liberation is analogous to that of the colonized territories in that it does not result from any well-planned strategy on his part but from the capricious hand of Lady Luck (or the mother country). Thus Santosh could say: "The victory I had was not something I had worked for, but luck; and that luck was only fate's cheating, giving an illusion of power" (*IFS*, 55–56). This "illusion of power" engaged Naipaul's interest in this phase of his development.

The fortuitous manner in which independence was achieved meant that once the colonial master abandoned the colonies, only gloom and doom could follow. Santosh personifies that lost condition:

Walking, through streets that were now so simple to me, I thought how nice it would be if the people in Hindu costumes in the circle were real. Then I might have joined them. We would have taken to the road; at midday we would have halted in the shade of big trees; in the late afternoon the sinking sun would have turned the dust clouds to gold; and every evening at some village there would have been welcome, water, food, a fire in the night. But that was a dream of another life. I had watched the people in the circle long enough to know that they were of their city; that their television life awaited them; that their renunciation was not like mine. No television life awaited me. It didn't matter. In this city I was alone and it didn't matter what I did. (*IFS*, 59–60)

Despite the obvious nostalgia for home, the political truth remains. Having attained freedom, Santosh is unable to use its essential qualities in a meaningful or productive way. Abandoned and alone, he can feel only loneliness, placelessness, and void.

For Santosh, then, freedom offers nothing substantively different from his previous condition except an illusion and a sense of alienation. His alienation and loss, however, become revulsion at being separated from the master and the dominant culture rather than separation from his own essence. More important, because his liberation "in a free state," as it were, is posited within the context of an isolated individual subject away from the shared social relations of a community, it becomes a meaningless and deceptive act. Thus the story ends on a note of despair:

I am a simple man who decided to act and see for himself, and it is as though I have had several lives. I do not wish to add to these. Some afternoons I walk to the circle with the fountain. I see the dancers but they are separated from me as by glass. Once, when there were rumours of new burnings, someone scrawled in white paint on the pavement outside my house: *Soul Brother*. I understand the words; but I feel, brother to what or to whom? I was once part of the flow, never thinking of myself as a presence. Then I looked in the mirror and decided to be free. All that my freedom has brought me is the knowledge that I have a face and have a body, that I must feed this body and clothe this body for a certain number of years. Then it will be over. (*IFS*, 61)

The liberation of the colonized subject is reduced to the mere fulfillment of his physical needs. As such, it becomes meaningless.

Yet there are two last reveries in the story that serve as a final farewell to the world of *A House for Mr. Biswas* and an anticipation of the attitudes that would prevail in the society of *A Bend in the River*. The allegoric scene in *A House for Mr. Biswas* in which Mr. Biswas, after his wedding, returns to his mother's house for sanctuary from the stifling influence of Hanuman House is displaced by Santosh's reminiscence (or wish-fulfillment) of a time when he had an organic relationship with his social environment, when life was much simpler and more meaningful. Such a time and place (of *home* and *security*, as Mr. Biswas's return to his mother's house suggested) is no longer possible at the end of "One out of Many."

But the alternative that the narrative suggests, that of renouncing one's past, is almost as impossible. One gets a sense of this position when, early in the story, Priya pleads: " 'Ah, Santosh, why do we do it? Why don't we renounce and go and meditate on the river-bank?' He waved about the room [with its good luck objects]. 'The yemblems of the world, Santosh. Just yemblems' " (*IFS*, 46). Because of Santosh's isolation and displacement, he cannot be considered paradigmatic of the postcolonial condition. And, most assuredly, he cannot be considered *the* "one out of many."

"TELL ME WHO TO KILL"

The sense of loss and hopelessness is almost the same in "Tell Me Who to Kill" as in "One out of Many," except that Frank, the major protagonist in "Tell Me Who to Kill," accepts his fate less helplessly than Santosh does. If only Frank could find the person responsible for his condition, all might not be so hopeless. The feeling of helplessness and loss are apparent at the beginning of the story. According to Frank, a postcolonial subject who is adrift in London, "Since I come to this country that is something I can't do. I can't see where I am going. I can only wait to see what is going to turn up" (*IFS*, 66).

For Frank, the problem is obvious. Despite all his best endeavors, everything goes wrong. Worse, he cannot explain why. Someone or something must be responsible for the wreck he has made (or that has been made) of his life. Yet he faces the quandary of quandaries: Who is the enemy? He does not know, and, like Santosh, he has no home to which to return:

But what I see in my mind [about my home] is in no place at all. Everything blot out except the rain and night coming and the house and the mud and the field and the donkey and the smoke from the kitchen and my father in the gallery and my brother in the room on the floor.

And it is as though because you are frightened of something it is bound to come, as though because you are carrying danger with you danger is bound to come. (*IFS*, 68)

He is equally lost in London. He has no place to go and sees his life finished: "The life is over. I am like a man who is giving up. I come with nothing, I have nothing, I will leave with nothing" (*IFS*, 101). Dayo, his brother, the source of much of his trouble and in whom he has poured all his love and hopes, is equally lost. A "tired, foolish boy," he possesses "the face of someone lost" (*IFS*, 100).

This emptiness and gloom are not far from the apocalypticism at the end of "One out of Many":

I used to think of him going back to the basement that day and finding nobody there, and nobody coming home; and I used to think of that as the end of the world. But he do better without me; he don't need me. I lose him. I can't see the sort of life he get into, I can't see the people he is going to mix with now. Sometimes I think of him as a stranger, different from the man I did know. Sometimes I see him as he was, and feel that he is alone, like me. . . .

All kinds of rubbish on top of the flat roofs over projecting back rooms, and sometimes a little plant in a pot inside, behind windows running with wet and steam. Everybody on his shelf, in his little place. But a man can leave everything, a man can just disappear. Somebody will come after him to clean up and clear away, and that new person will settle down there until his own time come. (*IFS*, 103)

Likewise, gloom and hopelessness accompany Dayo's wedding:

A taxi stop. It is my brother. He have a thin white boy with him, and the two of them in suits. Taxi today, wedding day. No turban, no procession, no drums, no ceremony of welcome, no green arches, no lights in the wedding tent, no wedding songs. Just the taxi, the thin white boy with sharp shoes and short hair, smoking, and my brother with a white rose in his jacket. He is just the same. The ugly labourer's face, and he is talking to his friend, showing everybody he is very cool. I don't know why I did think he would get different in three years. (*IFS*, 105)

The terrain is the same as in *A House for Mr. Biswas* and "One out of Many." With allegoric abundance, the author takes us from the obsolescence of the past to the hopelessness of the present. The welcome Mr. Biswas received in *A House for Mr. Biswas* and the nostalgia Santosh seems to feel in "One out of Many" are not present in "Tell Me Who to Kill." The world is but a remembrance of the past. It is no more. It is simply one of loss and denial.[18] Thus the wedding, which is supposed to be a celebration of life and nuptial bliss, is depicted in terms of death and denial of life:

I looked down, I do what Frank do, and all the time the taste is in my mouth. I don't look at my brother and the girl until it is all over. Then I see this girl in white, with her veil and flowers, like somebody dead, and her face is blank and broad and very white, the little make-up shining on cheeks and temples like wax. She is a stranger. I don't know how my brother allow himself to do this thing. It is not right. *He is a lost man here.* You can see it on everybody's face except the girl's. (*IFS*, 106; emphasis added)

When Frank bids Dayo farewell as he leaves for his honeymoon, he knows that his end is inevitable. He sends a message back home saying that he is dead: "And for all this time I am a dead man" (*IFS*, 107).

And so, like Santosh's, the life of a colonial subject is one of pointlessness and emptiness. Frank's inability to come to terms with his life, to structure his life independent of his brother's or the colonizer's, means it can never be meaningful. Like Santosh, Frank is alone and lost and completely bewildered in his new state of social development. The notion that there is some inscrutable force with which the colonized person must contend but which he does not quite know or understand is as persuasive in this work as in "One out of Many."

Correspondingly, Frank's condition is analogous to that of the colonial. In speaking about the colonizers, Frank argues:

I love them. They take my money, they spoil my life, they separate us. But you can't kill them. O God, show me the enemy. Once you find out who the enemy is, you can kill him. But these people here they confuse me. Who hurt me? Who spoil my life? Tell me who to beat back. I work four years to save my money, I work like a donkey night and day. My brother was to be the educated one, the nice one. And this is how it is ending, in this room, eating with these people. Tell me who to kill. (*IFS*, 107)

Who, indeed, is the enemy? For Naipaul, the enemy is beyond comprehension. As in "One out of Many," Naipaul structures "Tell Me Who to Kill" in such a way that he is unable to pose the question of the postcolonial dilemma: that is, what strategies can the postcolonial subject use to extricate himself from the discourses and practices of the colonialist-imperialist world? In "Tell Me Who to Kill" and "One out of Many," these strategies are beyond the intellectual and rational grasp of the postcolonial subject and certainly impossible to structure outside the social context of his world.

"IN A FREE STATE"

In "In a Free State" Naipaul makes his first creative venture into the African world. But although the central action of the story moves away from Washington and London, the setting remains virtually the same. The story is set in "an English-Indian creation in the African wilderness. It owed nothing to African skill; it required none. Not far from the capital were bush villages, half-day excursions for tourists" (*IFS*, 111). The Americans supported everything in that part of Africa, so it is simply an English-speaking outpost in the midst of the African wilderness.

In this newly liberated state, where there were only blacks and whites (no Asians),

the Africans were young, in their twenties, and plump. They could read and write, and were high civil servants, politicians or the relations of politicians, non-executive directors and managing directors of recently opened branches of big international corporations. They were the new men of the country and they saw themselves as men of power. They hadn't paid for the suits they wore; in some cases they had had the drapers deported. They came to the New Sharopshire to be seen and noted by white people, however transient; to be courted; to make trouble. There were no Asiatics in the bar: the liberations it offered were only for black and white. (*IFS*, 112)

These Africans are a new variation of the mimic men. They create nothing and possess no identity independent of that of their white benefactors. Like the characters of "One out of Many" and "Tell Me Who to Kill," the Africans in this story are the products of white civilization, incapable of independent thought or economic activity. They are the parasitical elements par excellence of the twentieth century.

It is in this setting that Bobby, an English homosexual, and Linda, a "man-killer," are placed to work out their problems of identity and to discover their purposes in life. The central theme, however, revolves not around Bobby and Linda but around the "nihilism" of Africa, which Naipaul described candidly in "A New King for the Congo: Mobutu and the Nihilism of Africa." Bobby's depiction of Africa is as debilitating and animalistic as Santosh's of the *hubshi* of Washington, D.C.:

Africa was for Bobby the empty spaces, the safe adventure of long fatiguing drives on open roads, the other Africans, boys built like men. "You want lift. You big boy, you no go school? No, no, you no frighten. Look, I give you shilling. You hold my hand. Look, my colour, your colour. I give you shilling buy schoolbooks. Buy books, learn read, get big job. When I born again I want your colour. You no frighten. You want five shillings?" Sweet infantilism, almost without language: in language lay mockery and self-disgust. (*IFS*, 117)

In all three stories, the blacks remain in a state of "sweet infantilism," without language and without basic intelligence. If spoken to harshly, they forget their petulance and childishness. Such a depiction of the blacks in Africa and the United States can be seen as the continuation of the response that began in *The Middle Passage*, although a certain honesty seems to characterize the latter, whereas only a deep sense of cynicism attends the former.

In this story, the identification of Africans with the bush is reiterated and reemphasized. They are depicted as coming out from the bush, a situation from which seventy years of colonialism did not entirely relieve them. They swear their oaths, eat excrement, and "hold hands and dance naked in the dark" (*IFS*, 130). Of course, such primitive behavior also occurs in *The Loss of El Dorado*. Here, however, it is presented as the general condition of all colonial peoples in postcolonial societies.

Later in the text, the people are described as being "barbaric," "savage," "without dignity," "smelling," extremely stupid, and as inauthentic people who pretend to be civilized: "They're close enough. Somewhere up there they've taken off their nice new clothes and they're dancing naked and holding hands and eating dung. The president probably sent them a nice piece of dung. You could disappear here without trace. You know what happened on the other side, don't you? The rivers ran red. But that again is something that never happened" (*IFS*, 173). And although Bobby and Linda consider themselves "white and neutral," the savages are seen as diabolical and debased.

Despite Naipaul's banal attitude toward these Africans, it is the stupidity of Peter and his relationship with the colonel that reiterates the colonial encounter in "One out of Many" and "Tell Me Who to Kill" and that holds these seemingly disparate stories together:

"What do you think of me, Peter?"
"I like you, sir."
"He likes me. Peter likes me."
"You take me in when I was small. You give me job, you give me quarters. You look after my children."
"He has fourteen. He's living with three of those animals right now. So polished. So nice. So well-spoken. You wouldn't believe he doesn't even know how to hold a pen in those hands. You wouldn't believe the filth he comes out of. But you like dirt, don't you, Peter? You like going in to some black hole to eat filth and dance naked. You will steal and lie to do that, won't you?"
"I like the quarters, sir."
"While I live you will stay there. You won't move in here, Peter. I don't want you to bank on that. If I die you will starve, Peter. You will go back to bush. (*IFS*, 189–90)

This threat to have the natives return to the bush and to oblivion when the master is gone and the absolute stupidity of the blacks become the dominant themes of the third phase of Naipaul's work. The bush becomes a metaphor for the backwardness and stupidity of all colonial peoples, a theme that is elaborated on in "A New King for the Congo: Mobutu and the Nihilism of Africa" and *A Bend in the River*.

Against this background there is a slight, almost irrelevant story about an African king and the responses of an English homosexual and his "man-killing" companion. The former is bent on mindless revenge, whereas the English pair are anxious to work out their private problems of identity in Africa. The story is not so much about the colonized person looking at himself, however, as it is about the colonizer's reaction to the mindless nihilism in an African state. These savages have no redeeming qualities. A colonial country struggling with the problems of transition cannot confer meaningful purpose upon its people. Thus the presumed political problem of the society is characterized as a gigantic game of deception the people play among themselves:

"Of course it was all bluff, all this talk about secession and an independent kingdom and so on. That was always Simon Lubero's private view, by the way. The king was just a London playboy. He impressed a lot of people over there. But I'm sorry to say he was a very foolish man."

"That's what everybody says. And I suppose that's why I didn't believe it. I thought it was too foolish to be true. All that Oxford accent and London talk. I thought it was an act. (*IFS*, 222)[19]

Once more, there is mimicry and borrowing. Like the earlier victims, the Africans can be neither authentic nor serious. At any rate, this is what Naipaul would like us to believe.

Nothing here can be real. The educated people only pretend to be real but are as fraudulent as their uneducated brothers. Even at the university, there is fraudulence. As Linda continues her tirades against the Africans, we come face to face with these unreal people:

You go out driving with Sammy Kiesenyi, making educated conversation, and you see a naked savage with a penis one foot long. You pretend you've seen nothing. You see two naked boys painted white running about the public highway, and you don't talk about it. Sammy Kiesenyi reads a paper on broadcasting at the conference. He's lifted whole paragraphs from T. S. Eliot, of all people. You say nothing about it, you can't say anything about it. Outside you encourage and encourage. In the compound you talk and talk. Everybody just lies and lies and lies. (*IFS*, 225)

Here we are not far from the notion of savagism expressed earlier on. All the stereotypes of the savage are advanced, even down to the size of his penis. And even though Bobby reproves Linda for her perception of the society, in the end it is depicted as savage, cruel, and unreal, the total creation of the other.

Clearly, the narrator has a great aversion for African society. Despite the apparent sophistication of the characters, they are only vehicles to allow the author to continue his tirades against colonial peoples. In "One out of Many," the tirades are against Afro-American peoples, whereas in "In a Free State" African peoples are attacked. But here Naipaul asserts that the problem is much larger. Frank, Dayo, and Santosh are representatives of colonial peoples who "even after they make assumptions about their place in the world . . . still have these enormous personal problems that can make their power seem meaningless to them, make it merely the background to their own anguish."[20]

All these views have been expressed before. In *The Middle Passage* Naipaul argued that the society created or achieved nothing; in *The Overcrowded Barracoon* he argued that those islands, dark and poor, were dangerous only to themselves. By *In a Free State* there is total absence of meaningful activity among the subjects or within the postcolonial state. As he says in "In a Free State": "Perhaps nothing that happens here is more interesting than any other thing that happens. Perhaps in a place like this there isn't any news. Sammy Kiesenyi can put out the Lord's prayer every day and call it news" (*IFS,* 152). Whether the king wins or loses, the African society (and, by extension, colonial peoples) is almost sure to lose because it is a society that lacks hope. Nothing of any importance can ever take place there, for it is at the edge of the world, partaking of the doctrine of the last days. Nothing, it would seem, can arise from this society. Nihilism and apocalypticism are its only choices.

In the end, the factual prologue and epilogue can only be perceived as futile acts meant to compensate for the gloom and hopelessness in the fictional part of the text. From his act of futility at Luxor (his inability to counteract the humiliation the Egyptian children feel), to the fragility and vanity of the tramp in the epilogue, to the final questioning of the primordial innocence (primitiveness) of African peoples at the end of the text, the author makes only feeble attempts to counterpose the disgust, humiliation, and loss depicted in the fictional narrative. There can be no redemption for those benighted people who were silly enough to cast off the tutelage of organized societies; and not even Naipaul's feeble gestures at disgust can counteract that picture of loss.

The novella, concerned as it is with an "extreme" and one-dimensional situation, does not adequately examine the complexities of these new relationships. Caught up in this transitional phase of social development and distanced from these societies, Naipaul is unable to determine their capacities, or the absence thereof, for renewal and regeneration. As Georg Lukács argues, "The novella frequently appears either as a precursor to a conquest of reality by the great epic and dramatic forms, or as a rearguard, a termination at the end of a period."[21] Naipaul's novellas of this period (reinforced by his essays) express the worst rear-guard literary activity, occasioned by his obvious reactionary views toward these societies.

Because the novella (and, in this case, the novelist) is concerned with an "extreme" situation, no indisputable truths about the societies under examination are revealed. Naipaul's inability to understand the larger social and political situation out of which his characters arise thus diminishes the importance of many of his insights. If it is true, as Lukács contends, that because the novella is so concerned with the "extreme" situation that it tends to "omit the social genesis of the characters, their relationships, the situations in which they act,"[22] then such omissions are palpably obvious in this third phase of his development. Needless to say, it prevents him from presenting a well-rounded picture of the evolving social relations of postcolonial societies. His truths (or the truths of the stories) must therefore be taken within the context of their limited applicability.

"A NEW KING FOR THE CONGO: MOBUTU AND THE NIHILISM OF AFRICA"

After the publication of *In a Free State* Naipaul repeated many of the insights he exhibited in the first phase of his work. In *The Return of Eva Perón,* acknowledging that much of what he offered in the period between *In a Free State* and *Guerrillas* was of an "obsessional nature" and that "the themes repeat, whether in Argentina, Trinidad or the Congo," Naipaul expressed his political views without the interference of the fictive mode.[23] This theme is clearest in "A New King for the Congo: Mobutu and the Nihilism of Africa," which repeats the notion of the superiority of the European mode of organizing the state and the conviction that, with the departure of the Europeans, the society would return to bush, the central metaphor for colonial backwardness and futility:

The bush grows fast over what were once great events or great disturbances. Bush has buried the towns the Arabs planned, the orchards they planted, as recently, during the post-independence troubles, bush buried the fashionable eastern suburbs of Stanleyville, near the Tshopo falls. The Belgian villas were abandoned; the Africans came first to squat and then to pillage, picking the villas clean of metal, wire, timber, bathtubs and lavatory bowls (both useful for soaking manioc in), leaving only ground-floor shells of brick and masonry. In 1975 some of the ruins still stand, and they look very old, like a tropical, overgrown Pompeii, cleared of its artifacts, with only the ruins of the Chateau de Venise nightclub giving a clue to the cultural life of the vanished settlement. (*ROEP,* 190)

The concept of mimicry, the central concern of *The Mimic Men,* is also repeated almost verbatim in this essay, as is the growing notion that postcolonial subjects lacked a rudimentary capacity for sharing ideas and acting responsibly and creatively. Speaking about the difficulty of getting to know some of the Africans, Naipaul argues:

Simon only answers questions; he is incapable of generating anything like a conversation; because of his dignity, his new sense of the self, the world has closed up for him again; and he appears to be hiding. But his resentment of the former manager must have a deeper cause than the one he has given. And gradually it becomes apparent, from other replies he gives, from his belief in "authenticity," from his dislike of foreign attitudes to African art (to him a living thing: he considers the Kinshasa museum an absurdity), from the secretive African arrangement of his domestic life (to which he returns in his motorcar), it gradually becomes apparent that Simon is adrift and nervous in this unreal world of imitation. (*ROEP*, 194–95)

Eight years later, Naipaul added a further complication to his concept of mimicry. He argued that the postcolonial subject now feels "a resentment of the people imitated, the people now known as *nostalgiques*" (*ROEP*, 194).

Subject to the same fantasy as their counterparts in *The Loss of El Dorado*, all the subjects of these newly freed states participate in the collective frenzy of their ancestors:

So Mobutuism becomes the African way out. The dances and songs of Africa, so many of them religious in origin, are now officially known as *séances d'animation* and are made to serve the new cult; the dancers wear cloths stamped with Mobutu's image. Old rituals, absorbed into the new, their setting now not the village but the television studio, the palace, the conference hall, appear to have been given fresh dignity. Africa awakes! And, in all things, Mobutu offers himself as the African substitute. (*ROEP*, 197)

Thus *The Loss of El Dorado* is updated and the fantasy of the slaves is taken to the administrative level of the newly freed state. The conclusions in this text, however, are not meant to serve Africa alone. They apply to the entire postcolonial situation:

So the borrowed ideas—about colonialism and alienation, the consumer society and the decline of the West—are made to serve the African cult of authenticity; and the dream of an ancestral past restored is allied to a dream of a future of magical power. The confusion is not new, and is not peculiar to Zaire. Fantasies like this animated some slave revolts in the West Indies; and today, in Jamaica, at the university, there are people who feel that Negro redemption and Negro power can only come about through a return to African ways. The dead Duvalier of Haiti is admired for his Africanness; a writer speaks, with unconscious irony, of the Negro's need for a "purifying" period of poverty (unwittingly echoing Duvalier's "It is the destiny of the people of Haiti to suffer"); and there are people who, sufficiently far away from the slaughter ground of Uganda, find in Amin's African nihilism a proof of African power. (*ROEP*, 198–99)[24]

Here in a final sweep Naipaul combines all his previous sentiments about postcolonial societies. Africans join Afro-Caribbeans and blacks of the United States in a unified fantasy. We are asked to believe that Mobutu and Amin are representative examples of Africa, even though Julius Nyerere condemned the actions of Amin as early as 1973 (long before the imperialist powers did) and France, the United States, and South Africa turned out to be the biggest supporters of Mobutu and Mobutuism when the liberation forces attempted to overthrow Mobutu's regime in 1978.[25] Duvalier is tossed in with Mobutu, and the colonial compact of doom is sealed. The reader is asked to believe simultaneously that Simon and Mulele are the most representative examples of liberated Africans and that they are the finest examples of the new African subjects in the postcolonial era.

Yet, without being able to answer the question he raised in *In a Free State*, Naipaul continues to be concerned about the individual subject in these newly freed states. He asks how, away from the "worship" of Mobutuism, "a new attitude to life" begins. He asks further, "Where, in Kinshasa, where so many people 'shadow' jobs, and so many jobs are artificial and political, part of an artificial administration, where does the sense of responsibility, society, the state, begin?" (*ROEP*, 200–201). Because he presents an atypical situation and characters, he can offer no structured alternative to the nihilism he argues is characteristic of the society. In fact, the question is really the complement of the one he asked earlier: How, indeed, is the futility of these islands to be written? At this level of his development, he asks: How, indeed, can the nihilism of these African societies be explained? The frame has been widened. It now consists of the West Indies, the United States, and Africa. But because he does not provide a comprehensive examination of the sociopolitical realities of these new societies—he relies too much on clichés—or a historical understanding of them, he is unable to answer the questions he raises.

Naipaul is, of course, acutely aware that some postcolonial states simplify the social and political tasks of independence. He argues that the approaches of most postcolonial states to social development, in this case Mobutuism, "simplif[y] the world, the concept of responsibility and the state, and simplif[y] people" (*ROEP*, 202). Because the leaders of these new societies did not have to work out plans for social and economic development, "creativity itself" appeared as "something that might be looted, brought into being by decree" (*ROEP*, 202). Yet, although much of what he says is true, he also tends to simplify and distort the role of the African past by accepting the original conquest and subsequent looting of Africa (both her resources and her labor power) as having no meaningful importance in the social evolution of the society. Although Mobutuism (which is peculiar to Zaire and represents one of the worst aspects of Africa's postcolonial development) cannot be considered to be synonymous with African social development, coming to terms with the evils of Mobutuism and Aminism is a necessary condition for the revaluation of the nature of social development in postcolonial societies.[26]

Because he can provide no larger framework for the examination of the society (this problem is circumscribed by the nature of the novella), Naipaul's final prognosis for the society consists only of the same laments we have heard before:

The kingship of Mobutu has become its own end. The inherited modern state is being dismantled, but it isn't important that the states should work. The bush works; the bush has always been self-sufficient. The administration, now the court, is something imposed, something unconnected with the true life of the country. The ideas of responsibility, the state and creativity are ideas brought by the visitor; they do not correspond, for all the mimicry of language, to African aspirations. (*ROEP*, 204)

Here is Rodney's argument about the nature of the African state before European colonization. He noted that one could argue for the superiority of the European concept of the state if one were prepared to disregard the importance of the social relations that existed in these early African states. By privileging the European concept of the state as the highest level of social development, Naipaul could arrive at no other conclusion than that the African state, as currently constituted, represented the lowest level of social, political, and intellectual development, a natural and inherent condition of the people.

That justice, equality, and liberty are the goals of all states is not a concept that can be challenged. What does lead to challenge, and always has, is the determination of the best way to attain these goals. To argue that the desire for justice and the attempt to organize a state to achieve these goals are based on borrowed concepts, one has to demonstrate not only that they do not apply to a specific society but that the people of such a society are inherently nonsocial. To offer the workability and self-sufficiency of the "bush" as alternatives to these desirable social goals is to engage in a crude racism that cannot be called analysis.

It is only in this context that one can understand the crudity of Naipaul's conclusions at the end of "A New King for the Congo" and the apocalyptic vision of the society he presents:

To arrive at this sense of a country trapped and static, eternally vulnerable, is to begin to have something of the African sense of the void. It is to begin to fall, in the African way, into a dream of a past—the vacancy of river and forest, the hut in the brown yard, the dugout—when the dead ancestors watched and protected, and the enemies were only men. (*ROEP*, 204)

These conclusions have been uttered before; only now they are "eternal." By repeating these ideas and presenting them with mastery, Naipaul makes them convincing and totally acceptable to First World admirers.

He writes with clarity and distinction. His prose flows elegantly, and his concentration on the details of his characters' experiences is impressive. He has achieved the gift of making complex ideas simple—too simple perhaps. Yet his concern with the formalist aspects of his prose prevents him from looking deeply at his society.[27] As a result, he reduces postcolonialism to nihilism, an unacceptable justification for what he interprets as the failure of these three societies.

On closer examination, however, the notion of nihilism is entirely inadequate to describe postcolonial reality. In fact, because nihilism does not acknowledge any objective basis for moral or ethical truth (nihilism by definition denies any objective basis for truth, especially moral truth), no such truths can emerge from these societies. Moreover, because Naipaul's portrayal of postcolonial societies is so one-sided, their organic evolution and social development cannot be revealed.

Nor do Naipaul's naturalistic excesses enable the reader to understand the motives behind the actors he portrays. They certainly do not exist simply to reveal the nature of their nihilism. One does not get the sense that these postcolonial subjects are struggling to construct a social order equal to their capacities as human beings. There is no sense of contestation that could reveal their capacity for meaningful social activity. They exist as nonhumans almost bereft of social essence. In other words, there is nothing remarkable about Santosh, Frank, or the inhabitants of the Zairian world. They simply exist, their lives a prelude to nothing.

With nihilism as a prerequisite, apocalypticism cannot be far behind. In *Guerrillas* and *A Bend in the River* (whose basic idea is found in "A New King for the Congo") Naipaul's apocalypticism is revealed in its strongest light. Because there is no *metanoia* in his work and because of its naturalistic excesses, there can be no moral vision of the person. As he explained to Mrs. Harwick: "Africa [and all postcolonial peoples] has no future."

THE RETURN OF EVA PERÓN AND "CONRAD'S DARKNESS": NAIPAUL AND HIS ART

At this late stage of his career, Naipaul became more conscious of his art. Even though he had moved a long way from examining the East Indian community of Trinidad, the tone of much of his examinations reflected his unresolved conflicts with his home and society. His distance from and noninvolvement in the society led to a change in his method of analysis as well.

The Return of Eva Perón (1972–74) attempts to link the South American dilemma with that of the Caribbean and the colonial condition. Naipaul draws a parallel between the South American condition and the Haitian Revolution, led by Toussaint L'Ouverture:

The parallel [of Peronism] is not with any country in Europe, as Argentine writers sometimes say. The parallel is with Haiti, after the slave rebellion of Toussaint: a barbarous colonial society similarly made, similarly parasitic on a removed civilization, and incapable of regenerating itself because slavery provided the only pattern of human behavior, and to be a man meant only to be able to assuage that pain about the other, to be like the master. (*ROEP*, 167)

Naipaul began *The Middle Passage* by quoting from Froude to demonstrate that the Haitians, and, by extension, all colonial people of the Third World, were not "real people in the true sense of the word." This formula became the point of departure for much of his work in the early period.

In the essays in *The Return of Eva Perón* Naipaul extends his vision of loss to include all the people of the Third World who live in "these dark or remote places who, for whatever reason, are denied a clear vision of the world" (*ROEP*, 215). Absolute anarchy is the condition of the Third World:

It is as if all the energy of the state now goes into holding the state together. Law and order has become an end in itself: it is part of the Argentine sterility and waste. People are brave; they torture and are tortured; they die. But these are private events, scattered, muffled by a free but inadequate press that seems incapable of detecting a pattern in the events it reports. And perhaps the press is right. Perhaps very little of what happens in Argentina is really news, because there is no movement forward; nothing is being resolved. The nation appears to be playing a game with itself; and Argentine political life is like the life of an ant community or an African forest tribe: full of events, full of crises and deaths, but life is only cyclical, and the year always ends as it begins. (*ROEP*, 100–101)

In other words, there can be no transindividualized subject in Argentina or any colonial territory. Naipaul arbitrarily lumps all the Third World countries together, and the encompassing principle, expressed so clearly in "A New King for the Congo," is repeated once more: because the mother country leaves, there can be no future for these "half-made societies." All must return to bush.

In spite of his repetitions (perhaps because of them), Naipaul once more articulates what his art ought to be and, as a result, more closely identifies himself with Conrad. Acknowledging the value of Conrad's work, he offers in his own defense the reminder that "the great novelists wrote about highly organized societies. I had no such society; I couldn't share the assumptions of the writers; I didn't see my world reflected in theirs. My colonial world was more mixed and secondhand, and more restricted" (*ROEP*, 213–14).

Naipaul had spoken about these problems before, in 1958, but then he saw the "unformed nature" of his society as a source of strength rather than a weakness. In "The Regional Barrier" he said that he wrote for an English audience and, rejecting the use of sex and race as cornerstones for his work, he argued that the only way he could have become a successful writer was by ceasing to be "a regional writer." In 1964, he argued that because Trinidad was a "formless, unmade society . . . without mythology, all literatures were foreign. Trinidad was small, remote and unimportant, and we knew we could not hope to read in books of the life we saw about us." As a result, the books that came from afar offered only fantasy. And even though he felt betrayed by his society because it lacked mythologies and materials that were "sufficiently hallowed by tradition," it was in the writing of his first short stories that he felt a sense of how writing could shape his vision of society. In that period, he argued that his "taste for literature developed into a love of language, the word in isolation," and in time he began to reject much of what he had read in his youth.[28]

The writing of *The Mimic Men* also allowed him to reflect upon his writing and what he was trying to do. Arguing that *The Mimic Men* allowed him to deal with "my own problem, the disassociation of a man from the simplicity around him," he posited that the central image of the novel "is a very private image, not at all political. Just a sense of loss and rootlessness and despair—a very consoling image for these things."[29] He believed that it was the private aspect of the novel's central image that was responsible for its success in England. At this stage of his career, he attempted to separate his art from the political context (even though he asserted later that he wanted to write about the peculiar subject that was created by postcolonialism) to enable him to break out of the regional context in which he was imprisoned.

Naipaul's clearest statement about his writing was made in a radio interview in New Zealand in 1972 in which he made three important observations. First, he argued that "one is a changed man at the end of every book one writes; one has discovered more about one's self, more of one's skills; one has discovered depths of responses that one never really knew existed before." Second, he spoke about how his early life in Trinidad shaped his experiences, his desire to rejoin the "Old World," and how his Hindu ancestry fashioned his toleration and his sense of humor: "Coming from a place like Trinidad which I always felt existed on the edge of the world, far away from everything else, not only physically but also in terms of culture, I felt I had to try very hard to rejoin the Old World. So I had this great drive to achievement."[30] This desire to reintegrate himself into the Old World motivated his denunciation of most of the social and political activities of the people of the Third World, and these sentiments became the driving force in his work.

Finally, Naipaul addressed the question of the concerns that should undergird an analysis of his writing:

I am not sure one really knows what one does in one's writing. One knows what one is trying to do, but this is not always the same as what comes out. It is very much for other people who read one's work to judge though it is wrong for them to look for philosophies or basic beliefs. One goes to a writer for a particular kind of mental adventure, and perhaps therefore one should just look for a particular kind of sensibility, a particular way of looking at the world—a kind of morbidity—these are the things you have to recognize. As to the writer himself, if he knows what kind of vision he has, then he will probably start guying himself. And if he does that, he won't be a good writer. Frankly, I don't think one knows what one is really writing.[31]

In an interview with Ian Hamilton in 1974, he reiterated many of the sentiments he had expressed in the former but added that because of the lack of a responsive audience in Trinidad, his art had become a private experience. Looking back at his earlier work with embarrassment, he said it took him a long time to realize "that he had no society to write about," and this made him "look at the world afresh."[32] He now felt peripheral to English society, and that, too, affected the way he viewed the world.

"Conrad's Darkness" (1974) reiterated many of the concerns he had expressed before and added that "most imaginative writers discover themselves, and their world, through their work" (*ROEP*, 220). For Naipaul, writing was not only a therapeutic exercise but one in which he came to understand his world. His identification with Conrad and his interpretation of Conrad's work provide insights, as Linda Anderson explains.

Conrad offers Naipaul ideas with which he can strongly identify; unable to write from within the stability and security of an accepted relationship with his social context, he delved into the problematics of the individual's relationship with his society, converting what is usually an implied relationship into a major theme. It is through this theme, the relationship between the individual and his society, that Naipaul's and Conrad's common interests are the most obviously displayed.[33]

Naipaul's interpretation of Conrad suggested much about his own art:

All Conrad's subjects, and all his conclusions, seem to have existed in his head when he settled down to write. *Nostromo* could be suggested by a few lines in a book, *The Secret Agent* by a scrap of conversation and a book. But, really, experience was in the past; and the labor of the writing life lay in dredging up this experience, in "casting round"—Conradian words—for suitable subjects for meditation. (*ROEP,* 221)

Naipaul came full circle to his 1958 comment that "unless I am able to refresh myself by travel—to Trinidad to India—I fear that living here [in England] will eventually lead to my own sterility."[34] Wherever Naipaul traveled, he drew on the ambivalent experiences of his early years, and those experiences shaped his response to new material. Like Conrad, he was a victim of his past.

But unlike Conrad, who had some reverence for the past, Naipaul's narrators could never say, as the narrator of *Nostromo* did, "For life to be large and full, it must contain the care of the past and of the future in every passing moment of the present. Our daily work must be *done to the glory* of the dead, and for the good of those who come after."[35] Conrad believed that one can free oneself from the loneliness and despair of the past; with sufficient commitment, one can transcend feelings of alienation. In Naipaul's thought no such transcendence is possible. Without compassion for the past and some belief that the colonial person could transcend his alienated condition, there could be no understanding of the future. Therein lies one of his major shortcomings: his prose, though lucid, is trapped in the eternal fluidity of the present.

Naipaul pointed to another of his own difficulties when he argued that "Conrad's experience was too scattered; he knew many societies by their externals, but he knew none in depth" (*ROEP,* 226). It is this diffusion of efforts, this lack of a stable body of responses from a certain homogeneous society, that led Naipaul to reaffirm his convictions about the private nature of his writing:

The great societies that produced the great novels of the past have cracked. Writing has become more private and more privately glamorous. The novel as a form no longer carries conviction. Experimentation, not aimed at the real difficulties, has corrupted response; and there is a great confusion in the minds of readers and writers about the purpose of the novel. The novelist, like the painter, no longer recognizes his interpretative function; he seeks to go beyond it; and his audience diminishes. And so the world we inhabit, which is always new, goes by unexamined, made ordinary by the camera, unmediated on; and there is no one to awaken the sense of true wonder. That is perhaps a fair definition of the novelist's purpose, in all ages. (*ROEP,* 227)[36]

In 1981, in his conversation with Charles Michener, Naipaul seemed to be more aware of this problem when he argued that "there is a kind of falsity

about the usual novel" and confessed that he was reading Proust to understand how the novel ought to be constructed.[37] Thus it is from the failure of
this form, which Naipaul recognized but did not see a solution for, that we
begin to see his reversal into a naturalism that could not convey the complexities of postcolonial realities in a sophisticated way. He could not hope
to use the usual form that was designed to depict great bourgeois societies
when writing about developing postcolonial societies.

To overcome these difficulties, Naipaul turned inward to the private
world of his feelings. He moved from the society to the private individual—
independent of any social ties—for a new source of vision. But as "One out
of Many," "Tell Me Who to Kill," and "In a Free State" demonstrate,
separating the individual from the social relations of his community meant
the loss of any organic or healthy basis upon which to (re)construct the new
postcolonial subject. Hence the major problem of Naipaul's art at this time
in his literary development was his inability to deal with the problems of
postcolonial societies in a form that was adequate to express their content.

There is, of course, a parallel point Naipaul may have missed. Although
the "great societies" may have cracked, the small, remote Third World
countries—"the half-made societies" of the world—that were emerging
could and do provide innumerable sources of inspiration for any novelist.
Lord Jim wondered about these remote places of the world and pondered:
"For a time, I stood there thinking most of the living who, buried in remote
places out of the knowledge of mankind, still are fated to share in its tragic
or grotesque miseries. In its noble struggles, too—who knows. The human
heart is vast enough to contain all the world. It is valiant enough to bear the
burden, but where is the courage that would cast it off."[38] Conrad saw the
remote possibility that these benighted people could share in the "noble
struggles" of the world. For Naipaul, no such possibility existed. Conrad's
formula of novelistic grandeur may have been appropriate at the end of the
nineteenth century, but at the end of the twentieth a formula is needed that
will express the content of those persons buried and living in the remote
places of the world.

Lukács, in his work Solzhenitsyn, has argued that great literature has
always contented itself with showing "how a given social condition, a stage
of development, a developmental tendency, has intrinsically influenced the
course of human existence, human development, the dehumanization and
alienation of man himself."[39] That Naipaul was concerned in the first two
phases of his development with these processes is not to be doubted. During
his last phase, however, Naipaul has not been remotely concerned about the

developmental possibilities of Third World peoples. He believed they could experience no social development; they are condemned to a life of ignominy and backwardness, which cannot be prevented. For those subjects, as Anderson has suggested, "Freedom does not just mean full knowledge of one's own individuality but is experienced as a sense of rage against oneself and others, a rage which leads inevitably to anarchy."[40] Such, also, are the tidings of *Guerrillas*.

Whereas in his earlier work Naipaul sought an appropriate form to express the given content of colonial and early postcolonial reality, during the later phase, though his prose was sharp and lucid, it had very little content. His only function was to interpret prophecies of doom and to propagate them in written form. He became an apocalyptist of the Third World, and his exegeses were welcomed by the First World.

8. Doom and Despair: The Eternal
Condition of Colonial Peoples

You see, I began at a time when the world was beginning to change. Empires were withdrawn, and I had the kind of childish faith that there was going to be a reorganization of the world. That it was going to be all right. The discovery has been, you know, you have to come face to face with a simple question: why is it that certain countries and certain peoples have allowed themselves to be exploited and abused? What is it in them that permits this? What is their flaw? And you will find that perhaps their flaws are still with them, that the flaws aren't always external, in other people's hostility. Flaws might be within, in the limitations of particular peoples, the limitations of their civilization or their culture.
—V. S. Naipaul, *Vogue* (August 1981)

Language is then, positively, a distinctively human opening of and opening to the world: not a distinguishable or instrumental but a constitutive faculty.
—Raymond Williams, *Marxism and Literature*

"MICHAEL X AND THE BLACK POWER KILLINGS IN TRINIDAD"

The killing in 1972 of three people associated with Michael X in Trinidad, for which he was hanged at the Royal Gaol in 1975, provided Naipaul with the impetus to expand on four themes explored in *The Overcrowded Barracoon* and *In a Free State*. First, he continued to attack the concept of black power and what he called the "chic" interest of some white liberals in it. Second, he attacked liberal whites who not only identified with the oppression of blacks but went to Africa and the Caribbean "in search of some sort of personal fulfillment."[1] Third, he attacked the use of language and the ideas he believed were taken verbatim from the metropolitan centers and used without creative application in former colonial territories. And finally, in the style of Conrad, he attempted to demonstrate the apparent inability of individual colonial subjects to free themselves from the debilitating effects of their past.[2]

The killings could not have come at a more appropriate time to provide Naipaul with a concrete example to prove his points.[3] They seemed to fulfill his prophecy that the "protest leader will appear and the millennium will . . . come, [bearing] the rage of primitive men coming to themselves."[4] Naipaul correctly diagnosed Michael Abdul Malik's (Michael X) malaise when he argued that "England gave him friends, a knowledge of elegance, a newspaper fame which was like regard, and money" (*ROEP*, 30). Yet he seemed to have no compunction about using Malik to denigrate the concept of black power and attack the aspirations of Caribbean peoples. Black power, he argued, "added something very old to a rational protest: a mystical sense of race, a millennarian expectation of imminent redemption" (*ROEP*, 39). In *A Bend in the River* this formula was transformed:

The Africans had called up this war; they would suffer dreadfully, more than anybody else; but they could cope. Even the raggedest of them had their villages and tribes, things that were absolutely theirs. They could run away again to their secret worlds and become lost in those worlds, as they had done before. And even if terrible things had happened to them they would die with the comfort of knowing that their ancestors were gazing down knowingly at them.[5]

Naipaul reserved his harshest criticism, however, for liberal middle-class whites, particularly women, who identified with oppressed blacks. He argued that such people had no firm views and saw the black power struggle as merely another playful diversion. These people "keep up with 'revolution' as with the theatre, the revolutionaries who visit centers of revolution, but with return air tickets, the people for whom Malik's kind of Black Power was an exotic but safe brothel" (*ROEP*, 29). Naipaul particularly criticized Gale Benson, the white woman who was among the people murdered in Trinidad in 1972. He found her the ultimate fake, the perfect example of the "great uneducated vanity of the middle-class dropout" (*ROEP*, 6). The reason for Naipaul's vehement attack on these whites seems related to his growing sense of despondence about the behavior of these repositors of white civilization and culture. Perhaps he was detecting cracks in the solidity of their sanctified world. Intense violence against liberal white women is depicted in *Guerrillas* and *A Bend in the River*.

The killings in Trinidad precipitated a violent response in Naipaul. After all, the society that produced Malik had also made Naipaul. Both men had come from Trinidad and described similar characters in their works. They went to sister schools in Trinidad (St. Mary's and Queen's Royal College), deserted their societies at an early age, and married women their mothers disliked (Malik a black woman, Naipaul a white). Both considered the press irresponsible and agreed that white liberals were damaging the black cause.

"Things," as it is said in Trinidad, "were coming too close to home for [Naipaul's] comfort."

Naipaul not only opposed Malik's phoniness but also may have disagreed with his distinction between the black and white elements of Trinidadian society and race prejudice in Trinidad. Malik said that when he was growing up, his mother taught him that "white is pretty" and "black is ugly." "It was her way of saying white people were superior and that we should pattern ourselves on them. It expressed the feeling that too many black people have had for too long."[6] In his earlier work, Naipaul had rejected George Lamming's position that his childhood ought to be perceived strictly in black and white.[7] Malik's comments on the society's racial cleavage may have precipitated Naipaul's savage attack against Malik's half-white origins. Naipaul claimed that Malik portrayed the Negro as "a grotesque: not American, not West Indian, but an American caricatured by a red man from Trinidad for a British audience. West Indians are not black Americans. American blacks are an excluded minority. West Indians come from countries with black majorities and black administrations; they have a kind of political tradition" (*ROEP*, 31–32). In attacking the "chic" nature of the American black power movement and the interest of liberal whites in it, Naipaul argued that

the American Black Power movement is a bogus sort of television revolution. I don't see what it has to do with people over here [England]. If you are interested in Blacks, in England, then you do have Blacks at hand, Blacks whose situation is infinitely worse than that of the American Blacks. I mean the West Indian blacks who are without any representation in the world whatsoever. Now, here is a cause. But this cause has not been sanctified; it has not been sanctified by chicness.[8]

Malik's career, however, offered Naipaul an opportunity to launch an almost hysterical attack against Trinidadian society:

It proves how much of Black Power—away from its United States source—is jargon, how much a sentimental hoax. In a place like Trinidad, racial redemption is as irrelevant for the Negro as for everybody else. It obscures the problems of a small independent country with a lopsided economy, the problems of a fully "consumer" society that is yet technologically untrained and without the intellectual means to comprehend the deficiency. It perpetuates the negative, colonial politics of protest. It is, in the end, a deep corruption: a wish to be granted a dispensation from the pains of development, an almost religious conviction that oppression can be turned into an asset, race into money. While the dream of redemption lasts, Negroes will continue to exist only that someone might be their leader. Redemption requires a redeemer; and a redeemer, in these circumstances, cannot but end like the Emperor Jones:

contemptuous of the people he leads, and no less a victim, seeking an illusory personal emancipation. In Trinidad, as in every black West Indian island, the too easily awakened sense of oppression and the theory of the enemy point to the desert of Haiti. (*ROEP*, 70)

Though many of these ideas were expressed in *The Loss of El Dorado*, the substance of the statement comes directly from *The Overcrowded Barracoon*, in which Naipaul argues that "Black Power as rage, drama and style, as revolutionary jargon, offers something to everybody: to the idealistic, the dropout, the Communist, the politically frustrated, the anarchist, the angry student returning home from humiliations abroad, the racialist, the old fashioned preacher who has for years said at street corners that after Israel it was to be the turn of Africa" (*OB*, 248). In the two passages quoted above one can find the formula for *Guerrillas* and the subsidiary theme of *A Bend in the River*. He echoed the same sentiments about the aborted Grenadian Revolution.[9]

Apart from the almost religious context of this analysis, however, Naipaul presents the societies he writes about as though their people faced no problems, historical or contemporaneous. To Naipaul, race and oppression are simple codes that are used to hide the major problems of economic backwardness, which these societies lack the intellectual means to comprehend.

Of more importance, however, are the inconsistencies in Naipaul's arguments. He admits that Michael Abdul Malik, the creation of white liberal society, was a pimp, a fraud, and a fake of the worst kind, who in Trinidad became "a 'character,' a Carnival figure, a dummy Judas to be beaten through the streets on Good Friday" (*ROEP*, 22). Yet the reader is asked to accept Malik as the representative revolutionary of that society. Because Malik was peripheral to the society, Naipaul used "Michael X and the Black Power Killings in Trinidad" as a vehicle to promulgate his own repetitious views. The article added nothing new to the ideas he had presented in earlier works.

The hysterical tone of the article suggests an aspect of Naipaul's relationship to his society that was not apparent before: his desire to assuage his guilt about the society by offering a subtle correction to Malik's distortions of childhood life in Trinidad, as he pleads, "Don't associate me with Malik. We may have come from the same country but most certainly we are not cut from the same piece of cloth." Naipaul had confessed some five years after the publication of *Guerrillas* that he had always been "fighting a hysteria" that plagued him as a child, "the old fear of extinction, and I don't mean of dying. I mean the fear of being reduced to nothing, of feeling crushed. It's partly the old colonial anxiety of having one's individuality destroyed. And it also goes back to the family I grew up in—a typically Indian extended family."[10] The panic evident in "Michael X and the Black Power Killings in Trinidad" is traceable to that fundamental fear of annihilation and Naipaul's close identification with Malik's childhood experiences.

In *Guerrillas* many of the ideas of Naipaul's previous work come full circle; he restates much of what he had outlined before. In this text, Naipaul repeats his frequent criticisms of the society. He argues that on the Ridge "everyone lived in a state of suppressed hysteria";[11] the island was "a community without rules" (*G*, 114); and the villages seemed to be "stranded in time, belonging to another era, an era that contained no possibility of a future" (*G*, 235). The society was not "organized for work or for individual self respect" (*G*, 236), and it consisted of "a dependent people, [who] . . . needed other people's approval" (*G*, 237). In *A House for Mr. Biswas* and *The Mimic Men* there is a positive sense of hope, aspiration, and possibilities for the colonial and postcolonial subjects in their attempts to negotiate the difficult business of colonialism and independence. In *Guerrillas* such integrity informing the lives of the characters is missing.

As a result, the novel is merely a comparison between life in the past and in the present, showing how the children of *A House for Mr. Biswas* and *The Mimic Men* begin to function in the new society. In *Guerrillas* Naipaul attempts to update the position of the postcolonial subject even though the language, in some parts, predates that of *A House for Mr. Biswas* and takes us back to the era of bad-Johnism and the legendary midnight robbers of the carnival season. The text also reflects Naipaul's limitations with his subject matter: his inability to understand the evolution of postcolonial societies at their most essential and dynamic moment of development.

Guerrillas attempts to prove that the subject has failed to realize the promise of independence and the possibilities offered by the new social order. Thus the subject's apparent futility in *A House for Mr. Biswas* and the frenzy in "A Flag on the Island" become a collective sense of madness and desolation in *Guerrillas*. Meredith, the only sane person in the novel, concludes that it is "madness [that] keeps the place going" (*G*, 157). There is no way out of the darkness that had descended upon postcolonial peoples.

Such hysterical judgment must be seen in the larger context of the author's neurotic fear of the society. When Naipaul returned to Trinidad in 1960, he expressed a tremendous fear of the place: "I had never examined this fear of Trinidad. I had never wished to. In my novels I had only expressed this fear; and it is only now, at the moment of writing, that I am able to attempt it."[12] Naipaul was responding in the classical manner of the neurotic for whom, as Anika Lemaire expressed it, "the experience which is the object of repression is already structured, it has, that is, entered into the circuit of discourse and has already been spoken, or has at least been brought into existence, before being rejected. As the neurotic has passed a judgment of existence on the repressed signification, that signification will always be capable of being re-evoked by analysis and of being re-integrated into the flow of discourse."[13] Naipaul's return to the site of his repressed fears "re-evoked" and "re-integrated" the neurotic content of his experiences, which, by a process of transference, became a part of his literary discourse.

This repressed fear, this neurotic behavior, becomes explicit in *Guerrillas*. Such behavior, however, can be examined only through the subject's accession to language, that is, through his or her conscious and unconscious discourses. And because language, as Lemaire asserts, "distances the 'I' which speaks and believes itself to be telling the truth about its essence from the unconscious reality which founds it in its truth,"[14] an interpretation of *Guerrillas* must concern itself with the locutory and fabular behavior of the subject. Because much of the content of this text is the same as in Naipaul's previous work, the neurotic behavior of the subject in *Guerrillas* seems to be reflective of a man who failed to discover any psychological balance in his life, even though he returned to his original home (Trinidad) and later visited his ancestral home (India).

Naipaul's final failure in the text, however, occurred when the values of the mother country, in which he had placed his trust and sought safety, began to crack in front of his eyes. It was almost as though his love for the colonial mother went unheeded, triggering a neurotic condition that produced "the drama of the obsessional or that of the hysteric."[15] Naipaul alluded to this idea in his author's note to *The Return of Eva Perón* when he explained that the "obsessional nature" of the pieces he wrote from 1972 to 1975 "bridged a creative gap: from the end of 1970 to the end of 1973 [when] no novel offered itself to me." Much of *Guerrillas*, then, ought to be read as a script of Naipaul's unconscious, a neurotic response to his country.

Within this context, the behavior of Jane (fashioned after Gale Ann Benson in "The Black Power Killings in Trinidad") signifies the powerful sense of disappointment and betrayal Naipaul must have felt when this "nice" and "cultured" Englishwoman began to involve herself with black power advocates and to work for some of the liberal causes associated with the Third World. After having gone to England to save his soul from such involvement, he must have been distressed to find white women losing their souls and bodies in the black power movement. No wonder, then, Naipaul "reserves for Jane the most bitter attack he has ever launched in fiction or non-fiction."[16]

Naipaul's sense of outrage against this particular white, liberal woman from the class that was responsible for his own financial and literary success can be explained only in this light. If there was anything new in *Guerrillas,* it was not the portrayal of Jimmy Ahmed, who hardly appears in the novel and who is a composite of many of the characters in Naipaul's past work. It is the portrayal of Jane that offers us another dimension of Naipaul's hysteria, reflecting his sense of betrayal at her calumny and bad taste.

Robert Hemenway has observed that "the relationship between Jane and Jimmy becomes an allegory of the way a Third World nation conceives of its former colonial masters."[17] Hana Wirth-Nesher, drawing on Hemenway, has written that Jane recognized her position of marginality and powerlessness in her society, and in her attempt to make up for white complicity in "colonial racism" she becomes the ultimate "scapegoat for colonialism." "Her sense of inferiority is not that different from the feelings of a man like Jimmy," and because of her dual self-hatred, as white and woman, "it is logical that she should seek revenge and abuse at the hands of a black male." Referring to Jimmy's "unresolved anger at being black," Wirth-Nesher argues that he takes revenge on Jane "to substitute a surrogate target for the one that is unattainable, the white male." She then makes the contestable statement: "The colonized native male who has been humiliated by colonialism has only one kind of power left—his greater physical strength as a male to overpower the female."[18] There are obvious echoes here of the same discredited positions that Eldridge Cleaver took in *Soul on Ice.* Such a position, however, simply repeats Naipaul's racist attitudes toward blacks and presents them as accepted and proven facts. There is certainly a more complex relationship between Naipaul's treatment of women and his own sexuality, a problem to which Hemenway alludes but does not really work out.[19] This complex psychoanalytical relationship will be analyzed more carefully in the next chapter to demonstrate why Naipaul treats the women in his later fiction the way he does and what it says about questions of power and his own sexuality.

Within this context, however, it is not entirely fruitful to reduce Naipaul's treatment of women or his depiction of sexuality to mere genitality, sadomasochism, "fear of faith in the future," or "hatred and contempt for female sexuality."[20] These questions are important, but the nature of human sexuality ought to be examined more in terms of "a system of conscious and unconscious human fantasies involving a range of excitations and activities that produce pleasure beyond the satisfaction of any basic psychological need. It arises from various sources, seeks satisfaction in many different ways and makes use of many diverse objects for its aim of achieving pleasure."[21] More specifically, sexuality ought to be seen as "a highly charged and volatile signifier for differentials of power that take their shape from the sociopolitical concomitants of gender difference."[22]

Sexuality, then, cannot be seen as pregiven fact but as the manner in which human subjects have been constructed by their histories. As Juliet Mitchell notes, "the issue of female sexuality always brings us back to the question of how the human subject is formed,"[23] and this is why the manner in which Naipaul depicts women, particularly in his later texts, raises so many important questions about his own sexuality and the question of power in postcolonial societies. If we accept Lacan's position that there is no certainty or authority in the notions of psychic or sexual life, the sexual lives that Naipaul describes may well reflect a crisis in his own life. For, as the intensity of Naipaul's alienation increases, the question of identification becomes sharper, and this is reflected in the increased attention he gives to sexual encounters and his somewhat pathological descriptions of them. Perhaps something of the "veiling effect," as Lacan calls it, occurs as Naipaul attempts to come to terms with his own identification.[24]

Also, I do not think that it is particularly useful to argue, as Jeffrey Robinson has, that Naipaul's depiction of sex forecloses the possibility of some "act of faith in the future" or as Elaine Fido has that "Naipaul, as much as any pornographic writer, may be profiting from the side-effects of conventional sexual mores, rather than trying (as Fallaci and Mailer do) to comprehend the sickness in men and women which gives rise to such behavior as he portrays."[25] Indeed, the question might not be so much why Naipaul chooses his sexual topics to "illuminate his world view" as how these topics choose him as ways to illuminate his views of himself and his world. In other words, Naipaul might not have had complete power over his way of depicting women.

To be sure, there is a sense in which Naipaul's "deep hostility towards the woman reaches a horrifying [racist] climax in *Guerrillas*"[26] (the pun, I hope, is not intended), and certainly there is a way in which Jimmy's battle with Jane "is simultaneously a battle with loved and hated aspects of himself, femininity and a desire for Englishness [imperialist culture]."[27] Jane's activities could also be seen as totally irrelevant to the central homosocial bonding that takes place between Jimmy and Roche, in which she functions as the conduit through which these desires are routed, and her sexuality is depicted as being corrosive, punishing, and eventually horrifyingly punished.[28] And isn't it important that Naipaul is more concerned about a foreign woman in a postcolonial culture than he is with a local woman within her own culture? After all, as most of these critics note, Jane is made almost entirely by the actions of the men who come into her life and her buggery/rape is meant to validate Jimmy's rather than Jane's existence. Perhaps the more important questions are these: what are the historical relationships of power and the political mechanisms that produce Naipaul's discourse on sexuality and how is that discourse reflective of the society's development?[29]

There is, then, the nexus of gender, race, and power, within a cultural, social, and economic context that has to be worked out very carefully before one can untangle the critical issues that are at stake in any discussion of Naipaul and sexuality, especially as they relate to his later novels. One cannot merely condemn the nature of sexuality in these novels without trying to determine what they say about the issues of power, race, and gender as they are restructured in the postcolonial state. Surely, whatever power Roche or Jimmy possess and the extent to which they confirm each other's value are in direct proportion to the extent to which Jane is made to be seen as contemptible and irresponsible.[30] One cannot proceed as though nothing specific is at stake in Naipaul's depiction of Jane and argue, as Sanna Dhahir has, that Jane is "the victim of her own nature and her tendency to misuse her sexuality which brings real violation to her body. Behind Jane's rape and murder lies Naipaul's belief in the sacredness of the human body [whatever this means] and his disapproval of nonchalant attitudes towards it."[31] *Guerrillas* reveals a major crisis was at work in Naipaul's life (and perhaps in the societies he describes), which is reflected in the signifying relation of sex to power and sexual alienation to political expression in his texts. As one analyzes these relations it is of "serious political importance," as Sedgwick notes, that the tools with which we examine them "be subtle and discriminate ones, and that our literary knowledge of the most crabbed and oblique paths of meaning not be oversimplified in the face of panic-inducing images of real violence, especially the violence of, around, and to sexuality. To assume that sex signifies power in a flat, unvarying relation of metaphor or synecdoche will always

entail a blindness, not to the rhetorical and pyrotechnic, but to such historical categories as class and race."[32]

Guerrillas, then, is an extended version of "Michael X and the Black
Power Killings in Trinidad," bringing together many bits and pieces of
Naipaul's earlier work and continuing his attempt to berate colonial people.
The society he describes in *Guerrillas* had "produced no great men and its
possibilities were now exhausted" (*G*, 59). Such a society is undermined by
internal decay. Although Jimmy is the vehicle through which most of the
author's concerns are expressed, the way he is portrayed is meant to suggest
that he is created by the words of others. His words do not convey his
individuality; they are merely instrumental and expressive of his former
master's will. His destiny is linked inextricably to his words, and thus when
we first meet him he is depicted as feeling "unsupported by his words, and
then separate from his words; and he had had a vision of darkness, of the
world lost forever, and his own life ending on that bit of wasteland" (*G*, 36–
37).

The text chronicles the separation of Jimmy Ahmed from his words and
his ultimate sense of loss when he no longer controls his words, which are,
in fact, the words of another. In anticipation of his demise, the narrator
argues: "Words, which at some times did so much for him, now did not
restore him to himself. He was a lost man, more lost than he had been as a
boy, in his father's shop, at school, in the streets of the city, when he saw and
knew nothing" (*G*, 42). Jimmy turns inward, becoming a mute being who
does not possess even his own language and who can be programmed for
any purpose. Language, which is seen normally as constituting one's individuality, is used here to express someone else's concern. Separated from
his words and the guidance of his master, Jimmy seems irrevocably lost.
Following the death of Jane, perhaps the only person who genuinely cared
for him, he enters a void and is lost forever, "lost since the beginning of
time. But time had no beginning. And he was disembodied. He was nothing
more than this sense of loss that grew deeper and deeper as he awakened to
it" (*G*, 241). The anticipated doom is fulfilled, the detective nature of the
novel is accomplished, and we are asked to accept and understand the
inevitable doom which is the destiny of the subject.

Unlike what we find in *A House for Mr. Biswas* and *The Mimic Men*,
there is no sense of character development in Jimmy Ahmed. He is just
there, a brooding presence, a reflection of many negatively accumulated
responses. There is no attempt to integrate him into the society, and there is
no indication of why he is the way he is. The narrator announces that Jimmy

has been made by another culture and that his words and ideas are not his own. He is simply thrust into the society, and despite Meredith's and Henry's concerns about him, he exists simply to satisfy the desire of some force outside of the society and the text. Unlike Mr. Biswas and Ralph Singh, Jimmy has not been created by the society, except in the most peripheral and mechanical sense. *Guerrillas* might have been a romance in the best Conradian sense with its "half-breeds," its "fantasies of native power and sexuality," "crippling visions of power," and so on, as the back cover of the novel announces. It certainly is not a realistic portrayal of the society. Although there is a diversity of social types and speech styles, there is no feeling of the social and living discourse of a society.

Guerrillas, therefore, becomes almost a verbal performance. The strategic use of language reinforces the author's perception of the society but also indicates the distance between the author and his society. In fact, as Naipaul becomes more distanced from his society, he relies increasingly upon ideas rather than on lived experiences to construct his fiction. As a result, verbal play predominates over an examination of a society that is becoming, and an entire literary subtext is introduced to grant the work authenticity. Naipaul draws upon Emily Brontë's *Wuthering Heights,* Charlotte Brontë's *Jane Eyre,* Thomas Hardy's *The Woodlanders,* and Joseph Conrad's *The Secret Agent* to structure the novel.[33] Precisely because of this strategy—this sense of literariness—the quality of shared experiences which is encountered in *The Mystic Masseur,* the graphic depiction of a society in transformation which is observed in *A House for Mr. Biswas,* or the illuminating portrayal of psychological reality which is demonstrated in *The Mimic Men* are not found in *Guerrillas.* These earlier works evidenced a close involvement with the society and an authentic integration of social types, whereas *Guerrillas* remains a purely literary construct.

Naipaul's problems with *Guerrillas* cannot be reduced simply to his distance from the society. They are also related to his acceptance of most of the theories of European civilization, primarily the notion that all of history can be reduced to a progressive, unilinear development which culminates with European civilization at the apogee of human progress.[34] By accepting this position, Naipaul cannot see language as a constitutive function of colonial subjects, shaped by the social realities of their lives. He simply presents language as possessing a formed and static quality, already given and having no meaning other than that the colonizer has given it. Thus, language is presented in *Guerrillas* as a "fixed, objective and . . . 'given' system," which takes "theoretical and practical priority" over the utterances of the inhabitants of colonial societies. As such, "the living speech of human beings in their specific social relationships in the world [is] . . . theoretically reduced to instances and examples of a system which lay beyond them."[35]

For Naipaul, the language of the colonized person can never be perceived as what all language is: "a persistent kind of creation and re-creation: a dynamic presence and a constant regenerative process."[36] It can be seen only as the production of the dominant culture. Thus to the narrator of *Guerrillas* Jimmy's language was "London words; London phrases." Although Jimmy's ideas may have been influenced by London ideas, it should be understood that language is transformed in the process of revolutionary struggle and that Jimmy also exists outside of his London words and phrases. In his idealist formulation of language, Naipaul examines language as a mere reflection and expression of materiality, fixed and structured by the other. And if, as some critics have argued, Jimmy is marginal to the society, it seems inconsistent to argue that he reveals "the pathological dimensions of the colonial encounter."[37] The pathology, it seems, resides more in Naipaul's than in the colonial psyche.

This use of language constitutes the real difference between the creative and innovative processes of *A House for Mr. Biswas* and *The Mimic Men,* in which the author explores a real society with real substantive relationships, and the mere verbal play that characterizes *Guerrillas.* The nature of the discourse in *Guerrillas* has value, for as Lacan noted, no matter how "empty this discourse may appear, it is only so if taken at its face value. . . . Speech, even when almost completely worn out, retains its value as a tessera. Even if it communicates nothing, even if it denies the evidence, it affirms that speech constitutes truth."[38] Because all social process is an activity between real individuals, "individuality, by the fully social fact of language (whether as 'outer' or 'inner' speech), is the active constitution, within distinct physical beings, of the social capacity which is the means of realization of any individual life."[39] Jimmy cannot be perceived as an active part of his society, socially conditioned by the experiences of that society, and thus can make no claims for an individuality as the product of his society. He is an imposition, existing in a vacuous region with no organic relationship to his society. He merely acts out some acquired English fantasies which he has accumulated abroad.

INDIA: A WOUNDED CIVILIZATION

Naipaul's violent response to such things as the killings in Trinidad and the sense of guilt revealed in *Guerrillas* received much fuller treatment in

India: A Wounded Civilization. Following the same historical trajectory as in *The Middle Passage, An Area of Darkness,* and *The Loss of El Dorado,* Naipaul examined his past to understand himself. In this text, his nonfictional work comes full circle and examines the manner in which the past intrudes upon the present and vice versa. Thus he argues that even though he has been washed clean of many of his Indian attitudes, it had taken him a long time to come to grips with "the strangeness of India, to define what separates me from the country; and to understand how far the 'Indian' attitudes of someone like myself, a member of a small and remote community in the New World, have diverged from the attitudes of people to whom India is still whole."[40]

Naipaul's visit to India soon after his visit to Trinidad cannot be separated from the neurotic response to Trinidad displayed in "Michael X and the Killings in Trinidad," for it corresponds to his psychotic response to his ancestral home. According to Lacan, if the neurotic represses "the psychical content which is destined to become unconscious, the psychotic represses [or forecloses] the real." More important, as his 1962 visit to India demonstrated, Naipaul diligently attempted to "foreclose" or repudiate the land of his forefathers. The first visit, in 1962, ended in "futility and impatience, a gratuitous act of cruelty, self-reproach and flight." Following his third trip to India, Naipaul argued that any further inquiry into India had to begin with himself because "in myself, like the split-second images of infancy which some of us carry, there survive, from the family rituals that lasted into my childhood, phantasmal memories of old India which for me outline a whole vanished world. . . . In India I know I am a stranger; but increasingly I understand that my Indian memories, the memories of that India which lived on into my childhood in Trinidad, are like trapdoors into a bottomless past" (*I,* x–xi). Naipaul's psychotic relationship to India prevented him from possessing his father's land in any meaningful and satisfactory manner. Writing about India "exorcised nothing," as he said in *An Area of Darkness* (p. 280) because he did not possess a lived relationship with India as he had with Trinidad. He possessed only the substance of a "primal hole" that could be patched imperfectly.

Thus, whereas Naipaul is able to reevoke his Trinidad experiences and to reinterpret them in his literary discourse, there were no such possibilities with his Indian experiences because he never possessed that country in any lived, physical manner. He could not integrate his Indian experiences into the web of his personal discourse, nor could he structure them in any symbolic fashion because in psychosis, unlike neurosis, there can be no substitution for lived experiences. In neurosis, the subject substantiates some symbol for the lived experience which is repressed, and this is one reason why no novels ever came out of his Indian experiences, except in a somewhat sublated form in *Mr. Stone and the Knights Companion.*

Naipaul visited India in 1975 during the state of emergency that had been announced by Prime Minister Indira Gandhi. He felt that the situation reflected India's deeper moral crisis, a result of a failed Hindu ideal of self-realization. *India: A Wounded Civilization* concentrates on Hindu India to the neglect of India's Islamic heritage and that of the other religious minorities that play an important part in all spheres of Indian life. As Helga Chaudhary noted, the book might have been more appropriately titled "Hindu India: A Wounded Civilization."[41] Naipaul argues that India's inability to develop an alternative vision of herself after almost forty years of formal independence demonstrated the nation's historical deficiency, a manifestation of a "thousand years of defeat and withdrawal . . . an older, deeper Indian violence . . . [which] remained untouched by foreign rule and had survived Gandhi. It had become part of the Hindu social order, and there was a stage at which it became invisible, disappearing in the general distress" (*I*, 40–42). The larger moral crisis of the society lay within this deeper historical base.

This sense of retreat, Naipaul argues, is analogous to the crisis in Africa after it gained its formal independence. The corruption of India, like the corruption of Africa, is that yearning for the past which has been the bane of the civilization from its inception. The withdrawal of the colonial powers— the English and Muslim dominance in India or the Belgian and Arab dominance in the Congo—could only lead to a recurrence of the violence and chaos of the past. Thus India could not provide the new code of behavior which independence demanded. Inevitably, society breaks down, "discovering again that it was cruel and horribly violent" (*I*, 42), and with independence the age-old distress and the cruelties that had always lain below her apparent stability remain. Accordingly, the "intellectual confusion" of the country during independence is seen as greater than it was during the British rule.

As in "A New King for the Congo," Naipaul continues to study the "moral" malaise of the colonial society and seems to suggest that its roots lie deep within its social history. Capable of nothing, the colonial peoples could never hope to achieve anything. Transposing those ideas to India, Naipaul suggests that the moral malaise of that society inheres in its historical attachment to Hinduism (manifested primarily in the concepts of *dharma* and *karma*), which prevents the Indians from actually observing or

analyzing their society. Thus British colonialism, which at first may have
been thought to be evil, is presented as something good, for it postpones
India's ultimate decay. For buried deep within this society (and other such
societies) are the seeds of destruction, and no fancy-sounding development
programs could rescue them from their doom. Because they retreated into
their least impregnable defenses, into "their caste, their *karma,* their un-
shakable place in the scheme of things" (*I,* 26), the Indians could never
become individuals. They possessed "obsessions" which, when transposed
to the political arena, led to a "decline into barbarism" (*I,* 121). The
underdeveloped ego of India is analogous to the underdeveloped and childlike behavior of the Africans.

Naipaul's argument stopped with chronicling the shortcomings of the
society; he knew nothing of its strengths. As a result, he could not go
beyond the formula of *The Mimic Men,* in which the behavior of all
colonized people is characterized by their capacity for mimicry. Thus his
tirades against the people of India continue in the same vein as those in the
past:

Complex imported ideas, forced through the retort of Indian sensibility, often come
out cleansed of content, and harmless; they seem so regularly to lead back, through
religion and now science, to the past and nullity: to the spinning wheel, the bullock
cart. . . . Mimicry within mimicry, imperfectly understood idea within imperfectly
understood idea. . . . There are times when the intellectual confusion of India seems
complete and it seems impossible to get back to clarifying first principles. (*I,* 129–
32)

Where in Naipaul's earlier work intellectual confusion led to "chaos" and
"nihilism," in this text it leads to "nullity" and "barbarism." To arrive at
this conclusion, Naipaul had to bend Indian historical thought to fit his own
needs. Sudha Rai has demonstrated Naipaul's misreading of Gandhi,
Narayan, and Kaker—all of whom Naipaul relied upon to demonstrate
India's "intellectual confusion"—and his tendency to impose Western in-
terpretations onto purely Eastern problems.[42]

Apart from a simple misreading, however, Naipaul's response to India
reflects a particular class bias. A different picture emerges in Dilip Hiro's
Inside India Today. Like Naipaul, Hiro is an Indian who, after having left
India for a number of years, returned and analyzed the society. And even
though he pointed out its shortcomings, he did so in a more rational manner,
noting the class basis of India's poverty and inequality and presenting the
Indian peasant as an essentially sensible person trying to come to grips with
the problems confronting his society.

Naipaul, to be sure, is partially correct when he attributes many of India's problems to Hinduism. But this is by no means the entire or essential reason for India's failures. India's central problem resides in a feudal economic arrangement supported by a religious system that keeps millions of Indians tied to their masters and, where it is profitable, to the land. The corruption and political chicanery of the rich and the powerful reinforce this system of oppression.

Nor are the problems of industrial and nonindustrial India as far apart as Naipaul would have us believe; the former always affects the latter. Yet it is the gap between these two sectors of the economy that creates the slums of Bombay and all the other large cities of India. The dispossession of the peasants from their land is not so much an Indian as a social phenomenon, which occurs in the transition from feudal to capitalist relations. It happens primarily when a society begins to industrialize. More important, as Hiro suggests by his examples, it is an active rather than a passive process that occurs when people struggle to maintain their individual selves, in spite of the power of medieval ways. As in all social upheaval, some individuals are crushed and impoverished by such a transition.

There is both progress and backwardness. But in reading Hiro one gets a balanced and rational picture of a society trying to come to grips with its many problems. In contrast, *India: A Wounded Civilization* is the frantic and frenetic outpourings of a man who is primarily concerned with dealing with the problems of his own identity by confronting his ancestral home, a man undecided about his own subjectivity and about those with whom he comes into contact.

Thus, in trying to come to terms with that primal absence, that attempt to anchor his subjectivity in the "bottomless past" of his uncertain relationship with India, V. S. Naipaul reverted to the Indian concepts of *karma* and *dharma* (products of his early childhood experiences and his major shared relationship with India) to interweave his experiences with theirs, that is, to patch (to continue Lemaire's analogy) the full cloth of their mutual Indian experience. Paradoxically, such an emotional response to his Indian experience prevents Naipaul from understanding the basic dynamic of the social relations of Indian society in its transformation from feudalist to capitalist production.

It is pertinent to contrast Naipaul's and Hiro's examples of the social ills of the society. In one of the stories with which Naipaul ends *India: A Wounded Civilization,* he declares:

Five years ago in Delhi I heard this story. A foreign businessman saw that his untouchable servant was intelligent, and decided to give the young man an education. He did so, and before he left the country he placed the man in a better job. Some years later the businessman returned to India. He found that his untouchable was a latrine-cleaner again. He had been boycotted by his clan for breaking away from them; he was barred from the evening smoking group. There was no other group he could join, no woman he could marry. His solitariness was insupportable, and he had returned to his duty, his *dharma;* he had learned to obey. (*I*, 188)

This story is meant to support Naipaul's argument about the evils of *dharma* and its centrality in the social order.

At the beginning of his book, Hiro tells the story of Kalipada Kundu, a sixty-eight-year-old weaver-cultivator. The story resembles the one Naipaul recounts but arrives at quite a different conclusion:

He [Kundu] had other frustrations, or rather his youngest son, Narhari, had. "Narhari was a good student and got a government scholarship to go to a technical college," he said. "He secured a diploma in weaving—three years ago. He sent out many applications for a job; but not even once did he get an interview. In the end he gave up. He began weaving at home." He pointed to the room at the back which had handlooms and where Narhari was then weaving. "What is the use of all that education and expense?" he asked. "Now Narhari is doing exactly what my other son is doing, working on a handloom at home; and that one never even went to high school. We are all going down the hill here." The man sitting next to him on the veranda nodded agreement.[43]

What conclusions can we draw from these stories? Both men, despite their education, were unable to move out of their traditional positions. Naipaul ascribes the reason to *dharma,* whereas Hiro ascribes it to the general weakness of the economic condition. After telling his story, Naipaul explodes at the "obvious" moral conclusion one can draw:

Obedience: it is all that India requires of men, and it is what men willingly give. The family has its rules; the caste has its rules. For the disciple, the guru—whether holy man or music teacher—stands in the place of God, and has to be implicitly obeyed, even if—like Bhave with Gandhi—he doesn't always understand why. Sacred texts have to be learned by heart; school texts have to be learned by heart, and university textbooks, and the notes of the lecturers. . . . So India ever absorbs the new into its old self, using new tools in old ways, purging itself of unnecessary mind, maintaining its equilibrium. The poverty of the land is reflected in the poverty of the mind; it would be calamitous if it were otherwise. (*I*, 188–89)

It could be argued that Naipaul seeks to explain the society through the metaphysics of his rhetoric and that Hiro does the same through the examples of inequality and statistical information.

In the end Naipaul sees only blackness, "that of a decaying civilization, where the only hope lies in further swift decay (*I*, 191). In his turn, Hiro sees a certain degree of hope and suggests that the only way to stop the further impoverishment of the society (not the decay of a civilization) is to effect "an equitable distribution of what is produced—that is, in practical terms, putting more money into the pockets of the poor *at the cost of the rich*— curbing the superfluous consumption of the rich; and mopping up their excessive income through an honest and efficient system of tax assessment and collection, and investing it as capital for the economic development of the country."[44]

Hiro stresses the economic dimension of development, whereas Naipaul directs his attention to social and cultural matters. Both approaches could be used to arrive at entirely different conclusions about the society. Yet the bleakness which Naipaul sees is a manifestation of a personal and metaphysical vision of the society fashioned by his interpretation of colonial history and his need to justify his particular vision of the society. Naipaul does not seem to have moved very far from his "small and remote community in the New World," and the focus of his work remains on his perennial question about his position in the world. As a consequence, most of the central concerns in this text reecho many of the concerns expressed in his earlier work.

In his review of *India: A Wounded Civilization*, even though he admired Naipaul's dazzling prose, William Boarders felt constrained to conclude that the book left many important questions unanswered. "But at least," he said, "it poses and ponders them with startling clarity, offering no clear outline of how things could be improved, but only an anguished and articulate cry against the way they are."[45] And this is precisely the problem with Naipaul's latter works. They are all cries of anguish or hysteria, reflections of his own inadequacies placed in the social context and presented as the limitations of the society he is examining. And it is this anguished relationship with the "vanished world" of the past that becomes the central principle that orders much of his later work.

At the end of *India: A Wounded Civilization*, Naipaul argues that the individual subject (and by definition, all postcolonial subjects) cannot be liberated from his past until he distances himself from that past. Moreover he argues that the "past has to be seen as dead; or the past will kill" (*I*, 191). But Naipaul's neurotic response to Trinidad and India does not let him see the past as dead. It is an exploration of this relationship—between a subject and his past—which becomes the main focus of *A Bend in the River*. The

manner in which the major protagonist liberates himself from the past will
be suggested as the manner in which postcolonial subjects ought to liberate
themselves from the tyranny of their culture and civilization.

A BEND IN THE RIVER: BAD TIDINGS OF THE LAST DAYS

A Bend in the River, the title of which might have been taken from a line
in the *Ramayana* that reads "At the bend in the Ganges, they paused to take
a look at the land they were leaving,"[46] opens with and is structured by the
same idealistic approach to society that was so obvious in "A New King for
the Congo" and *India: A Wounded Civilization.* In fact, many of the central
ideas of these books are used in *A Bend in the River,* a dramatization of
Naipaul's apocalyptic vision of the society. He begins the text by emphasiz-
ing the denied possibilities for those societies ("The world is what it is; men
who are nothing, who allow themselves to become nothing, have no place in
it.")[47] and ends with a vision of utter darkness and hopelessness when
Ferdinand, the only African of any consequence in the novel, declares:
"We're all going to hell, and every man knows this in his bones. We're
being killed. Nothing has any meaning. That is why everyone is so frantic.
Everyone wants to make his money and run away. But where? That is what
is driving people mad. They feel they're losing the place they can run back
to" (*BR,* 272).

As in earlier works, Naipaul stresses the society's dependence on Europe
for ideas:

All that I know of our history and the history of the Indian Ocean I have got from
books written by Europeans. If I say that our Arabs in their time were great
adventurers and writers; that our sailors gave the Mediterranean the lateen sail that
made the discovery of the Americas possible; that an Indian pilot led Vasco da Gama
from East Africa to Calicut; that the very word *cheque* was first used by our Persian
merchants—if I say these things it is because I have got them from European books.
They formed no part of our knowledge or pride. Without Europeans, I feel, all our
past would have been washed away, like the scuff marks of fishermen on the beach
outside our town. (*BR,* 11–12)

The most distinctive part of the text is its examination of the relationship
between the past and the present, the overpowering symbolism of bush and
blood, and Naipaul's inversion of Conrad's *Heart of Darkness* to fit his own
purposes.[48] As he did in *Guerrillas,* Naipaul demonstrates his continuing
inability to examine postcolonial societies in any depth. He has become too
distant from these societies; his response to them is unbalanced, and so his
anxieties become those of the society. He is constrained to return to the

original problematic of his people in an alien world, and this idea becomes central to the text. As Larry Husten notes, in this work Naipaul "fully explores the possibilities of a fiction which connects his own personal concerns to the larger world viewed in specifically political and historical terms."[49]

The theme of A Bend in the River is the gradual darkening of African society as it returns to its age-old condition of bush and blood. Continuing in the language and sentiments of Guerrillas, in which each individual attempts to fulfill his needs in a chaotic and anachronistic manner, A Bend in the River proposes that the final reckoning has arrived, forcing all the postcolonial people to return to a primitive condition. This is why Salim interprets the work of Father Huismans, the liberal whom the narrator believes assumes too much about Africa, in the following manner: "True Africa he saw as dying or about to die. That was why it was so necessary, while that Africa still lived, to understand and collect and preserve its things" (BR, 64). Salim suggests that Father Huismans's overemphasis of the cultural artifacts deflects attention from the central problems of the society.

Relying on the Conradian theme of repetition of the past in the present, A Bend in the River examines the homeless condition of the East Indian adrift in a world he cannot call home. Naipaul proposes that the only way the Indian can rid himself of a past that kills is to trample on it, so as to establish a liberating relationship with his present. Thus, it is not entirely accurate to argue, as Irving Howe has in New York Times Book Review, that in A Bend in the River Naipaul "struggles with the ordeals and absurdities of living in new 'third world' countries."[50] The novel is concerned primarily with Salim's attempt to free himself from the constricting ties of his society's past.

The novel begins in blood. Driving through a country that is "full of blood," where "the bush muffled the sound of murder, and the muddy rivers and lakes washed the blood away" (BR, 53), Salim, African-born of Muslim heritage, leaves the nullity and decay of his civilization to start up again at an outpost in deepest Africa, where he hopes to achieve a sense of personal liberation and to structure a new discourse with his world. At an early age, Salim recognized that his feudal community had fallen behind, and he made the decision to break out of it: "I could no longer submit to Fate. My wish was not to be good, in the way of our tradition, but to make good" (BR, 20). And it is from this posture that he begins his journey toward achieving a specific identity.

Yet the town at the bend in the river where Salim begins his quest for freedom looks "like the site of a dead civilization. The ruins, spreading over so many acres, seemed to speak of a final catastrophe. But the civilization wasn't dead. It was the civilization I existed in and in fact was still working towards. . . . You felt like a ghost, not from the past, but from the future. You felt that your life and ambition had been already lived out for you and you were looking at the relics of that life. You were in a place where the future had come and gone" (*BR*, 27).

Salim realizes that his old way of life is gone forever and that his condition is analogous to that of the native Africans. Significantly, the past life is perceived as existing within the protagonist's mind rather than in the activities of his real life. Indar, who has been Salim's intellectual guide, argues that the only way to free oneself from the past is to reject it:

I began to understand at the same time that my anguish about being a man adrift was false, that for me that dream of home and security was nothing more than a dream of isolation, anachronistic and stupid and very feeble. I belonged to myself alone. I was going to surrender my manhood to nobody. For someone like me there was only one civilization and one place—London, or a place like it. Every other kind of life was make-believe. Home—what for? To hide? To bow to our great men? For people in our situation, people led into slavery, that is the biggest trap of all. We have nothing. We solace ourselves with that idea of the great men of our tribe, the Gandhi and the Nehru, and we castrate ourselves. "Here, take my manhood and invest it for me. Take my manhood and be a greater man yourself, for my sake!" No! I want to be a man myself. (*BR*, 151–52)

These sentiments are the central theme of the novel. First, as in his earlier work, Naipaul considers London the "real world," that is, "the bigger, harder world" (*BR*, 270). Second, because a sense of identity—that is, one's manhood—can be achieved only in London or a similar city, Salim goes to London. The Big Man theme, which becomes the third part of the novel, concerns the ability of the great men of the colonial world to castrate the aspirations of individual subjects.

Yet the great lesson that Indar teaches Salim through his example is that one can be rescued from the past only by removing oneself from a society that denies the implicit worth of one's humanity. The certainties offered by London and similar places are unavailable in India or Africa because of the arbitrariness of those societies. In such societies all civilized discourse has broken down. As Mahesh, the old Indian of the town, explains to Salim: "It isn't that there's no right and wrong here. There's no right" (*BR*, 92). This sentiment reflects the sense of apocalyptic doom prevalent in the society.

Salim argues that he achieved "the idea of my manliness I had grown to need" (*BR*, 202) through his relationship with Yvette, a white woman from Europe. He asks: "Wasn't my attachment to her an attachment to that idea?" (*BR*, 202). He had discovered that if he were not to become like Mehest and Shoba, "empty in Africa, and unprotected, with nothing to fall back on" (*BR*, 228), he had to leave the society as quickly as possible.

Therefore, Salim goes to London, and, like Indar, he is able to retrieve his manhood and his humanity. He rejects all the ideas his traditional society had imposed upon him, "the ideas of home and ancestral piety, the unthinking worship of his great men, the self-suppression that went with that worship and those ideas" (*BR*, 230). Significantly, at the moment when he realizes his sense of individuality, he experiences the same feelings of childlike wonder that Ralph Singh experienced in *The Mimic Men*. In London, he resolves:

There could be no going back; there was nothing to go back to. We had become what the world outside had made us; we had to live in the world as it existed. The younger Indar was wiser. Use the airplane; trample on the past, as Indar had said he had trampled on the past. Get rid of that idea of the past; make the dream-like scenes of loss ordinary. (*BR*, 244)

Like Indar, Salim accepts his separation from his society, and his return to Africa is symbolic. In London he begins to enjoy his newly acquired liberation. Salim and Indar believe it is hopeless to try to build a postcolonial society. The only problem is that not all Africans and Indians could escape to London.

In the end the novel returns to the bloodshed with which it began. The society is seen as returning to the beginning of time, and the last images of the town at the bend of the river are of the estates and great houses of colonial days, the only remaining examples of Africa's past.

A subsidiary theme in the novel is the contrast of Salim's life with that of Ferdinand, who represents the new African man. Newly arrived from the African bush, Ferdinand is capable of being programmed for any purpose. Incapable of independent thought, Ferdinand becomes another mimic man possessing only fetishes of the world. Where the Indian possessed "obsessions" rather than "ideas," the African possesses "fetishes." Thus Salim, Ferdinand's mentor, observes:

And when I pushed him past the stage where he could repeat bits of what he had heard at the lycée, I found that the ideas of the school discussion had in his mind become jumbled and simplified. Ideas of the past were confused with ideas of the present. In his lycée blazer, Ferdinand saw himself as evolved and important, as in the colonial days. At the same time he saw himself as a new man of Africa, and important for that reason. Out of this staggering idea of his own importance, he had reduced Africa to himself; and the future of Africa was nothing more than the job he might do later on. *(BR, 48)*

Ferdinand's social development is confined to his own self-importance and an inward-looking attitude that prevents him from seeing the world as existing beyond his immediate concerns. As a new man of Africa, Ferdinand perceives the outside world only in relation to Africa. Contrasted with Salim, who accepted his civilization, Ferdinand could never take his world lightly, and thus, as Salim says, "He could never be simple. The more he tried, the more confused he became. His mind wasn't empty, as I had begun to think. It was a jumble, full of all kinds of junk" *(BR, 54)*.

Ferdinand's social development is, of necessity, stymied. Capable of nothing, getting everything too quickly, Ferdinand (and other Africans) could have no firm grasp of the world primarily because they were never "doers and makers" of anything. Salim, intent on reducing Ferdinand's life to the most basic and absurd level, argues:

You took a boy out of the bush and you taught him to read and write; you levelled the bush and built a polytechnic and you send him there. It seemed as easy as that, if you came late to the world and found ready-made those things that other countries and peoples have taken so long to arrive at—writing, printing, universities, books, knowledge. The rest of us had to take things in stages. I thought of my own family, Nazruddin, myself—we were so clogged by what the centuries had deposited in our minds and hearts. Ferdinand, starting from nothing, had with one step made himself free, and was ready to race ahead of us. *(BR, 102–3)*

As is to be expected from Ferdinand's uncritical and unreflective development, pain and confusion follow, and this same condition will be the fate of the nation. Meeting with Salim for the last time, Ferdinand is obsessed with the society's degeneration and the impending gloom; he believes everything and everybody is going to hell. The people revert back to the bush and the primitive organization of their society. The same frenzy that attended the people in "A Flag on the Island" characterizes the people at the bend in the river.

The central concern in this novel, as I have pointed out, is not the social development of the African. It is the relationship between an Indian (from whom the East Indian has descended) and his past. Like the *hubshi* in "One out of Many" and the Africans in "In a Free State," the Africans in this novel function as social fodder against which these subjects can come to terms with their world. Thus, when Howe argued that Naipaul "offers no intimations of hope or signals of perspective . . . [and that] one may wonder whether, in some final reckoning, a serious writer can simply allow the wretchedness of his depicted scene to become the limit of his vision," he pinpoints one of the major problems of Naipaul's vision or lack thereof. He observes, however, that "it may be that the reality he grapples with allows him nothing but grimness of voice. There is a complicated literary-moral problem here that cannot be solved in a few sentences, if solved at all."[51] This statement indicates that Howe has missed the major intent of the work, which is not to examine the society but to continue his struggle with his own ambiguous relationship with his society. As Larry Husten has noted, "Naipaul fails to convince us that the perverse sex and violence of the novel are central and constituent elements of our world and not quirks of Naipaul's character."[52]

Naipaul made this position clear in an interview with Elizabeth Hardwick, when, in response to her question: "What is the future, in Africa?" Naipaul stated, "Africa has no future."[53] Such a position does not give rise to a "complicated literary-moral problem." It is the deeply entrenched belief of an individual that fashions and, to a large degree, obscures the artistic vision of the author and leads him to misrepresent what he sees, a condition that Naipaul alluded to in *The Middle Passage*. Nor is it valid to argue as Robert Hemenway does that Naipaul remains a "philosophical idealist . . . a technically superb artist who uses politics to illustrate a personal vision which keeps him from greatness."[54] Naipaul has become a nihilist and can see no good coming out of these societies, and this is the central theoretical position of his later work. Naipaul is a self-exile who, as Martin Amis suggests, goes out among the ruins, "always on the lookout for mimicry, falsity, [and] any pretence of civilisation."[55] Condemned to travel, he is condemned to find nothing new in postcolonial societies.

Naipaul, then, is a classic self-exile, who, wishing to affirm the basic liberties of men, realizes that even though the rights he asserts may be called individual, the condition of their guarantee is inevitably social. For as Raymond Williams notes in his analysis of George Orwell's work,

The exile, because of his own personal position, cannot finally believe in any social guarantee: to him, because this is the pattern of his own living, almost all association is suspect. He fears it because he does not want to be compromised (this is often his virtue, because he is so quick to see the perfidy which certain compromises involve). Yet he fears it also because he can see no way of confirming, socially, his own individuality; this, after all, is the psychological condition of the self-exile.[56]

Naipaul's condition of self-exile prevents him from affirming solidarity with any human community. It demands that he be a nihilist.

Thus, in *A Bend in the River* Naipaul is not concerned so much with the expression of his artistic sensibility as with the articulation of his formulated opinions. Arnold Kettle differentiates between the two concepts and argues that when in everyday life "we refer to a man as a 'socialist' or 'critical' we are usually referring to his formulated *opinions,* whereas the important thing about an artist is not his opinions (on this level) but his *sensibility,* his all-round apprehension and comprehension of things. . . . When we refer to a writer's point of view in the artistic sense we are referring to his sensibility rather than his opinions or intentions, though of course both of these are relevant factors."[57]

At this point in his career, the views Naipaul promulgates and the feelings these views generate can be considered imperialistic and are intended to satisfy the expectations of an audience that is neither Trinidadian nor Third World. In an interview with Bharati Mukherjee and Robert Boyers, Naipaul contemptuously dismissed his Asian and African readership. Of the former he said, they "do not read. . . . If they read at all, they read for magic. They read holy books, they read sacred hymns, or they read books of wisdom, books that will do them good." Of the Africans, he said, "I don't count the African readership and I don't think one should. Africa is a land of bush, again, not a very literary land."[58] As he said to Michiko Kakutani:

I can't be interested in people who don't like what I write, because if you don't like what I write, you're disliking me. . . . I can't see a Monkey—you can use a capital M, that's an affectionate word for the generality—reading my work. No, my books aren't read in Trinidad now—drum-beating is a higher activity, a more satisfying activity. . . . I do not have the tenderness more secure people can have towards bush people. . . . I feel threatened by them. My attitude and the attitude of people like me is quite different from people who live outside the bush or who just go camping in the bush on weekends. . . . These people [Trinidadians] live purely physical lives, which I find contemptible. . . . It makes them interesting only to chaps in universities who want to do compassionate studies about brutes.

In fact, Naipaul has imbibed the ideas of the dominant culture so thoroughly that he is willing to argue that *A Bend in the River* is a defense against "the enemies of the civilization which I cherish. . . . A fear of being swallowed up by the bush, a fear of the people of the bush, and it's a fear that I haven't altogether lost."[59]

The imperialist intent of Naipaul's work seems to make itself more manifest in his willingness to argue that "certain countries and certain peoples have allowed themselves to be exploited and abused" not because of the cruelty of others but because of their internal flaws and "the limitations of their civilization or their culture."[60] The blame of colonialism and imperialism is removed from its external, exploitative source and made into an internal and inherent flaw of the colonized. This is the central position that *A Bend in the River* seeks to demonstrate. Because such a position is more concerned with ideas and opinions than with sensibility and experience, the novel emerges as a political document rather than a fictional text, and this is its major difficulty.

Reflecting the new ideological content of his work, Naipaul's prose became sparse and acerbic, glib and shimmering. Long gone is the playfulness that characterized his earlier work. And so, even though his later prose style allows him to create the impression of hopelessness and doom, it merely reflects the surface reality of African life, a lack of desire to engage the serious content of the life of the continent.

As Naipaul emphasized in his formulated opinions, his prose can only apprehend the narrowest dimension of African life. His concern with his own anxieties remains paramount, as he revealed to Michiko Kakutani. Yet his novelistic technique is so structured that he is able to obscure the real motives of the novel (that is, his examination of Salim's life) by collapsing that life into a framework of a bloodied and vicious country that is presented as being capable of the worst human atrocities.

No colonial person can accept the gloom and apocalypticism which Naipaul proposes as the normal condition of these societies. There can be no return to the blissful ignorance of the bush. One must struggle to liberate oneself from the "bushlike" features that confront one's world. And though Salim may pour scorn upon the notion that the society was in transition from "the end of feudalism and the dawn of a new age" (*BR*, 29), such a process entails tremendous upheavals and disfunctioning of the given society.

Though many attempts have been made to obscure these facts, it should not be forgotten that an entire civilization was wiped out to "civilize" the New World and more than 100 million Africans were brought to till its soil and work its mines. In the process, many millions of Africans and Indians were killed.[61] One may not want to be patient with Africa or India, but one should not forget the history of the civilization which is given as the exemplar of civility and in which Salim finds solace and peace. England may provide a home for Salim, but it contributed immeasurably to the homelessness and hopelessness of the Salims and Ferdinands of the world and presumably toward the rage of primitive men who tend to dominate the landscape of African peoples in this text.

9. Language, Repression, Identity:
A Materialist Recuperation

Because all the practices that make up the social totality take place in language, it becomes possible to consider language as the place in which the social individual is constructed. In other words, man can be seen as *language,* as the intersection of the social, historical and individual. It is for this reason that work on language has created considerations of man as "subject," that is, the individual entity.
—Rosalind Coward and John Ellis, *Language and Materialism*

A strong egoism is protection against disease, but in the last resort we must begin to love in order that we may not fall ill, and must fall ill if, in consequence of frustration, we cannot love.
—Sigmund Freud, *General Psychological Theory*

The radical transformation in Naipaul's art over the course of his development, particularly on the psychological level, culminates in a disturbing and distorting outlook in his most recent work. At the unconscious level of his texts, subtended as they are by the repetition of previous themes, the larger contradiction of his work becomes clear: that is, the struggle to articulate his psychical and social identification and the manner in which his sentiments are bound up with the dominant imperialist discourse of the age.

To be sure, the entirety of Naipaul's work moves in this direction. Yet it is the intensity with which these themes are cathected that reveals Naipaul's psychological motivation. Undoubtedly, the insights of psychoanalysis and Western attitudes toward the East help place Naipaul's discourse in its correct materialist framework and bring a sense of closure to his literary production.

Psychoanalysis has argued that all repressions are rooted in one's sexuality, "which represents the model of every drive and probably constitutes the only drive in the strict sense of the term."[1] In this sense, sexuality cannot be confined to genital activity, perversions, and neuroses but must be extended to encompass all human activity. In Naipaul's work, not one character enjoys a sexually satisfying experience. In fact, each sexual relation is perverted. The manner in which these relationships are depicted gives us a good clue as to what is at stake in his work: that repressed sexuality subverts Naipaul's understanding of the nature of the subject's construction and tends thereby to falsify his depiction of the emerging subject in postcolonial societies.[2]

Naipaul's work tells a great deal about the author himself (a certain libidinal investment), which is related to his desire to construct his ego within the context of his work. In an important interview with Curt Suplee, Naipaul revealed a correspondence between his own "narcissism" and the perceived deficiencies of the cultures he examined. Indeed, Naipaul's satisfied response to his narcissism resembled a form of autoeroticism, which, as Laplanche argued, is a form of self-preservation. Afraid to open up to his world, Naipaul remained smugly confident in his own love and his own little world.[3] Because the process of narcissism stands at the nether side of sexual difference and language, we are able to locate Naipaul's ego within his conflicting response to his two primary worlds—Trinidad and India—and the manner in which his ego locates itself within language.

This chapter will be concerned not so much with the manner in which the subject's discourse represents or misrepresents experience as with the positions allowed the subject within his or her discourse, the way the subject's sexuality signifies some specific meaning within the text, and the way this subjectivity (the human ego) of the postcolonial individual is shaped by the specific social relations of his or her time. In other words, how does the nature of the subject's sexuality signify the understanding of the subject's identity, and how does the social totality, in its economic, political, and ideological practices, construct a new subject within his or her language?

The use of language is important in the construction of the postcolonial subject or individual, in the definition of both his biological individuality and his psychic life. Relying on the work of Lacan, Colin McCabe, points out that

language introduces us to an existence which can never be satisfied, for, as a condition of our speech, something is always missing. And this missing thing is not an unimportant theoretical postulate but the necessarily recurrent question of our being. The process of loss which enables us to gain language produces for us a place and an identity (a name and its substitution rules) within language, but this place is produced by the necessary absence of the differences that constitute it. It is these repressed differences which make themselves heard in verbal slips where language once again reduces to the material from which it has been fashioned.[4]

For Lacan, the possibility of identification arises because of the inherent condition of language: the repressed differences that exist within language. Any examination of the psychical life of the postcolonial subject must necessarily begin as a play of differences and a multiplicity of conditioning contradictions.

Viewed from this perspective, the postcolonial subject cannot be perceived as some "ideal human essence" that preexists his or her entrance into the social totality. Rather than constructing the social totality, the individual is constructed by it. Correspondingly, there can be no "ideal" notion of sociality to which the postcolonial subject must conform, whether one admires that "universal civilization" or not.[5] Yet because Naipaul never questions the manner in which the emerging subject takes up his or her place in language, he is unable to depict the subject as an emerging consciousness or subjectivity of the postcolonial world.

Such a failure of vision, perforce, prevents Naipaul from depicting the postcolonial subject as an ensemble of specific social relations. This deficiency emerges most clearly when one contrasts *A House for Mr. Biswas* with *A Bend in the River*. In the former, a complex of social relations fixes Mr. Biswas in place, giving his existence a certain meaning. Such relations can be determined, analyzed, and understood in a materialist context. *A Bend in the River* offers no such web of social relations, no symbolic order into which Ferdinand can be inserted; there is no society that can reproduce a subject called Ferdinand and provide him with a plausible, consistent meaning. Nor does the privileged and dominant discourse given to Salim assist in providing any specific meaning for Ferdinand. A product of Hinduism, Salim is concerned about his own problem of identity and so is unable to situate Ferdinand in a symbolic order that could grant him authentic meaning.

Because of his commitment to the Western vision of the world Naipaul cannot understand the cosmology of the African world. We are told that Zabeth and Ferdinand come out of the bush and, rather derisively, that the only security they know is that they are protected by their ancestors. The text reveals virtually nothing of their world. There is an understanding of that world, however, that Naipaul fails to report. Wole Soyinka, for example, explained the three dimensions of the Yoruba world view: the world of the ancestors, the world of the unborn, and the world of the living. In *Myth, Literature, and the African World*, Soyinka notes the limits of an imposed Eurocentric view of Africa and the problems that arise when the former comes into conflict with the latter. He also recognizes some of the Islamic influences that fashion the African consciousness:

The past is the ancestors', the present belongs to the living, and the future to the unborn. The deities stand in the same situation to the living as do the ancestors and the unborn, obeying the same laws, suffering the same agonies and uncertainties, employing the same masonic intelligence of rituals for the perilous plunge into the fourth area of experience, the immeasurable gulf of transition.[6]

Even though the deities, the ancestors, and the unborn commune with man in his everyday life, a gap still separates these entities from man and creates the collective experience (or psyche) of the group. How this perception of the world affects Ferdinand is never discussed in *A Bend in the River*. Such shortcomings in Naipaul's later work make his limitations as a novelist painfully clear.

It is fairly obvious that Ferdinand and Zabeth are the products of a certain symbolic order, a world beyond Salim's knowledge and experience.[7] That these subjects are constructed by a symbolic order analogous to the materialist perception of the world seems to be confirmed by the Yoruba proverb: *Bi o s'enia, imale o si* (if humanity were not, the gods would not be). Yet *A Bend in the River* does not examine that world or the way these subjects are constructed by it. Ferdinand, it would appear, exists simply to absorb everything that is European.[8]

Naipaul's use of the realist (naturalist) method of inquiry prevents him from depicting Ferdinand as being constructed by his social totality. Contrasted with *A House for Mr. Biswas,* the great realist novel of its time, *A Bend in the River* and *Guerrillas* look pitiable and incomplete. For in looking back at the world of his grandparents, a world that was accessible through reasoned discourse and possessed an organic wholeness and order, Naipaul could have proceeded to examine the characters of that world as they related to his own language and world. Such a world was manageable even in a process of transition.

The African world Naipaul depicts in *A Bend in the River* cannot be seen in the same light. His constant attempt at negation does not begin to encompass the colonial world in transition wherein the subject has to reposition himself with regard to his language. And although the transition from feudalism to colonial-capitalism presumed the liberation of the individual ego in *A House for Mr. Biswas* (and Mr. Biswas personifies the partial liberation of that ego), the transition from colonialism to postcolonialism as depicted in *A Bend in the River* presumed the emergence of an individual shaped in his relationship to language and the cultural history of his people at a different historical moment.

A successful portrayal of the postcolonial subject during the transition out of colonialism demands a comprehensive examination of the unconscious nature of that experience. Such an examination should be concerned with the gaps in the subject's conscious discourse, the paratactical arrangement of ideas rather than the dominant discourse of the narrator, and should describe rather than explain events and the absence of a metalanguage that controls the discourse of the text. To have Salim as the one dominant center of intelligibility, standing majestically over the text, proclaiming that there is but one final and privileged way of seeing, feeling, and interpreting reality, is to deny the nature of the African individual as a subject that is being structured within his or her language and to accept that fixed human essence that Naipaul would have us believe constitutes the postcolonial person.

The construction of a postcolonial subject positioned differently in language is not antithetical to the literary experience of the Caribbean. Wilson Harris, a Guyanese writer, in *The Guyana Quartet,* was concerned with what he called "the genesis of fiction" and attempted to subvert the canons of realism by seeking to bring "the fictions I had in mind into parallel with profound myth that lies apparently eclipsed in largely forgotten so-called savage cultures." In *Palace of the Peacock,* the first novel of the quartet, Harris argues that all pretenses have to be broken down before one can begin to "walk again," before one can undertake a true journey of and into the self. In that text, he uses a certain "primitive" music "to invoke depth in space, oceanic/forested space, sound and sounding" in order to give an authentic vision to the mythic space of the Caribbean.[9]

In *The Eye of the Scarecrow,* Harris renders an alternative to Naipaul's depiction of the self-sufficient subject. Examining the unfolding of the psychical or unconscious development of the Guyanese people from 1920 to 1964, Harris attempts to bore beneath the known physical facts of the society—its history, economics, and so on—to understand how psychical experiences shaped the unconscious domain of the Guyanese people. By situating the central thematic movement of the text within the gaps of the conscious discourse of the subjects (that is, the society), by proceeding by paradox and indirection, displacement and condensation, the narrator authentically reconstitutes the psyche of the colonial subjects during that period of their history. The narrator of *The Eye of the Scarecrow* argues that "language is one's medium of the vision of consciousness. There are other ways—shall I say—of arousing this vision. But language alone can express (in a way which goes beyond any physical or vocal attempt) the sheer—the ultimate 'silent' and 'immaterial' complexity of arousal."[10]

In this text, the physical activity of the people is not emphasized unduly. Though the narrator recognizes that "the grave conflicts between capital and labour, between parties and powers, between institutions and masses," play an important part in the history of the Guyanese people, it is "a convulsion in the psyche of ordinary men and women"[11] caused by these events that concerns him more. For Harris, therefore, the unconscious (the subjectivity) of the colonial person is revealed through the psychical world of the imagination and memory, emotions and repressions, dreams and fantasies. The positions the subject is allowed to take up within the language allow him or her to become a person.

Harris goes further. Unlike Salim, the narrator of *The Eye of the Scarecrow* recognizes the obstructionist nature of fixed forms and self-sufficient entities and calls upon the subject to "empty" himself of such illusions. Calling for an "open surrender" to all experiences, the narrator argues that "the true beginnings of possible dialogue, the breadth of all unobstructive physicality one receives standing upon a borderline (as silent words stood on their speaking page) between an Imagination capable of reconciling unequal forms present and past and an Imagination empty of self-determined forms to come, black frames, indwelling non-resemblance, freedom from past, present, future form and formlessness. *It is in this unpredictable and paradoxical light one begins to forgive and be forgiven all.*"[12]

In the *The Mimic Men* Naipaul seemed to understand the necessity for the subject to undergo some sort of internal transformation as he moves from colonialism to postcolonialism. Harris, however, *overstood* (to use the language of the Rastafarians) and explored the psyche through the flickering functions of language, decentering the self-sufficient subject and allowing the reader, as Terry Eagleton pointed out in another context, no "secure position of knowledge and dominance in relation to the text."[13]

In *The Eye of the Scarecrow* the reader is allowed to participate actively in the making of the meaning of the text. All the "ideological certainties" with which one is confronted in a realist text such as Naipaul's "are threatened by a great swell of language which knows no absolutes, [and] gender-roles [are] ruptured by a kind of polymorphous perversity of the word."[14] In *The Eye of the Scarecrow* the elusiveness and problematic nature of the "truth" are counterposed to the vexedness and rigid ideological certainties Naipaul always seems to present as truth confirmed. No wonder the great realist and naturalist details of Naipaul's later work seem so inadequate for structuring the essential nature of the postcolonial psyche. Perhaps this is one reason Naipaul argued that he was taking a closer look at the work of Marcel Proust.

Concern for the construction of the essential nature of the subject and its positionality in language brings one to the function of repressed sexuality in the development of Naipaul's texts. In this regard, the world of the text cannot be clearly separated from the world of the author. Not that the author now becomes a major part of the concern, but there is the suggestion that the nature of his sexuality is related to the question of identity and the manner in which he formulated the central problematic of his work. I have alluded to the perverse nature of sexual relations in Naipaul's texts (understanding perversion both as the diversion of the sexual instinct as a vital and healthy function in the child and the sexual aberrations of the adult). That perversion could be the result of Naipaul's inability to come to terms with his early childhood experiences with his society. If we accept Laplanche's position that sexuality can be seen as the "repressed *par excellence*,"[15] it becomes clear that Naipaul's hysterical response to the societies he writes about can be read as a displacement of his early childhood experiences with Trinidad. Drawing on Freud's essay on repression ("Those objects to which men give their preference, that is, their ideals, originate in the same perceptions and experiences as those objects of which they have most abhorrence, and that the two originally differed from one another only by slight modifications"),[16] much of Naipaul's emotional response to his own and other postcolonial societies can be located, in large measure, in that perverse form of sexuality that shaped his younger life and is manifested in his later texts.

In the same essay quoted above, Freud argued that the device the subject uses to deflect the painful aspects of those things he abhors is joking, which lifts the depression only temporarily.[17] The comical elements in Naipaul's first three novels could be perceived as a device to deflect the pain associated with his experiences in Trinidad. And, acting in another classical manner for handling repression, he rushed to the mother country to avoid the pain that resulted from his living in a colonial society. Indeed, his final embrace of the mother (country) in *The Enigma of Arrival* simply attempts to state publicly that which is the necessary and logical trajectory of his whole being. But even that embrace, as we will see, is not as unequivocal and binding as it seems.

Such severe forms of repression, however, lead to hysteria, which finds expression through the circuitous paths of the unconscious.[18] As Laplanche has suggested, "Hysterics tend to lie. . . . They have taken their imagination for reality, and more fundamentally, they have translated—according to specific laws of transposition—their desire into reality." Naipaul's hysteria, therefore, tends to displace the reality of the postcolonial world. Thus, as we examine the work of Naipaul's later period, we are confronted less with a "subjective lie" than with a "transition from the subjective to a grounding—perhaps even to a transcendental dimension: in any event a kind of objective lie inscribed in the facts."[19]

Naipaul, in his later work, does not deliberately and consciously defame Third World societies, nor does he believe that he is not telling the "truth" as he perceives it. Rather, he accuses these countries of living a gigantic "lie" and justifies his fear of "the bush" by his "having lived in the bush": "a fear of being swallowed up by the bush, and it's a fear I haven't altogether lost. The [people of the Third World] are the enemies of the civilization which I cherish."[20]

Apparently, his original repression, resulting from his experiences in early childhood and expressed in the contradictory presence of "ideal" and "abhorrence," caused Naipaul's many hysterical outbursts against Third World societies; his favorite expressions of displeasure are words such as "rage," "outrage," "nihilism," and "nullity." One can argue, however, that these expressions of displeasure are merely an inversion of Naipaul's inability to reestablish and re-create a normal relationship with his past, to come to terms with his early life.

Undoubtedly, the human ego—the conflict of the splitting individual—that Naipaul seeks to reconstruct within his texts is intimately connected with an attempt at self-preservation and the establishment of his self as a living totality. Undeniably, sexuality threatens human integrity, though not directly the integrity of life. Naipaul seeks to articulate his identity within these two opposite tendencies. Moreover, his responses to Trinidad (his home), India (his ancestral home), and England (his adopted home) lead him to examine his position in the world, and this is one reason why he keeps recounting his childhood experiences, especially in his last two works.[21] As he said to Curt Suplee of the *Washington Post,* "What people say is my harshness, my hatred is really my looking, my self-analysis and self-discovery."[22] In the final analysis, this is the central conflict that continues to generate Naipaul's fiction.

AMONG THE BELIEVERS

Naipaul's journey to the Islamic world was the result of his internal quest for "self-analysis and self-discovery." Because the rise of Islam represented another challenge to the civilization Naipaul cherished and a continuing threat to the fragility of the dominant Christian culture with which he aligned himself, Naipaul was not well equipped to examine that culture. Naipaul went out "among the believers" to document how they had distorted the values of his adopted civilization and the "rage" and "anarchy" they had brought to the world. Implicit in this analysis, however, is the notion that the West is "the world" and all those movements that are not in agreement with its doctrines have no part in it.

Thus he begins his Islamic journey with the same fixity of vision and righteousness of cause that inform most of his later work. Needless to say, most of his themes are repeated here. The resulting work cannot pretend to be an objective version of "Islam at work" or a search for Islamic institutions. Rather, it is an attempt to find out how the "rage" and "anarchy" of Islamic people undermine his seemingly secure relationship with dominant Western society. It is not surprising therefore that Naipaul makes comparisons, noting the differences between the Hindu and Muslim experiences in the country of his birth, to demonstrate the incompleteness of Islamic thought:

Islam, going by what I saw of it from the outside, was less metaphysical and more direct than Hinduism. In this religion of fear and reward, oddly compounded with war and worldly grief, there was much that reminded me of Christianity—more visible and "official" in Trinidad; and it was possible for me to feel that I knew about it. The doctrine, or what I thought was its doctrine, didn't attract me. It didn't seem worth inquiring into; and over the years, in spite of travel, I had added little to the knowledge gathered in my Trinidad childhood.[23]

Thus he establishes the differences between himself, a Hindu, and Muslims and the notion that Islamic civilization has not reached the heights of (and presumably cannot be compared with) the European renaissance. Further, the deep antagonisms between the Hindus and the Muslims in India and in Trinidad, particularly around the time Naipaul was growing up, and that were manifested in *The Suffrage of Elvira,* had to be taken into consideration in Naipaul's analysis of Islam. To appear "objective" in his analysis, Naipaul had to obscure his "real" relationship to Islam, even though he made an enormous psychic investment in his examination.

In Iran, he reaffirmed the static nature of Trinidad's colonial society and condemned its "spiritual limitations." In Pakistan, he reiterated the oft-repeated indictment that he grew up in a society that did not allow for the development of the "idea of human quality" and once more noted his separation from that society. "I didn't belong to the colonial Trinidad I had grown up in. . . . Masood's panic now, his vision of his world as a blind alley (with his knowledge that there was activity and growth elsewhere), took me back to my own panic of thirty to thirty-five years before" (*AB*, 194).

In Malaysia the ambivalence of his early life came to the fore once more: "As a Kampong child Mohammed would have been aware of two worlds, two landscapes—more than I would have been in Trinidad. But how much had he really noticed? How much had his instinctive Malay village life permitted him to see?" (*AB*, 285). Unlike Naipaul, who was able to understand the promise of the superior Western Christian world, Mohammed could not separate himself from the world of Islam:

> He didn't deal in the concrete. It was hard for him—dependent on other people's words and thoughts, fitting those thoughts to his own wordless emotions—it was hard for him to be concrete. He wished only for the world to be remade and repossessed as suddenly as (in his memory, the village boy going to the mission school beside the cemetery) it had been taken away from him. This was the promise of his Islam. (*AB*, 289)

Naipaul had escaped from these "wordless emotions." Islam threatened to return him to that chaos, and he wished to protect himself from the fear of being "swallowed up" by this awesome and dreadful force. Hence his ideological onslaught against Islam was the result of his deeply entrenched fear that the Islamic way might subvert the "real" civilizing order in which he had placed so much faith.

Because he was unable to contain his fear, Naipaul's examination of Islam was not as fortuitous as he would have us believe. And though he tried to gloss over the antagonism between the Muslims and the Hindus when he lived in Trinidad, he could not extricate himself from the influence of his formative years. In surrendering his hand to Behzad (with whom he begins the text) to lead him through the maze of Tehran's traffic, Naipaul is symbolically returning to that unexplored area of his childhood consciousness:

> Without Behzad, without the access to the language that he gave me, I had been like a half-blind man in Tehran. And it had been especially frustrating to be without the language in these streets, scrawled and counterscrawled with aerosol slogans in many colours in the flowing Persian script, and plastered with revolutionary posters and cartoons with an emphasis on blood. Now, with Behzad, the walls spoke; many other things took on meaning; and the city changed. (*AB*, 6–7)

Nor should we overlook Naipaul's constant reminder that the central flaw of Islam is its need to go back to its infancy, which was the period of its greatest glory. Such an interpretation, though ostensibly about Islam, is also relevant to Naipaul's incessant quest for his identity. Thus in identifying with Shafi's (Naipaul's guide in Malaysia) sentiments, he reechoes his own grief and persistent preoccupations:

In Pakistan the fundamentalists believed that to follow the right rules was to bring about again the purity of the early Islamic way: the reorganization of the world would follow automatically on the rediscovery of the true faith. Shafi's grief and passion, in multi-racial Malaysia, were more immediate; and I felt that for him the wish to re-establish the rules was also a wish to re-create the security of his childhood, the Malay village life he had lost.

Some grief like that touches most of us. It is what, as individuals, responsible for ourselves, we constantly have to accommodate ourselves to. Shafi, in his own eyes, was the first man expelled from paradise. He blamed the world; he shifted the whole burden of that accommodation onto Islam. (*AB*, 242–43)

Yet Naipaul's predisposition toward Islam prevented him from seeing or understanding any of its social or political truths. He argues that "Islam was a complicated religion. It wasn't philosophical or speculative. It was a revealed religion, with a Prophet and a complete set of rules. To believe, it was necessary to know a lot about the Arabian origins of the religion, and to take this knowledge to heart" (*AB*, 7). From the beginning of his journey, therefore, he was locked into a specific perception of the religion which precluded his ever opening himself up to speculative inquiry. His journey served only to confirm his original charge against Islam: that it leads men backward rather than forward, cripples intellectual life, prevents the development of one's individuality, contradicts the rational quest for scientific knowledge (and hence is contradictory to technological advancement), and leads to hysteria and unreason. From this plateau, he is able to make his now-familiar conclusions about non-Western societies: "This late-twentieth-century Islam appeared to raise political issues. But it had the flaw of its origins—the flaw that ran right through Islamic history: to the political issues it raised it offered no political or practical solution. It offered only the faith. It offered only the Prophet, who would settle everything—but who had ceased to exist. This political Islam was rage, anarchy" (*AB*, 355). In his own way, the Iranian thinker Ali Shari'ati refuted Naipaul's position when he argued that Marxism and its various tendencies such as Leninism, Titoism, Trotskyism, Maoism, and so on were named after individuals and were the breeding ground of personality worship. He contended that the people of the West were "denying personality and maintaining that the individual, the hero, has not the slightest place in human life and history, while their schools take the form of leader-worship."[24]

Nothing could arise out of the anarchy and rage of "political Islam." Like Pakistan, the fate of all Islamic countries and their 700 million inhabitants is inevitable. "Step by step, out of its Islamic striving . . . [it] had undone the rule of law it had inherited from the British, and replaced it with nothing"

(*AB*, 169). Without the West and its Christian guidance, no new forms of thought or practice can emerge. The fate of Islamic people is analogous to that of African and Indian people. In India all is nullity and decay, and in Africa salvation lies in the return to the bush. In the Islamic countries, the people will lose themselves in blood. Islam, it turns out, is not much different from the vices of Hinduism and African ancestral-bush worship. Unable to extricate themselves from their past, people are condemned to an even darker future. And even though the Muslims, unlike the Hindus and the Africans, may have felt some conflict between their faith and their material aspirations, which their oil money from the West allowed them to fulfill, their denial of the West and its Christian light can only bode ill for these unfortunate people.

Yet this Islamic journey—entirely too long and boring in parts—never attempts to examine the Muslim's perception of his world in his own terms. To be sure, there are some interviews—entirely too staged and leading in their presentation—that cite some historical origins of Islam. But Naipaul never begins or frames his questions from the central conception of the philosophical and speculative basis of Islamic thought, which in his view consists solely in a confrontation with the West and its contradiction between the profession of faith and the need for Western technology.

To understand the limits of such an approach to Islam (and, incidentally, the peripheral nature of Naipaul's inquiry) I turn briefly to the insights of the Islamic philosopher Ali Shari'ati, who outlined some of the ideas that guided Islamic revolutionary thought. Shari'ati, convinced that the revolutionary ideas being propagated by the various popular and Islamic movements in Africa "could inspire a new intellectual dynamism in the social and political struggles of the Iranian Muslims,"[25] was influenced tremendously by Frantz Fanon and regarded Fanon's *Wretched of the Earth*, "with its profound sociological and psychological analyses of the Algerian revolution, as a valuable intellectual gift to be presented to all those engaged in the struggle for change in Iran."[26] He called for an "immediate cultural revolt against the [Iranian] regime through a return to Islam," and like the intellectuals of Africa, Asia, and Latin America called vigorously for colonial peoples to return to the roots of their culture.[27] Clearly, the anticolonialist and the anti-imperialist sentiments of the Iranian revolution cannot be ignored when one attempts to understand Islam as an ideology and its rise to prominence over the last decade. Though I do not agree with Shari'ati's critique of Marxism and Western liberal thought (it is much too mechanical and somewhat vulgar in its approach), he is useful for a brief understanding of the ideological roots of Islam.

In his essay "On Humanism," Shari'ati claims that both Western liberalism (or bourgeois thought) and Marxism are derived from the same Greco-Roman thought:

The former claims, by leaving individuals free to think and to pursue scientific research, intellectual encounter, and economic production, to lead to a blossoming of human talents. The latter claims to reach the same goal through the denial of those freedoms, through their confinement under a dictatorial leadership that manages society as a single organization, on the basis of a single ideology that imparts to peoples a monotonous uniformity. The real philosophy of man and life, however, is the same that lies dormant within the liberal bourgeois philosophy: the extension of the life of the bourgeoisie to all members of society.[28]

He believed that Marxism, like Western liberalism, leads to the "embourgeoisement" of all men within that system. Existentialism, which is but another branch of the same tree of Greco-Roman thought and follows necessarily from Marxism, as he sees it, leads only to "nihilism," which cannot be taken seriously in any discussion about human beings and their possibilities. To him, these three ideologies deny the "sacred substance" that differentiates man from all other animals.

Islam is therefore the only medium through which man can achieve a state of grace and free himself from the tyranny of ideologies. It challenges the doctrine of the separation of church and state, which bourgeois liberalism advances, and the denial of the church and glorification of the state, which Marxism offers. Shari'ati claims that Islam offers a rational basis for reliance upon faith in the construction of a new social order. Islam, the last link in the development of the world's historical religions, which arrived under the standard of the *tauhid* (the profession of divine unity),

offers a profound spiritual interpretation of the universe, one that is as noble and idealistic as it is logical and intelligible. In the second place, through the philosophy of the creation of Adam, Islam reveals in its humanism the conception of a free, independent, noble essence, but one that is as fully attuned to earthly reality as it is divine and idealistic. . . .

This future, which begins with the discarding of capitalism and Marxism, is neither predestined nor prefabricated. Instead, it remains to be built. There is no doubt that Islam will have an appropriate role in its construction, when it has freed itself from the effects of centuries of stagnation, superstition, and contamination, and is put forth as a living ideology.

That is the task of the true intellectuals of Islam. Only in this way will Islam—

after a renaissance of belief and an emergence from isolation and reaction—be able to take part in the current war of beliefs and, in particular, to command the center and serve as an example to contemporary thought, where the new human spirit is seeking the means to begin a new world and a new humanity.[29]

Though Shari'ati sees shortcomings in his society, his conclusions differ from Naipaul's. Naipaul, as an outsider, generalizes from the weaknesses of this society, which gives him a pessimistic outlook. Shari'ati looks at the strengths of his society and begins his criticisms from that point. As a result, he offers a more optimistic and solidly based analysis.

The perception of man as presented by Shari'ati ought not to be considered a blueprint for Islamic society. It is a self-critical document, a statement of a goal, and a necessary point of departure. When the Pilgrims and the Puritans came to North America, they did not possess a blueprint for development. They knew only that they were tired of the tyranny of their king and that they wanted to be free to worship their God and to create their city upon the hill. In short, they felt the need for a new beginning. As Shari'ati pointed out in a related context, though Europe stagnated until the Middle Ages, her method of investigating phenomena and of looking at the world resulted in her most productive period: her three centuries of development after the Renaissance.[30] Such is the case Islam makes for its own thought. It is not mindless opposition to Western modernism or Marxist "totalitarianism" but the articulation of a new beginning.

Naipaul, however, went to the Islamic world looking for a blueprint for development. Much to his chagrin, he found none. The predicament of many of the young and not-so-young people he interviewed was that they, like Shari'ati, knew the limitations of both Western liberal and Marxist thought but could not provide a master plan or the sophistication Naipaul required for building a new society. It is also evident, as one reads Shari'ati and other commentators on Islamic thought, that they presented their ideas in an elliptical, allusive manner in contrast to Naipaul's straightforward, no-nonsense approach. As Roy Mottahedeh argues, "Muslim thinkers loved to argue by using contraries (which meant developing and memorizing exhaustive lists of possible alternatives), but they loved even more to argue by contradictories."[31]

Naipaul could grant no validity to the Islamic conception of the world. Leaving the sanctity of a world whose values he cherished, replete in the certainty and correctness of his vision, he went on his Islamic journey, as Fouad Ajami suggests, not so much to understand the people he found there as to judge them. Thus, in his desire to discover "their hidden vulnerabilities and point out their contradictions . . . he tends to miss the drama and the real meaning of their situation. He forgets that it is part of the painful process of history that people are always made by the world they reject and that the rage at it they express is in large measure rage at themselves."[32] Freud made this very point on the nature of repression in his essay of the same name.

Yet another difficulty attended Naipaul's attempt to examine Islamic thought and practice. Because he did not speak the language of the people, understand their culture, or live among them long enough, it was difficult for him to penetrate their world and to arrive at profound insights into their culture. Shari'ati alluded to this difficulty when he argued that any analysis of the existing realities of Islamic societies was possible only through an understanding of their values, modes of conduct, and belief structures. Only through recourse to the terms, expressions, and concepts of Islamic philosophy, culture, religion, and literature, which are, in some cases, richer and more exact than their analogues in foreign languages, can one hope to understand the culture.[33]

Only the arrogance of a Western frame of reference could have permitted Naipaul such license. An Iranian, unable to speak English and having very little perception of Western culture, could not visit England, Canada, and the United States for six months, return to the Islamic world, pronounce a judgment on those societies, and then hope to be taken seriously by the West. More important, suppose on his visit to the United States this Iranian merely visited the South Bronx in New York, a Ku Klux Klan group training for an expected race war between blacks and whites, and then, for good measure, a meeting of Jerry Falwell and members of the Moral Majority who pronounce every doctor who ever performed an abortion a "baby-killer." Would we accept the results of such an exposure as *the* real perception of American society?

Nor can the ideological thrust of this work be ignored. The tendency to abstract and then emphasize the mystical and religious traditions of the societies he visited without any reference to their social context or the scientific and technological bases simply perpetuates the tendency to link "the irrational and obscurantist tradition that we [Asians] have been taught is our own, and only claim to ancient learning."[34]

But this was precisely Naipaul's thrust in arguing that the glories of Islam "were in the remote past; it had generated nothing like a Renaissance" (*AB,*

12). That he should use the European Renaissance as his point of departure to place Asia in the "remote past" is not coincidental. As A. Rahman, the Indian scientist, notes:

The linking of European scientific developments with the earlier tradition of Greeks was not merely to provide legitimacy to the developments during Renaissance against scholasticism, but was also to bypass the contributions of Asian nations, which were in truth tremendous, and to paint science and technology as a purely European phenomenon. . . . Renaissance Europe wished to rid itself of the influence of Arabic scientific and technological tradition and reacted by trying to minimize its achievements. Nor was this hostility to Asian thought new. The ancient Greeks had also reacted, with identical hostility to Asian and Egyptian scientific tradition to which their knowledge owed a great debt.[35]

Naipaul's main purpose, then, in continuing a well-defined European tendency to "delink" the religio-mystical tradition of Asia from its social and scientific roots and depict it as irrational was to negate all the achievements of Islam. In so doing, he could perpetuate the myth of Islamic inferiority and thereby justify the West's exploitation and intellectual domination of these societies.

Naipaul's inability to examine the central problems of Islam as a political force and religio-political ideology weakens his work. One critic argues that Naipaul's "obsession with lost people" makes *Among the Believers* a valuable study.[36] However, even though there are some good descriptive passages, the text does not possess the conviction, the sharpness of insights, or the tender play and subtle contradictions that illuminate his earlier nonfictional works. Where *The Middle Passage, An Area of Darkness,* and *The Loss of El Dorado* engage the societies portrayed in a rich and polemical manner and thereby make them more responsive to the major problematics of the society, no such responses are contained in *Among the Believers.* Where, in the former texts, Naipaul's ambivalence toward his society allowed him to be interestingly and circumspectly irreverent, such richness is not found in *Among the Believers.* Islam is an unknown quantity, and so, apart from his early relationship with the Muslims of Trinidad, which he prefers to minimize, Naipaul injects no central subjective tension to hold the text together, and it bears the burden of the vacuousness and thoughtlessness of its contents.

As a result, Naipaul's resentments against Islam ring false. Much of what he reports could have been found in *Newsweek* or *Time.* As most critics have suggested, there is nothing particularly perceptive about *Among the Believers* except Naipaul's uneasiness about his identity in connection with this intemperate, backward, and archaic religion, and this only seems to demonstrate the uneasy truce he has made with his native culture and the civilization he cherishes.

On the positive side, Naipaul's concern for the autonomy of the individual subject remains paramount. His fear that Islam proclaims the death of the subject in the face of the indifference of the masses—a problem with which Islam has not yet come to grips—continues to concern Naipaul greatly. Yet his inability to add any new dimensions to this genuine concern indicates that his work has reached a dead end. The farther he gets from his society (that is, the less genuine his relationship to his society becomes), the weaker his work becomes and the less perceptive he is as an observer of postcolonial reality. Naipaul stated it best many years ago when he said that no writer could deny his society and still hope to write perceptively and meaningfully about it. This is the dilemma in which he found himself after writing *Among the Believers*.

At that point of his career, his dynamism, his creative insights, and his quasi-philosophical observations all seemed to have dried up. His themes repeat, his prose becomes transparent, and he strains after effect. As a result, his work seems artificial and staged. Success has made him irresponsible. As he loses contact with his society and his self-contestation ceases, so too do the validity of his insights and the quality of his perceptions diminish.

FINDING THE ONTOLOGICAL CENTER

After writing *Among the Believers,* Naipaul undertook an autobiographical enterprise not so much to tell the story of his life as to account for "something less easily seized: my literary beginnings and the imaginative promptings of my many-sided background."[37] This step was necessary if he was to produce any more serious fiction. Conscious of a certain homelessness and an inability to determine just who he was and where he belonged, Naipaul turned once more to writing to examine the contradiction within himself. In so doing, he began to fetishize his writing, and it is within the space between his writing and his fetish about writing that we begin to locate the problematic nature of his being. In *The Enigma of Arrival,* he calls it the separation of "the man from the writer" and sees their coming together as the complete fulfillment of the man.[38] The quest for "self-discovery and self-analysis" that he announced earlier as his goal continued to plague him, and he reiterated it in his "Prologue to an Autobiography": "To become a writer, that noble thing, I had thought it necessary to leave.

Actually to write, it was necessary to go back. It was the beginning of self-knowledge" (FC, 34). He had left his society, but with each new book he rewrote himself back into his society in an attempt to define himself. As he noted in The Enigma of Arrival: "With me, everything started from writing. Writing had brought me to England, had sent me away from England; had given me a vision of romance; had nearly broken me with disappointment. Now it was writing, the book [In a Free State], that gave savor, possibility, to each day, and took me on night after night" (EOA, 169).

In this sense, "Prologue to an Autobiography," "The Crocodiles of Yamoussoukro," and The Enigma of Arrival are auto-bio-graphies, attempts to bring himself to life through language. As Janet Gunn notes, "It is by the means of language (graphie) that self both displays itself and has access to depth; it is also through language that self achieves and acknowledges its bios." It is his impulse to find an orientation in his world that pushes Naipaul toward this form of writing. He wishes not so much to escape time as to acknowledge his "temporal experience as a vehicle of meaning."[39] No wonder, then, at this moment of crisis in his development that he turned to autobiography. Whereas the earlier nonfictional texts such as The Middle Passage and An Area of Darkness had been written at one remove from the self in an attempt to make the traveler's document accessible to others (a private act of self-writing), "Prologue to an Autobiography" and The Enigma of Arrival were more direct and sought deliberately to probe through the introspection of the writer's eye to discover where he belongs (a cultural act of self-reading) through the position that he takes up in language. As much "a movement toward possibility as much as a turning around to the already achieved,"[40] the autobiographical act points heuristically toward the future.

As a result of this attempt at self-knowledge, "Prologue to an Autobiography" and The Enigma of Arrival cover similar ground, in that Naipaul attempts in both to recapture his ontological center through a return to beginnings. The latter takes up where the former leaves off. In "Prologue" Naipaul begins with Bogart, whose father and his (Naipaul's) grandfather had traveled from India together as indentured laborers; "at some time during the long and frightening journey they had sworn a bond of brotherhood; that was the bond that was being honored by their descendants" (FC, 6). In The Enigma of Arrival he goes back to his first arrival in London, to the years of solitude and loneliness when he struggled to find a language that could adequately describe his relationship to yet another unknown world. In contrast to Bogart in Venezuela and Angela, the first woman outside the family whom he got to know when he went to London, both of whose lives have turned out badly, Naipaul describes himself as steeped in his writing to preserve his balance, increase his knowledge of himself, and thereby prevent his disintegration:

So step by step, book by book, though seeking each time only to write another book, I eased myself into knowledge. To write was to learn. Beginning a book, I always felt I was in possession of all the facts about myself; at the end I was always surprised. The book before always turned out to have been written by a man with incomplete knowledge. And the very first, the one begun in the freelancers' room, seemed to have been written by an innocent, a man at the beginning of knowledge both about himself and about the writing career that had been his ambition from childhood. (*FC*, 19–20)

In a way, "Prologue to an Autobiography" is a desperate search for roots, *The Enigma of Arrival* an attempt at reconciliation and a quest for a new beginning. In the former, Naipaul receives the language to reconstruct himself in the death chamber of his aunt, in "her deathbed talk," in broken English and Hindi: "The language still strained her, but what she was saying was like her bequest to me. I had known her poor, living with a man of a cultivator caste. She wanted me to know now, before the knowledge vanished with her, what she—and my father—had come from. She wanted me to know that the blood was good" (*FC*, 51). Naipaul needed this knowledge if he was to reconcile himself with his past.

At the Port of Spain newspaper library of the *Trinidad Guardian,* where his father worked, he received yet another part of his family's history, his father's writings, and through them a knowledge of his father's legacy to him. Through those articles, his father not only transmitted his vocation but "his hysteria from the time when I didn't know him: his fear of extinction. That was his subsidiary gift to me. That fear became mine as well. It was linked with the idea of the vocation: the fear could be combated only by the exercise of the vocation" (*FC*, 72). Writing, and coming to terms with what he wrote, was the only way for Naipaul to reconcile his dilemma.

The Enigma of Arrival picks up where "Prologue to an Autobiography" leaves off in that it continues to examine the process of writing and Naipaul's attempt to locate himself in the future. In spite of all that he had written, Naipaul had not settled the question of his identity or his sense of belonging. The deaths of his sister Sati in 1984 and his brother Shiva in 1985 (to whom the book is dedicated) brought home to Vidya Naipaul the need to address the past—his life of denial—and the future with greater urgency. Without an honest confrontation with the past, there could be no meaningful future. As he says at the end of the book as he watches and contemplates, in Trinidad, his sister's mourning ceremonies even though she, like he, did not believe in Hindu pieties:

Every generation now was to take us further away from those sanctities. But we remade the world for ourselves; every generation does that, as we found when we came together for the death of this sister and felt the need to honor and remember. It forced us to look on death. It forced me to face the death I had been contemplating at night, in my sleep; it fitted a real grief where melancholy had created a vacancy, as if to prepare me for the moment. It showed me life and man as the mystery, the true religion of men, the grief and the glory. And that was when, faced with a real death, and with this new wonder about men, I laid aside my drafts and hesitations and began to write very fast about Jack and his garden. (*EOA*, 354)

The Enigma of Arrival, a sad and saddening book, reads very much like a "work of mourning" and allows Naipaul yet another opportunity to work out his psychical relationship to his original home. The traumatic effects of his siblings' deaths cause him to come to terms with his life and propels him to "work out," in a serious, psychical manner the implications of their lives for his continued living. In other words, what did their deaths mean to his future and in what way was he to anchor himself in his world? An autobiography, disguised as fiction, *The Enigma of Arrival* chronicles what Naipaul calls his "second childhood of seeing and learning, my second life, so far away from my first" (*EOA*, 87) and attempts to demonstrate the harmony with nature that he discovers for the first time. Thus, the text is not so much an autobiography of his sociocultural life, as it is about a linguistic unfolding of a consciousness, an attachment to a new land and the evolution of a new sensibility. The harmony evinced between Jack, an Englishman, and his garden grants Naipaul a paradigm of ordered existence. As he revealed to Melvyn Bragg in an interview on "The South Bank Show," in London:

I saw his [Jack's] life as genuine, rooted, fitting; man fitting the landscape. It did not occur to me when I first went walking that Jack's style of life might have been a matter of choice, a conscious act; that out of the little piece of earth which had come to him with his farm-worker's cottage he had created a special land for himself, a garden where he was more than content to live out his life and where, as in a version of a book of hours, he celebrated the seasons.

That instinct to plant, to see crops grow, might have seemed eternal, something to which the human heart would want to return. But in the plantation colony from which I came, a colony created for agriculture, for the great flat fields of sugar-cane, in that colony, created by the power and wealth of industrial England, that instinct had been eradicated.[41]

This, though, is just another variation of Naipaul's previous theme. Here he reaches back to an even deeper historical source to explain his origins through a "kind of language and a symbolic sequence, but loaded with elements of imagination; a structure, but activated by contingent elements."[42] Whatever the guise, Naipaul is always writing against a backdrop, the anchoring sensibility of which is his Trinidad experiences. Social phenomena (experiences) only mean as they relate to Trinidad. What was previously implicit is made explicit. England is accepted as home as he speaks about "the great love I had grown to feel for it [the English landscape], greater than for any other place I had known" and the great exchange that took place:

For me, for the writer's gift and freedom, the labor and disappointments of the writing life, and the being away from my home; for that loss, for having no place of my own, this gift of the second life in Wiltshire, the second, happier childhood as it were, the second arrival (but with an adult's perception) at a knowledge of natural things, together with the fulfillment of the child's dream of the safe house in the wood/[world]." (*EOA*, 88)

The English landscape provides the narrator (or Naipaul) with a safe haven (it possessed "more meaning . . . than the tropical street where I had grown up" [*EOA*, 5]) and thus is privileged over the latter. In the text, Naipaul tries so very hard to appropriate England. As he says: "I picked my way up and down and around each mound; I wanted in those early days to leave no accessible mound unlooked at, feeling that if I looked hard enough and long enough I might arrive, not at an understanding of the religious mystery, but at an appreciation of the labor" (*EOA*, 19). Here is Naipaul, the unapologetic, truth-telling colonial who, as Richard Cronin notes, "has travelled the world as a self-appointed missionary intent on the destruction of all human illusions"[43] willing to participate in an acknowledged fantasy to reclaim something that was not even his, that could never possibly be his. But English fantasies are more noble than Caribbean or African fantasies and so he keeps up the illusion of trying to appropriate England, thus making *The Enigma of Arrival* the most intense of all his fantasies.

He tells us that on his way back to Salisbury one autumn he reread *Sir Gawain and the Green Knight,* a poem he had read at Oxford as part of a Middle English course some twenty years previously, and at once he realized how much a part of England he had become: "So in tune with the landscape had I become, in that solitude, for the first time in England" (*EOA*, 21). In fact, he had really become G. Ramsay Muir, Esq., M.B.E., country squire, whom he had wanted to become fully one generation before in *The Mystic Masseur* (1957) and of which Elaine Campbell has written that there are sufficient continuities to raise the question: Does it express "the ambiguity of Naipaul's early expatriation in England?"[44] In this sense, *The Enigma of Arrival* should be read less as a second beginning and more as a kind of wish-fulfillment of Naipaul's fantasies. As Derek Walcott puts it, "To those of us for whom his direction has always been clear, this arrival (which, hastily interrupted, elects him to the squirearchy of club and manor) is neither enigmatic nor ironic, but predictable. . . . And if the cost to that spirit has meant virulent contempt toward the island of his origin, then rook, shaw, and hedgerow, tillage and tradition, will soothe him, because although he may reject his own soil, his own phantoms, the earth everywhere is forgiving, even in Trinidad, and rejects no one."[45]

In *The Enigma of Arrival,* people are never just people. They are romanticized beings shaped almost exclusively from the literary store of characters the autobiographer has accumulated in his head. Jack's father is "Wordsworthian, the subject of a poem Wordsworth might have called "The Fuel-Gatherer." In *Miguel Street,* for example, these characters would be made to appear rude, almost absurd. Here they are etherealized; fit subjects of romance and fantasy. They all walk in dignity. Like the mourners in Gray's "Elegy Written in a Country Churchyard," they all possess that rustic beauty, capable only of beauty and noble deeds. One only has to contrast the landscape of *Guerrillas* with that of *The Enigma of Arrival* to understand Naipaul's racism and ideological biases and why in *Miguel Street* he has one of his characters say: "The white man is God, you hear."

In England, a church is not just a church. It is a "part of the wealth and security of Victorian-Edwardian times. It was like the manor to which my cottage was attached; like many of the other big houses around" (*EOA*, 49). In England, the word "estate" reflects the idea of "grandeur and style"; in Trinidad it connoted "many small lives and small houses at the edges" (*EOA*, 195). In England, even sickness is welcomed and thought to be noble; one can even taste its nobility: "Now, in my welcoming cottage, deliciously, for the first time since my childhood, I felt I was having 'fever.' Exhaustion—work, travel—had brought it on: the doctor's diagnosis felt true" (*EOA*, 197). Everything in that world is magical. No wonder Walcott is constrained to ask, "Why is the sticky, insufferable humidity of any city summer preferable or more magical than the dry fierce heat of the Caribbean that always has the startling benediction of breeze and shade? Why is this heat magical in Greece or in the desert, and just heat in Trinidad?"[46] In those other places things are different: the world "is never absolutely new; there is always something that has gone before" (*EOA*, 51). In that world, graced by history and culture, he finds perfection and sees everything as "perfectly evolved" (*EOA*, 51). This perfection would be broken by the haunting memories of Trinidad (his "first childhood") but they would return again with new assurance to keep him comfortable in his new world. And his writing would preserve him.

The nature of Naipaul's responses, then, is obvious. It is almost as though they were deliberately induced and manipulated to satisfy a deeper psychological need. The nobility that he gives to a landscape and the new awareness that he purports to receive are merely retrospective reveries that have their origins beyond the physical reality of Trinidad's society; they seem to read more as a fantasy of origins. Writing on the nature of fantasy and the origins of sexuality, Jean Laplanche and P.-B. Pontalis argued that, "in their content, in their theme . . . original fantasies also indicate this postulate of retroactivity: they relate to origins. Like myths, they claim to provide a representation of, and a solution to, the major enigmas which confront the child. Whatever appears to the subject as something needing an explanation or theory, is dramatized as a moment of emergence, the beginning of a history."[47]

This search for his identity (ego)—or the representation of and solution to the major enigma of Naipaul's life—is closely bounded to his neurotic response to Trinidad, a response that reaches its most hysterical pitch whenever he encounters his society. As he reaches further and further back into the psychological trauma of his origins to explain his present, what emerges are not facts but, as Freud would say, "scenes in fantasy."[48] Such scenes are animated (made manifest) through the creative processes, and *The Enigma of Arrival* can be read as an attempt to explain the primal fantasy of Naipaul's origins.

Throughout the text, Naipaul's response to his society and his acceptance of England is spoken of as an act of fantasy or a kind of phantasmic experience. Indeed, his studied act of refusal/defense in calling *The Enigma of Arrival* a novel can be described as nothing more than an attempt to deflect the painful consequences of his decision; his inability to face up to the implications of his colonial origins. For example, when Naipaul for the first time feels himself a part of the English landscape, his response is: "Of literature and antiquity and the landscape Jack and his garden and his geese and cottage and his father-in-law seemed emanations" (*EOA*, 21). Surely such an embrace was related directly to the unbearability of the Trinidad landscape and reflected his unconscious desire to thrust Trinidad out of his mind. As early as 1975, Landeg White noted that Mr. Stone's behavior and existence, in Naipaul's earliest novel set in an English landscape, were "another version of what Mr. Biswas spends his life pursuing, a means of bringing what has been unbearable under control."[49]

This, however, is precisely the phenomenon that Homi Bhabha calls "the colonial fantasy." As he noted, "In shattering the mirror of representation, and its range of Western bourgeois social and psychic 'identifications,' the spectacle of colonial fantasy sets itself up as an uncanny 'double.' Its terrifying figures—savages, grotesques, mimic men—reveal things so profoundly familiar to the West that it cannot bear to remember them."[50] However, the act of forgetting, as Freud notes, gives rise "either to hysteria, or to obsession, or to an hallucinatory psychosis"[51] and in hysteria such unbearable ideas are transmuted into some bodily form of expression and are expressed in what Freud calls "the capacity for conversion."[52] It is in this sense that *The Enigma of Arrival* represents an expression of conversion, a process that Naipaul had started as early as *Mr. Stone and the Knights Companion*, developed in *The Mimic Men*, and culminated in *The Enigma of Arrival*. In other words, *The Enigma of Arrival* represents the culmination of his most intense childhood desires, and even though he may have tried to detach himself from the "affect" of the idea, "the idea itself remained in [his] consciousness, although weakened and isolated."[53] Through an effort of will Naipaul tried to thrust Trinidad out of his mind and to embrace England as home, to join "the real world again," as he said in 1971.[54] Yet his native land remained a part of his unconscious that was difficult to weed out. As in the case of the hysteric, the more he tried to forget the unbearable experience the more it seemed to remain a part of him.

The entire text therefore proceeds at this level of the splitting of consciousness. Naipaul's almost joyous response as he encounters the order and beauty of England is counterposed to the dis-order and absence of beauty in his colonial land. Like a child, he sets out to learn anew ("with an adult's perception," as he says) the new society that he has embraced. His description of that embrace seems dreamlike and magical even though it is carried forward by a turgid and wooden prose. Yet, all that *The Enigma of Arrival* seems to demonstrate is that, like Naipaul's life, it has been structured by the "phantasmic" which Laplanche and Pontalis argue "should not be conceived of merely as a thematic—not even as one characterized by distinctly specific traits for each subject—for it has its own dynamic, in that the phantasy structures seek to express themselves, to find a way out into consciousness and action, and they are constantly drawing in new material."[55] *The Enigma of Arrival* represents another emanation of Naipaul's consciousness.

By the time Naipaul arrives at *The Enigma of Arrival*, however, he realizes that he lives in a world in which change is inevitability. As he says, "My own presence in the valley, in the cottage of the manor, was an aspect of another kind of change. . . . Everyone was aging; everything was being renewed or discarded" (*EOA*, 32). In "Ivy" he says, "The world had changed; time had moved on. I had found my talent and my subject, ever unfolding and developing. My career had changed; my ideas had changed. And coming to the manor at a time of disappointment and wounding, I felt an immense sympathy for my landlord, who, starting at the other end of the world, now wished to hide, like me" (*EOA*, 191–92). In his "welcoming cottage where he deliciously accepted his fever, he confesses: "I was like a child again. As though I had at last, after twenty years, traveled to the equivalent of the fantasy I had had in mind when I left home" (*EOA*, 197). A new spring had begun, and with it a new way of seeing. In this fantasy he emerges as the major protagonist and participant, one whose intense desire to be a member of the "real world" is satisfied. After twenty years, Naipaul could be a child again and feel comfortable in the mother (country); "the fulfillment of the child's dream of the safe home in the wood." He had overcome his biggest handicap: "being born in Trinidad."[56]

In *The Enigma of Arrival* something very uncharacteristic happens, however: Naipaul is far more accommodating in accepting his history and his "Asian-Indian" background. He tries to give something back to his society, to reconcile himself with his past, and to celebrate his original home. In 1960, after he wrote *A House for Mr. Biswas*, "a book which I felt to be important" (*EOA*, 151), he returned to the island and seemed in a celebratory mood toward his country:

Everything I saw and felt and experienced then was tinged with celebration. . . .

If there was a place, at this stage of my career, where I could fittingly celebrate my freedom, the fact that I had made myself a writer and could now live as a writer, it was here, on this island which had fed my panic and my ambition, and nurtured my earliest fantasies. And just as, in 1956, at that first return, I had moved from place to place, to see it shrink from the place I had known in my childhood and adolescence, so now I moved from place to place to touch it with my mood of celebration, to remove from it the terror I had felt in these places for various reasons at different times. Far away, in England, I had recreated this landscape in my books. The landscape of the books was not as accurate or full as I had pretended it was; but now I cherished the original, because of that act of creation. (*EOA*, 151–52)

Such sentiments are a long way from the horror of the island that he expressed in *The Middle Passage*. If they do not represent an attempt of "associative absorption," then they certainly reflect an attempt to qualify his earlier view of the society so that he could move on, with less remorse and psychical trauma than he felt previously:

It was odd: the place itself, the little island and its people, could no longer hold me. But the island—with the curiosity it had awakened in me for the larger world, the idea of civilization, and the idea of antiquity; and all the anxieties it had quickened in me—the island had given me the world as a writer; had given me the themes that in the second half of the twentieth century had become important; had made me metropolitan, but in a way quite different from my first understanding of the world, when I had written "Gala Night" and "Life in London" and "Angela." (*EOA*, 153)

His acknowledgment of his debt to his original home, his recognition that it still held him in fief, and the realization that he could not arbitrarily renounce his emotional association with his original landscape were necessary acts of cognition before a new beginning could be made, or, to put it another way, before a psychical cure could be undertaken.

Completing *The Loss of El Dorado* seems to have given him a feeling of freedom. On returning to Trinidad while the island was experiencing racial tensions, he lost that celebratory mood and confessed almost in sadness, "So, as soon as I had arrived at a new idea about the place, it had ceased to be mine" (*EOA*, 158). Yet it is through writing that, "knowledge and curiosity feeding off one another—I had arrived at a new idea of myself and my world" (*EOA*, 158), and with this new knowledge, he moved to another stage of development. When, therefore, he received Angela's letter telling him about her life since he knew her, he could only confess that he had moved, intellectually and imaginatively, from where he was in 1950. The manner in which he treats Angela, after he had used her in life as well as in his fiction, is deplorable, but she and Bogart were in and of the past. They could form no part of his future.

Yet there remains in Naipaul's past one specific relation to which he continues to show definite hostility: his relationship to blacks. It, too, is part of his colonial legacy that he must negotiate if he wishes to continue as an imaginative writer of continuing importance and insight. In *The Enigma of Arrival* and "The Crocodiles of Yamoussoukro" Naipaul continues his tirades against black people. In commenting on London's change from a national to an international city, Naipaul sees it as a place "for learning and elegant goods and manners and freedom by all the barbarian peoples of the globe—people of forest and desert, Arabs, Africans, Malays" (*EOA*, 142).

All are forced to go to the mecca of sophistication to acquire goods and breeding. On his trip from New York to London in 1950, a Negro was brought to share his cabin for a night. His response is interestingly familiar:

Yet I was also ashamed that they had brought the Negro to my cabin. I was ashamed that, with all my aspirations, and all that I had put into this adventure, this was all that people saw in me—so far from the way I thought of myself, so far from what I wanted for myself. And it was shame, too, that made me keep my eyes closed while they were in the cabin. (*EOA*, 126)

His feelings of racism plagued Naipaul enormously. Although his behavior might have resulted in part from his Brahmin sense of difference, it also reflected his unresolved hostility toward black people. In his work Naipaul never depicted black people in a positive or complimentary manner, and this remained a serious deficiency. And though "Prologue to an Autobiography" and *The Enigma of Arrival* enable Naipaul to achieve a psychic truce with his "colonial-Hindu self," he refuses to negotiate similarly with the African dimension of his self, society, and the larger nonwhite world.

Significantly, it was while he was completing "In a Free State" in Wiltshire that Naipaul seemed to have manifested the severity of this problem. While writing the story, he projected Africa into the English landscape, and it "began to radiate or return African to me. So man and writer became one: the circle became complete." He continues:

The Africa of my imagination was not only the source countries—Kenya, Uganda, the Congo, Rwanda; it was also Trinidad, to which I had gone back with a vision of romance it had seen black men with threatening hair. It also now became Wiltshire. It was also the land created by my pain and exhaustion, expressed in the dream of the exploding head. A little over a year before, toward the end of the book about the New World, I had had the waking fantasy of myself as a corpse tossing lightly among the reeds at the bottom of a river (a river like the one in the Pre-Raphaelite painting of the drowned Ophelia, reproduced in the *Nelson's West Indian Reader* I had used in my elementary school in Trinidad, a river that turned out to be like the river in Wiltshire at the back of my cottage). Now every night at some stage an explosion in my head—occurring in a swift dream, giving me the conviction that this time I had to die, that this time I could not survive the great, continuing noise—awakened me.

Such violence in my Africa, in the security of my stone cottage, where I had a coal fire every night! So much had gone into that Africa of my fantasy. As a point of rest, as a refreshment, a promise of release, I allowed myself to play, lightly, with the ancient Mediterranean idea that had come to me from the de Chirico painting, "The Enigma of Arrival." (*EOA*, 171–72)

The Africa of his imagination had penetrated the safety of his English world. In fact, he had never left the African world of his childhood, the

Africa of his society, and therein lay the continuing problem. With the above image, he closed the frame that characterized his writing career from *Miguel Street* to *Among the Believers,* the book he was writing when he received Angela's letter. His relationship with Africa remains a puzzling enigma and brings him to a dead end. He can go no further creatively until he comes to terms with the African part of his heritage. The explosion that he hears, the corpse that he imagines, the fear of death, all emanate from that unresolved relation.

"The Crocodiles of Yamoussoukro" is also somewhat autobiographical, for it is part of Naipaul's struggle to come to terms with Africa and her postcolonial people. He visited the Ivory Coast because he thought it the only successful African country. Nevertheless, it resembles other African societies in one remarkable respect: it, too, was built by others. When the whites leave, Africa will certainly go back to bush, and the "wild" black men of Africa will be left with only their magic. As in his other works, most of his sentiments collapse back into the Caribbean world that he had known, and the African world emerges as illusory: "To the outsider, to the slave owner, the African night world might appear a mimic world, a child's world, a carnival. But to the African—however much, in daylight, he appeared himself to mock it—it was the true world: it turned white men to phantoms and plantation life into an illusion" (*FC,* 149).

Thus even what appears to be the most successful African colony is nothing but another form of mockery and an illusion. Even when these countries appear to be successful, they only reflect African magic, once removed from stupidity. The people participate in the same meaningless nonsense as their Caribbean counterparts: "It was a story that might have come from a Caribbean slave plantation two hundred years before. White men, creatures of the day, were phantoms, with absurd, illusory goals. Power, earth magic, was Africa and enduring; triumph was African. But only Africans knew" (*FC,* 165). African magic matches Caribbean magic, and for good measure the psychic sickness of American blacks is thrown in: "They are like everybody else who comes to do that [convert the Africans]. They bring their own psychic sickness to Africa. They are mad" (*FC,* 176).

One is not too sure who possesses the madness in this context and who "they" are. In *The Enigma of Arrival,* Naipaul spoke about an explosion in his head, having no place to go, feeling the end had come, almost anticipating his own death. At the end of "The Crocodiles of Yamoussoukro" he condemns the Afro-Americans who bring their "psychic sickness" to Africa and concludes that "they" (probably meaning all blacks) are mad. Because of their madness, black people have no place to go. Stated in his more famous words, "Africa has no future," even when one looks at the most successful experiment of African development.

In "Crocodiles of Yamoussoukro" Naipaul makes the ultimate statement when he acknowledges:

I travel to discover other states of mind. And if for this intellectual adventure I go to places where people live restricted lives, it is because my curiosity is still dictated in part by my colonial Trinidad background. I go to places which, however alien, connect in some way with what I already know. When my curiosity has been satisfied, when there are no more surprises, the intellectual adventure is over and I become anxious to leave. (*FC*, 90)

In the foreword to *Finding the Center*, he argues that "a writer after a time carries his world with him, his own burden of experience, human experience and literary experience (one deepening the other); and I do believe— especially after writing 'Prologue to an Autobiography'—that I would have found equivalent connections with my past and myself wherever I had gone" (*FC*, ix). In his interview with Melvyn Bragg in 1987, after the publication of *The Enigma of Arrival*, Naipaul still seemed prisoner of his past. Recognizing the inevitability of change, Naipaul argues that, as he grows older, he becomes acutely aware of how much he continues to live out the effects of his "family past" and the effect of his "father's early death. . . . And, you know, I think about 10 years ago one thought one had got rid of that. One thought one entered a new world. One was making one's own life. Then you find that no, you're still a prisoner, a prisoner of the past."[57]

The Enigma of Arrival, then, reveals no significant shift in Naipaul's vision. He refuses to grant any validity to the world of the other. He sees only African stupidity. In his interview with Melvyn Bragg, Naipaul argued that it took "a lot of trouble, a lot of writing, before I came to the conclusion that my subject was really the other."[58] In a remarkably perceptive essay, Thomas Mypoyi-Buatu demonstrates Naipaul's attempt to negate the reality of the other, particularly Africans, through the strategic deployment of his fiction and argues that the leitmotif in Naipaul's work is that "the black African demonstrates the extent to which their 'otherness' is indomitable, fundamentally demonic and, as a consequence, refuses the attempts at standardization (or 'normalization') made by the West."[59] Mypoyi-Buatu notes that in most of Naipaul's work a Westerner makes a long journey, sees selectively, and then discovers the frightening reality: that region of the world has no possible future. "The social and cultural depth of these countries through which he crosses escapes him entirely." Naipaul, he claims, sees only that which is dictated to him by his Western biases. He continues:

When the narration is extended to the indigenous people in having them say "I," this is nothing more than a convenient fiction. Their talk is determined by the point of view of the Western character: the Africans are lacking in psychology. Situating the narration within these characters is simply a way of animating them, much in the same way that one would make a marionnette move. If we assume that psychology takes shape within the context of a story, and that the story in turn implies the existence of the past, then it can be said that Naipaul denies his native characters a past of any kind. . . . The precise descriptions, which are scrupulous to a fault, reveal reality. The details separate reality into its various facets, stress certain aspects by isolating them and, given the fact that they constitute discontinuous moments of the story, generally hold the narrative immobile. History is an accumulation of details; however, history alone is capable of transcending the details, and thus absolves politics (which Naipaul calls stupidity) of all responsibility.

This "stupidity," however, is not Naipaul's obsession: *he seeks to show the confused overlapping of reality and fiction in order to express his refusal of the representation of reality through literature.* In this manner he rejects all hope and all possibility for a future. His choice has been made: we can do nothing to combat reality. Just like one of his characters who chooses London as the only possible place to live and the only possible center of civilization, Naipaul has chosen to speak out in favor of the quiet and unassuming charm of London life. He loudly proclaims himself to be in favor of "universal Western civilization." In reality, he has made the choice to deny "otherness," and in this he is a zealous, painstaking, "normalized" son of this Western world which for a long time and even now is being thought of positively only in the context of the negation of the Other."[60]

Such a strategy prevents Naipaul from granting any authenticity to the activities of any people that is not white and European. To think properly of itself, the West must think badly of the other and it is here that Naipaul fulfills the ideological task set forward for him by the Western imperialist world.

The task, then, of *The Enigma of Arrival* is to describe in a painstaking and meticulous way the manner in which Naipaul arrives at and accepts the universal civilization of the Western world. To do so, however, he must always deny the validity and the authenticity of the other's culture; hence the magic of Wiltshire. It must always be naturalized, neutralized, neuterized, and described in such a way that it can be easily managed, conscripted, and consumed by the dominant culture. It must be explicated only in language that is acceptable to the dominant power. Thus he confirms in his fictionalized autobiography what he has always said in his fiction. But even at this point of his development he is unwilling to expose this new "self" that he claims to have become to the unblinding light of day, except under the guise of fiction: hence, the convenient fiction/fantasy that the obviously autobiographical *The Enigma of Arrival* is, in fact, a novel. Reality must always be confused with fiction (perhaps in Naipaul's case they are one and the same). Somehow, it all isn't quite true. The past of which he is a prisoner would not allow him to do so.

This, then, is Naipaul's burden: in his attempt to work out his future, he transfers his neuroses onto others and thereby assures himself that he would always be "a prisoner of the past." Indeed, until he can see Africa and Africans for what they are and understand that any cultural or social analysis "can only be pursued with the help of appropriate paradigms and models derived from the culture of society itself, for only such paradigms can yield rules or principles whose structural autonomy is beyond rebuke,"[61] he will be unable to capture a balanced vision of Africa or of his society. He may continue to depreciate these societies, select whom he wishes to speak for them; but until he examines their positive aspects, seeking honestly to understand the social and cultural frames from which they operate, he will never get close to their or his truth, and the explosion in his cathedral will continue. Until he positions himself differently and more accurately within his speech (he says that he carries his human and literary experiences to these societies), the reconciliation of man and the writer which he seeks will continue to evade him. Writing may ease the pain momentarily but the man will always be alone and afraid.

I began this analysis by locating Naipaul's work within the context of Caribbean literature. I think it ought to remain there despite the growing tendency of his publishers (and I suspect Naipaul himself) to disassociate him from the society that is responsible for his most meaningful fiction. The dust jacket of *Among the Believers,* as well as that of *A Bend in the River,* describes Naipaul as "born in Trinidad, to which his grandfather had come from India, but he has lived most of his life in London." This factual statement does not begin to tell the truth about Naipaul's life, as he himself is beginning to acknowledge. The Caribbean—and its capacity for generating meaning in Naipaul's work—remains the wellspring of his art, whether he chooses to accept that reality or not. He may not want to accept it emotionally, but rationally his most creative fiction remains embedded in that primal reality.

NAIPAUL'S IMPERIALIST PREOCCUPATIONS

One ought not to end a reading of Naipaul's work with the vagaries of psychoanalysis alone, even if a strong case can be made for its centrality in understanding his personal dilemma. As I have argued, his work, particularly in the latest period, is surely and securely located within the dominant imperialist ideology and racist preoccupations of the age. Thus, if Naipaul has become the darling of the First World, it is because he has said so well what many white racists wanted to say all along but could not. Naipaul was not the first person to echo racist commentaries, nor is the *Wall Street Journal* original in its concern for the maintenance of the morality of international law.[62] In 1859, speaking about the general perception of its continental neighbor and using the racist codes of contemporary discourse ("civilized" versus "uncivilized"; "Christian Europe" versus "Asiatic despots"), John Stuart Mill spoke of the great distinction in the conduct of international affairs between "civilized" and "barbarian" nations:

To suppose that the same international customs, and the same rules of international morality, can obtain between one civilized nation and another, and between civilized nations and barbarians, is a grave error, and one which no statesman can fall into, however it may be with those, who from a safe and unresponsible position, criticise statesmen. . . . In the first place, the rules of ordinary international morality imply reciprocity. But barbarians will not reciprocate. They cannot be depended on for observing any rules. Their minds are not capable of so great an effort, nor their will sufficiently under the influence of distant motives. In the next place, nations which are still barbarous have not got beyond the period during which it is likely to be for their benefit that they should be conquered and held in subjection by foreigners. Independence and nationality, so essential to the due growth and development of a people further advanced in improvement, are generally impediments to theirs. The sacred duties which civilized nations owe to the independence and nationality of each other are not binding towards those to whom nationality and independence are either a certain evil, or, at best, a questionable good. . . . To characterize any conduct whatever towards a barbarous people as a violation of the law of nations, only shows that he who speaks so has never considered the subject. A violation of great principles of morality it may easily be; but barbarians have no rights as a *nation*, except a right to such treatment as may, at the earliest possible period, fit them for becoming one. The only moral laws for the relation between a civilized and a barbarous government are the universal rules of morality between man and man.[63]

Naipaul, it must be remembered, was acquainted with both the language and the content of this discourse, as is reflected in *The Middle Passage*. After all, John Stuart Mill belonged to the same school of thought that produced Anthony Froude, Thomas Carlyle, and Anthony Trollope. "A Few Words on Non-Intervention," from which the excerpt above is taken,

appeared in *Fraser's Magazine,* the same forum in which Carlyle introduced the world to his now famous discourse on the "Nigger Question."
Naipaul, a good scholar of this period of English history, must have been
acquainted with Mill's discourse on nonintervention.

I quote Mill at length to demonstrate that much of what Naipaul and the
editorial board of the *Wall Street Journal* said about the Iranian and Islamic
people came from the most reactionary period of racism and ethnocentrism,
both products of English imperialism. Naipaul's position had not changed
much from the initial concerns he expressed in *The Middle Passage* even
though he might have made a belated attempt to temper his position somewhat.

In light of these concerns, the question arises inescapably: for whom does
Naipaul write? In the *Times Literary Supplement* of August 15, 1958,
Naipaul articulated part of the problem he faced as a West Indian writer at
that time and his literary objectives:

The Americans do not want me because I am too British. The public here do not
want me because I am too foreign. . . . I live in England and depend on an English
audience. Yet I write about Trinidad, and more particularly the Indian community
there. . . . I write for England. . . . It is an odd, suspicious situation: an Indian
writer writing in English for an English audience about non-English characters who
talk their own sort of English. . . . The only way out [that is, to overcome public
indifference] is to cease being a regional writer. . . . I would like nothing better. But
now I feel I can never hope to know as much about people here as I do about Trinidad
Indians, people I can place almost as soon as I see them.[64]

Naipaul fulfilled his highest ambition when he wrote *The Enigma of Arrival.*
Written for an English audience, it went to the English best-seller list as
soon as it was published and he noted his delight at seeing the average
English reader reading his book. More than a regional writer, he has become
an international writer, speaking "truths" that the dominant bourgeois class
(be it French, English, or American) dearly loves to hear and so it has
acclaimed him the "best novelist writing in the English language today." In
March 1987, Melvyn Bragg, an English television presenter of one of
England's most popular television programs, introduced Naipaul as "one of
our most distinguished novelists," and, as I noted at the beginning of this
book, Patrick Swinden in *The English Novel of History and Society, 1950–
1980* (1984) not only argued that Naipaul's experience prepared him "in a
special way for the occupation of being an English writer" but claimed that
"an English writer is what Naipaul is."[65] By 1987 Naipaul's career had
gone full circle. He had fulfilled his most cherished desire: he was accepted
as an English writer.

Because of such an embrace, Naipaul's writing cannot be abstracted from its class content, nor can we ignore the battle of readings that takes place in any analysis of his work. Literary texts are practices that do something to us. Terry Eagleton, writing in *Social Text,* has argued that since "all literary texts are in some sense ideological—that is to say, aligned somewhere on a spectrum of significations which contribute either to transforming the conditions of existence or the dominant social relations of production—it follows that to read is to become engaged in the class struggle."[66] V. S. Naipaul has clearly aligned himself and his writing on the side of the dominant class. The *Washington Post,* the *New York Times,* the *Boston Globe, Vogue,* and *Newsweek* (to name a few United States publications) continue to praise him. The oppressed brothers and sisters in Kingston, Port of Spain, Tehran, New Delhi, or Accra would recognize him automatically as the bourgeois surrogate spokesman he has become.

Thus, whether Naipaul continues to serve the oppressor class because of subjective "psychological" or practical "material" reasons, his ideas, more than ever, are securely entrenched within the dominant imperialist discourse of the age. Needless to say, these ideas are welcomed and accepted with amazing gratitude, and they are almost uncritically disseminated by inundating Naipaul with the most precious symbols of appreciation: literary awards. And so he wanders through the Western world, "a prophet without God," marked with "blessed purity," uttering his malevolent incantations as he interprets the fate of those barbarous peoples who live in the remote parts of the globe, confident that he and his work will be rewarded by those with whom he is aligned and whose ideas he promulgates in a not-so-unconscious manner.

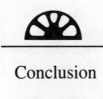

Conclusion

V. S. Naipaul, by far the most prolific and important novelist of the West Indies, is also its most cherished. As Derek Walcott noted, "Despite his horror of being claimed, we West Indians are proud of Naipaul, and that is his enigmatic fate as well."[1] After nineteen books and a career that spans over thirty years, Naipaul's central concern still remains his desire to make a truce with his world so that he could move on to conquer other worlds. Although his search has led him to embrace England as his home, his problematic and ambivalent relationship with his original home still remains the source of his creative power and all his works have to be evaluated against that central conflict.

As I have argued, his most important, interesting, and arresting work (up to and including *The Mimic Men*) takes place in the early part of his career, after which most of his ideas repeat and become more intensely racist and openly hostile to the Third World. Although he may have become more technically proficient in his later period, his morbid preoccupation with himself limits the overall applicability and persuasiveness of his work, particularly to readers of the Third World.

That Naipaul has made immeasurable contributions to the examination of the subject in colonial and postcolonial societies is not to be doubted. My contention is that *A House for Mr. Biswas* and *The Mimic Men* are his two most important works, even though some First World critics, primarily those in the United States, have tended to grant this honor to *Guerrillas*. Because First World scholars are concerned with lauding Naipaul's virtues, they have failed to see his many shortcomings and to interpret his work within the context of West Indian literature and what can be called post-colonial discourse.

Naipaul will continue to be praised by the West, but for the wrong reasons. He will continue to say what Westerners want to hear and will receive the necessary publicity for his pains. With greater success, his darkened vision of the world will drift over even to those of the First World who will praise him until he is rebuked. Until that time, however, he will continue to believe that his apocalypticism correctly mirrors the world of his fathers and brothers, as he struggles ever so intensely to prevent himself from being overtaken by the "monkey-sensibility" of his people.

A House for Mr. Biswas will remain a great piece of literature because it captures the complexity of a colonial subject caught up in the transition from feudalism to capitalism and the various forms of alienation that such a condition engenders. *Guerrillas* and *A Bend in the River* will fade into obscurity because they do not speak to any active self-contestation within the individual subject as he or she struggles to realize his or her human potential. As a society seeks to transform itself from social and economic backwardness to some degree of self-sufficiency and decency, it cannot use a literature that presents madness, desolation, and nihilism as the predominant human emotions. Such sentiments cannot be the major impulses that fashion successful fiction, simply because they negate human possibilities and are of inherently limited literary value.

For critics and scholars who are only too willing to uncritically and unequivocally accept the words of V. S. Naipaul, as they write from the security of America or Britain, it is not nearly as comfortable to remember that in the settling of America an entire civilization was wiped out by the Europeans, that 100 million Africans were brought to the New World to be enslaved over a period of two hundred years, and that innumerable cruelties were committed against the peoples of whom V. S. Naipaul writes. It is comfortable to feel relaxed by the barbarity in which he depicts these people because somehow it assuages the conscience of the First World. Yet the societies of which Naipaul writes are going through tremendous upheavals and may endure many more atrocities as they seek to come to terms with the world in which they live. The question, though, is not how bad things are but whether these societies contain any good. This ought to be the context in which most of Naipaul's later texts are examined.

It might be wise to see the plight of these people, as they move from a state of colonialism to postcolonialism or from feudalism to capitalism, as being no better and certainly no worse than their European counterparts. They respond as they must to an ever-changing present, undergoing tremendous hardships as they assert themselves in their world. Naipaul increasingly, as he goes through the apocalyptic period of his career, attempts to portray these people as barbarous and at the end of the world, presumably fit candidates for extermination. Such depictions ought to be resisted for the ideological analyses they are. While it is true that the dominant bourgeois class dominates the intertextual production of meaning, it is the responsibility of those of us from the dominated group to break through the silence that is imposed upon our group, recognizing, as some feminist scholars have, that "those who have the power to name the world are in a position to influence [its direction]."[2]

In 1979 Naipaul discussed his work with David Pryce-Jones and noted, almost exuberantly, that he was "recording and chronicling this extraordinary period of ours [the social transformation from colonialism to post-colonialism]. The books will have to stand by their truth or otherwise. If I'm wrong then the books won't continue to survive."[3] Naipaul could not have spoken more correctly, since his work is welcomed and accepted so uncritically by the West. Sooner, rather than later, though, he will be seen for the misanthrope that he has become. Later, rather than sooner, his work will be given the measured treatment it deserves, and that which is socially useful and morally uplifting will be treasured and retained. I hope that this analysis is but the beginning of such a process.

Notes

INTRODUCTION

1. Patrick Swinden, *The English Novel of History and Society, 1940–1980* (New York: St. Martin's Press, 1984), p. 210.

2. V. S. Naipaul, "Prologue to an Autobiography," *Vanity Fair* 46 (April 1983).

3. See the Bibliography for a listing of these works.

4. Swinden, *The English Novel*, p. 210.

5. Louis Althusser, "The Importance of Theory," *Theoretical Review* 20 (January–February 1981): 14.

6. By "literary work" I mean the entire corpus of Naipaul's writings. By "literary text" I mean Naipaul's fictional and nonfictional books. For a useful distinction between the "text" and the "work," see Roland Barthes, "From Work to Text," *Image, Music, Text*, trans. Stephen Heath (New York: Hill and Wang, 1977), pp. 155–66.

7. Leonard Green, "Materialist Readings in Modernism: T. E. Hulme and T. S. Eliot" (Ph.D. diss., Cornell University, 1979), pp. 24–25.

8. Kenneth Ramchand, "History and the Novel: A Literary Critic's Approach," *Savacou* 5 (June 1971): 103.

9. Pierre Macherey, *A Theory of Literary Production*, trans. Geoffrey Wall (London: Routledge & Kegan Paul, 1978), p. 42.

10. The term "problematic" is used as Louis Althusser defines it in *For Marx*, trans. Ben Brewster (London: Penguin, 1969), pp. 253–54.

11. Wilson Harris, *Tradition, the Writer, and Society* (London: New Beacon, 1967), pp. 31, 28.

12. Such readings are not confined to critics of West Indian literature. Biodun Jeyifo makes the same case against certain First World readings of Wole Soyinka's plays. See "Soyinka Demythologized: Notes on a Materialist Reading of *A Dance of the Forests, The Road,* and *Kongi's Harvest*," Ife Monographs on Literature and Criticism, 1st ser., no. 2 (University of Ife, Ife, Nigeria, 1984).

13. Macherey, *Theory of Literary Production*, p. 100.

14. Dominick La Capra, in *Preface to Sartre: A Critical Introduction to Sartre's Literary and Philosophical Writings* (Ithaca: Cornell University Press, 1978), p. 38, makes the same point about Sartre's nonfictional writings.

15. Elaine Campbell, "West Indian Fiction: A Literature of Exile" (Ph.D. diss., Brandeis University, 1981), p. 184.

16. Michael Thelwell's novel *The Harder They Come* (New York: Grove Press, 1980) has won praise for the "authentic manner" in which it depicts the reality of Jamaican people in particular and Third World people in general. Chinua Achebe, the African novelist and critic, has argued that *The Harder They Come* "is a magnificent achievement, moving, eloquent, defiant. It is a milestone in the cultural history of black people. Michael Thelwell has put us all in his debt." Achebe's assessment of Thelwell's work is in direct opposition to his reading of Naipaul's work and to Elizabeth Hardwick's response. See "Viewpoint," *Times Literary Supplement,* February 1, 1980; *New York Times Book Review,* June 24, 1979; Irving Howe, "A Dark Vision," *New York Times Book Review,* May 13, 1979.

17. Gordon Rohlehr, "The Ironic Approach: The Novels of V. S. Naipaul," in Louis James, ed., *The Islands In Between* (London: Oxford University Press, 1968); Edward Lucie-Smith, *London* 8 (July 1968): 96.

18. Helen Tiffin, "The Lost Ones: A Study of the Works of V. S. Naipaul" (Ph.D. diss., Queens University, 1972), p. 117; William Walsh, *V. S. Naipaul* (New York: Barnes and Noble, 1973), p. 5.

19. Jean Kramer, "From the Third World," *New York Times Book Review,* April 13, 1980, p. 1; emphasis added.

20. Rohlehr, "The Ironic Approach," p. 123.

21. See, for example, Fred Halliday, "The Misanthrope," *Nation,* October 24, 1981, pp. 415–16; and Edward Said, "Expectations of Inferiority," *New Statesman* 102 (October 16, 1981): 21–22; Chris Searle, "Naipaulicity: A Form of Cultural Imperialism," *Race and Class* 26, no. 2 (Autumn 1984): 45–62; Derek Walcott, "The Garden Path," *New Republic,* April 13, 1987, pp. 27–31; and Alan Brien, "A Person of Refinement," *New Statesman,* March 13, 1987, pp. 26–27.

22. Paul Theroux, *V. S. Naipaul: An Introduction to His Work* (New York: Africana, 1972), p. 7.

23. The terms "tradition" and "influence" are used here not to mean expressive causality in which there is an allusion to prior cause and a sense of teleological unfolding, "a principle of coherence and the outline of future unity" (Michel Foucault, *The Archaeology of Knowledge,* trans. A. M. Sheridan Smith [New York: Harper and Row, 1972], p. 22), but in the materialist sense, that is, as structures that are radically overdetermined, representing positionality rather than causality in the discursive field. Although I would not argue that one author, Naipaul, for example, exists because of a causal process called Caribbean literature, his work obviously cannot be understood fully unless we have recourse to the discursive field of knowledge called Caribbean literature, a field that possesses its own limits and discontinuities.

24. Quoted in S. Mozhyagun, ed., *Problems of Modern Aesthetics* (Moscow: Progress Publishers, 1969), p. 187.

25. Walcott, "The Garden Path," p. 30.

26. See Roland Barthes, "The Death of the Author," in *Image, Music, Text,* and Roland Barthes, *Writing Degree Zero and Elements of Semiology,* trans. Annette Lavers and Colin Smith (Boston: Beacon Press, 1970).

27. J. H. Collens, *A Guide to Trinidad: A Handbook for the Use of Tourists and Visitors,* 2d ed. (London: Elliot Stock, 1888), p. 233.

28. See J. C. Jha, "Indian Heritage in Trinidad, West Indies," *Caribbean Quarterly* 19, no. 2 (1973): 32–33, for a meticulous description of Indian culture in Trinidad. Upon reading this work, one critic suggested that the influence of East Indian cultural life (he did not say Hindu) upon Naipaul's work is so obvious that one need not mention its pervasive influence in the culture. In spite of this "apparent" pervasiveness, not one of Naipaul's critics (apart from Sudha Rai, *V. S. Naipaul: A Study in Expatriate Sensibility* [New Delhi: Arnold-Heinemann, 1982]) was perspicacious enough to demonstrate how this cultural heritage influenced his work.

29. Jonathan Culler, *Roland Barthes* (New York: Oxford University Press, 1983), p. 32. Barthes elaborates on the notion of "second-order memory" in *Mythologies,* trans. Annette Lavers (New York: Hill and Wang, 1973). Hinduism and its myths act as the second-order memory in Naipaul's writings. See also Noor Kumar Mahabir, *The Still Cry: Personal Experiences of East Indian Indentures in Trinidad and Tobago, 1845–1917* (Tacarigua: Calaloux Publications, 1985), for a discussion of the evolution of the East Indian language in Trinidad and Tobago during indenture.

30. V. S. Naipaul, *An Area of Darkness* (London: André Deutsch, 1964), pp. 37–38.

31. Mulk Raj Anand, *An Apology for Heroism* (London: Lindsay Drummond, 1945), pp. 7, 23, 95.

32. Mulk Raj Anand, "Old Myth, New Myth: Recital versus Novel," in C. D. Narasimhaiah, ed., *Indian Literature of the Past Fifty Years, 1917–1967* (Prasaranga, India: University of Mysore, 1970), p. 120.

33. Ibid., p. 110.

34. As Georg Lukács has noted in his many works on realism, the epic form, by its very nature, is not constructed to ask questions, because the hero is always organically connected to the values of his society. The novel, on the other hand, arises at the very moment that people begin to become alienated from their society. The novel, as a form, therefore, is able to question the nature of the fragmentation of a society, whereas the epic is prepared to state, with especial vigor, the certainties of its world.

35. V. S. Naipaul, "Critics and Criticism," *Bim* 38 (1964): 75. See also Kerry McSweeney, *Four Contemporary Novelists* (Montreal: McGill-Queen's University Press, 1983), pp. 152–94, for a discussion of what Naipaul views as the function of the novel.

36. Anand, *Apology for Heroism,* p. 45.

37. Naipaul's acceptance of the "civilizing" aspects of Christianity is clear in the following comment: "I am devoted to the idea of the life of the mind. I'm interested in the spread of human values. I went to a Catholic wedding in Essex about two weeks ago; I was gripped by the experience. It was all new to me, very fresh! I saw the altar, the wine and the wafer. I saw the links with the classical world of the bloody sacrifice. And I saw what had been added by Christianity to the old idea of appeasement of the gods as this endless message of love, of *charity* man to man. Not that Christianity hasn't done harm, but that Christian idea of love, added to the Roman idea of law, of contracts, is what has made Western civilization" (Charles Michener, "The Dark Visions of V. S. Naipaul," *Newsweek,* November 16, 1981, p. 110).

38. R. S. Singh, *The Indian Novel in English* (Atlantic Highlands, N.J.: Humanities Press, 1978), p. 168.

39. Between 1845 and 1917, some 238,000 Indians were brought to the West Indies. The term "East Indian" was first used to refer to these indentured laborers in 1896 in the protector of immigrants report. E. F. Woods used the term in his report of 1922 to distinguish the indentured Indians from American Indians and West Indians of African descent.

40. Many aspects of African culture, however, remained intact well into the nineteenth century. Bridget Brereton gives a good account of the retention of African life in Trinidad in chapter 7 of her history. See *Race Relations,* pp. 130–51. See also Melville Herskovits, *Trinidad Village* (New York: Knopf, 1947), for a study of one such Trinidadian community.

41. V. S. Naipaul, *The Middle Passage* (London: André Deutsch, 1962), p. 82.

42. The term "British Caribbean" is used interchangeably with "West Indies" to mean the English-speaking countries of the Caribbean.

43. A. R. F. Webber, *Those That Be in Bondage: A Tale of Indian Indentures and Sunlit Western Ways* (Demerara, British Guiana: Daily Chronicle, 1917), was the first novel written by someone from Trinidad and Tobago; Edgar Mittleholzer, *Corentyne Thunder* (London, 1941; reprint, London: Heineman, 1970); Seepersad Naipaul, *Gurudeva and Other Indian Tales* (Port of Spain, 1946; reprinted as *Gurudeva and Other Stories,* London: André Deutsch, 1976); and Samuel Selvon, *A Brighter Sun* (London, 1952; reprint, London: Longman Caribbean, 1971).

44. V. S. Naipaul, *The Overcrowded Barracoon* (Harmondsworth: Penguin, 1967), p. 9.

45. Walcott, "The Garden Path," p. 30.

1. TRADITION, *MIGUEL STREET,* AND OTHER STORIES

1. The social development of Trinidad and Tobago can be divided into four periods: 1833–1870, when new villages were established by the former slaves and when large numbers of East Indians, Portuguese, and Chinese arrived; 1870–1900, when the society evolved into a more cohesive pattern, though still demarcated along class lines; 1900–1940, when the development of social consciousness among the black masses (both the East Indians and the Africans) took center stage; and 1940–1962, when national independence was achieved. See Bridget Brereton, *Race Relations in Colonial Trinidad, 1870–1900* (Cambridge: Cambridge University Press, 1979), for a discussion of the first two periods.

Raphael Sebastien argues for a Marxist division of the society along the lines of political economy. He lists three periods: 1797–1833, when slave labor became generalized and systematic colonization of the society took place; 1833–1921, when agrarian capitalism was organized and an urban-industrialized proletariat formed; and 1921–1956, when the national bourgeoisie consolidated its dominance over the economy. See "The Political Economy of Capitalism of Trinidad and Tobago," *Tribune* 1 (1981): 5–52.

2. Brereton, *Race Relations,* p. 58.

3. Jose Bodu, quoted in Anthony de Verteuil, *The Years of Revolt: Trinidad, 1881–1888* (Port of Spain: Paria, 1984), p. 233.

4. In subsequent years, the list of banned publications included the *Negro Worker,* all publications of the National Campaign Committee of the Communist party of the U.S.A., the *Daily Worker,* the *Young Worker, Russia Today,* pamphlets by the Trinidadian George Padmore, the father of pan-Africanism, *Negro Anthology* by Nancy Cunard, and many others.

5. See the excerpt from Sander's interview with Alfred Mendes in Reinhard Sander, *From Trinidad: An Anthology of Early West Indian Writing* (New York: Africana, 1978), p. 4. See also Ralph de Bossiere's account of that period in "On Writing a Novel," *Journal of Commonwealth Literature* 17 (1982): 1–12. De Bossiere's first novel, *Crown Jewel,* is set in the turbulent 1930s.

6. Sander, *From Trinidad,* p. 1.

7. W. I. Carr ("Reflections on the Novel in the British Caribbean," *Queens Quarterly* 70 [Winter 1964]: 585) and Gerald Moore (*The Chosen Tongue* [London: Longmans, Green, 1969], p. 6) argue that West Indian literature merited serious attention in 1949.

8. I will argue that the essential aspect of the culture resides at the unofficial level, in the "culture of carnival," as I call it. Needless to say, I do not endorse the argument for a "life without fiction" prior to a written culture, except in its most narrow sense (see Kenneth Ramchand, *The West Indian Novel and Its Background* [London: Faber, 1970]). Neither do I privilege the written discourse over the nonwritten. Calypsos, for example, still remain an extremely effective means of communicating with the populace of Trinidad and Tobago. See Selwyn R. Cudjoe, "Revolutionary Struggle and the Novel," *Caribbean Quarterly* 25 (December 1979), for some notion of how the novel functioned before and after the achievement of independence.

9. Sander, *From Trinidad,* pp. 36, 39.

10. Ibid., p. 27.

11. Ibid., p. 28.

12. Ibid., p. 31.

13. See Selwyn R. Cudjoe, "Tradition, *Miguel Street,* and Other Stories," *Trinidad and Tobago Review* 5 (1982), and 6 (1983) for an examination of the short stories of the period.

14. Landeg White, *V. S. Naipaul: A Critical Introduction* (New York: Barnes & Noble, 1975), p. 50.

15. Seepersad Naipaul, *The Adventures of Gurudeva and Other Stories* (Port of Spain: Guardian Commercial Printery, 1946), p. 19.

16. BBC Written Archives Centre, "Caribbean Voices Scripts," September 24, 1950. All quotations are taken from this source.

17. V. S. Naipaul, *An Area of Darkness* (London: André Deutsch, 1964), p. 45.

18. Helen Tiffin, "The Lost Ones: A Study of the Works of V. S. Naipaul" (Ph.D. diss., Queens University, 1972), p. 14.

19. "This Is Home," BBC Written Archives Centre, "Caribbean Voices Scripts," June 24, 1951.

20. See V. S. Naipaul, *Finding the Center* (New York: Knopf, 1984).

21. This story appears in *A Flag on the Island* (Harmondsworth: Penguin, 1969) but is changed somewhat from the original version. I quote from the original text as it appeared in 1951: "The Mourners," BBC Written Archives Centre, "Caribbean Voices Scripts," September 16, 1951.

22. BBC Written Archives Centre, "Caribbean Voices Scripts," April 27, 1952.

23. In 1972 Naipaul spoke about his sense of shame at being among the poor relatives in his family and his lifelong ambition to be wealthy: "I think that perhaps one was ashamed of the poverty because one was so close to what was a great deal of wealth. I think that my father's uncle who was killed the other day—he died a millionaire—and I think that my mother's family, after all, were quite well off. But our little group within the clan was impoverished and I think that one sensed the disgrace of this poverty because one was fairly close to people who had a certain amount of money. . . . For a long, long time, I used to worship people who had made their own money. I would look at them as nearly divine beings" ("Myself When Young," August 24, 1972, BBC Radio Broadcast).

24. "The Old Man," BBC Written Archives Centre, "Caribbean Voices Scripts," April 26, 1953.

25. "A Family Reunion," BBC Written Archives Centre, "Caribbean Voices Scripts."

26. *A Flag on the Island,* p. 9.

27. *Times* (London), January 2, 1964.

28. In reviewing Selvon's *Turn Again Tiger,* his sequel to *A Brighter Sun,* Naipaul wrote: "Mr. Selvon is without the stamina for the full-length novel, and he has here found the undemanding form which suits his talents best: the flimsiest of frames which can, without apparent disorder, contain unrelated episodes and characters. . . . Mr. Selvon's gifts may not be important but they are precious" (*New Statesman,* December 6, 1958, pp. 826–27).

29. BBC Written Archives Centre, "Caribbean Voices Scripts," January 22, 1956.

30. "Pooter," *Times Saturday Review,* November 9, 1968, p. 23.

31. Quoted in Victor Ramraj, "A Study of the Novels of V. S. Naipaul" (Ph.D. diss., University of New Brunswick, 1968), pp. 117, 11.

32. "Myself When Young," BBC Radio Broadcast, August 24, 1972.

33. Ibid.

34. Letter to Grenfell Williams, BBC Written Archives Centre.

35. "Unfurnished Entrails—the Novelist V. S. Naipaul in Conversation with Jim Douglas Henry," *The Listener,* November 25, 1971, p. 721.

36. V. S. Naipaul, "Prologue to an Autobiography," *Vanity Fair* 46 (April 1983), tells how *Miguel Street* was born. One ought not, however, be carried away by Naipaul's romantic and somewhat idealist recounting of that process some thirty years later.

37. *The Overcrowded Barracoon* (Harmondsworth: Penguin, 1967), p. 27.

38. V. S. Naipaul, *Finding the Center: Two Narratives* (New York: Alfred Knopf, 1984), p. 20.

39. That "The Enemy," written as a part of *Miguel Street* (it later appeared in *A*

Flag on the Island), could be extracted from the text without damaging its unity demonstrates that *Miguel Street* ought not to be considered a novel. Writing in the *Times Literary Supplement* on April 24, 1959, a reviewer concluded: *"Miguel Street* is not properly a novel at all but a series of character sketches, concerned with the most singular or significant of the street's inhabitants, most of whom turn up in one another's sketches" (p. 237). Naipaul confirms this view in "Prologue to an Autobiography."

40. V. S. Naipaul, *Miguel Street* (London: Heineman, 1959), p. 216; hereafter *MS*.

41. Geoffrey Broughton, "A Critical Study of the Development of V. S. Naipaul as Reflected in His Four Major West Indian Novels" (Master's thesis, University of London, 1968), p. 18.

42. *Times* (London), February 1, 1964.

43. See the introduction to the abbreviated version of *The Perfect Tenants and the Mourners*, ed. Francis Curtis (Cambridge: Cambridge University Press, 1977).

44. *The Overcrowded Barracoon*, pp. 9–10.

45. C. L. R. James, *The Future in the Present* (London: Allison & Busby, 1977), pp. 191, 188.

46. Walter Rodney, *The Groundings with My Brothers* (London: Bogle L'Ouverture, 1969), p. 68.

47. Ibid., pp. 33–34.

48. In his work *Jesus: An Experiment in Christology,* trans. Hurbert Hoskins (New York: Seabury Press, 1979), Schillebeeckx identified three different planes of history which he says "enfold and interpenetrate one another": (a) "ephemeral" history, which consists of everyday events; (b) "conjectural" history, which is more expansive and comprehensive but possesses a slower rate of change than the first: (c) "structural" history, which lasts for centuries and borders "on the central point of what moves and what does not, although not standing outside history" (p. 577). There is a suggestion in Schillebeeckx's understanding of history that certain historical judgments which are made and solidified by intellectuals (usually of the dominant class) become so impermeated in the minds of men that it takes a broad epochal movement (perhaps revolutionary struggle) to break its hold. The difference between Rodney's and Naipaul's judgments can be thought of as lying at the "conjectural" and "ephemeral" planes of historical judgments.

49. Nancy Fitch, "History Is a Nightmare" (Ph.D. diss., University of Michigan, 1981), p. 28.

2. THE COLONIAL SOCIETY

1. V. S. Naipaul, *The Middle Passage* (London: Penguin, 1969), p. 88. Morton Klass, *East Indians in Trinidad* (New York: Columbia University Press, 1961), p. 3, argues that the East Indian community he studied in 1957–58 "is structurally Indian rather than West Indian." The major characteristics of feudalism in the East Indian community of Trinidad during its early history are a strong communal basis for property relations and a close family structure; the presence of indentured laborers who controlled their labor power, as opposed to slaves, who had no rights over their

labor; and a sharp hierarchical division within the society and the absence of social mobility. Within the estate system, a resident proprietor or an absentee landlord was at the top of the hierarchical order; an estate manager, who lived on the estate, an overseer, who superintended the gangs and overlooked the planting and weeding of the sugar estates, and a foreman, who was the immediate supervisor of each gang. Among the Hindus there were also four Vana castes: the Brahmins, who were the highest caste, the Kshatriyas, the Vaisyas, and the Sundras. During indenture these caste relations were reproduced and adhered to strictly. The dissolution of feudalism also saw the gradual dissolution of these relations. Capitalism in Trinidad can be seen as arising out of the emancipation of the ownership of the means of production from a communal base of production, even though Raphael Sebastien would argue that the sugar plantations were merely an extension of capitalist relations. In Trinidad, however, the commercial production of oil from 1914 and the presence of Americans did much to speed up growth of capitalism. Capitalism was characterized, generally, by the rise of individualism, competitiveness, social mobility, and the intensification of wage labor.

2. V. S. Naipaul, *The Mystic Masseur* (London: André Deutsch, 1959), pp. 10–12; hereafter *MM*.

3. Visnu, which is symbolic of the external and internal aspects of the East Indians in Trinidad and Tobago, is the name given to the *sattva* quality in the "cosmological trinity" of Hindu mythology. It is this principle that "holds the universe together [and] which is the cause of all concentration, hence of light, of matter, of life. It pervades all existence, hence it is known as the Pervader" (Alain Daniélou, *Hindu Polytheism* [New York: Pantheon Books, 1964], p. 149). On the external level, therefore, Visnu represents the cohesive or centripetal tendency of the universe and thereby holds all things together. On the internal level, Visnu represents the inner dimension of East Indian existence, perpetual life and infinite wisdom. For those who see the light and are faithful to his Being, he offers human power by which to understand one's life. Visnu holds a conch, a discus, a mace, and a bow in his four arms, which represent the three fundamental qualities and the notion of individuality from which all existence arises (p. 150).

4. According to Hindu mythology, by his very nature a person wants to be liberated from the illusory condition of this world but can achieve this goal only if he prepares himself for that condition. To do so, the Hindu must go through the four *asramas* or stages of human development, which consist of youth, manhood, middle age, and old age. The *asramas* are related to the moral development of the individual, which is related finally to the four castes of Hindu life. See Satischandra Chatterjee, *The Fundamentals of Hinduism* (Calcutta: Das Gupta, 1950).

5. In Naipaul's early novels he places special importance on the act of writing, and although it exists initially at an ontic level of cognition, it gradually assumes a position of full-scale ontological importance and becomes one of his essential devices for explaining the East Indian experience in Trinidad and Tobago. The term "ontic level of cognition" is the domain of knowledge Heidegger relegated to the positive sciences. According to Heidegger, "The ontic is a separate sphere from the ontological and is less fundamental, it not being concerned with the Being of Being-there which is an ontological entity, but only with the Being of entities other than

Being-there" (quoted in Lucien Goldman, *Lukács and Heidegger,* trans. William Q. Boelhower [London: Routledge & Kegan Paul, 1977], p. xvi). The former is the purely mechanical application of knowledge and the latter is the philosophical exploration of one's being.

6. In Hindu mythology, Gaṇeśa, another name for Ganapati, the Lord of Categories, is represented as an "elephant-headed man to express the unity of the small being, the microcosm, that is man, and the Great Being, the macrocosm, pictured as an elephant." He is considered the remover of all obstacles "who, by giving immortality, removes the fear inherent in time and duration" (Daniélou, *Hindu Polytheism,* pp. 293–94). The most worshiped of Hindu gods, Ganesha represents "to the poor hard-working villager . . . the height of successful achievement and the reward of a lifelong struggle" (E. Osborn Martin, *The Gods of India* [New York: E. P. Dutton, 1956], p. 190).

7. See Louis Fischer, *The Life of Mahatma Gandhi* (New York: Collier Books, 1962).

8. W. T. Stace, *Mysticism and Philosophy* (Philadelphia: J. B. Lippincott, 1960), pp. 335–36.

9. Evelyn Underhill, *Practical Mysticism* (New York: E. P. Dutton, 1915), p. 4.

10. R. C. Zaehner, *Mysticism: Sacred and Profane* (London: Oxford University Press, 1969), p. 134.

11. Underhill, *Practical Mysticism,* p. 29.

12. Zaehner, *Mysticism,* p. 130.

13. *The Suffrage of Elvira* (New York: Penguin, 1969), p. 11; hereafter *SOE.*

14. Broughton, "The Development of V. S. Naipaul," p. 42.

15. The picture on Chitteranjan's wall is a copy of a photograph taken in England while Mahatma Gandhi was attending the second session of the Round Table Conference at St. John's Palace from September to December, 1931. During his stay in England Gandhi went to Buckingham Palace to have tea with King George V and Queen Mary and "wore a loincloth, sandals, a shawl, and his dangling watch" (Fischer, *Life of Mahatma Gandhi,* p. 285).

16. M. K. Gandhi, *Indian Home Rule* (Madras, India: S. Ganesan Publishers, 1922), p. 55.

17. In *Indian Home Rule,* Gandhi differentiates between "brute force," which England used to gain its dominance over India, and soul-force, "or more popularly passive resistance," a force that is "indestructible." As he said, "The force of arms is powerless when matched against the force of love or the soul" (p. 67).

18. *Times,* January 2, 1964.

19. Broughton, "The Development of V. S. Naipaul," p. 41.

3. A PROSE-TRAGEDY

1. Swinden, *The English Novel,* p. 223.

2. Leban Omella Erapu, "The Novels of V. S. Naipaul: A Symbolic Approach" (Master's of Letters thesis, University of Edinburgh, 1971), p. 4.

3. In many ways *A House for Mr. Biswas* is the great realist novel of Caribbean literature. In speaking about the major contributions that inhere in all important

transitory periods of human history, Georg Lukács argued that "a new type of man always come[s] into being in the course of an untitled though contradictory process. In such critical transitional periods the tasks and responsibility of literature are exceptionally great" (*Studies in European Realism*, trans. Edith Bone [London: Hillway Publishing, 1950], p. 10).

4. Christopher Land and Jerry Ventry on a BBC broadcast for schoolchildren in early 1982 observed that Mr. Biswas was born into a rigid order and that "his search for an identity in Trinidad is in part at least a rebellion against a kind of order which has condemned him to the position of a mere non-identity. . . . Mr. Biswas comes to feel that Hanuman House is a type of order; that there is hierarchy in Hanuman House and his problem is that it is not a hierarchy which he can accept." Victor Ramraj, in "A Study of the Novels of V. S. Naipaul," has argued that this sense of fate is present in embryonic form in all the early novels of Naipaul. Ramraj undercuts the importance played by one's fate or *karma* in the feudal community of the East Indians, however, by arguing that Naipaul "believes that chance and environmental circumstances, not fate, play a role in Ganesh's success" (p. 40). The presence of fate, Ramraj says, also extends to Harbans, who, like Ganesh, "believes in predestination and fate" (p. 56). He does not relate the question of fate to the feudal nature of the society.

5. V. S. Naipaul, *A House for Mr. Biswas* (New York: Penguin, 1969), p. 15; hereafter *HFMB*.

6. Rejecting the orthodoxy of Hinduism, Mr. Biswas is the nascent Trinidad person who tries to cope with the pressures of his new order through self-effacing humor. He gives us our first glimpse at the Trinidadian man who seeks to release himself from the philistinism of the new world.

7. Gordon Rohlehr, "The Ironic Approach," in Louis James, ed., *The Island in Between: Essays in West Indian Literature* (London: Oxford University Press, 1968), p. 135.

8. I use the term "animal being" to differentiate it from man's "sensuous being" as Karl Marx used the term in his *Economic and Philosophical Manuscripts of 1844*. This dichotomy is also found in Hindu religion and philosophy, which admits that *karma-yoga* leads to liberation through self-purification and self-realization. As Satischandra Chatterjee argues in *The Fundamentals of Hinduism:* "It is extremely difficult for a man to rise above his animal nature and to be free from the influence of ordinary passions and impulses of life, of his natural desire for pleasure and aversion towards painful objects" (p. 147). Therefore, in this life, pain and suffering are more desirable than pleasure in that they act as incentives to make a person put forward his or her best efforts to overcome evil.

9. Annie Verut, "Alienation and Delimitation of Space in V. S. Naipaul's *A House for Mr. Biswas,*" in *The Other in Anglo-Saxon Sensibility* (Reims, France: Presses Universitaires de Reims, 1983), p. 124.

10. Ibid., p. 127.

11. Lukács, *European Realism*, pp. 10, 13.

12. Homi Bhabha, "Representation and the Colonial Text: A Critical Exploration of Some Forms of Mimeticism," in Frank Gloversmith, ed., *The Theory of Reading* (New Jersey: Barnes & Noble, 1984), pp. 115, 117–18.

13. The *Ramayana*, one of India's best-known epics, is reputed to have been written by the Indian sage Valmiki. The poem consisted of six books. The seventh, the *Uttara Kanda*, was added later. The epic tells of the "ancient traditions of two powerful races, the Kosalas and the Videhas, who lived in Northern India between the twelfth and tenth centuries before Christ" (Romesh Dutt, ed., *The Ramayana and the Mahabharata* [London: Everyman's Library, 1976], p. v). The hero of the poem is Rama of Kosalas, and the heroine is Sita, the daughter of the Janak king of the Videhas, who was "born miraculously of a field of furrow" (ibid., p. 34). The epic depicts two ideal societies whose characters embody either an ideal good or an ideal evil. It was therefore designed to inculcate certain moral and ethical principles and to serve as a guide to Hindu life.

14. I will call this creative transformation of the *Ramayana* the inversion-distortion, by which I mean the complete turning upside-down of the epic (inversion) and the creative picking apart and rearrangement to fit the Trinidadian situation (distortion). Therefore, distortion is used here in a positive rather than a negative sense. The East Indians recited the *Ramayana* in the cane fields of Trinidad in the latter part of the nineteenth century, using it as a means of solace in that alien land. Their clinging to the *Ramayana* gives us a sense of its central importance in their lives and substantiates the case for its necessary transformation in the Wilderness. See James H. Collens, *A Guide to Trinidad*, 2d ed. (London: E. Stock, 1888) and Selwyn R. Cudjoe, "The Language of the East Indians," in Noor Kumar Mahabir, *The Still Cry* (Tacarigua, Trinidad: Calaloux, 1985).

15. To understand the use to which the *Ramayana* has been put in this new world, it is necessary to recognize that the Hindu epics have many characteristics similar to those of the Western world. As a form used to carry forward a content that consisted of noble deeds and a lofty conception of life, the *Ramayana* and the *Mahabharata* share many features with the *Odyssey* and the *Iliad*.

16. Walter Benjamin, *The Origin of German Tragic Drama*, trans. John Osborne (London: New Left Books, 1977), pp. 16–17.

17. Dutt, ed., *Ramayana and Mahabharata*, p. 191.

18. Ibid., pp. 2–3; hereafter Dutt's edition of *The Ramayana and the Mahabharata* will be abbreviated as *R*.

19. Sister Nivedita and Ananda K. Coomaraswamy, *Myths of the Hindus & Buddhists* (London: George G. Harp, 1913), pp. 21–22.

20. Benjamin, *The Origin of German Tragic Drama*, p. 160.

21. Georg Lukács, *The Meaning of Contemporary Realism* (London: Merlin, 1972), p. 40.

22. Benjamin, *The Origin of German Tragic Drama*, p. 166.

23. Chatterjee, *The Fundamentals of Hinduism*, p. 93.

4. THE CONFLICT OF WORLD VIEWS

1. Dominick La Capra, *Preface to Sartre* (Ithaca, N.Y.: Cornell University Press, 1978), p. 20.

2. V. S. Naipaul, *The Middle Passage* (London: André Deutsch, 1962), p. 27; hereafter *MP*.

3. See *Thomas Carlyle's Collected Works*, vol. 19 (London: Chapman and Hall, 1870), pp. 209–37, for a discussion of the importance of the "doer" as opposed to the "thinker."

4. Sylvia Wynter, "Reflections on West Indian Writing and Criticism" (Part 11), *Jamaica Journal* 3 (1969): 30.

5. Quoted in *The Middle Passage*, p. 66.

6. A. C. Derrick, "The Uncommitted Artist" (M.Phil. diss., Leeds University, 1967), p. 305.

7. V. S. Naipaul, *An Area of Darkness* (London: André Deutsch, 1964), p. 29; hereafter *AD*.

8. Not even Naipaul, independent and unto himself, can measure accurately the intensity of the "supporting philosophy" of his Hinduism and the effect it had upon his writing; nor can he disregard the "solidity" of his world and the effect it had upon the development of his consciousness. For Aleksandr R. Luria's theories on cognitive development, see his *Cognitive Development* (Cambridge, Mass.: Harvard University Press, 1976), pp. 9–10.

9. C. D. Narasimhaiah, "Somewhere Something Has Snapped," *Literary Criterion* 6 (1965): 84, 90.

10. Ibid., p. 86.

11. "Areas of Promise," *Times Literary Supplement*, September 24, 1964, p. 879.

12. "Mr. Naipaul's Passage to India," *Times Literary Supplement*, September 24, 1964, p. 881.

13. Quoted in Paul Theroux, "V. S. Naipaul," *Modern Fiction Studies* 30, no. 3 (Autumn 1984): 454; Peggy Nightingale, *Journey through Darkness: The Writing of V. S. Naipaul* (St. Lucia: University of Queensland Press, 1987), p. 79.

14. Larry Alan Husten, "From Autobiography to Politics: The Development of V. S. Naipaul's Fiction" (Ph.D. diss., State University of New York at Buffalo, 1983), pp. 42–43; John Thieme, "Naipaul's English Fable: *Mr. Stone and the Knights Companion*," *Modern Fiction Studies* 30 (Autumn 1984): 498.

15. V. S. Naipaul, *Mr. Stone and the Knights Companion* (Harmondsworth: Penguin, 1973), pp. 16–17; hereafter *MSKC*.

16. Fritjof Capra, *The Tao of Physics* (New York: Bantam Books, 1977), pp. 29–30.

17. Elaine Campbell, "West Indian Fiction: A Literature of Exile" (Ph.D. diss., Brandeis University, 1981), pp. 230–31.

18. Sanna Dhahir, "Women in V. S. Naipaul's Fiction: Their Role and Relationships" (Ph.D. diss., University of New Brunswick, 1985), pp. 66, 71.

5. AT THE "RIM OF THE WORLD"

1. In his important essay "The Love Axe (1): Developing a Caribbean Aesthetic, 1962–1974," in Houston A. Baker, Jr., ed., *Reading Black: Essays in the Criticism of African, Caribbean, Black American Literature* (Ithaca, N.Y.: Africana Studies and Research Center, Cornell University, Monograph Series No. 4, 1976), p. 21, Edward Brathwaite has called this important literary period the "implosion of people

and thought." In his attempt to explain the theoretical and philosophical postulates that characterized that period, Brathwaite has argued that "ideological Cuba, then the academic voices of [C. L. R.] James, [Elsa] Goveia, [Eric] Williams; the increasingly conscious West Indian University of the West Indies; these are some of the founding factors of the New Movement" (p. 21). Although the essay must be faulted for the hegemonic role it ascribes to the intellectuals and artists in the "founding" of the new movement and the superficial (almost incidental) manner in which it treats the political activity of the earlier period of Caribbean history, it does convey a sense of the urgent cultural activity that took place in the period.

2. Brathwaite, "The Love Axe (1)," p. 20; Norman Manley, "Roger Mais—The Writer," in *The Three Novels of Roger Mais* (London: Jonathan Cape, 1966), p. 20.

3. V. S. Naipaul, *A Flag on the Island* (Harmondsworth: Penguin, 1976), p. 24; hereafter *FOI*.

4. I do not believe that this is the only way to understand the carnival celebration. The motif is picked up frequently in Naipaul's works and is raised to an epistemological dimension in *The Loss of El Dorado* and *The Overcrowded Barracoon,* and I will contextualize this concept in the next chapter.

5. Although the term "social formation" can be understood as analogous to "society," I use the term as Louis Althusser used it to mean the economic, political, and ideological practices that constitute the social whole at a certain place and stage of social development.

6. Anika Lemaire, *Jacques Lacan,* trans. David Macey (London: Routledge & Kegan Paul, 1977), p. 40.

7. Although the island of Isabella resembles Trinidad in many respects, it ought not to be equated with Trinidad, as many commentators have done. For example, Molly Mahood has argued that "*The Mimic Men* is about Trinidad, but because the story culminates in fictional political events, the island has to be renamed Isabella" (*The Colonial Encounter* [London: Rex Collins, 1977], p. 142). Naipaul intends Isabella to be representative of a postcolonial society and for Ralph Singh to be a colonial subject rather than a specific and identifiable "Trinidadian" man.

8. V. S. Naipaul, *The Mimic Men* (Harmondsworth: Penguin, 1969), p. 192; hereafter *MM*.

9. As Meredith Ann Skura has noted, psychoanalysis is not concerned only with the discovery of the unconscious or diseases and primitive experiences. It "offers instead a theory and a method of studying how the whole mind works—for understanding another human being as he tries to describe his world in words and to draw on all his resources, both conscious and unconscious" (*The Literary Use of the Psychoanalytic Process* [New Haven: Yale University Press, 1982], p. 2). A psychoanalytic reading can be seen, then, as complementing the text's manifest (or conscious) reading, as an additional device to gain greater insight into the behavior of the subject.

10. The Imaginary is the transformation that takes place in the subject at the formative mirror phase, when it assumes a discrete image which allows it to postulate a series of equivalences, sameness, identities, between the objects of the surrounding world. See Homi K. Bhabha, "The Other Question: The Stereotype and Colonial Discourse," *Screen* 24, no. 6 (1983): 29, and Jacqueline Rose, "The

Imaginary," in Colin MacCabe, *The Talking Cure* (New York: St. Martin's Press, 1981), p. 138, for a discussion of the function of the Imaginary.

11. Jacques Lacan introduced the concept of the "mirror phase" of development to describe an individual's formation of the "I." In this phase, which occurs between the ages of six and eighteen months, the infant is physically powerless but anticipates on the mental plane of his or her development (the Imaginary level) a transformation into an autonomous being. The primary alienation of the child from himself or herself occurs and the subsequent discovery of the self takes place. In this period, the child, upon recognizing his or her image in a mirror, usually mimics him or herself in a jubilant flutter of activity. Lacan called this preexistent and undifferentiated stage of the individual the "ideal I" and identified it as the stage in which the self acquires its social identification, the "social I." Moreover, Lacan sees this mirror stage as a period in intense fragmentation, in which there is the fantasy of the body in pieces. Anika Lemaire describes this concept as "the advent of coenaesthetic subjectivity preceded by the feeling that one's own body is in pieces. The reflection of the body is, then, salutary in that it is unitary and localized in time and space" (*Jacques Lacan*, p. 81). The mirror stage is not only the first step in self-recognition but also a moment in which the child situates himself socially by comparing himself with another. It is in the other that the subject first lives and registers himself. For a discussion of the mirror stage of development, see Jacques Lacan, *Ecrits: A Selection*, trans. Alan Sheridan (New York: Norton, 1977), chaps. 1 and 2.

12. This process of separation, of tearing away from the mother (country), manifested in the fragmentation, the loss, and the fantasy of the body in pieces, can be understood only in the context of the pain that results from the struggle for separation that takes place between the colonial mother (and father) who has been in authority for so long and the child who must be "prepared for autonomy." Colonial peoples have always referred to the metropole, the source from which all power emanated, as the "mother country." This is one reason why Ralph Singh takes solace in London (the bosom of the mother, as it were) and writes his story from there. See Vic Reid, *New Day* (London: Heineman Educational Books, 1949), p. 337, for a good depiction of this relationship.

13. Lacan has argued that although the aggressive tendency takes different forms, it "proves to be fundamental in certain series of significant states of the personality, namely the paranoid and paranoic psychoses" (*Ecrits*, p. 16). Paranoic knowledge is defined as corresponding "in its more or less archaic forms to certain critical moments that mark the history of man's mental genesis, each representing a stage in objectifying identification" (ibid., p. 17).

14. Martin Thom, "The Unconscious Structured as a Language," in Colin MacCabe, *The Talking Cure*, p. 8.

15. Quoted in ibid., p. 144.

16. Lacan, *Ecrits*, p. 27.

17. The question of psychological space arises in Naipaul's fictional and nonfictional texts not only in *The Mimic Men* but in "A Flag on the Island" (p. 164), "Conrad's Darkness," in *The Return of Eva Perón* (pp. 214–15), "The Little More," *Times*, July 13, 1964, in a BBC conversation reported in the *Trinidad*

Express, and many other writings. It becomes a certain form of condensation which overdetermines this particular condition of the life of the colonial subject.

18. Gordon Rohlehr refers to this condition as an intellectual "crampedness" which one finds in the colonial territories. (See "Gordon Rohlehr on V. S. Naipaul: An Interview with Selwyn R. Cudjoe." This interview was reproduced as "Talking about Naipaul" in *Carib* 2 [1984]). K. Garebian also argues that in the works of Naipaul "the myth of the land, while seeking to discover and define an integral psychic center from where the artist can chart a moral geography for his characters and himself, acquires a negativism which contrasts with the positive place-sensibility of writers who belong physically to a homeplace" ("V. S. Naipaul's Negative Sense of Place," *Journal of Commonwealth Literature* 10 [1975]: 23). He attributes this negativism to Naipaul's inability "to possess in a spiritual sense the land one has in a physical sense." I believe this "negativism" (or failure) ought to be seen much more as a function of the historical condition that inheres in the sociopolitical reality of colonialism than as simply inability on the part of the writer to possess his place. At any rate, the notion of "psychic crampedness" seems to be a much more inclusive concept.

19. Consuelo López de Villegas, "Identity and Environment: Naipaul's Architectual Vision," *Revista/Review Interamericana* 10, no. 2 (Summer 1980): 221.

20. If one accepts the notion that Europe's conquest of the Caribbean involved, among other things, the animal need for the conquest of space as a function of its own expansion, then one has to concede that this notion also demanded the denial of such psychological space to colonial peoples and became a necessary condition for the articulation of its own greatness. Such notions are manifest in the concept of the second-rate nature of anything that is small ("the smallness of the island") or the unworthiness of anyone who comes from a small island (he or she cannot think in global terms). Naipaul endorsed this imperialist need for additional space when he spoke in rapt admiration of what he called Trollope's "mid-Victorian certainty" ("The Little More," *Times,* July 13, 1964).

21. Naipaul's notion of the mimicry, helplessness, and disgust of the subject inherent in the postcolonial condition in the absence of revolutionary violence may be contrasted with Fanon's notion of "mockery" (the opposite of mimicry) and disdain for white, colonial values which occur in the aftermath of independence where there has been revolutionary violence. See Fanon, *The Wretched of the Earth,* trans. Constance Farrington (New York: Grove Press, 1967), p. 35.

22. See *The Return of Eva Perón* (New York: Knopf, 1980), p. 219.

23. Lemaire, *Jacques Lacan,* p. 215.

24. Ibid., p. xxi.

25. *The Return of Eva Perón,* pp. 220, 224, 215–16.

26. Homi K. Bhabha in his essay "The Other Question" describes "the minimum conditions and specifications" of the colonial discourse: "It is an apparatus that turns on the recognition and disavowal of racial/cultural/historical differences. Its predominant strategic function is the creation of a space for a 'subject peoples' through the production of knowledges in terms of which surveillance is exercised and a complex form of pleasure/unpleasure is incited. It seeks authorisation for its strategies by the production of knowledges of coloniser and colonised which are stereo-

typical but antithetically evaluated. The object of colonial discourse is to construe the colonised as a population of degenerate types on the basis of racial origin, in order to justify conquest and to establish systems of administration and instruction. . . . Therefore, despite the 'play' in the colonial system which is crucial to its exercise of power, colonial discourse produces the colonised as a fixed reality which is at once an 'other' and yet entirely knowable and visible" (p. 23). Abdul R. JanMohammed, in "The Economy of Manichean Allegory: The Function of Racial Difference in Colonialist Literature (*Critical Inquiry* 12, no. 1 [Autumn 1985]: 59–87) refutes Bhabha's somewhat idealist definition of colonial discourse and argues that Bhabha's definition represses "the political history of colonialism which is inevitably sedimented in its discourse." He goes on to argue that one can better understand colonial discourse "through an analysis that maps its ideological function in relation to actual imperialist practices."

27. Bhabha, "The Other Question," p. 18.

28. See Paul Brown, " 'This thing of darkness I acknowledge mine': *The Tempest* and the Discourse of Colonialism," in Jonathan Dollimore and Alan Sinfield, eds., *Political Shakespeare* (Ithaca, N.Y.: Cornell University Press, 1985).

29. In an article entitled "What's Wrong with Being a Snob?" Naipaul argued for the security history provides and quoted Stendhal in his defense. He argued that in *The Charterhouse of Parma*, "Stendhal could with perfect calm dismiss America as an absurd democratic land where grocers had to be courted. It therefore wasn't suitable, even as a place of refuge, for Europeans of breeding. Unlike some of today's writers, Stendhal didn't need the protection of being considered old-fashioned, a character or an eccentric. He was simply stating an important fact about American life which he expected his readers to find disagreeable" (*Saturday Evening Post*, June 3, 1967, p. 12).

30. Naipaul, "The Little More," p. 12.

31. Naipaul, "What's Wrong with Being a Snob?" p. 12.

32. Derwent May, "A Black Tale," *Times*, November 1, 1969.

33. V. S. Naipaul, *The Loss of El Dorado: A History* (New York: Knopf, 1970), p. 27; hereafter *LED*.

34. There were four classes of society in Trinidad at the end of the eighteenth century: the Europeans, or whites; the coloreds (part European and part African); the free Negroes, who had gained their freedom from slavery either by purchase or escape; and at the bottom of the social ladder, the slaves.

35. Naipaul, "What's Wrong with Being a Snob?" p. 12.

36. Bhabha, "The Other Question," pp. 27–28.

6. IDEOLOGY, CULTURE, AND NATIONAL IDENTITY

1. Bernard Sheehan, *Savagism and Civility* (Cambridge: Cambridge University Press, 1980), p. 12.

2. Henri Baudet, *Paradise on Earth: Some Thoughts on European Images of Non-European Man,* trans. Elizabeth Wentholt (New Haven: Yale University Press, 1965), pp. 11, 13.

3. Sheehan, *Savagism and Civility,* p. 21.

4. Ibid., p. 2.

5. See Baudet, *Paradise on Earth,* chap. 2.

6. Sheehan, *Savagism and Civility,* pp. 26, 21.

7. Gordon Rohlehr, "The Ironic Approach," p. 124.

8. V. S. Naipaul, *The Overcrowded Barracoon* (Harmondsworth: Penguin, 1976), p. 26; hereafter *OB*.

9. Mikhail Bakhtin in his work *Rabelais and His World,* trans. Helene Iswolsky (Cambridge, Mass: MIT Press, 1968), p. 12, argues that the "satirist whose laughter is negative places himself above the object of his mockery" and differentiates such negative laughter from the "wholeness of the world's comic aspect," which is found in the people's laughter. Bakhtin differentiates between the laughter of the Middle Ages and that of the modern satirist.

10. George Lamming, who accused Naipaul initially of being incapable of moving "beyond a castrated satire" in his first three novels (*The Pleasure of Exile* [London: Michael Joseph, 1960], p. 225), goes on to accuse him of avoiding "that total encounter which is the experience of any Trinidadian" ("A Trinidadian Experience," *Time and Tide,* October 5, 1961, p. 1657), a charge that Naipaul rejected and that seems a little beyond the mark. Rohlehr, in a much more perceptive analysis, argued that this sense of laughing at the society tends to reveal itself as early as *The Mystic Masseur.* He argues, however, that Naipaul's early satire is couched in "considerable sympathy" for the society ("The Ironic Approach," pp. 121–22).

11. The reality of these societies was certainly more complex than Naipaul makes them. As Bridget Brereton reports, during the period of which Naipaul speaks the Negroes had many secret societies derived from the secret societies of West Africa. These societies had their own kings, dauphins, grand judges, soldiers, and alguazils. They possessed their own rituals and forms of initiation for their young men and women. They were a continuation of the social organization of African life. The East Indians, like the Africans, followed the same pattern in reproducing their culture as it existed in India. Although Naipaul knows and understands the rituals and practices of his East Indian group, he knows very little of the rituals and practices of the African group, and so he reduces their activity to "fantasy." Herein lies the critical difference in Naipaul's interpretation of these two groups. Naipaul depicts the Negroes as simply savages.

12. On the jacket cover of the original edition of *The Loss of El Dorado,* the publisher described the book as follows: "Only a novelist of his quality and range could have made such an illuminating and entertaining use of the people involved. . . . It is an astonishing performance. Perhaps it is history as it should be written: an artist has chosen to explore a clearly defined aspect of events because it is one which he can interpret according to his own genius, using scrupulous scholarship to ends beyond documentation." It is difficult to understand how "scrupulous" scholarship can be entertaining. The questions that must be asked are, Who is being entertained and at whose expense, and what are the "ends" beyond which these documents of history are placed?

13. In his works *For Marx* (trans. Ben Brewster [London: New Left Review, 1969]) and *Lenin and Philosophy* (trans. Ben Brewster [New York: Monthly Review

Press, 1971]), Louis Althusser outlines the manner in which ideology functions in the social totality. He differentiates between what he calls "ideological history, whose values and verdicts are decided even before investigation starts" (*For Marx*, p. 70) and "real history," which examines men and their activity in their own material world. He argues: "History that fails, makes no headway and repeats itself is, as we know only too well, still history" (ibid., p. 82). The task of the examiner, however, is to grant such history its own integrity and autonomy and to determine its internal dynamics.

14. In discussing the unofficial world of the colonized, I have opted for using the term "the culture of carnival," as distinct from "Trinidad Carnival" or merely "carnival," as Naipaul has used the term. Naipaul used the term to refer to the pageantry of carnival. When I speak of the culture of carnival, I mean not only the pageantry of the carnival celebrations but all the necessary and contingent aspects that make it so important to the life of the islands. More important, I understand the "ritual" of the annual carnival celebrations as only one aspect of the larger mosaic of the folk life of Trinidad and Tobago, expression of the unofficial social and cultural life of the people which gives them a sense of meaning and self-worth.

In any such definition, calypsos, stick fighting, and the rhetoric which accompanies these performances, the dances, and so on, are all aspects of this larger culture of the people. Drawing on Bakhtin's study, we can perceive the carnival of culture as being constituted of (1) ritual spectacle: carnival pageantry, comic shows, démarche gras, dances before carnival, preparation for carnival, the activity at the calypso tents and in the band yards; (2) verbal compositions (that is, the literature of carnival): the calypso, the parodies of the official life, the robber talk of the midnight robbers, the language of stick fighting, and so on; (3) ritual dances: camboulay, calenda, innovative calypso dances made up for the celebrations; (4) ritual meaning: what carnival means and what the band leaders, the calypsonian, and others try to say at each annual ceremony. What does carnival itself mean to the people who participate in it and why the urgent necessity to carry it on year after year? Most important, the culture of carnival must be seen as existing distinct from the official culture, a constant affirmation of the integrity of a way of life of the oppressed. No wonder so many attempts, particularly in the nineteenth century, were made to stop this important affirmation and celebration of life.

15. Bakhtin, *Rabelais and His World*, p. 6.

16. Ibid.

17. Karl Marx and Frederick Engels, *Collected Works*, vol. 5 (New York: International Publishers, 1976), p. 36. As a materialist, Marx began his examination of history from what he called "real, active men, and on the basis of their real life process" (p. 36). It is from this point that Marx arrived at the basic conception of historical science or historical materialism. He argued, "It is not the consciousness that determines life, but life determines consciousness" (p. 37). When such an approach to history is contrasted to that of Naipaul's approach, the latter can only be called idealistic or, as Althusser suggested, "ideological history."

18. Homi Bhabha, "Some Problems in Nationalist Criticism," pp. 113–14.

19. Naipaul's attitude toward Indian society is basically the same as that which he

displays toward African civilization and culture. The recent interest that the West has taken toward the East "is like a cruel revenge joke played by the rich, many-featured West on the poor East that possesses only mystery" (*OB*, 88).

20. Nissim Ezekeil, *Literary Criticism*, pp. 73–74.

21. Capra, *The Tao of Physics*, pp. 25, 29.

22. One needs to reread the conclusion of *The Mimic Men* to see the manner in which Naipaul repeats himself.

23. Naipaul also seeks to thrust the Rastafarians into the same condition of carnival lunacy even though his assumptions about this group are entirely incorrect. For a good discussion of the origins of the Rastafarian movement, see "African Redemption: The Rastafarian and the Wider Society, 1959–69," in Rex M. Nettleford, *Mirror Mirror* (Kingston: Williams Collins and Sangster, 1970).

24. Eugene Genovese, in his book *From Rebellion to Revolution: Afro-American Slave Revolts in the Making of the Modern World* (Baton Rouge: Louisiana State University Press, 1979), a somewhat mechanistic analysis of the slave rebellions in the Americas, makes a strong argument for the central significance of the Haitian Revolution in international affairs at the end of the eighteenth and early nineteenth centuries. I do not accept his "restorationist" interpretation of the slave and maroon movements (that is, that these movements "looked toward the restoration of as much of a traditional African way of life as could be remembered and copied" [p. 82]) because it leads to incorrect conclusions about the character of these struggles (that is, "in the unfolding of the blacks' complex struggle, the early slave revolts—to the extent to which they remained imprisoned in the early maroon vision—developed in a way not merely contradictory but tragic" [p. 83]). Pride of place in the Caribbean revolutionary firmament of glorious achievements ought not to go to the French Revolution but to the Haitian Revolution.

25. This statement is, of course, the perfect formula for (and the birth of) Jimmy Ahmed of *Guerrillas*.

26. Bhabha, "Some Problems in Nationalist Criticisms," p. 114.

27. V. S. Naipaul, "An Island Betrayed," *Harper's*, March 1984, pp. 62–63, hereafter "IB." The same article appeared in the *Sunday Times Colour Magazine* (London), February 12, 1984, under the title "V. S. Naipaul: Heavy Manners," pp. 23–31.

28. See Chris Searle, "Naipaulicity: A Form of Cultural Imperialism," *Race and Class* 26, no. 2 (Autumn 1984): 45–62. See also Selwyn R. Cudjoe, *Grenada: Two Essays* (Tacarigua: Calaloux, 1984).

29. Searle, "Naipaulicity," p. 50.

30. Ibid., p. 60.

31. Ibid., p. 61.

32. See Selwyn R. Cudjoe, *Movement of the People* (Tacarigua: Calaloux, 1983), and Selwyn R. Cudjoe, *A Just and Moral Society* (Tacarigua: Calaloux, 1984), for a discussion of this problem.

33. See Amilcar Cabral, *Return to the Source* (New York: Monthly Review Press, 1973).

34. Errol Hill, *The Trinidad Carnival: Mandate for a National Theatre* (Austin: University of Texas Press, 1972).

35. G. W. F. Hegel, *The Phenomenology of Mind,* vol. 1, trans. J. B. Baile (New York: Macmillan, 1910), p. 175.

7. THE POSTCOLONIAL SOCIETY AND THE INDIVIDUAL SUBJECT

1. Mikhail Bakhtin, *The Dialogic Imagination: Four Essays,* trans. Caryl Emerson and Michael Holquist (Austin: University of Texas Press, 1981), p. 23.

2. Schillebeeckx, *Jesus: An Experiment in Christology,* pp. 119–20.

3. Ibid., pp. 120, 124.

4. Bakhtin, *Dialogic Imagination,* pp. 276–77, 293–94.

5. Bakhtin uses the term "heteroglossia" to express the mutually interrelated manner in which utterances are shaped and communicated at any given moment in history. First, there is the language of the dominant group, which represents a fixed system of transcription and tends to have a homogenized effect upon language (centripetal-unitary). Second, there is the language of the oppressed group (the common folks), which is innovative and always tends to confront the official language of the oppressor and must be understood always in its specific social context (centrifugal-individual). It is the interrelationship of these two aspects of language (utterance) that allows for its development. Social discourse cannot fail "to be oriented toward the 'already uttered,' the 'already known,' the 'common opinion' and so forth" (ibid., p. 279).

6. Chris Searle, *Words Unchained: Language and Revolution in Grenada* (London: Zed Books, 1984), p. xxii.

7. Ibid., p. 88.

8. Carrington describes "languaging" as a form of speech which uses language not for meaning or clarity but simply for itself and the glorification of the speaker. Here words are valued for their sound and length rather than their meaning. See ibid., pp. 30, 36.

9. Amilcar Cabral, *Unity and Struggle: Speeches and Writings,* trans. Michael Wolfers (London: Heineman, 1980); "Mikey Smith: Dub Poet," interviewed by Mervyn Morris, *Jamaica Journal* 18 (May–July 1985): 39. Jamaican "dub poetry" incorporates reggae rhythms, is usually in Jamaican Creole, and often affirms the cultural strength of the Jamaican people.

10. Gustav Morf argues that Lord Jim "is the projection of Conrad's unconscious wishes for compensation" and that "in *Lord Jim,* Conrad experienced, in a symbolic fashion, the deepest conflicts that arose from the Polish-English within him" (*The Polish Heritage of Joseph Conrad* [London: Sampson Low, Marston, 1930], pp. 161, 166). The psychoanalytic balance that pervades *A House for Mr. Biswas* (and, less so, *The Mimic Men*) gives way to an intense ambivalence in *Guerrillas,* which may be considered a symbolic representation of Naipaul's traumatic experiences with his country. Despite his posturing, it may be that Naipaul, like Conrad, never really came to grips with the duality of his experience.

11. Edward Said, *Joseph Conrad and the Fiction of Autobiography* (Cambridge, Mass.: Harvard University Press, 1966), p. vii.

12. Linda Anderson, "Ideas of Identity and Freedom in V. S. Naipaul and Joseph Conrad," *English Studies* 59, no. 6 (December 1978): 510.

13. V. S. Naipaul, "Without a Place," *Savacou* 9–10 (1974): 125–26. The distinction between "creating" and "making" a novel is examined by Bakhtin in "Discourse in the Novel."

14. In this story, the blacks, seen from the consciousness of Santosh, are depicted as "that wild race [which] existed in numbers in Washington and were permitted to roam the streets so freely." They were "very wild-looking . . . with dark glasses and their hair frizzled out, but it seemed that if you didn't trouble them they didn't attack you" (*In a Free State* [London: André Deutsch, 1971], p. 33; hereafter *IFS*). Like animals, they hardly speak, they merely grunt. Thus when Santosh learns his first few words of English, he is taught by a black girl to say: " 'Me black and beautiful.' . . . Then she pointed to a policeman with the guns outside and taught me 'He pig' " (*IFS*, 38). When the blacks in Washington begin to riot, Santosh's employer responds: "The *hubshi* have gone wild, Santosh. They are burning down Washington" (*IFS*, 44). Thus does his depiction of blacks continue throughout the text, similar to descriptions of the blacks in *The Middle Passage*.

15. The same racist approach continues in "Tell Me Who to Kill." In the only reference to Africans in the story, the narrator, seeing some Africans in London with their jackets, ties, and briefcases, concludes: "I don't know what good these studies they are taking will ever do them" (*IFS*, 98).

16. Naipaul, "Without a Place," p. 125.

17. Santosh's sense of freedom is always accompanied by a feeling of exhilaration. Such nervous or emotional responses to the concept of freedom ought to be contrasted with the feeling of "drama" which independence brought in *The Mimic Men*. The nature of colonial reality is such that the colonized subject is incapable of any deeper response to the concept of liberation. His response is simply animalistic or "primitive."

18. In *A House for Mr. Biswas*, Mr. Biswas returns from his marriage to Sharma and seeks solace in his mother's arms. In this instance, however, such solace is not even expected. Frank, as narrator, simply notes its absence.

19. Naipaul will depict Jimmy Ahmed in this manner in *Guerrillas*.

20. Naipaul, "Without a Place," pp. 125–26.

21. Georg Lukács, *Solzhenitsyn* (Cambridge, Mass.: MIT Press, 1981), p. 7.

22. Ibid., p. 8. Naipaul recognized this position implicitly when he compared Gandhi's function in India to that of the novelists. He said: "Like a novelist who splits himself into his characters, unconsciously setting up the consonances that give his theme a close intensity, the many-sided Gandhi permeates modern India. . . . The creator does not have to understand the roots of his obsessions; his duty is merely to set events in motion" (*India: A Wounded Civilization* [New York: Knopf, 1977], p. 189).

23. V. S. Naipaul, *The Return of Eva Perón: with the Killings in Trinidad* (New York: Vintage, 1981), author's note; hereafter *ROEP*.

24. I cannot agree with Phyllis Rose's assessment that "although these essays [in *The Return of Eva Perón*] deal with the Third World phenomena, it would be a mistake to read their indictments as directed at the Third World alone" ("Of Moral

Bonds and Men," *Yale Review* 70 [October 1980]: 151). I would insist that in spite of all of the accidental commentaries that Naipaul makes about European societies, his strongest attacks are directed essentially at Third World peoples. None of the essays (or other novels) ever examine the corruption of European civilization in any central manner. In fact, when Naipaul goes to his next set of essays in *India: A Wounded Civilization,* he makes the same attacks against the Indian civilization that he makes against the African civilization in this essay.

25. "With a Lot of Help from His Friend," *New York Times,* May 28, 1978, Sec. 4, p. 1.

26. The atypical nature of Mobutuism and Aminism cannot be emphasized too strongly. Clearly, Naipaul would not consider the way whites in South Africa treat the blacks as the best manifestation of Western Christian social development.

27. This almost narcissistic concern for his prose style comes through clearly when Alfred Kazin, in his interview with Naipaul, reports that "the part of his life which rouses him in the telling [of his stories] is his love and mastery of the English language" ("V. S. Naipaul, Novelist as Thinker," *New York Times Book Review,* May 1, 1977, p. 7).

28. Naipaul, *The Overcrowded Barracoon,* pp. 14, 27.

29. Quoted in Gordon Rohlehr, "The Creative Writer in West Indian Society," *Tapia,* August 18, 1974, p. 6.

30. "V. S. Naipaul Tells How Writing Changes a Writer," *Tapia,* December 2, 1973, p. 11.

31. Ibid.

32. Naipaul, "Without a Place," p. 122.

33. Anderson, "Ideas of Identity and Freedom in V. S. Naipaul and Joseph Conrad," p. 510.

34. Naipaul, *The Overcrowded Barracoon,* pp. 16–17.

35. Joseph Conrad, *Nostromo* (New York: New American Library, 1960), p. 414.

36. As I have suggested, much of Naipaul's definition of the function of the writer is taken from Conrad's 1897 preface to *The Nigger of Narcissus,* which states, "The changing wisdom of successive generations discards ideas, questions facts, demolishes theories. But the artist appeals to the part of our being which is a gift and not an acquisition—and, therefore, more permanently enduring. He speaks to our capacity for delight and wonder, to the sense of mystery surrounding our lives; to our sense of pity, and beauty, and pain; to the latent feeling of fellowship with all creation" (*Typhoon and Other Tales* [New York: New American Library, 1980], pp. 19–20). Naipaul refers to the grandeur of the novel, a product of the great societies of the past.

37. "The Dark Visions of V. S. Naipaul," *Newsweek,* November 26, 1981, p. 104.

38. Joseph Conrad, *Lord Jim* (New York: New American Library, 1980), p. 239.

39. Lukács, *Solzhenitsyn,* p. 34.

40. Anderson, "Ideas of Identity and Freedom in V. S. Naipaul and Joseph Conrad," p. 516.

8. DOOM AND DESPAIR

1. See "Without a Place," *Savacou* 9–10 (1974): 121, 126.

2. See Said, *Joseph Conrad and the Fiction of Autobiography.*

3. "Michael X and the Black Power Killings in Trinidad" first appeared in the London *Sunday Times Magazine* as "The Life and Trials of Michael X: The Killings in Trinidad," obviously intended to appeal to the sensibilities of the readers, to discredit the doctrine of black power, and to profit from the tragedy of the Jonestown massacre in Guyana. Jack Beatty in the *New Republic* called the Michael X incident a "Jonestown in a minor key, and as at Jonestown the tragedy lies in the slaughter of the followers" ("The Return of Eva Perón," *New Republic,* April 12, 1980, p. 38).

4. V. S. Naipaul, *The Return of Eva Perón: with the Killings in Trinidad* (New York: Knopf, 1980).

5. V. S. Naipaul, *A Bend in the River* (New York: Vintage, 1980), p. 71; hereafter *BR.*

6. Michael Abdul Malik, *From Michael de Freitas to Michael X* (London: André Deutsch, 1968), p. 7.

7. See Naipaul, *An Area of Darkness,* p. 37.

8. Naipaul, "Without a Place."

9. Naipaul, *The Overcrowded Barracoon,* p. 248; see Naipaul, "An Island Betrayed," *Harper's* (1982): 61–72.

10. Charles Michener, "The Dark Visions of V. S. Naipaul," *Newsweek,* November 16, 1981, p. 105.

11. V. S. Naipaul, *Guerrillas* (New York: Vintage, 1975), p. 108; hereafter *G.*

12. V. S. Naipaul, *The Middle Passage* (London: André Deutsch, 1962), p. 41.

13. Lemaire, *Jacques Lacan,* p. 228.

14. Ibid., p. 215.

15. Ibid., p. 228.

16. Campbell, "West Indian Fiction: A Literature of Exile," p. 250.

17. Robert Hemenway, "Sex and Politics in V. S. Naipaul," *Studies in the Novel* 14 (Summer 1982): 200.

18. Hana Wirth-Nesher, "The Curse of Marginality: Colonialism in Naipaul's *Guerrillas,*" *Modern Fiction Studies* 30 (Autumn 1984): 543, 540, 542.

19. See Hemenway, "Sex and Politics in Naipaul."

20. See Helen Pyne-Timothy, "Women and Sexuality in the Later Novels of V. S. Naipaul," *World Literature in English* 25 (1985): 298–306; also Jeffrey Robinson, "V. S. Naipaul and the Sexuality of Power," pp. 69–77; Elaine Fido, "Psychosexual Aspects of the Woman in V. S. Naipaul's Fiction," pp. 79–94; and Cheryl Griffith, "The Woman as Whore in the Novels of V. S. Naipaul," pp. 95–105, all in Mark McWatt, ed., *West Indian Literature and Its Social Context: Proceedings of the Fourth Annual Conference on West Indian Literature* (Cave Hill: Department of English, University of the West Indies, 1985).

21. Juliet Mitchell and Jacqueline Rose, eds., *Feminine Sexuality: Jacques Lacan and the école freudienne* (New York: Norton, 1983), p. 2.

22. Eve Kosofsky Sedgwick, *Between Men: English Literature and Male Homosocial Desire* (New York: Columbia University Press, 1985), p. 151.

23. Mitchell and Rose, eds., *Jacques Lacan,* p. 27.

24. See especially "The Meaning of the Phallus," and "Guiding Remarks for a Conference," in ibid.

25. Fido, "Psycho-sexual Aspects of the Woman in V. S. Naipaul's Fiction," pp. 84, 79.

26. Griffith, "The Woman as Whore in the Novels of V. S. Naipaul," p. 98.

27. Robinson, "V. S. Naipaul and the Sexuality of Power," p. 75.

28. See Sedgwick, *Between Men,* esp. chap. 1. As Sedgwick notes in a discussion on Shakespearean sonnets, "To say that a woman is present is not to say anything about her, or that she is the subject of consciousness; although she is a subject of action" (p. 36).

29. In this context, see Michel Foucault, "The History of Sexuality: Interview," trans. Geoff Bennington, *Oxford Literary Review* 4 (1980): 3–14; and Michel Foucault, *The History of Sexuality,* vol. 1, *An Introduction,* trans. Robert Hurley (New York: Random House, 1980).

30. See Sedgwick, *Between Men,* esp. chap. 8.

31. Sanna Dhahir, "Women in V. S. Naipaul's Fiction: Their Roles and Relationships" (Ph.D. diss., University of New Brunswick, 1985), p. 122. This work is a defense of Naipaul's "uncomplimentary treatment" of the women in his fiction and their sexual relationships with men rather than a study of *why* he (mis)treats them the way he does and the perverse manner in which he depicts their sexual relationships. Dhahir does not examine the manner in which the violence Naipaul perpetrates against these women relates to his sexuality and what it reveals about his identity.

32. Sedgwick, *Between Men,* pp. 10–11.

33. See John Thieme, " 'Apparition of Disaster': Brontëan Parallels in *Wide Sargasso Sea* and *Guerrillas,*" *Journal of Commonwealth Literature* 14, no. 1 (1979). See also Ling-Mei Lim, "V. S. Naipaul's Later Fiction: The Creative Constraints of Exile" (Ph.D. diss., Indiana University, 1984), pp. 188–96, and Wirth-Nesher, "The Curse of Marginality," for a discussion of the manner in which Naipaul used these English classics to structure *Guerrillas.*

34. See Raymond Williams's comments on Herder's *Philosophy of Mankind* in his work, *Marxism and Literature* (Oxford: Oxford University Press, 1977), p. 17.

35. Ibid., p. 27.

36. Ibid., p. 31.

37. Wirth-Nesher, "The Curse of Marginality," p. 545.

38. Lemaire, *Jacques Lacan,* p. 216.

39. Williams, *Marxism and Literature,* pp. 41–42.

40. V. S. Naipaul, *India: A Wounded Civilization* (New York: Knopf, 1977), p. ix; hereafter *I.*

41. Helga Chaudhary, "V. S. Naipaul's Changing Vision of India: A Study of *An Area of Darkness* and *India: A Wounded Civilization,*" *Literary Half-yearly* 23 (January 1982): 111.

42. Sudha Rai, *V. S. Naipaul: A Study in Expatriate Sensibility* (New Delhi: Arnold Heinemann, 1982), p. 7.

43. Dilip Hiro, *Inside India Today* (London: Routledge & Kegan Paul, 1976), p. 16.

44. Ibid., p. 281.

45. William Boarders, *New York Times,* August 17, 1977, C19.

46. See Lim, "V. S. Naipaul's Later Fiction," p. 199.

47. V. S. Naipaul, *A Bend in the River* (New York: Vintage, 1980), p. 3; hereafter *BR*.

48. See Lynda Prescott, "Past and Present Darkness: Sources of V. S. Naipaul's *A Bend in the River,*" *Modern Fiction Studies* 30 (Autumn 1984): 547–59.

49. Larry Alan Husten, "From Autobiography to Politics: The Development of V. S. Naipaul's Fiction" (Ph.D. diss., State University of New York at Buffalo, 1983), p. 109.

50. Irving Howe, "A Dark Vision," *New York Times Book Review,* May 13, 1979, p. 1.

51. Ibid., p. 37.

52. Husten, "From Autobiography to Politics," pp. 106–7.

53. Howe, "A Dark Vision," p. 36.

54. Hemenway, "Sex and Politics in V. S. Naipaul," p. 192.

55. Martin Amis, "More Bones," *New Statesman* 100 (July 4, 1980): 20.

56. Raymond Williams, "George Orwell," in *Culture and Society, 1780–1950* (New York: Columbia University Press, 1958), p. 291.

57. Arnold Kettle, "Dickens and the Popular Tradition," in David Craig, ed., *Marxists on Literature: An Anthology* (Harmondsworth: Penguin, 1975), p. 216.

58. Bharati Mukherjee and Robert Boyers, "A Conversation with V. S. Naipaul," *Salmagundi* 54 (Fall 1981): 5–6.

59. Michiko Kakutani, "Naipaul Reviews His Past from Afar," *New York Times,* December 1, 1980, C15.

60. Cathleen Medwick, "Life, Literature, and Politics: An Interview with V. S. Naipaul," *Vogue,* August 1981, p. 130.

61. See Walter Rodney, *How Europe Underdeveloped Africa* (London: Bogle L'Ouverture, 1972).

9. LANGUAGE, REPRESSION, IDENTITY

1. Jean Laplanche, *Life and Death in Psychoanalysis,* trans. Jeffery Mehlman (Baltimore: Johns Hopkins University Press, 1976), p. 8.

2. Naipaul's men constantly degrade themselves and brutalize women. Ralph Singh and Salim can relate only to whores, Bobby is a homosexual, and Jimmy is bisexual. Linda is a "man-killer"; Jane is buggered by Jimmy before he violently murders her. Salim beats up Yvette (she loves him most when he is brutal) and spits in her vagina after a moment of lovemaking. Such sexual violence is closely related to the author's own perception of his sexuality and relates specifically to the question of his identity.

3. See *Washington Post,* November 19, 1961, C17.

4. Colin McCabe, *James Joyce and the Revolution of the Word* (London: Macmillan, 1977), pp. 6–7.

5. Curt Suplee, "Voyager with the Dark and Comic Vision," *Washington Post,* November 19, 1981, C1, 17.

6. Wole Soyinka, *Myth, Literature, and the African World* (London: Cambridge University Press, 1976), p. 148.

7. Chinua Achebe, in *Things Fall Apart* (New York: Astor-Honor, 1959), gives a good description of the African world before the Europeans arrived and its subsequent dissolution following contact with the European "civilization." Sembene Ousmane, *God's Bits of Wood,* trans. Francis Price (Garden City, N.Y.: Doubleday, 1962), depicts the construction of the new African postcolonial subject in relation to the language as she/he arises from the African-Islamic perception of the world. Naipaul, therefore, was not original when he proposed that the only salvation for Africa lies in its return to the bush. As early as 1962, Ousmane ridiculed this bias against Africans in the words of one of his European characters: "You'll see . . . you have to learn how to forget. Twenty years ago there was nothing here but an arid wilderness. We built this city. Now they have hospitals, schools and trains, but if we ever leave they're finished. Bush will take it all back. There wouldn't be anything left" (p. 225).

8. In *India: A Wounded Civilization* Naipaul studied some creative Indian texts to understand the deeper impulses of the Hindu world. No such evidence is at work in his examination of Africa.

9. Wilson Harris, *The Guyana Quartet* (London: Faber and Faber, 1985), pp. 7, 8.

10. Wilson Harris, *The Eye of the Scarecrow* (London: Faber and Faber, 1974), p. 95.

11. Ibid., p. 8.

12. Ibid., p. 98.

13. Terry Eagleton, "Molly's Piano," *New Statesman* 100, no. 2583 (September 1, 1980): 21.

14. Ibid., p. 21.

15. Laplanche, *Life and Death in Psychoanalysis,* p. 29.

16. Sigmund Freud, *Collected Papers,* vol. 4, trans. Joan Riviere (New York: Basic Books, 1959), p. 89.

17. Ibid.

18. See "The Libido Theory," in ibid.

19. Laplanche, *Life and Death in Psychoanalysis,* pp. 33–34.

20. Michiko Kakutani, "Naipaul Reviews His Past from Afar," *New York Times,* December 1, 1980, p. C15.

21. See *Finding the Center* and *The Enigma of Arrival.*

22. Curt Suplee, "Voyager with the Dark Vision," *Washington Post,* November 19, 1981, p. C17.

23. V. S. Naipaul, *Among the Believers* (New York: Knopf, 1981), p. 12; hereafter *AB.*

24. Ali Shari ati, *Marxism and Other Western Fallacies: An Islamic Critique,* trans. R. Campbell (Berkeley: Nizam Press, 1980), p. 108.

25. Ali Shari ati, *On the Sociology of Islam,* trans. Hamid Algar (Berkeley: Nizam Press, 1979), p. 24.

26. Ibid., p. 23.

27. Roy Mottahedeh, *The Mantle of the Prophet: Religion and Politics in Iran* (New York: Simon and Schuster, 1985), p. 330.

28. Shari ati, *Marxism and Other Western Fallacies*, p. 21.

29. Ibid., pp. 95–96.

30. Shari ati, *On the Sociology of Islam*, p. 58.

31. Mottahedeh, *The Mantle of the Prophet*, p. 88.

32. Fouad Ajami, "In Search of Islam," *New York Times Book Review*, October 25, 1981, p. 30.

33. See Shari ati, *On the Sociology of Islam*.

34. A. Rahman, "Science and Technology in Medieval India," *Journal of Scientific and Industrial Research* 40 (October 1981): 616.

35. Ibid., p. 615.

36. Dinesh Mohan, "A Flawed Mirror," *Book Review* 4 (January–February 1982): 197–202.

37. V. S. Naipaul, *Finding the Center: Two Narratives* (New York: Knopf, 1964), p. viii; hereafter *FC*.

38. *The Enigma of Arrival*, p. 147; hereafter *EOA*.

39. Janet Varner Gunn, *Autobiography: Toward a Poetics of Experience* (Philadelphia: University of Pennsylvania Press, 1982), p. 9.

40. See ibid., chap. 1, for a discussion of the distinction between a self-writing and a self-reading; quote is on p. 18.

41. "Post Production Script," transmitted March 8, 1987, pp. 13–14.

42. Jean Laplanche and J.-B. Pontalis, "Fantasy and the Origins of Sexuality," *The International Journal of Psychoanalysis* 49 (1968), part 1, p. 10.

43. Richard Cronin, "Quite Quiet India: The Despair of R. K. Narayan," *Encounter* 64, no. 3 (March 1985): 59.

44. Campbell, "West Indian Fiction: A Literature of Exile," p. 202.

45. Walcott, "The Garden Path," pp. 27–28.

46. Ibid., p. 29.

47. Laplanche and Pontalis, "Fantasy and the Origins of Sexuality," p. 11.

48. Quoted in ibid., p. 3.

49. White, *V. S. Naipaul: A Critical Introduction*, p. 134.

50. Homi Bhabha, "Representation and the Colonial Text: A Critical Exploration of Some Forms of Mimeticism," in Frank Gloversmith, *The Theory of Reading* (New Jersey: Barnes & Noble, 1984), pp. 119–20.

51. "The Defence of Neuro-psychoses," in *Collected Papers of Sigmund Freud*, Vol. 1, trans. Joan Riviere (London: Hogarth Press, 1956), p. 62.

52. Ibid., p. 65.

53. Ibid., p. 72.

54. "Unfurnished Entrails—the Novelist V. S. Naipaul in Conversation with Jim Douglas Henry," *The Listener*, November 25, 1971, p. 721.

55. J. Laplanche and J.-B. Pontalis, *The Language of Psychoanalysis*, trans. Donald Nicholson-Smith (New York: Norton, 1973), p. 317.

56. Quoted in Campbell, "West Indian Fiction: A Literature of Exile," p. 197.

57. "Post Production Script," p. 33.

58. Ibid., p. 11.

59. Thomas Mypoyi-Buatu, "Le refus de l'Autre," *La Quinzaine Litteraire,* October 16–31, 1983, p. 8 (my translation).

60. Ibid., p. 8.

61. Sunday O. Anozie, *Structural Models and African Poetics: Towards a Pragmatic Theory of Literature* (London: Routledge & Kegan Paul, 1981), p. 44.

62. See the *Wall Street Journal* editorial, "Civilization Receding," November 20, 1979, in which it is argued that "the events in Iran . . . [were] the latest and most dramatic symptoms of a more general collapse of established values and conventions of conduct. Throughout the world, civilization is receding before our eyes." Such a sad state of affairs, they concluded, resulted from a decline in American power, will, and influence over the last decade and could only be made right by a demonstration of American power in that part of the world.

63. John Stuart Mill, *Dissertations and Discussions: Political, Philosophical, and Historical,* Vol. 3 (New York: Henry Holt, 1882), pp. 252–53.

64. Naipaul, *The Overcrowded Barracoon,* pp. 9–15.

65. "Post Production Script," p. 1, and Swinden, *The English Novel of History and Society, 1950–1980,* p. 210.

66. Terry Eagleton, "Ideology, Fiction, Narrative," *Social Text* 2 (Summer 1979): 66.

CONCLUSION

1. Walcott, "The Garden Path," p. 30.

2. See Toril Moi, *Sexual/Textual Politics: Feminist Literary Theory* (London: Methuen, 1985), chap. 8. The quotation is taken from Cheris Kramarae, *Women and Men Speaking: Frameworks for Analysis* (Rowley, Mass.: Newbury House, 1981), p. 165.

3. "The Book Programme—V. S. Naipaul," Saturday BBC 2, *Radio Times,* 1979.

Bibliography

This bibliography consists of three sections: texts by V. S. Naipaul and important interviews that he granted; major critical texts and essays on Naipaul's work; and all other important texts (including reviews) that were used to explicate his work. In the first category, the texts are listed in chronological order. The other two categories are in alphabetical order. I do not attempt to list each piece of work written by or about V. S. Naipaul but have listed only the most important sources for this study.

TEXTS BY NAIPAUL, INCLUDING INTERVIEWS

"Two-Thirty A.M." Caribbean Voices Scripts, BBC Written Archives, 1950.
"This Is Home." Caribbean Voices Scripts, BBC Written Archives, 1951.
"Potatoes." Caribbean Voices Scripts, BBC Written Archives, 1952.
"Old Man." Caribbean Voices Scripts, BBC Written Archives, 1953.
"A Family Reunion." Caribbean Voices Scripts, BBC Written Archives, 1954.
The Mystic Masseur. London: André Deutsch, 1957.
"A Letter to Maria." *New Statesman* 56 (July 1958): 14.
"New Novels." *New Statesman* 56 (December 1958): 826–27.
The Suffrage of Elvira. 1958. Reprint. Harmondsworth: Penguin, 1969.
Miguel Street. London: Heinemann, 1959.
"New Novels." *New Statesman* 60 (July 1960): 97–98.
A House for Mr. Biswas. 1961. Reprint. Harmondsworth: Penguin, 1969.
"Trollope in the West Indies." *The Listener,* March 15, 1962, p. 461.
The Middle Passage. London: André Deutsch, 1962.
"Tea with an Author." *Bim* 9, no. 34 (January–June 1962): 79–81.
Mr. Stone and the Knights Companion. 1963. Reprint. Harmondsworth: Penguin, 1973.
"Critics and Criticism." *Bim* 10, no. 38 (January–June 1964): 74–77.
"Jamshed into Jimmy." *New Statesman,* January 25, 1963, pp. 129–30.
"India's Cast-Off Revolution." *Sunday Times* (London), August 25, 1963, p. 17.
"The Little More." *The Times* (London), July 13, 1964, p. 12.
"Interview with Frank Winstone." *Sunday Mirror* (Trinidad), 1964.
An Area of Darkness. London: André Deutsch, 1964.
"Images." *New Statesman,* September 24, 1965, pp. 452–53.
"What's Wrong with Being a Snob?" *Saturday Evening Post,* June 3, 1967, p. 12.
The Mimic Men. 1967. Reprint. Harmondsworth: Penguin, 1969.
"Pooter." *Times Saturday Review,* November 9, 1968, p. 23.

A Flag on the Island. 1967. Reprint. Harmondsworth: Penguin, 1969.

The Loss of El Dorado. 1969. Reprint. New York: Alfred Knopf, 1970.

"V. S. Naipaul: A Transition Interview by Adrian Rowe-Evans." *Transition* 40 (1971): 56–62.

"V. S. Naipaul in Conversation with Ian Hamilton: Without a Place." 1971. Reprint. *Savacou* 9–10 (1974).

In a Free State. London: André Deutsch, 1971.

"Interview with Nigel Bingham." *The Listener* 88, no. 9 (1972): 641.

The Overcrowded Barracoon and Other Articles. 1972. Reprint. Harmondsworth: Penguin, 1976.

"Without a Dog's Chance." *New York Review of Books,* May 18, 1972, pp. 29–31.

"The Corpse at the Iron Gate." *New York Review of Books,* August 10, 1972, pp. 3–7.

"Comprehending Borges." *New York Review of Books,* October 1972.

"V. S. Naipaul Tells How Writing Changes a Writer." *Tapia,* December 2, 1973, pp. 11–12.

"A Country Dying on Its Feet." *New York Review of Books,* April 4, 1974, pp. 21–33.

"The Life and Trials of Michael X." *The Sunday Times Magazine,* May 12, 1974, pp. 16–35; May 19, 1972, pp. 24–41.

"Argentina: The Brothels Behind the Graveyard." *New York Review of Books,* September 1974.

"A New King for the Congo." *New York Review of Books,* June 1975.

Guerrillas. New York: Vintage, 1975.

India: A Wounded Civilization. New York: Alfred Knopf, 1977.

"V. S. Naipaul, Novelist as Thinker." Interview by Alfred Kazin. *New York Times Book Review,* May 1, 1977, pp. 7, 20–21.

"Meeting V. S. Naipaul." Interview by Elizabeth Hardwick. *New York Times Book Review,* May 13, 1979, pp. 1, 36.

"The Book Programme—V. S. Naipaul." Saturday BBC 2. *Radio Times,* 1979.

A Bend in the River. 1979. Reprint. New York: Vintage, 1980.

A Congo Diary. Los Angeles: Sylvester & Orphanos. 1980.

The Return of Eva Perón: with the Killings in Trinidad. New York: Alfred Knopf, 1980.

Among the Believers. New York: Alfred Knopf, 1981.

"The Dark Visions of V. S. Naipaul." Interviewed by Charles Michener. *Newsweek,* November 16, 1981, pp. 104–17.

"Life, Literature, and Politics: An Interview with V. S. Naipaul. Interview by Cathleen Medwick. *Vogue* (1981).

"Voyager with the Dark Vision." Interview by Curt Suplee. *Washington Post* (1981).

"Introduction." *East Indians in the Caribbean: Colonialism and the Struggle for Identity.* New York: Kraus International Publishers, 1982.

"A Note on a Borrowing by Conrad." *New York Review of Books,* December 16, 1982, pp. 37–38.

"Prologue to an Autobiography." *Vanity Fair* 46 (April 1983).

"Writing 'A House for Mr. Biswas.' " *New York Review of Books,* November 24, 1983, pp. 22–23.

"An Island Betrayed." *Harper's* 268, no. 1606 (March 1984): 62–72.

"V. S. Naipaul: 'It Is Out of This Violence I've Always Written.' " *New York Review of Books,* September 16, 1984, pp. 45–46.

"Among the Republicans." *New York Review of Books,* October 25, 1984, pp. 5, 8, 10, 12, 14–17.

Finding the Center: Two Narratives. New York: Alfred Knopf, 1984.

"The Enigma of Arrival." *New Yorker,* August 11, 1986, pp. 26–62.

The Enigma of Arrival. New York: Alfred Knopf, 1987.

"The South Bank Show—V. S. Naipaul." London Weekend Television. Interview by Melvyn Bragg, March 8, 1987.

MAJOR CRITICAL TEXTS AND ESSAYS ON NAIPAUL

Ahmad, Naheed F. "The Quest for Identity in the West Indian Novel, with Special Reference to John Herne, George Lamming, Roger Mais, Dennis Williams, and V. S. Naipaul." B. Litt. thesis, Wolfson College, Oxford University, 1973.

Ajami, Fouad. "In Search of Islam." *New York Times Book Review,* October 25, 1981, pp. 7, 30–32.

Alisharam, Stephen Sheik. "V. S. Naipaul: A Study of Four Books." Masters thesis, Mt. Allison University, 1965.

Amis, Martin. "More Bones." *New Statesman,* July 4, 1980, pp. 19–20.

Anderson, Linda. "Ideas of Identity and Freedom in V. S. Naipaul and Joseph Conrad." *English Studies* 59, no. 6 (December 1978): 510–17.

Angrosino, Michael V. "V. S. Naipaul and the Colonial Image." *Caribbean Quarterly* 21, no. 3 (September 1975): 1–11.

Anniah Gowda, H. H. "Naipaul in India." *Literary Half-yearly* 11, no. 2 (July 1970): 163–70.

———. "India in Naipaul's Artistic Consciousness." *Literary Half-yearly* 16, no. 1 (January 1975): 27–39.

———. "Visions of Decadence: William Faulkner's *Absolom, Absolom!* and V. S. Naipaul's *The Mimic Men.*" *Literary Half-yearly* 23, no. 1 (January 1982): 71–80.

Argyle, Barry. "Commentary on V. S. Naipaul's 'A House for Mr. Biswas.' A West Indian Epic." *Caribbean Quarterly* 16, no. 4 (December 1970): 61–69.

———. "Commentary on V. S. Naipaul's 'A House for Mr. Biswas.' " *Literary Half-yearly* 14, no. 2 (July 1973): 81–95.

Asnani, Shyam M. "Quest for Identity Theme in Three Commonwealth Novels." In Avadhesh K. Srivastava, ed., *Alien Voice: Perspectives on Commonwealth Literature.* Lucknow, India: Print House, 1981; Atlantic Highlands, N.J.: Humanities, 1982.

Ayen, Anthony Wing Chong. "V. S. Naipaul: A Study in Alienation." Ph.D. diss., University of Toronto, 1978.

Balandier, Georges. "Naipaul et le grand chambardement." *La Quinzaine Litteraire,* October 16–31, 1983, pp. 5–6.

Balliett, Whitney. "Books: Soft Coal: Hard Coal." *New Yorker,* August 27, 1960, pp. 97–101.

Barloewen, Constantin von. "Auf der Suche nach Metropolis: Zur Kulturphiloso-phie V. S. Naipauls." *Neue Rundschau* 93, no. 4 (1982): 124–44.

Bayley, John. "New Novels." *The Spectator* (May 1957).

Beatty, Jack. "*The Return of Eva Perón* by V. S. Naipaul." *New Republic* (April 1980).

Belitt, Ben. "The Heraldry of Accommodation: A House for Mr. Biswas." *Sal-agundi* 54 (Fall 1981): 23–43.

Birkerts, Sven. "V. S. Naipaul and Derek Walcott: A Multiplicity of Truths," *New Boston Review* 5, no. 4 (August–September 1980): 19–21.

Blakemore, Steven. "An Africa of Words: V. S. Naipaul's *A Bend in the River.*" *South Carolina Review* 18, no. 1 (Fall 1985): 15–23.

Blodgett, Harriet. "Beyond Trinidad: Five Novels by V. S. Naipaul." *South Atlantic Quarterly* 73, no. 3 (1974): 388–403.

Boxhill, Anthony. "The Concept of Spring in V. S. Naipaul's *Mr. Stone and the Knights Companion.*" *Ariel* 5, no. 4 (October 1975): 21–28.

———. "The Little Bastard Worlds of V. S. Naipaul's *The Mimic Men* and *A Flag on the Island.*" *International Fiction Review* 3, no. 1 (January 1976): 12–19.

———. *V. S. Naipaul's Fiction: In Quest of the Enemy.* Fredrickton, N.B.: York Press, 1983.

———. "V. S. Naipaul's Starting Point." *Journal of Commonwealth Literature* 10, no. 1 (August 1975): 1–9.

Boyers, Robert, "Confronting the Present." *Salmagundi* 54 (Fall 1981): 77–97.

Breslin, Patrick. "Naipaul and the Empire of Discontent." *Washington Post Book World,* March 30, 1980, pp. 1, 6.

Brien, Alan. "A Person of Refinement." *New Statesman,* March 13, 1987, pp. 26–27.

Broughton, Geoffrey. "A Critical Study of the Development of V. S. Naipaul as Reflected in His Four Major West Indian Novels." Master's thesis, University of London, 1968.

Brown, John L. "V. S. Naipaul: A Wager on the Triumph of Darkness." *World Literature* 57, no. 2 (Spring 1983): 223–27.

Campbell, Elaine. "A Refinement of Anger: V. S. Naipaul's *A Bend in the River.*" *World Literature Written in English* 18, no. 2 (1979): 394–406.

———. "West Indian Fiction: A Literature of Exile." Ph.D. diss., Brandeis University, 1981.

Carnegie, Jimmy. "Rediscovering from the Outside: A Review." *Savacou* 5 (June 1971): 125–28.

Charles, Henry J. "A Theological-Ethical Appraisal of the Disclosure of Possibility for the Post-Colonial Caribbean via an Analysis of Selected Literary Texts." Ph.D. diss., Yale University, 1982.

Chatterjee, R. N. "*The Mystic Masseur* and Its Style." *Literary Half-yearly* 25, no. 2 (July 1984): 95–111.

Chaudhary, Helga. "V. S. Naipaul's Changing Vision of India: A Study of *An Area of Darkness* and *India: A Wounded Civilization.*" *Literary Half-yearly* 23, no. 1 (January 1982): 98–114.

Coleman, John. "Last Words." *The Spectator,* April 24, 1959, p. 595.

Conde, Maryse. "Naipaul et les Antilles: Une histoire d'amour?" *La Quinzaine Litteraire* 403 (October 16–31, 1983): 6–7.

Cooke, John. "A Vision of the Land: V. S. Naipaul's Later Novels." *Caribbean Quarterly* 25, no. 4 (December 1979): 31–47.

Cooke, Michael G. "Rational Despair and the Fatality of Revolution in West Indian Literature." *Yale Review* 71, no. 1 (Autumn 1981): 28–38.

Cudjoe, Selwyn R. "Gordon Rohlehr on V. S. Naipaul: An Interview with Selwyn Cudjoe." *Carib* 2 (1981).

———. "Kenneth Ramchand on V. S. Naipaul: An Interview with Selwyn Cudjoe." *Antillia* 1, no. 1 (1981).

———. "Tradition, *Miguel Street,* and Other Short Stories." *Trinidad and Tobago Review* 5, nos. 11 and 12 (Governor Plum, 1981): 12–16; 6, nos. 1 and 2 (Independence, 1982): 19, 21, 23; 6, no. 3 (Back to School, 1982): 14, 17, 19, 21; 6, no. 4 (Xmas, 1982): 22–24.

———. "V. S. Naipaul and the Question of Identity." In William Luis, ed., *Voices from Under: The Black Narrative in Latin America and the Caribbean.* Westport, Conn: Greenwood, 1984.

Davies, Barrie. "The Personal Sense of a Society—Minority View: Aspects of the 'East Indian' Novel in the West Indies." *Studies in the Novel* 4, no. 2 (1972): 284–95.

Demott, Benjamin, "Lost Worlds, Lost Heroes." *Saturday Review,* October 15, 1975, pp. 23–24.

Deodat, Rovindrada. "V. S. Naipaul's Fiction, 1954–1971: Fragmentation and Rootlessness." M.A. thesis, Mt. Allison University, 1975.

Derrick, Alphonsus Clement. "Naipaul's Technique as a Novelist." *Journal of Commonwealth Literature* 7 (1969): 32–44.

———. "The Uncommitted Artist: A Study of the Purpose and Method of Satire in the Novels of V. S. Naipaul." M.Phil. thesis, Leeds University, 1968.

Dhahir, Sanna. "Women in V. S. Naipaul's Fiction: Their Roles and Relationships." Ph.D. diss., University of New Brunswick, 1985.

Dinish, Mohan. "A Flawed Mirror." *Book Review* 4, no. 4 (1982): 197–202.

Doerkson, Nan. "*In a Free State* and *Nausea.*" *World Literature Written in English* 20, no. 1 (Spring 1981): 105–13.

Dunwoodie, Peter. "Commitment and Confinement: Two West Indian Visions." *Caribbean Quarterly* 21, no. 3 (September 1975): 15–27.

Erapu, Leban Omella. "The Novels of V. S. Naipaul: A Symbolic Approach." Master's of Letters thesis, University of Edinburgh, 1971.

Eyre, M. Banning. "Naipaul at Wesleyan." *South Carolina Review* 14, no. 2 (Spring 1982): 34–47.

Ezekiel, Nassim. "Naipaul's India and Mine." *Literary Criterion,* Summer 1965, pp. 30–45.

Ferracane, Kathleen K. "Images of the Mother in Caribbean Literature: Selected Novels of George Lamming, Jean Rhys, and V. S. Naipaul." Ph.D. diss., State University of New York, Buffalo, 1987.

Fido, Elaine. "Psycho-sexual Aspects of the Woman in V. S. Naipaul's Fiction." In Mark McWatt, ed., *West Indian Literature and Its Social Context: The Proceed-*

ings of the Fourth Annual Conference on West Indian Literature. Cave Hill: University of the West Indies, 1985.

Fido, Martin. "Mr. Biswas and Mr. Polly." *Ariel* 5, no. 4 (October 1974): 30–37.

Figueroa, John. "Introduction: V. S. Naipaul: A Panel Discussion." *Revista/Review Interamericana* 6, no. 4 (Winter 1976–77): 554–73.

Fitch, Nancy. "History Is a Nightmare: A Study of the Exile in the Life and Works of James Joyce, V. S. Naipaul, and Edna O'Brien." Ph.D. diss., University of Michigan, 1981.

Garebian, Keith Stephen. "The Spirit of the Place: A Comparative Study of R. K. Narayan and V. S. Naipaul." Ph.D. diss., Queens University, 1973.

———. "V. S. Naipaul's Negative Sense of Place." *Journal of Commonwealth Literature* 10, no. 1 (1975): 23–25.

Goldie, Terry. "The Minority Men." *Thalia: Studies in Literary Humor* 4, no. 2 (Fall–Winter 1981): 15–20.

Goodheart, Eugene. "Naipaul and the Voices of Negation." *Salmagundi* 54 (Fall 1981): 44–58.

———. "V. S. Naipaul's Mandarin Sensibility." *Partisan Review* 50, no. 2 (1983): 244–56.

Gornick, Vivian. "Terror and Rhetoric in Hot Places: V. S. Naipaul's Travels." *Esquire*, April 1980, p. 22.

Gottfried, Leon. "A Skeptical Pilgrimage." *Modern Fiction Studies* 30, no. 3 (Autumn 1984): 505–18.

Gray, Paul. "Burnt-Out Cases." *Time,* December 1, 1975, pp. 84–86.

Green, Benny. "News from Nowhere." *Nation,* June 30, 1979, pp. 791–93.

Greenwald, Roger Gordon. "The Method of V. S. Naipaul's Fiction, 1955–1963." Ph.D. diss., University of Toronto, 1978.

Griffith, Cheryl. "The Woman as Whore in the Novels of V. S. Naipaul." In Mark McWatt, ed., *West Indian Literature and Its Social Context: Proceedings of the Fourth Annual Conference on West Indian Literature*. Cave Hill: University of the West Indies, 1985.

Guinness, Gerald. "Naipaul's Four Early Trinidad Novels." *Revista/Review Inter-americana* 6, no. 4 (Winter 1976–77): 564–73.

Gurr, A. J. "Third-World Novels: Naipaul and After." *Journal of Commonwealth Literature* 7, no. 1 (June 1972): 6–13.

———. *Writers in Exile: The Identity of Home in Modern Literature*. Atlantic Highlands, N.J.: Humanities Press, 1981.

Halliday, Fred. "The Misanthrope." *Nation,* October 24, 1981, pp. 415–16.

Hamner, Robert. "An Island Voice: The Novels of V. S. Naipaul." Ph.D. diss., University of Texas at Austin, 1971.

———. *V. S. Naipaul*. New York: Barnes & Noble, 1973.

———. "V. S. Naipaul: A Selected Bibliography." August 1975.

Hanen, David Jad Markham. "Naipaul's Unnecessary and Unaccommodated Man." M.A. thesis, University of Calgary, 1975.

Hassan, Dolly. "West Indian Response to V. S. Naipaul's West Indian Works." Ph.D. diss., George Washington University, 1986.

Healy, J. J. "Friction, Voice, and the Rough Ground of Feeling: V. S. Naipaul after Twenty-Five Years." *University of Toronto Quarterly* 55, no. 1 (Fall 1985): 45–63.

Hearne, John. "The Snow Virgin: An Inquiry into V. S. Naipaul's 'Mimic Men.' " *Caribbean Quarterly* 23, no. 3 (September 1977): 31–37.

Hemenway, Robert. "Sex and Politics in V. S. Naipaul." *Studies in the Novel* 14, no. 2 (Summer 1982): 189–200.

Henry, Jim Douglas. "Unfurnished Entrails—The Novelist V. S. Naipaul in Conversation with Jim Douglas Henry." *The Listener,* November 25, 1971, p. 721.

Hermassi, Elbaki. *The Third World Reassessed.* Berkeley: University of California Press, 1980.

Howe, Irving. "A Dark Vision." *New York Times Book Review,* May 13, 1979, pp. 1, 37.

Hughes, Shaun F. D. "Two Books on V. S. Naipaul: An Essay-Review." *Modern Fiction Studies* 30, no. 3 (Autumn 1984): 573–80.

Husten, Larry Allen. "From Autobiography to Politics: The Development of V. S. Naipaul's Fiction." Ph.D. diss., State University of New York at Buffalo, 1983.

Jefferson, Margo. "Misfits." *Newsweek,* December 1, 1975, pp. 102–4.

Johnson, Patrice. "The Third World According to V. S. Naipaul." *Black Scholar* 15, no. 3 (May–June 1984): 12–14.

Johnstone, Richard. "Politics and V. S. Naipaul." *Journal of Commonwealth Literature* 14, no. 1 (1979): 100–8.

Jones, D. A. N. "Little Warriors in Search of a War." *Times Literary Supplement,* September 12, 1975, p. 1013.

Kakutani, Michiko. "Naipaul Reviews His Past from Afar." *New York Times,* December 1, 1980, C15.

Karameheti, Indira. "Tradition and Originality in Third World Literature: V. S. Naipaul and Aime Cesaire." Ph.D. diss., University of California, Santa Barbara, 1987.

Kaul, Suvir. "Compelling Story." *The Sunday Observer* (Bombay), April 26, 1987, p. 20.

King, Bruce. "V. S. Naipaul." In Bruce King, ed., *West Indian Literature.* London: Macmillan, 1979.

King, John. " 'A Curiously Colonial Performance': The Ec-centric Vision of V. S. Naipaul and J. L. Borges." *Yearbook of English Studies* 13 (1983): 228–43.

Kramer, Jane. "From the Third World." *New York Times Book Review,* April 13, 1980, pp. 1, 30–32.

Krikler, Bernard. "V. S. Naipaul's *A House for Mr. Biswas.*" *The Listener,* February 13, 1964, pp. 270–71.

Lacovia, R. M. "The Medium Is Divide." *Black Images* 1, no. 2 (Summer 1972): 3–6.

Larson, Charles R. "Watching the Revolution Go By." *The Nation,* December 13, 1975, pp. 627–28.

Lee, R. H. "The Novels of V. S. Naipaul." *Theoria* 27 (October 1966): 31–46.

Leonard, John. "Books of the Times." *New York Times,* March 13, 1980, C21.

Levin, Martin. "How the Ball Bounces down Trinidad Way." *New York Times Book Review*, April 12, 1959, p. 5.

Lim, Ling-Mei. "V. S. Naipaul's Later Fiction: The Creative Exile." Ph.D. diss., Indiana University, 1984.

Lockwood, Bernard. "V. S. Naipaul's *The Middle Passage*." *Revista/Review Interamericana* 6, no. 4 (Winter 1976–77): 580–86.

López de Villegas, Consuelo. "Identity and Environment: Naipaul's Architectural Vision." *Revista/Review Interamericana* 10, no. 2 (Summer 1981): 220–29.

———. "The Paradox of Freedom: Naipaul's Later Fiction." *Revista/Review Interamericana* 6, no. 4 (Winter 1976–77): 574–79.

Lyn, Gloria. "Naipaul's *Guerrillas:* Fiction and Its Social Context." In Mark McWatt, ed., *West Indian Literature and Its Social Context: Proceedings of the Fourth Annual Conference on West Indian Literature*. Cave Hill: University of the West Indies, 1985.

MacDonald, Bruce. "The Birth of Mr. Biswas." *Journal of Commonwealth Literature* 11, no. 3 (1977): 50–53.

———. "Symbolic Action in Three of V. S. Naipaul's Novels." *Journal of Commonwealth Literature* 9, no. 3 (April 1975): 41–52.

Maes-Jelinek, Hena. "The Myth of El Dorado in the Caribbean Novel." *Journal of Commonwealth Literature* 6, no. 1 (June 1971): 113–28.

———. "V. S. Naipaul: A Commonwealth Writer." *Revue des Langues Vivantes* 33 (1967): 113–28.

Manning, Margaret. "Grim View from Naipaul." *Boston Globe*, March 31, 1980, p. 27.

Martin, Murray S. "Order, Disorder, and Rage in the Islands: The Novels of V. S. Naipaul and Albert Wendt." *Perspectives on Contemporary Fiction* 10 (1984).

Mason, Nondita. "The Fiction of V. S. Naipaul: A Study." Ph.D. diss., New York University, 1980.

McSweeney, Kerry. *Four Contemporary Novelists: Angus Wilson, Brian Moore, John Fowles, V. S. Naipaul*. Kingston: McGill-Queen's University Press, 1983.

———. "V. S. Naipaul: Sensibility and Schemata." *Critical Quarterly* 18, no. 3 (Autumn 1976): 73–79.

Miller, Karl. "In Scorn and Pity." *New York Review of Books*, December 11, 1975, pp. 3–5.

———. "Naipaul's Emergent Country." *The Listener*, September 28, 1967, pp. 402–3.

———. "V. S. Naipaul and the New Order." *Kenyon Review* 29, no. 5 (November 1967): 685–98.

Mohan, Dinesh. "A Flawed Mirror." *Book Review* 4 (January–February 1982): 197–202.

Moore, Gerald. "East Indians and West: The Novels of V. S. Naipaul." *Black Orpheus*, no. 7 (June 1960): 11–15.

Morris, Mervyn. "Some West Indian Problems of Audience." *English* 16, no. 94 (Spring 1967): 127–31.

Morris, Robert K. *Paradoxes of Order: Some Perspectives on the Fiction of V. S. Naipaul*. Columbia: University of Missouri Press, 1975.

Mpoyi-Buatu, Thomas. "Le refus de l'autre." *La Quinzaine Litteraire,* October 16–31, 1983, p. 8.

Mukherjee, Bharati, and Robert Boyers. "A Conversation with V. S. Naipaul." *Salmagundi* 54 (Fall 1981): 4–22.

Mustafa, Fawzia. *Africa Unbound: Works of V. S. Naipaul and Athol Fugard.* Ph.D. diss., Indiana University, 1986.

Nachman, Larry David. "The Worlds of V. S. Naipaul." *Salmagundi* 54 (Fall 1981): 59–76.

Nandakumar, Prema. *The Glory and the Good.* New York: Asia Publishing House, 1965.

Narashimhaiah, C. D. "Somewhere Something Has Snapped." *Literary Criterion* 4, no. 4 (1965).

Nazareth, Peter. " 'The Mimic Men' as a Study of Corruption." *East Africa Journal* 7, no. 7 (July 1970): 18–22.

———. "Out of Darkness: Conrad and Other Third World Writers." *Conradianna* 14, no. 3 (1982): 173–87.

Neill, Michael. "Guerrillas and Gangs: Frantz Fanon and V. S. Naipaul." *Ariel* 13, no. 4 (October 1982): 21–62.

Nightingale, Margaret. *Journey through Darkness: The Writing of V. S. Naipaul.* St. Lucia: University of Queensland Press, 1987.

———. "V. S. Naipaul as Historian." *Southern Review* 13, no. 3 (1980): 239–50.

O'Connor, John. "T V: Naipaul Responds to Cavett's Questions." *New York Times,* December 29, 1980, C20.

Ormerod, David. "In a Derelict Land: The Novels of V. S. Naipaul." *Contemporary Literature* 9, no. 1 (Winter 1968): 74–90.

———. "Theme and Image in V. S. Naipaul's *A House for Mr. Biswas.*" *Texas Studies in Literature and Language* 8, no. 4 (Winter 1967): 589–602.

Owens, R. J. "*A House for Mr. Biswas* by V. S. Naipaul." *Caribbean Quarterly* 7, no. 4 (April 1962): 217–19.

Payne, Robert. "Caribbean Carnival." *Saturday Review,* July 2, 1960, p. 18.

Perez Minik, Domingo. "Los simuladores, de V. S. Naipaul." *Insula: Revista de Letras y Ciencias Humanas* 39, nos. 456–57 (November–December 1984): 19.

Prescott, Lynda. "Past and Present Darkness: Sources of V. S. Naipaul's *A Bend in the River.*" *Modern Fiction Studies* 30, no. 3 (Autumn 1984): 547–66.

Pyne-Timothy, Helen. "V. S. Naipaul and Politics: His View of Third World Societies in Africa and the Caribbean." *College Language Association Journal* 28, no. 3 (March 1985): 247–62.

———. "Women and Sexuality in the Later Novels of V. S. Naipaul." *World Literature Written in English* 25, no. 2 (1985): 298–306.

Raghavacharyulu, D. V. K. "Beyond Exile and Homecoming: A Preliminary Note." In *Alien Voice: Perspectives on Commonwealth Literature.* Lucknow, India: Print House, 1981; Atlantic Highlands, N.J.: Humanities, 1982.

Rai, Sudha, *V. S. Naipaul: A Study in Expatriate Sensibility.* New Delhi: Arnold Heinemann, 1982.

Rajan, P. K. "Patterns of Cultural Orientation in the Approach to Indian Reality: A

Study Based on the Writings of V. S. Naipaul, E. M. Forster, Nirad C. Chaudhuri, and Mulk Raj Anand." *Jawaharlal Nehru University School of Languages* 8, nos. 1 and 2 (1981–82): 121–35.

Ramamurti, K. S. "Kanthapura, Kederam, Malgudi, and Trinidad, as Indias in Miniature: A Comparative Study." In *Alien Voice: Perspectives on Commonwealth Literature*. Lucknow, India: Print House, 1981; Atlantic Highlands, N.J.: Humanities, 1982.

Ramchand, Kenneth. "From Street to House." *Trinidad and Tobago Review,* Independence 1982, pp. 11, 14.

———. "The World of *A House for Mr. Biswas*." *Caribbean Quarterly* 15, no. 1 (March 1969): 65–78.

Ramraj, Victor. "A Study of the Novels of V. S. Naipaul." Master's thesis, University of New Brunswick, 1968.

———. "The Irrelevance of Nationalism." *World Literature Written in English* 23, no. 1 (Winter 1984): 187–96.

Rao, K. I. Madhusudana. "The Complex Fate: Naipaul's View of Human Development." In *Alien Voice: Perspectives on Commonwealth Literature*. Lucknow, India: Print House, 1981; Atlantic Highlands, N.J.: Humanities, 1982.

———. "V. S. Naipaul's *Guerrillas:* A Fable of Political Innocence and Experience." *Journal of Commonwealth Literature* 14, no. 1 (1979): 90–99.

Riis, Johannes. "Naipaul's *Woodlanders*." *Journal of Commonwealth Literature* 14, no. 1 (August 1979): 42–47.

Robinson, Jeffery. "V. S. Naipaul and the Sexuality of Power." In Mark McWatt, ed., *West Indian Literature and Its Social Context: Proceedings of the Fourth Annual Conference on West Indian Literature*. Cave Hill: University of the West Indies, 1985.

Rohlehr, Gordon. "Character and Rebellion in *A House for Mr. Biswas*." *New World Quarterly* 4, no. 4 (Cropover 1968): 53–59.

———. "The Ironic Approach: The Works of V. S. Naipaul." In Louis James, ed., *The Islands In Between*. London: Oxford University Press, 1968.

———. "Predestination, Frustration and Symbolic Darkness in Naipaul's *A House for Mr. Biswas*." *Caribbean Quarterly* 10, no. 1 (March 1964): 3–11.

Rose, Phyllis. "Of Moral Bonds and Men." *Yale Review* 70, no. 1 (October 1980): 149–56.

Said, Edward. "Expectations of Inferiority." *New Statesman,* October 16, 1981, pp. 21–22.

Sandall, Roger. "Naipaul's 'Colonia.' " *Quadrant* 28, no. 4 (April 1984): 68–72.

Searle, Chris. "Naipaulicity: A Form of Cultural Imperialism." *Race and Class* 26, no. 2 (Autumn 1984): 45–62.

Sedenberg, Peter C. "Faulkner, Naipaul, and Zola: Violence and the Novel." In Benjamin R. Barber and Michael J. Garges McGrath, eds., *The Artist and Political Vision*. New Brunswick: Transaction, 1982.

Seukeran, Angela Ahlia. "The Development of V. S. Naipaul as a Writer." M.A. thesis, McMaster University, 1975.

Sharma, T. R. S. "Chinua Achebe and V. S. Naipaul: One Version and Two Postures on Post-colonial Societies." In *The Colonial and the Neo-colonial Encounters in Commonwealth Literature*. Mysore: Prasaragana University, 1983.

Shepherd, R. Z. "Half World." *Time*, April 7, 1980, pp. 87, 90.

Simpson, Louis. "Disorder and Escape in the Fiction of V. S. Naipaul." *Hudson Review* 37, no. 4 (Winter 1984–85): 571–77.

Singh, H. B. "V. S. Naipaul: A Spokesman for Neo-Colonialism." *Literature and Ideology*, no. 2 (Summer 1969): 71–85.

Singh, R. S. *The Indian Novel in English*. Atlantic Highlands, N.J.: Humanities Press, 1978.

Singh, Vishudat. "Naipaul's New Indians." *Trinidad and Tobago Review Literary Supplement* 6, nos. 11–12 (1983): 3–8.

Small, John. "Sexuality and Cultural Aesthetic in the Novels of V. S. Naipaul." In Mark McWatt, ed., *West Indian Literature and Its Social Context: Proceedings of the Fourth Annual Conference on West Indian Literature*. Cave Hill: University of the West Indies, 1985.

Smyer, Richard. "Experience as Drama in the Works of V. S. Naipaul." *Kunapipi* 3, no. 2 (1981): 33–41.

———. "Naipaul's *A Bend in the River:* Fiction and the Post-Colonial Tropics." *Literary Half-yearly* 23, no. 2 (July 1982): 59–67.

Spurling, John. "The Novelist as Dictator." *Encounter* 45, no. 6 (December 1975): 73–79.

St. Omer, Garth. "The Colonial Novel: Studies in the Novels of Albert Camus, V. S. Naipaul, and Alejo Carpentier," Ph.D. diss., Princeton University, 1975.

Subramani, K. T. "Search for a Country: A Study of V. S. Naipaul's Fiction and Non-Fiction." Ph.D. diss., University of New Brunswick, 1972.

Swinden, Patrick. *The English Novel of History and Society, 1940–1980: Richard Hughes, Henry Green, Anthony Powell, Angus Wilson, Kingsley Amis, V. S. Naipaul*. New York: St. Martin's Press, 1984.

Tewarie, Bhoendradatt. "A Comparative Study of Ethnicity in the Novels of Saul Bellow and V. S. Naipaul." Ph.D. diss., Pennsylvania State University, 1983.

Theroux, Paul. "An Intelligence from the Third World." *New York Review of Books*, November 16, 1975, pp. 1–2.

———. "V. S. Naipaul." *Modern Fiction Studies* 30, no. 3 (Autumn 1984): 445–54.

———. *V. S. Naipaul: An Introduction to His Work*. New York: Africana Publishing Corporation, 1972.

Thieme, John. " 'Apparitions of Disaster': Brontëan Parallels in *Wide Sargasso Sea* and *Guerrillas.* " *Journal of Commonwealth Literature* 14, no. 1 (1979): 116–32.

———. "Authorial Voice in V. S. Naipaul's *The Middle Passage.* " *Prose Studies* 5, no. 1 (May 1982): 139–50.

———. "Calypso Allusions in Naipaul's *Miguel Street.* " *Kunapipi* 3, no. 2 (1981): 18–32.

———. "A Hindu Castaway: Ralph Singh's Journey in *The Mimic Men.* " *Modern Fiction Studies* 30, no. 3 (Autumn 1984): 505–18.

———. "Naipauliana." *Caribbean Review* 7, no. 1 (1975): 32–35.

———. "Naipaul's English Fable: *Mr. Stone and the Knights Companion.*" *Modern Fiction Studies* 30, no. 3 (1984): 497–503.

———. "V. S. Naipaul's Third World: A Not So Free State." *Journal of Commonwealth Literature* 10, no. 1 (August 1975): 10–22.

Thorpe, Marjorie. " 'The Mimic Men': A Study of Isolation." *New World Quarterly* 4, no. 4 (Cropover 1968): 55–59.

Tiffin, Helen. "The Lost Ones: A Study of the Novels of V. S. Naipaul." Ph.D. diss., Queens University, Kingston, Ontario, 1972.

———. "V. S. Naipaul's 'Outposts of Progress.' " *World Literature Written in English* 22, no. 2 (Autumn 1983): 309–19.

Verut, Annie. "Alienation et delimitation de l'espace dans *A House for Mr. Biswas* de V. S. Naipaul." In *L'Autre dans la sensibilite anglo-saxonne.* Reims: Presses Universitaires de Reims, 1983.

Wade, C. Alan. "The Novelist as Historian." *Literary Half-yearly* 11, no. 2 (July 1970): 179–84.

Walcott, Derek. "The Garden Path." *New Republic,* April 13, 1987, pp. 27–31.

Walsh, William. "Commonwealth Literature: Context and Achievement." In *Rhetorique et communication.* Paris: Didier-Erudition, 1980.

———. "Necessary and Accommodated: The Work of V. S. Naipaul." *Lugano Review* 1, nos. 3 and 4 (Summer 1975): 169–81.

———. *V. S. Naipaul.* New York: Barnes & Noble, 1973.

Warner, Maureen. "Cultural Confrontation, Disintegration and Syncretism in *A House for Mr. Biswas.*" *Caribbean Quarterly* 16, no. 4 (December 1970): 70–79.

Webb, Peter. "The Master of the Novel." *Newsweek,* August 18, 1980, pp. 34–38.

White, Landeg. *V. S. Naipaul: A Critical Introduction.* London: Macmillan, 1975.

Wichkenden, Dan. "Stories Told under the Sun of Trinidad." *New York Herald-Tribune Book Review,* May 22, 1960, p. 10.

Wickham, John. "Naipaul Risks Self-Revelation." *Caribbean Quarterly* 12, no. 8 (January 1985): 15.

Williams, Ronald Alexander. "Third World Voices: An Analysis of the Works of Chinua Achebe, George Lamming, and V. S. Naipaul." Ph.D. diss., Lehigh University, 1982.

Wirth-Nesher, Hana. "The Curse of Marginality: Colonialism in Naipaul's *Guerrillas.*" *Modern Fiction Studies* 30, no. 3 (Autumn 1984): 531–45.

Wood, Percy. "Tale of Hindus in Trinidad." *Chicago Tribune Sunday Magazine of Books,* July 12, 1959, p. 5.

Wyndham, Francis. "Services Rendered." *New Statesman,* September 19, 1975, pp. 339–40.

———. "V. S. Naipaul." *The Listener,* October 7, 1971, pp. 461–62.

Zinkhan, Elaine Joan. "Vidia Naipaul: Artist of the Absurd." M.A. thesis, University of British Columbia, 1972.

Zverev, Aleksei, "Raznye vremena na Migel-strit." *Literaturnoe Obozrenie* 9 (September 1985): 66–69.

OTHER IMPORTANT WORKS

Achebe, Chinua. *Things Fall Apart*. New York: Astor-Honor, 1959.

Ajami, Fouad. "The Fate of Non-Alignment." *Foreign Affairs* 58, no. 2 (1980).

Althusser, Louis. *For Marx*. Translated by Ben Brewster. London: Allen Lane, 1969.

———. "The Importance of Theory." *Theoretical Review* 20 (1981).

———. *Lenin and Philosophy and Other Essays*. Translated by Ben Brewster. New York: Monthly Review Press, 1971.

Anand, Mulk Raj. *An Apology for Heroism*. London: Lindsay Drummond, 1945.

———. "Old Myth, New Myth: Recital versus Novel." In C. D. Narashimhaih, ed., *Indian Literature of the Past Fifty Years, 1917–1967*. Parasaranga: University of Mysore, 1970.

Anozie, Sunday O. *Structural Models and African Poetics: Towards a Pragmatic Theory of Literature*. London: Routledge & Kegan Paul, 1981.

Bahdur, S. P. *The Ramayana of Goswamin Tulsidas*. Bombay: Jaico Publishing House, 1970.

Bakhtin, Mikhail. *The Dialogic Imagination: Four Essays*. Translated by Caryl Emerson and Michael Holquist. Austin: University of Texas Press, 1981.

———. *Rabelais and His World*. Translated by Helene Iswolsky. Cambridge: MIT Press, 1968.

Bakunin, Mikhail. *God and the State*. New York: Dover Publications, 1970.

Barreda, Pedro. *The Black Protagonist in the Cuban Novel*. Translated by Page Bancroft. Amherst: University of Massachusetts Press, 1979.

Barthes, Roland. *Image, Music, Text*. Translated by Stephen Heath. New York: Hill and Wang, 1977.

———. *Writing Degree Zero and Elements of Semiology*. Translated by Annette Levers and Colin Smith. Boston: Beacon Press, 1970.

Baudet, Henri. *Paradise on Earth: Some Thoughts on European Images of Non-European Man*. Translated by Elizabeth Wentholt. New Haven: Yale University Press, 1965.

Benjamin, Walter. *The Origin of German Tragic Drama*. Translated by John Osborne. London: NLB, 1977.

Bennett, Tony. *Formalism and Marxism*. London: Methuen, 1979.

Bhabha, Homi K. "The Other Question: The Stereotype and Colonial Discourse." *Screen* 24, no. 6 (1983): 18–36.

———. "Representation and the Colonial Text: A Critical Exploration of Some Forms of Mimeticism." In Frank Gloversmith, ed., *The Theory of Reading*. Brighton, Sussex; Totowa, N.J.: Barnes & Noble, 1984.

———. "Some Problems in Nationalist Criticism."

Brathwaite, Edward Kamau. "The African Presence in Caribbean Literature." *Daedalus* 103, no. 2 (1974): 87–109.

———. "The Love Axe (1): Developing a Caribbean Aesthetic, 1962–1974." In Huston A. Barker, Jr., ed., *Reading Black: Essays in the Criticism of Africa,*

Caribbean, and American Literature. Ithaca: Africana Studies and Research Center, Cornell University, 1976.

Brereton, Bridget. *Race Relations in Colonial Trinidad, 1870–1900*. Cambridge: Cambridge University Press, 1973.

Brown, Paul. " 'This thing of darkness I acknowledge mine': *The Tempest* and the Discourse of Colonialism." In Jonathan Dollimore and Alan Sinfield, eds., *Political Shakespeare*. Ithaca: Cornell University Press, 1985.

Cabral, Amilcar. *Return to the Source*. New York: Monthly Review Press, 1973.

———. *Unity and Struggle: Speeches and Writings*. Translated by Michael Wolfers. London: Heinemann, 1980.

Campbell, Horace. "Rastafari: Culture of Resistance." *Race and Class* 22, no. 1 (Summer 1980): 1–22.

Capra, Fritjof. *The Tao of Physics*. New York: Bantam Books, 1977.

Carlyle, Thomas. "Occasional Discourse on the Negro Question." *Frazer's Magazine* 90, no. 240 (December 1849): 670–79.

———. *Thomas Carlyle's Collected Works*. Vol. 19. London: Chapman and Hall, 1870.

Carpentier, Alejo. "The Cultures of the Caribbean Peoples." *Granma* (1979).

Carr, W. I., "Reflections on the Novel in the British Caribbean." *Queens Quarterly* 70 (Winter 1964): 570–86.

Chatterjee, Satischandra. *The Fundamentals of Hinduism*. Calcutta: Das Gupta, 1940.

Collens, James Henry. *A Guide to Trinidad: A Handbook for the Use of Tourists and Visitors*. 2d ed. London: Elliot Stock, 1888.

Conrad, Joseph. *Lord Jim*. New York: New American Library, 1980.

———. *Typhoon and Other Tales*. New York: New American Library, 1980.

———. *Youth and Two Other Stories*. New York: Doubleday Page, 1923.

Coomaraswamy, Ananda K., and Sister Nivedita. *Myths of the Hindus and Buddhists*. New York: Dover Publications, 1967.

Coward, Rosalind, and John Ellis. *Language and Materialism*. London: Routledge & Kegan Paul, 1977.

Craig, David, ed. *Marxists on Literature: An Anthology*. Harmondsworth: Penguin, 1975.

Cronin, Richard. "Quite Quiet India: The Despair of R. K. Narayan." *Encounter* 64, no. 3 (March 1985): 52–59.

Cudjoe, Selwyn R. *Grenada: Two Essays*. Tacarigua: Calaloux, 1984.

———. *Movement of the People: Essays on Independence*. Tacarigua: Calaloux, 1983.

———. *Resistance and Caribbean Literature*. Athens: Ohio University Press, 1980.

———. "Revolutionary Struggle and the Novel." *Caribbean Quarterly* 25, no. 4 (1979): 1–30.

Culler, Jonathan. *Roland Barthes*. New York: Oxford University Press, 1983.

Dabaydeen, David. *Slave Song*. Mundelstrup: Dangaroo Press, 1984.

Daniélou, Alain. *Hindu Polytheism*. New York: Pantheon, 1964.

Davis, N. Darnell. *Mr. Froude's Negrophobia or Don Quixote as a Cook's Tourist.* Demerara: Argosy Press, 1888.

de Bossière, Ralph. "On Writing a Novel." *Journal of Commonwealth Literature* 17, no. 1 (1982): 1–12.

de Verteuil, Anthony. *The Years in Revolt: Trinidad, 1881–1888.* Port of Spain: Paria, 1984.

Drayton, Arthur. "West Indian Consciousness in West Indian Verse." *Journal of Commonwealth Literature* 9 (1970).

Eagleton, Terry. *Criticism and Ideology.* London: Verso, 1978.

———. "Ideology, Fiction, Narrative." *Social Text* 2 (Summer 1979): 62–80.

———. "Molly's Piano." *New Statesman,* September 19, 1980, p. 21.

Eliot, T. S. *The Sacred Wood.* London: Methuen, 1943.

Fanon, Frantz. *The Wretched of the Earth.* New York: Grove Press, 1967.

Fischer, Louis. *The Life of Mahatma Gandhi.* New York: Collier Books, 1962.

Foucault, Michel. *The Archeology of Knowledge.* Translated by A. M. Sheridan Smith. New York: Harper & Row, 1972.

———. *The History of Sexuality: An Introduction.* Vol. 1. Translated by Robert Hurley. New York: Random House, 1980.

———. "The History of Sexuality: Interview." Translated by Geoff Bennington. *Oxford Literary Review* 4, no. 1 (1980): 3–14.

Freud, Sigmund. *Collected Papers.* Vol. 4. Translated by Joan Riviere. New York: Basic Books, 1959.

———. "The Defence of Neuro-psychoses." In *Collected Works of Sigmund Freud.* Vol. 1. Translated by Joan Riviere. London: Hogarth Press, 1956.

Froude, James Anthony. *The English in the West Indies or, the Bow of Ulysses.* London: Longmans, Green and Co., 1888.

———. *Thomas Carlyle: A History of His Life in London.* Vol. 11. London: Longmans, Green and Co., 1884.

Gandhi, Mahatma. *The Collected Works of Mahatma Gandhi.* Vol. 48. Publication Division of Information and Broadcasting, Government of India, New Delhi, 1932.

———. *The Gospel of Selfless Action, or the Gita According to Gandhi.* Translated by Mahadev Desai. Ahmedabad: Navajivan Publishing House, 1946.

Genovese, Eugene. *From Rebellion to Revolution: Afro-American Slave Revolts in the Making of the Modern World.* Baton Rouge: Louisiana State University Press, 1979.

Goldman, Lucien. *Lukács and Heidegger.* London: Routledge & Kegan Paul, 1977.

Goveia, Elsa. *Historiography of the British West Indies.* Mexico, 1956. Reprint. Washington, D.C.: Howard University Press, 1980.

Gras, Vernon, ed. *Literary Theory and Practice: From Existential Phenomenology to Structuralism.* New York: Dell, 1973.

Green, Leonard O. "Materialist Readings in Modernism: T. E. Hulme and T. S. Eliot." Ph.D. diss., Cornell University, 1979.

Gunn, Janet Varner. *Autobiography: Toward a Poetics of Experience.* Philadelphia: University of Philadelphia Press, 1982.

Halliday, Fred. *Iran: Dictatorship and Development*. Harmondsworth: Penguin, 1979.

———. "Theses on the Iranian Revolution." *Race and Class* 21, no. 1 (1979): 81–97.

Harlow, V. T. *Ralegh's Last Voyage*. London: Argonaut Press, 1932.

Harris, Wilson. *The Eye of the Scarecrow*. London: Faber and Faber, 1974.

———. *Guyana Quartet*. London: Faber and Faber, 1984.

———. *Tradition, the Writer, and Society*. London: New Beacon, 1967.

Hegel, G. W. F. *The Phenomenology of Mind*. Vol. 1. Translated by J. B. Baile. New York. Macmillan, 1910.

Herskovits, Melville. *Trinidad Village*. New York: Knopf, 1947.

Hill, Errol. *The Trinidad Carnival: A Mandate for a National Theatre*. Austin: University of Texas Press, 1972.

Hiro, Dillip. *Inside India Today*. London: Routledge & Kegan Paul, 1976.

Howe, Irving. "A Dark Vision." *New York Times Book Review,* May 13, 1979, pp. 1, 37.

Hylton, Patrick. "The Politics of Caribbean Music." *Black Scholar* 7, no. 1 (September 1975): 23–29.

Indian Round Table Conference (Second Session) 7 September 1931–1 December 1931. London: His Majesty's Stationary Office, 1932.

Jahn, Jahneinz. *Muntu: New African Culture*. Translated by Marjorie Greene. New York: Grove Press, 1961.

James, C. L. R. *Beyond a Boundary*. London: Stanley Paul, 1963.

———. *Black Jacobins*. New York: Grove Press, 1963.

———. *The Case for West Indian Self Government*. London: Leonard and Virginia Woolf at the Hogarth Press, 1933.

———. *The Future in the Present*. London: Allison & Busby, 1977.

———. "The West Indian Intellectual." Introduction to J. J. Thomas, *Froudacity*. London, 1889. Reprint. London: New Beacon, 1969.

———. "Rastafari at Home and Abroad." *New Left Review* 25 (1964).

Jameson, Fredric. *The Political Unconscious*. Ithaca: Cornell University Press, 1981.

JanMohammed, Abdul R. "The Economy of Manichean Allegory: The Function of Racial Difference in Colonialist Literature. *Critical Inquiry* 12, no. 1 (Autumn 1985): 59–87.

Jeyifo, Biodun. "Soyinka Demythologized: Notes on a Materialist Reading of *A Dance of the Forests, The Road,* and *Kongi's Harvest.*" Ife Monographs on Literature and Criticism, 1st ser., no. 2. Ife, Nigeria: University of Ife, 1984.

Jha, J. C. "Indian Heritage in Trinidad, West Indies." *Caribbean Quarterly* 19, no. 2 (June 1973): 28–38.

Kingsley, Charles. *At Last: A Christmas in the West Indies*. New York: Harper and Brothers, 1871.

Klass, Morton. *East Indians in Trinidad*. New York: Columbia University Press, 1961.

Lacan, Jacques. *Ecrits: A Selection*. Translated by Alan Sheridan. New York: W. W. Norton, 1977.

———. *Feminine Sexuality: Jacques Lacan and the école freudienne.* Edited by Juliet Mitchell and Jacqueline Rose; translated by Jacqueline Rose. New York: Norton, 1983.

———. *The Language of Self: The Function of Language in Psychoanalysis.* Translated by Anthony Wilden. Baltimore: Johns Hopkins University Press, 1968.

La Capra, Dominick. *Preface to Sartre: A Critical Introduction to Sartre's Literary and Philosophical Writings.* Ithaca: Cornell University Press, 1978.

Lamming, George. *The Pleasure of Exile.* London: Michael Joseph, 1960.

———. *The Season of Adventure.* London: Allison & Busby, 197.

———. "A Trinidad Experience." *Time and Tide,* October 5, 1961, p. 1657.

Laplanche, Jean. *Life and Death in Psychoanalysis.* Translated by Jeffrey Mehlman. Baltimore: Johns Hopkins University Press, 1976.

Laplanche, Jean, and J.-B. Pontalis. "Fantasy and the Origins of Sexuality." *International Journal of Psycho-Analysis* 49, no. 1 (1968): 1–18.

———. *The Language of Psychoanalysis.* Translated by Donald Nicholson-Smith. New York: Norton, 1973.

Lemaire, Anika. *Jacques Lacan.* Translated by David Macey. London: Routledge & Kegan Paul, 1977.

Lukács, Georg. *The Meaning of Contemporary Realism.* Translated by John and Necke Mander. London: Merlin Press, 1972.

———. *Solzhenitsyn.* Translated by David Graf. Cambridge: MIT Press, 1981.

———. *Studies in European Realism.* Translated by Edith Bone. London: Hillaway, 1950.

Luria, A. R. *Cognitive Development, Its Cultural and Social Foundations.* Translated by Martin Lopez-Morillas and Lynn Solotaroff. Cambridge: Harvard University Press, 1976.

MacCabe, Colin. *James Joyce and the Revolution of the Word.* London: Macmillan, 1979.

Macherey, Pierre. *A Theory of Literary Production.* Translated by Geoffrey Wall. London: Routledge & Kegan Paul, 1978.

Mahood, M. M. *The Colonial Encounter: A Reading of Six Novels.* London: Rex Collins, 1977.

Malik, Michael Abdul. *From Michael de Freitas to Michael X.* London: André Deutsch, 1968.

Martin, Edward Osborne. *The Gods of India.* New York: E. P. Dutton, 1956.

Marx, Karl, and Friedrich Engels, *Collected Works.* Vol. 5. New York: International Publishers, 1976.

May, Derwent. "A Black Tale." *The Times* (London), November 1, 1969, (Books), p. 5.

Mbiti, John. *African Religions and Philosophies.* New York: Doubleday, 1970.

McLeod, A. L. *The Commonwealth Pen: An Introduction to the Literature of the British Commonwealth.* Ithaca: Cornell University Press, 1961.

Mill, John Stuart. *Dissertations and Discussions: Political, Philosophical, and Historical.* Vol. 3. New York: Henry Holt, 1882.

Mittelholzer, Edgar. *Corentyne Thunder.* London: Heinemann, 1970.

———. "Of Casuarianas and Cliffs." *Bim* 2, no. 5 (1945): 6–7, 53.

Moi, Toril. *Sexual/Textual Politics: Feminist Literary Theory.* London: Methuen, 1985.

Morf, Gustav. *The Polish Heritage of Joseph Conrad.* London: Sampson Low, Marston, 1910.

Morris, Mervyn. "Mikey Smith: Dub Poet." Interviewed by Mervyn Morris. *Jamaica Journal* 18 (May–July 1985): 38–45.

Mottahedeh, Roy. *The Mantle of the Prophet: Religion and Politics in Iran.* New York: Simon and Schuster, 1985.

Mozhyagun, S., ed. *Problems of Modern Aesthetics.* Moscow: Progress Publishers, 1969.

Naiasimhaiah, C. D. *Indian Literature and the Past Fifty Years, 1917–1967.* Prasaranga, India: University of Mysore, 1970.

Naipaul, Seepersad. *The Adventures of Gurudeva and Other Stories.* London: André Deutsch, 1976.

Nettleford, Rex. *Mirror, Mirror.* Kingston: William Collins and Sangsters, 1970.

Ousmane, Sembene. *God's Bits of Wood.* Translated by Francis Price. New York: Doubleday, 1962.

Rahman, A. "Science and Technology in Medieval India." *Journal of Scientific and Industrial Research* 40 (October 1981): 615–22.

Ralegh, Walter. *The Discoveries of Guiana and the Discovery of the World.* Cleveland: World Publishing Company, 1966.

Ramchand, Kenneth. "Concern for Criticism." *Caribbean Quarterly* 16, no. 2 (1970): 51–60.

———. "History and the Novel: A Literary Critic's Approach." *Savacou* 5 (June 1971): 103–14.

———. *The West Indian Novel and Its Background.* London: Faber and Faber, 1970.

Redding, Saunders. "Literature and the Negro." *Contemporary Literature* 9, no. 1 (1968): 135–38.

Reid, Vic. *New Day.* London: Heinemann Educational Books, 1949.

Rodney, Walter. *The Groundings with My Brothers.* London: Bogle L'Ouverture, 1969.

———. *How Europe Underdeveloped Africa.* London: Bogle L'Ouverture, 1972.

Rohlehr, Gordon. "The Creative Writer in the West Indian Society." *Tapia* (1974).

Rose, Jacqueline. "The Imaginary." In *The Talking Cure: Essays in Psychoanalysis and Language.* Edited by Colin MacCabe. New York: St. Martin's Press, 1981.

Said, Edward. *Joseph Conrad and the Fiction of Autobiography.* Cambridge: Harvard University Press, 1966.

———. *Orientalism.* New York: Pantheon, 1978.

Salmon, C. S. *The Caribbean Confederation.* London: Cassell, 1888.

Samaroo, Brinsley. "The Presbyterian Canadian Mission as an Agent of Integration in Trinidad during the Nineteenth and Early Twentieth Centuries." *Caribbean Studies* 14, no. 4 (January 1975): 41–55.

Sander, Reinhard W. *From Trinidad: An Anthology of Early West Indian Writing.* New York: Africana Publishing, 1978.

―――. "An Index to *Bim.*" In *Art and Civilization Series* 2. St. Augustine, Trinidad, University of the West Indies, Extra-Mural Unit, 1973.

Schillebeeckx, Edward. *Jesus: An Experiment in Christology.* New York: Seabury Press, 1979.

Searle, Chris. *Words Unchained: Language and Revolution in Grenada.* London: Zed Books, 1984.

Sebastien, Raphael. "The Political Economy of Capitalism in Trinidad and Tobago: An Overview." *Tribune* 1 (June 1981): 40–48.

Sedgwick, Eve Kosofsky. *Between Men: English Literature and Male Homosocial Desire.* New York: Columbia University Press, 1985.

Selvon, Samuel. "The Baby." *Bim* 3, no. 10 (1949).

―――. *A Brighter Sun.* London: Longman Caribbean, 1971.

Shari'ati, Ali. *Marxism and Other Western Fallacies.* Translated by R. Campbell. Berkeley: Mizan Press, 1980.

―――. *On the Sociology of Slavery.* Translated by Hamid Algar. Berkeley: Mizan Press, 1979.

―――. "Reflections of a Concerned Muslim: On the Plight of Oppressed Peoples." *Race and Class* 21, no. 1 (1979): 33–40.

Sheehan, Bernard. *Savagism and Civility.* Cambridge: Cambridge University Press, 1980.

Singh, R. S. *The Indian Novel in English.* Atlantic Highlands, N.J.: Humanities Press, 1978.

Skura, Meredith. *The Literary Use of the Psychoanalytic Process.* New Haven: Yale University Press, 1982.

Soyinka, Wole. *Myth, Literature, and the African World.* Cambridge: Cambridge University Press, 1976.

Stance, W. T. *Mysticism and Philosophy.* New York: J. P. Lippincott, 1960.

Thelwell, Michael. *The Harder They Come.* New York: Grove Press, 1980.

Thom, Martin. "The Unconscious Structured as a Language." In *The Talking Cure: Essays in Psychoanalysis and Language.* Edited by Colin MacCabe. New York: St. Martin's Press, 1981.

Thomas, J. J. *Froudacity: The West Indian Fables by James Anthony Froude.* London: T. Fisher Unwin, 1889.

Trollope, Anthony. *The West Indies and the Spanish Main.* London: Chapman and Hall, 1860.

Underhill, Evelyn. *Practical Mysticism.* New York: E. P. Dutton, 1915.

Warner, George F. *The Voyage of Robert Dudley to the West Indies.* London: Hakluyt Society, 1899.

Webber, A. R. F. *Those That Be in Bondage.* Demerara, British Guyana: Daily Chronicle, 1917.

Williams, Eric. *British Historians of the West Indies.* New York: Scribner's, 1966.

―――. *Capitalism and Slavery.* Chapel Hill: University of North Carolina Press, 1944.

―――. *History of the People of Trinidad and Tobago.* Port of Spain: PNM Publishing Company, 1962.

Williams, Raymond. "George Orwell." In *Culture and Politics, 1780–1950*. New York: Columbia University Press, 1958.

————. *Marxism and Literature*. Oxford: Oxford University Press, 1977.

Wilson, David. *Mr. Froude and Mr. Carlyle*. London: William Heinemann, 1898.

Wynter, Sylvia. "Reflections on West Indian Writing and Criticism, Part 11." *Jamaica Journal* 3, no. 1 (March 1969): 21–42.

Zaehner, R. C. *Mysticism: Sacred and Profane*. New York: Oxford University Press, 1969.

Zakaria, Rafig. "Interesting Probe." *Illustrated Weekly of India,* July 17, 1977, p. 32.

Index